From the Inside Ou

MW01282991

Urban and Industrial Environments

Series editor: Robert Gottlieb, Henry R. Luce Professor of Urban and Environmental Policy, Occidental College

For a complete list of books published in this series, please see the back of the book.

From the Inside Out

The Fight for Environmental Justice within Government Agencies

Jill Lindsey Harrison

The MIT Press
Cambridge, Massachusetts
London, England

This book was set in Stone Serif and Stone Sans by Westchester Publishing Services. Printed and bound in the United States of America.

Library of Congress Cataloging-in-Publication Data is available.

Names: Harrison, Jill Lindsey, 1975- author.
Title: From the inside out : the fight for environmental justice within
    government agencies / Jill Lindsey Harrison.
Description: Cambridge, MA : The MIT Press, 2019. | Series: Urban and
    industrial environments | Includes bibliographical references and index.
Identifiers: LCCN 2019001210 | ISBN 9780262537742 (pbk. : alk. paper)
Subjects: LCSH: Environmental justice--Governmental policy--United States. |
    Environmental policy--United States. | Administrative agencies--United States--
    Decision making.
Classification: LCC GE230 .H37 2019 | DDC 363.7/05610973--dc23 LC record
    available at https://lccn.loc.gov/2019001210

10 9 8 7 6 5 4 3 2

For Teresa DeAnda

In moving EJ [environmental justice] at this agency and at other agencies, there has to be a cultural shift.... We just celebrated the 20th anniversary of the Executive Order [on Environmental Justice], and the Office of Environmental Justice [at U.S. EPA] has been around since 1992. So, the question is, how long does evolution actually have to take? [I tell my colleagues,] folks in the community don't get a chance to leave. They have to live with these things, day in and day out. People are still getting sick. People are still dying.... I work on EJ issues because it is my passion.... You have to bring that level of commitment, because you are not always going to be able to say and do things that are going to make everybody happy inside of this building. That is not why we are here. We are here because there is an injustice.... That is the way we were raised when Dr. Gaylord was Director of the Office of EJ. She said, "Be bold. You are an advocate for communities." ... If you are at the EPA, remember that your job is about protecting the health and the environment of folks.... [S]tay focused on the most vulnerable communities and making sure that we are doing everything in our power to help improve their lives and to stand up against injustice in whatever form or fashion that may present itself. When we raised our right hand, that oath that we took was to make sure that we were doing those things.

—Jamie, government agency EJ staff person

You have no idea how difficult it is until you walk into the agency and work there.... You are going up against the standard way of doing business.... People have no idea what the EJ staff people are dealing with on the inside.

—Nicky, government agency EJ staff person

Contents

Contents

Preface

I have written this book during a dark moment in the history of environmental regulation. The Trump administration's attacks on environmental protections and other civil rights are devastating in scope and consequence. Scholars, environmental and human rights activists, journalists, retired government staff, and even some current staff in unprecedented public protest have criticized the Trump administration's attacks on environmental protections.[1] Their actions reveal what scholars have shown: that environmental regulatory agencies like the U.S. Environmental Protection Agency (U.S. EPA) are staffed with people who identify as public servants, environmental stewards, and scientists, and who take great pride in protecting the environment and public health. Since their inception, agencies have endured budget cuts and been forced to defend their authority to regulate industry. Staff feel beleaguered by antiregulatory attack and have accomplished a lot within those constraints. I stand with them in their protest of the current administration.[2] I believe deeply in the importance of a strong state that protects human and environmental rights. My research and teaching show how, despite the many problems with current public institutions, we need them.

Yet, environmental regulatory protections have never been evenly applied. Working-class, racially marginalized, and Native American communities have always been disproportionately exposed to deadly environmental hazards relative to wealthier, white communities. Moreover, as I show in this book, environmental regulatory agency staff who express deep pride in their work also express disinterest in or even hostile resistance to "environmental justice" (EJ) reforms designed to improve conditions in the nation's most environmentally burdened and vulnerable communities. In so doing, these well-meaning people, widely regarded as politically progressive, engage in practices that undermine prospects for social justice and equity. In this book, I grapple with this contradiction to provide new insights into why agencies have such a hard time implementing EJ reforms that would systematically extend environmental protections to racially marginalized, working-class communities.

My argument in this book is that, while changes in administration most certainly shape regulatory practice and environmental outcomes in significant ways (Dillon et al. 2018; Fredrickson et al. 2018), so do some of the everyday practices through which staff defend their understanding of their agency's priorities and commitments. This book is about the shapes staff resistance to EJ takes, how persistent it has been, where it comes from, and what its consequences are. Importantly, this pushback against EJ reforms endures from one administration to the next. Staff make these agencies what they are and will continue their work into future administrations. Even under the best of circumstances at the federal level—during the Obama administration, whose top leadership actively endorsed EJ, appointed high-level EJ staff, and assigned EJ training to all employees—EJ-supportive staff felt that their efforts were stymied by the ways some of their own colleagues responded to proposed EJ reforms and treated EJ staff. To truly support environmental justice, government agencies not only need supportive leadership and resources, but also need to look within and address their own cultural dynamics through which some bureaucrats undermine EJ reforms. Business as usual won't cut it; changes have to be made.

I have multiple goals in writing this book. Academically, my findings about environmental regulatory culture contribute novel insights into why government agencies' EJ efforts fall so short of EJ advocates' principles. On a more practical level, I want to generate conversation about what standards society should use to judge the fairness and effectiveness of environmental regulation. I believe that environmental equity should be a key metric according to which we judge these public institutions. However, some staff do not. That feels problematic to me and something that should be subject to democratic debate. Additionally, I write this book to show that staff are active participants when it comes to their agencies' progress on EJ reforms, and that they have choices about what impact to have on such work. Clearly, their work is highly constrained by resource limitations, environmental law, analytical tools, and other factors largely outside their control. They work hard and often feel that they have little room to maneuver. However, staff also reveal that they have discretion over how to do various tasks, which, understandably, they cherish. Moreover, bureaucrats, like the rest of us, carry into their jobs ambitions and ideas about the right and best ways to do their work. So, in characterizing bureaucrats' work, our narratives cannot only be about the material constraints within which they find themselves. We also have to attend to *how* bureaucrats do their jobs—their sense of what is right, and the actions they take—because, as I will show, bureaucrats' practices undermine those trying to fight for EJ reforms to regulatory practice.

While I honor bureaucrats' sense of commitment to environmental protection, I also honor the legitimate, profound grievances of people in Flint, Standing Rock, Uniontown, Diamond, Delano, New Orleans, and so many other overburdened and vulnerable communities. My principle commitment is to those most harmed by environmental hazards and abandoned by state institutions that otherwise are quick to proclaim that everything is fine. I wrote this book to help fight for government that uncompromisingly strives for environmental justice.

Some of my friends and students expressed surprise that I would write something critical of the U.S. EPA while it suffers serious attack by antiregulatory elites. Should we raise critical concerns about the internal workings of such an important organization at a moment when the cards are stacked against it? Colleagues at other universities, knowing about my research, have written to me asking for advice on this topic. I understand this concern. Yet crisis is not a time to abandon our standards and principles, especially our commitments to equity and justice. The U.S. EPA is a crucial public institution that, like others, is needed to protect public health and the environment because industry and everyday citizens will not and cannot adequately do so on their own. I am certain that none of us would ever want to trade our current environment for one from the days before environmental regulation. Yet neither those accomplishments nor federal agencies' current predicament mean that we should turn a blind eye to government's oversights. Defending a public institution is not the same as refusing to critique it. While environmental conditions have improved in many ways, we do not all experience this equally. America's poorest communities, communities of color, and Native American communities suffer environmental hazards in ways other Americans do not, and their residents will pay for it with illness and suffering. These inequalities are inexcusable, and we cannot dismiss them by pointing to the aggregated, overall improvements in air and water quality or to the hostile attacks by the current administration. I write this book because I feel we have a responsibility to hold public institutions to high standards and specify how they must improve.

I offer my critique as a way to help build a stronger movement for EJ within these agencies. Elements of my recommendations that feel unrealistic during the current federal administration can be understood as recommendations for state agencies and for the next federal administration. Many state agencies are not under the same degree of attack that federal agencies are. Many of the Trump administration's proposals face significant legal challenges. Leadership will change.

Now is precisely the time to be clear about what needs to be done for agencies to support environmental justice. Prior regulatory regimes were insufficient; justice requires something new. This book aims to contribute to conversations about what an environmental regulatory state prioritizing social justice might entail. As we deliberate which changes are required from environmental regulatory agencies, we must keep justice at the center of that conversation.

Acknowledgments

This book is a product of conversation with so many generous, thoughtful, and very smart people. My research participants selflessly took time out of their busy days to thoughtfully and candidly share with me their commitments, convictions, and challenges. Special thanks to those who met with me multiple times, and to a few who secured permission for me to attend internal agency meetings.

I conducted initial, exploratory fieldwork for this project while on the faculty at the University of Wisconsin–Madison. My colleagues kindly helped me create space in my teaching schedule and encouraged me in the new project. I conducted the rest of this project while on the faculty at the University of Colorado Boulder. Many thanks to my colleagues for their encouragement, especially to Lori Peek and Kathleen Tierney for covering some of my responsibilities so that I could disappear on sabbatical to write this book, and to Lori Hunter, Janet Jacobs, Lori Peek, and Kathleen Tierney for mentoring me over the years.

I am indebted to those who took time to read and comment on written drafts of my work from this project, including William Boyd, Max Boykoff, Phil Brown, Joe Bryan, Matt Desan, Simone Domingue, Danny Faber, Mara Goldman, David Goodman, Julie Guthman, Sanyu Mojola, Stef Mollborn, Rachel Rinaldo, Matt Rowe, Laura Senier, Christi Sue, and Emily Yeh, as well as two environmental regulatory agency representatives who, due to confidentiality protections, I cannot name. Marianne Engelman-Lado generously helped me think through the history of Title VI of the Civil Rights Act at U.S. EPA. Other scholars provided thoughtful, crucial input on my ideas along the way, including Alyse Bertenthal, Ellen Kohl, Raoul Liévanos, Jonathan London, David Pellow, and Cedrick-Michael Simmons. Michael Bell, Michael Mascarenhas, and David Pellow buoyed me with encouragement along the way. I feel especially grateful to David Pellow for pushing me to delve into literatures that have broadened my thinking. Bob Gottlieb, Beth Clevenger, and their staff at MIT Press all helped strengthen and nurture this project in no small way.

Many, many thanks to those who invited me to present my work in progress and asked tough, excellent questions that helped me tighten my arguments: participants of the University of Georgia Workshop on Culture, Power, and History; the University of Colorado Boulder Geography Department Colloquium; the University of Colorado Boulder Center for Science and Technology Policy Research; the Social Science Environmental Health Research Institute at Northeastern University; the Sociology Department at Northwestern University; the Conference on the Plurality and Politics of Environmental Justice at the University of East Anglia; and the Indiana University School of Environmental and Public Affairs. I also presented earlier versions of this work at several annual meetings of the American Sociological Association and the Association of American Geographers, and I gained valuable new insights through the communities of scholars I have interacted with there.

William Boyd graciously allowed me to audit his environmental law graduate seminar in 2017 and patiently answered my many questions. What a gift to be able to immerse myself in another discipline's perspective, to continue to learn in a structured formal way. I especially appreciate his insistence to his students that they honor EJ concerns.

Several fantastic research assistants helped me at different points in this project. Simone Domingue collected and analyzed the Federal Employee Viewpoint Survey data described in chapter 6. Dan Downs observed and took notes at several agency EJ meetings. Trisha Yoon helped analyze the numerous EJ grant program abstracts. Elizabeth Bittel also helped analyze EJ grant program abstracts and reviewed scholarship on EJ policy implementation.

Several agency staff kindly and helpfully fulfilled my public records requests and carefully organized many documents for me: Anne Eng at City of San Francisco Department of Environment, Jessica Diedesch and Malinda Dumisani at California EPA, and Lisa Kranick and David Witt at New York State Department of Environmental Conservation.

Fieldwork for this project was supported with funding from the University of Colorado Boulder and a Franklin Research Grant from the American

Philosophical Society. An impeccably timed Sabbatical Fellowship from The American Council of Learned Societies enabled me to take the year away from teaching I needed to write this book.

My parents get credit for this book too—they got me thinking about justice and fairness from an early age and instilled in me that, in society, we need to care about and for each other. Finally, and most especially, thank you Max. You have been so supportive, so understanding, and bring incomparable joy to my life. I am incredibly grateful for you.

1 Introduction

The Environmental Justice (EJ) movement is composed of people from communities of color, indigenous communities, and working-class communities who are focused on combating environmental injustice—the disproportionate burden of environmental harm facing these populations. For the EJ movement, social justice is inseparable from environmental protection.
—David Naguib Pellow (2018, 2)

Our most successful tool has been building relationships with government....We know our way there now. Never underestimate the relationships with people in government. We are living in a difficult time. But not an impossible time.
—Luis Olmedo from EJ organization Comité Cívico del Valle

The U.S. Environmental Protection Agency (EPA) and the state-level environmental regulatory agencies it supports curb the harms of industrial growth in ways that other actors will not and cannot do—neither industry, with its focus on profits, nor individuals and environmental organizations, who lack the power to force polluters to act. Environmental and other civil rights protections have been under attack for as long as they have existed, and the Trump administration has accelerated this assault to an unparalleled degree. It has instituted racist immigration policies that further scapegoat certain immigrant groups and tear families apart, condoned white supremacist violence, eviscerated health care policy, and rolled back protections for transgender people. Its attack on environmental protections has been particularly pronounced: pulling out of the Paris Climate Agreement, rolling back the Clean Power Plan and dozens of other environmental regulations, approving the Keystone XL and Dakota Access pipelines, reversing the EPA's own ban on the neurotoxic pesticide chlorpyrifos, shrinking the size of wildlife refuges and National Monuments held as sacred by Native American tribes and opening those lands to oil and gas development, stacking EPA science advisory boards with industry representatives, prohibiting government analysts from using many independent scientific studies, removing contaminated sites from the Superfund list, and cutting grants that help fund state and tribal regulatory agencies (Bomberg 2017; Davenport 2017b, 2018a, 2018b; Dillon et al. 2018; Eilperin and Cameron 2018; ELI 2018; Federman 2018; Fredrickson et al. 2018; Gustin 2017; Harvard Law School 2018; Leber 2018; Paris et al. 2017; PEER 2017; Popovich, Albeck-Ripka, and Pierre-Louis 2018; Sellers et al. 2017; Shear 2017; Turkewitz 2017; UCS 2018, 2019).

These moves to weaken the agency have enraged environmental advocates and EPA staff alike (Dillon et al. 2018; Fredrickson et al. 2018; Paris et al. 2017; Sellers et al. 2017; UCS 2018). In uncharacteristic political activism, some EPA staff publicly protested the nomination of Scott Pruitt to EPA administrator (Davenport 2017a; Sellers et al. 2017), hundreds of former EPA staff wrote a scathing letter of protest and formed activist organizations to defend the agency (Davenport 2017a; Gardner 2017; Save EPA 2017), staff have resigned in protest of the Trump administration and its practices (e.g., Friedman, Affo, and Kravitz 2017), and staff surreptitiously inform journalists and researchers about controversial pending reforms.

While these budget cuts and promises to shrink EPA's authority will harm all Americans, they are especially problematic for working-class, racially marginalized, and Native American communities, who have scarcely benefitted from the environmental protections that legislation and regulatory enforcement afford to many people. These communities endure not only substandard housing, crumbling infrastructure, and underfunded public education, but also higher exposures to toxic pollution, weaker enforcement of environmental laws, and access to fewer parks and playgrounds. They also have disproportionately high rates of lead poisoning, cancer, asthma, and other diseases that experts have linked to environmental hazards. EPA and other environmental regulatory agencies do important work—but they have never protected all people equally.

Such environmental inequalities gain the public's attention in particularly acute moments, such as Hurricane Katrina in 2005, which showed Americans that working-class black communities are not as protected from natural disasters as their wealthier white neighbors. Government agencies failed to aid working-class and racially marginalized residents desperately in need of help during the floods, the media used racist stereotypes in portraying black residents as lawless and violent, and recovery efforts fell short of meeting communities' basic needs and in some cases harmed them further (Allen 2007; Pastor et al. 2006; Sze 2006; Tierney, Bevc, and Kuligowski 2006). Similarly, the water contamination crisis in the predominantly black and working-class city of Flint, Michigan, reveals racial and class disparities in access to clean drinking water. Government mismanagement of the city's drinking water caused at least a hundred thousand people to be exposed to lead at levels known to cause brain damage, learning disabilities, and behavioral problems; 200 or more fetal deaths; and at least a dozen people to be killed by Legionnaires' disease (Flint Water Advisory Task Force 2016; Ingraham 2017; Michigan Civil Rights Commission 2017). Far from outliers, these cases exemplify conditions that characterize everyday life for racially marginalized, Native American, and working-class communities across America, and that contribute to vast racial and class inequalities in illness and death. This book sheds new light on why government agencies, essential for providing certain services that industry and individuals will not or cannot provide, allow these grossly unfair and devastating inequalities to persist.

These environmental inequalities are the focus of the U.S. *environmental justice (EJ) movement*. Working at the intersection of the environmental and civil rights movements, grassroots EJ advocates argue that justice requires that the state reduce environmental hazards in the most vulnerable and overburdened communities and that members of those communities have more control over government decision-making.

The U.S. EPA and numerous state-level agencies establish acceptable industrial practices and pollution levels, assign permits to restrict the pollution of industry and other actors, enforce environmental laws and regulations, monitor air and water quality, clean up contaminated sites, and help fund state and tribal agencies' environmental programs. Many have responded to EJ movement pressure by adopting EJ policies and hiring "EJ staff" tasked with proposing EJ reforms to regulatory practice. Yet, although EJ advocates and agencies' EJ staff have proposed and fought hard for many important regulatory reforms that could protect overburdened and vulnerable communities from dangerous environmental hazards, agencies have institutionalized few of them.

This book lifts the veil on the U.S. EPA and its state-level environmental regulatory agency counterparts, examining the challenges faced by their staff who fight for EJ reforms to regulatory practice as a way to gain new insights into why these agencies fail to reduce harmful toxics and other hazards in our nation's most overburdened communities. It shows that, to understand why agencies have allowed environmental inequalities to persist, we must go inside and talk to bureaucrats within them. Other scholars have emphasized that material factors outside the control of agency staff—budget cuts, limits to regulatory authority, industry pressure, and under-developed analytical tools—constrain the possibilities for EJ reforms. This book builds upon that work by demonstrating that agencies' EJ efforts are also undermined by elements of regulatory workplace culture that transcend institutions and changes in administration. Specifically, through extensive interviews with and observations of staff at numerous environmental regulatory agencies, I show that agencies' EJ efforts have also long been undermined by ways in which staff defend what they think the goals and priorities should be of the organizations they work for and to which they feel very committed—with some staff outright rejecting proposed EJ reforms, and others promoting "environmental justice" in principle but in ways that deviate from key tenets of the EJ movement. That is, the disappointing pace of agencies' EJ efforts stems not only from hostile acts of conservative political elites and industry pressure to deregulate, but also from everyday practices through which some staff, in reacting to proposed EJ reforms, define how these institutions should best protect public health and the environment. By exploring these interacting factors, this book exposes how, at all levels of government, agencies are failing to keep some communities safe, despite the concerted efforts of their EJ-supportive staff, EJ advocates, and the communities they fight for. It also shows how, despite these constraints, EJ staff and their EJ-supportive colleagues fight for environmental justice by trying to change both regulatory practice and regulatory culture from the inside out.

As activists, scholars, bureaucrats, and the public strive to defend environmental regulatory protections and rebuild them in the coming years, we have an opportunity to re-envision our government institutions' commitments and priorities. To protect our most overburdened and vulnerable communities, we cannot restore our environmental regulatory system to its previous form. The fight for environmental justice—and social justice broadly—requires that we craft government institutions that systematically reduce inequalities and dismantle the structures of oppression that uphold them. This book aims to help inform the resistance against unjust political elites and their attacks on human rights by providing a set of concrete recommendations for crafting a future environmental regulatory regime that is both strong and *just*.

Environmentalism and the Environmental Justice Movement

In interviews with me, and as other scholars have documented, EPA and other environmental regulatory agency staff express deep pride in their work, their agency, its accomplishments, and the role of environmental regulation in protecting public health and the environment (Mintz 2012; Pautz and Rinfret 2011, 2014; Rinfret and Pautz 2013; Robertson 2010; Taylor 1984). Environmental legislation and regulation played a key role in reducing certain forms of air and water pollution in the United States. For example, since 1990, national ambient concentrations of lead improved by 85 percent, carbon monoxide by 84 percent, sulfur dioxide by 67 percent, and nitrogen dioxide by 60 percent (EPA 2017c), dramatically curtailing Americans' risks of death and illness from exposure to these hazards.

Yet these aggregate improvements mask a landscape of remarkable environmental inequality, where some communities are overburdened with pollution, hazardous facilities, dilapidated infrastructure, and other environmental harms. Community organizations around the country have protested the hazards within their neighborhoods, condemning the fact that environmental problems are not distributed randomly or evenly but instead are disproportionately clustered in working-class, racially marginalized, and Native American communities. The environmental justice movement today encompasses all of these organizations. Many EJ activists are personally and immediately affected by environmental hazards, and they draw connections between these hazards and patterns of illness they have observed in their families, workplaces, schools, and neighborhoods. They are angry at polluters for exploiting their communities and at government agencies and mainstream environmental organizations for ignoring their concerns and conditions. They have formed hundreds of community-based EJ organizations across the United States and work in alliances with scientists, attorneys, and other supporters.

EJ activism is part of a long history of struggle against racist oppression in the United States (Taylor 2014a). Such struggle gained momentum during the civil rights movement, as illustrated, for example, in conflict over a hazardous waste dump in Warren County, North Carolina, in 1982. State officials there sought a location for disposing of soil contaminated with polychlorinated biphenyls. Officials selected a site in the poorest county in the state and the one with the highest percentage of black residents, despite the fact that its shallow water table and residents' reliance on local wells for drinking water made the town an environmentally terrible choice. Residents, outraged at the discriminatory siting decision, protested the landfill and were ultimately joined by members of national civil rights organizations in physically blocking the waste-loaded trucks from being able to enter the site. This protest, in which more than five hundred people were arrested for acts of civil disobedience, was the first time anyone in U.S. history had been jailed for trying to halt a toxic waste landfill.

EJ activists' fights for improved environmental conditions in the most overburdened and vulnerable communities also include immigrant farmworkers' fights for stronger pesticide regulations. Activists emphasize that industry coerces agencies to weaken pesticide regulations, while poverty, legal status issues, and racism impede farmworkers and their families in reporting pesticide exposures and result in them not being taken seriously when they do (Harrison 2011; Pulido 1996). EJ activism also includes working-class white Appalachian communities' battles against mountain-top-removal coal mining, in which activists emphasize how the coal industry pressures the state to allow mining practices that destroy rivers and livelihoods while residents, lacking other employment opportunities, feel unable to criticize it (Bell 2016). Additionally, EJ activists fight against food insecurity rampant in working-class communities and for food justice, the right of all people to accessible, affordable, nutritious, and culturally appropriate food (Gottlieb and Joshi 2010). And furthermore, EJ activism includes the climate justice movement, whose members condemn the ways Indigenous communities in the Arctic and low-income communities in the global south have been forced to bear the burden of the climatic changes destroying their homes and livelihoods for which they bear little responsibility (Ciplet, Roberts, and Khan 2015). Conflicts over the Dakota Access Pipeline in North Dakota at Standing Rock in 2016 and 2017 are a recent case of EJ activism, where Native Americans sought to protect their water resources and sacred sites from a new oil pipeline. Activists criticized the fact that the pipeline had been rerouted away from the predominantly white city of Bismarck to protect its drinking water, as well as the fact that U.S. government agencies used military violence, violated tribal sovereignty, and ignored due process to foster pipeline construction (Hayes 2016; Petrella and Loggins 2016).

EJ activist organizations are largely grassroots and tend to embrace cross-class and multiracial alliances. Some have formed regional EJ networks and other EJ coalitions to more effectively share resources and shape state and federal policy (Bullard 1990; Cole and Foster 2001; Faber 1998; Gottlieb 2005; Hofrichter 1993; Pezzullo and Sandler 2007a,b). Importantly, the 1991 First National People of Color Environmental Leadership Summit, where participants adopted 17 "Principles of Environmental Justice," helped the budding EJ movement gain coherence and identity (Principles 1991). Numerous subsequent EJ conferences have further helped EJ advocates build alliances with each other and their supporters in academia and elsewhere.

EJ activists have been strongly influenced by the civil rights movement, the labor movement, grassroots anti-toxics activism, and struggles for Native American sovereignty (Cole and Foster 2001). EJ activists' use of marches, protests, and other direct action reflects the tactics of these "tributary" movements (Cole and Foster 2001). As much as EJ activists can be understood as part of the environmental movement, they are also deeply critical of mainstream environmental organizations for focusing on protection of endangered species, wilderness areas, and other environmental concerns of the relatively wealthy; ignoring the environmental knowledge of and environmental harms borne disproportionately by working-class, racially marginalized, and Native American communities; using tactics that often directly harm marginalized people; and doing little to diversify their own leadership and staff (Brulle 2000; Cole and Foster 2001; Di Chiro 1996, 1998; Gottlieb 2005; Pezzullo and Sandler 2007a,b; Taylor 2000, 2014b).

Scope and Roots of Environmental Inequalities

Environmental inequalities research has helped substantiate and investigate EJ activists' concerns and convictions. Scholarship has overwhelmingly demonstrated that environmental problems are highest in low-income communities, communities with a high percentage of racially marginalized residents, and those that are highly racially segregated (e.g., Ard 2015,

2016; Bullard et al. 2007; Bullock, Ard, and Saalman 2018; Campbell, Peck, and Tschudi 2010; Clark, Millet, and Marshall 2014; Crowder and Downey 2010; Downey 2006; Downey and Hawkins 2008; Faber and Kreig 2002; Grant et al. 2010; Grineski and Collins 2018; Liévanos 2015; Liévanos and Horne 2017; Mikati et al. 2018; Mohai, Pellow, and Roberts 2009a, Mohai et al. 2009b, 2011; Mohai and Saha 2007, 2015; Pastor, Sadd, and Hipp 2001; Taylor 2014a; WHO 2016a).[1] Additionally, scholars have demonstrated race- and class-based disparities in government agencies' enforcement of environmental laws (Konisky and Schario 2010; Pulido 2015). Scholars have shown that environmental inequalities have remained persistent over time (Ard 2015) and contribute to racial and socioeconomic disparities in health and educational attainment (Mohai et al. 2011; Morello-Frosch and Jesdale 2006; Morello-Frosch et al. 2011).

These findings are conservative, undoubtedly underestimating the scope and severity of environmental inequalities. Massive gaps in scientific knowledge limit researchers' abilities to definitively link many illnesses to environmental harms. We know very little about the industrial history of lands converted to residential and other urban uses, the extent of various illnesses, the causal links between illnesses and environmental hazards, the full range of physiological and psychological effects of exposure to most hazards, how actually existing mixtures of hazards affect human bodies, and how those effects vary among people given the diversity of activity patterns, stress levels, and other factors known to affect our responses to environmental hazards (Brown 2007; Frickel and Elliott 2018; Langston 2010; Tesh 2001). Some have shown how standard scientific norms of proof and other key elements of regulatory science serve the interests of industry rather than the public (Brown 2007; Cordner 2016; Langston 2010; Nash 2006; O'Brien 2000; Raffensperger and Tickner 1999; Thornton 2000; Tickner 2003; Vogel 2012; Whiteside 2006).

These inequalities stem from many factors. To some extent, environmental inequalities stem from the utilitarian nature of environmental governance in the United States, in which government has prioritized policies that provide the greatest net benefit for the population overall, irrespective of how those benefits are distributed within society (Andrews 1999; S. Foster 2000; Harrison 2011, 2014; Harvey 1996; Low and Gleeson 1998). As EJ scholars Bob Bullard and colleagues have noted, "The mission of the federal EPA was never designed to address environmental policies and practices that result in unfair, unjust and inequitable outcomes" (Bullard et al. 2007, 8). Environmental regulatory agencies' progress is measured in utilitarian, aggregated measures (e.g., changes in the number of expected deaths from exposure to air pollution nationwide) (EPA 2017c). Indeed, the EJ movement is unique in insisting that the government be held accountable instead to its progress on reducing environmental inequality.

Additionally, in working-class communities in which residents struggle to make ends meet, they lack the free time, scientific support, credibility, and other resources needed to fight powerful industries. Their elected officials feel compelled to welcome industrial development in exchange for jobs and tax revenues, despite the accompanying hazards—a dynamic Bullard (1992) characterizes as "environmental blackmail." Also, fear of retaliation often makes workers reluctant to report or challenge environmental problems. These dynamics, as well as lower property values, make such communities attractive to hazardous industries (Mohai and Saha 2015).

The clustering of environmental problems in communities of color is also an enduring legacy of centuries of industry practices and government policies that have created residential segregation and systematically afforded material resources—from wealth to clean air—disproportionately to whites (Bonilla-Silva 2014; Lipsitz 1995, 2011; Mascarenhas 2016; Mohai and Saha 2015; Morello-Frosch 2002; Pulido 2000, 2015; Taylor 2014a). Some of these institutions are explicitly and unabashedly racist, including slavery, Jim Crow laws, and "redlining" and other racist lending practices. Others are less explicitly racist but effectively so, such as highway development projects, government urban "renewal" programs, weak environmental laws in occupational sectors largely employing immigrants and other racially marginalized groups, and uneven enforcement of environmental and civil rights laws. They also include employers' racist hiring practices that allocate the best-paying jobs to whites, the U.S. government's violation of treaties with Native American tribes that have whittled away reservations' resources, immigration enforcement policies that target certain racially marked groups and leave them afraid to report environmental or other social problems, and racist housing covenants that enabled whites to exclude people of color and environmental hazards alike from their suburban enclaves (Huber 2013; Pulido 2000).

Scholars have long shown that environmental problems stem from the fact that U.S. environmental regulatory agencies have been subject to "capture" by the industries they are charged with regulating (Brown 2007; Cordner 2016; Davidson and Frickel 2004; Downey 2015; Faber 2008, 2018; J. B. Foster 2000; Freudenburg and Gramling 1994; Harvey 2005; Langston 2010; Layzer 2012; Mintz 2012; Nash 2006; O'Brien 2000; O'Connor 1998; Raffensperger and Tickner 1999; Schnaiberg and Gould 1994; Thornton 2000; Tickner 2003; UCS 2008, 2018, 2019; Vogel 2012; Whiteside 2006). The "revolving door" of elites between industry and government agencies and associated regulatory capture have reached new heights in the current administration (Dillon et al. 2018; Fredrickson et al. 2018). Trump's first EPA administrator, Scott Pruitt, stridently defended industry from government regulations as Oklahoma's attorney general and, as EPA administrator, met consistently with industry and not with environmental NGOs (Buford 2017c; Davenport 2017b; Lipton and Friedman 2017a). Similarly, other top appointees in the agency have strong histories of defending industry and fighting environmental regulations (Henry 2017; Lipton 2017a).

Although environmental inequalities have always existed, the neoliberal shift in environmental regulation and activism in recent decades has further rendered environmental and health protections a privilege largely available to the relatively wealthy. Since the 1980s, conservative elites have slashed the budgets for environmental regulation, health care, public education, and programs designed to help the unemployed and disabled; weakened environmental and labor regulations; cut corporate taxes; increasingly privatized prisons, drinking water systems, and other public services; and encouraged individuals to take responsibility for their own health through their shopping decisions, dietary habits, fitness regimens, and other personal behaviors (Auyero 2010; Bakker 2010; Brenner, Peck, and Theodore 2010; Centeno and Cohen 2012; Guthman 2011; Harrison 2014; Harvey 2005; Heynen et al. 2007; Lockie 2013; Mascarenhas 2012; Peck and Tickell 2002; Wacquant 2009). Neoliberal reforms across the state have been driven both by a belief that the best way to solve social problems is not through government intervention but instead through economic growth and free trade, as well as by racist resentment of civil rights protections and affirmative action programs that sought to extend the benefits of early twentieth-century New Deal-era programs to women and people of color (Harrison 2011, 2014; Hochschild 2016; Huber 2013; Omi and Winant 2015; Pulido 2015). Scholars have shown that this retrenchment renders government agencies less able to regulate polluters, leaves overburdened communities more vulnerable to environmental harms, and absolves the state of responsibility for environmental and health problems.

Many mainstream environmental organizations have accommodated this broader context by increasingly relying on neoliberal practices: shifting their own resources away from fighting for regulatory and policy reforms and increasingly advocating for private-sector "solutions" such as green consumerism and pollution markets like carbon cap-and-trade (pollution permit trading) systems (Faber 2008; Guthman 2008a; Harrison 2008, 2011, 2014; Heynen et al. 2007; London et al. 2013; McCarthy 2005; Park and Pellow 2011). At the same time, scholars have observed a neoliberalization of popular culture, in which everyday people vocally dismiss the state and instead advocate for and rely on voluntary, individual, charitable, and market-based measures to address their environmental concerns (Guthman 2008a, 2011; Maniates 2001; Szasz 2007). All of these trends leave environmental problems underregulated, especially for the vulnerable communities who bear the greatest burden of environmental problems and are unable to buy their way out of them.

Key Tenets of Environmental Justice

Within these contexts that create and reinforce environmental inequalities, EJ organizations have fought to improve environmental conditions in the most overburdened and vulnerable communities.[2] Notwithstanding the complexity of ideas and practices within the EJ movement, EJ activist organizations have shared numerous overarching tenets that have cohered them as a movement. I draw these tenets from EJ advocates' published declarations (e.g., Principles 1991; Michigan Environmental Justice Work Group Report 2018), my own observations of EJ advocacy, and scholars' overviews of EJ activism (Benford 2005; Bullard 1990; Bullard et al. 2007; Cable and Shriver 1995; Capek 1993; Cole and Foster 2001; Di Chiro 1998; Faber 2008; Faber and McCarthy 2003; Holifield, Chakraborty, and Walker 2018; Low and Gleeson 1998; Pellow 2018; Pellow and Brulle 2005; Sandweiss 1998; Schlosberg 2007; Shrader-Frechette 2002; Taylor 2000; Walker 2012). Although EJ advocacy has not always lived up to them, they constitute aspirational principles for what justice ultimately requires. Therefore, in this book, I use the following tenets to judge agencies' EJ policies, programs, and practices.

First, *environmental justice requires that the state protect the rights of all people to live free from environmental harm.* While EJ activists use many tactics, they have insisted that justice requires pursuing change through regulatory and policy protections. EJ activists argue that freedom from environmental harm should be a *right* to be protected by the state, not a privilege available only to those with means to buy their way into safer environments. For example, in his now-classic treatise on the EJ movement, *Dumping in Dixie* (1990), scholar-activist Robert Bullard described trends in EJ mobilization, highlighted activists' demand that environmental protections are rights to be guaranteed by the state, and articulated a model EJ framework that foregrounds the pursuit of change through regulatory and policy protections (Bullard 1990, 113, 122). As Jonathan London and colleagues (London et al. 2013) emphasize, EJ advocacy rejects the neoliberal shift in environmentalism and environmental regulation for treating environmental protection as a commodity available only to those with means:

> Environmental justice scholarship and social movements have launched critiques of the retrenchment of state regulation and the ascendency of market-based public policy as perpetuating unjust distributions of environmental hazards. … A preference for public over private sector solutions by many environmental justice advocates derives from a relatively positive generational history of civil rights legislation and litigation on the one hand and the experience of being "dumped on" by corporations operating according to market logics on the other. … Advocates emphasize the importance of social movement pressure on the state apparatus to ensure alignment with environmental justice values and to regulate the market to reduce its structural inequities. (792, 795)

For these reasons, EJ advocates have argued that environmental justice requires reforming regulatory practice in line with EJ principles. These include *race-conscious* government policies to target and reduce racial environmental inequalities. To be sure, EJ advocacy in practice sometimes deviates from this tenet. Notably, whereas EJ advocacy historically has opposed neoliberal regulatory rollback and the associated reliance on market-based environmental change, I show in chapter 7 that some EJ activists have problematically abandoned this non-neoliberal stance.

Second, EJ activists argue that government agencies and environmental organizations need to explicitly identify and prioritize environmental improvements in communities facing the greatest cumulative environmental impacts. Cumulative impacts are a function of both the full scope of environmental stressors a community faces (including environmental hazards and any deficits in important environmental amenities such as parks and playgrounds) and the community's vulnerability to harm from those stressors (including poverty, racism, and geographic isolation, which render the effects of exposure to environmental hazards more serious in some communities than others; see Cutter, Boruff, and Shirley 2003; EPA 2017k, 10–19; NEJAC 2014; Solomon et al. 2016). These improvements will require reducing contamination, fostering community revitalization, and protecting against gentrification.

Third, environmental justice requires *reducing environmental inequality and other forms of material inequality*. That is, in addition to reducing cumulative impacts in the most overburdened and vulnerable communities, justice also requires that environmental regulatory agencies create environmental equity among communities (also characterized as reducing environmental disparity or disproportionality of environmental harm). Other aspects of material inequality—such as those that pertain to wealth, health care, education, shelter, and food—are beyond the purview of environmental regulatory agencies and thus need to be addressed by other state institutions. This commitment to distributive justice sets EJ advocacy apart from the utilitarianism of mainstream environmental politics and guides EJ activists' criticisms of environmental regulation (Harrison 2011, 2014).

Fourth, EJ advocates have insisted that environmental justice requires *making environmental decision-making processes more democratic*. EJ activists have criticized the undemocratic nature of regulatory agencies' decision-making processes, in which industry actors enjoy consistent access to and deferential treatment by regulators while community members' participation is limited to points late in the decision-making process, their knowledge is often treated dismissively by state actors and industry representatives, and their input rarely changes regulatory outcomes.

Strengthening public participation in environmental decision-making enables residents of marginalized communities and the organizations who represent their interests to monitor, analyze, and critically challenge proposed agency decisions. Community members and their advocates contribute valuable knowledge, ask questions experts have not been asking, point out data gaps, and raise critical questions about the ethical basis of standard scientific norms (Brown 2007; Brulle 2000; Cole and Foster 2001; Di Chiro 1998; Pezzullo and Sandler 2007a,b). This includes risk assessment, which, although typically communicated and conducted in technocratic ways, warrants being conducted more democratically. Risk assessment requires many subjective decisions—such as how to account for data gaps, how to characterize the full array of risks to which communities are exposed, and how to resolve scientific disagreement (which can be frequent and significant). The fact that communities tend to conceptualize risk in very different terms than bureaucrats do underscores the point that assessing risk is not an objective exercise for which there is one correct answer (S. Foster 2000; Kuehn 1996; O'Brien 2000; O'Neill 2000; Tesh 2001; Whiteside 2006).

Fifth, environmental justice requires that government agencies *use the precautionary principle* to more assertively reduce environmental problems (Brown 2007, 220–221; Faber 2008; Harrison 2011; Liévanos 2012; Morello-Frosch, Pastor, and Sadd 2002; NEJAC 2004; NJDEP EJAC 2009, 4; Sze and London 2008). This principle holds that, when current data and analytical techniques indicate that hazards likely pose serious risks to human health or the environment, agencies must take action to reduce those risks—even without full scientific certainty (O'Brien 2000; Raffensperger and Tickner 1999; Thornton 2000; Whiteside 2006). Precautionary principle advocates highlight the limits of risk assessment, asserting that regulatory agencies should strive to prevent pollution and find alternatives to harmful products and practices.

Sixth, environmental justice requires economic and racial justice: *challenging and breaking down structures of exploitation and oppression that produce unjust inequalities* throughout social life. EJ advocates emphasize that environmental injustices stem from systems of economic inequality (manifesting as poverty, the racial wealth gap, labor exploitation, and consolidation of corporate power) and cultural oppression (including racism, sexism, and disregard for Native American communities' sovereignty and rights). As Cole and Foster (2001) explain, many EJ activists "view environmental problems in their communities as connected to larger structural failings—inner-city disinvestment, residential segregation, lack of decent health care, joblessness, and poor education. Similarly, many activists also seek remedies that are more fundamental than simply stopping a local polluter or toxic dumper. Instead, many view the need for broader, structural reforms as a way to alleviate many of the problems, including environmental degradation, that their communities endure" (33). To be sure, the EJ movement has not been as anti-capitalist as some EJ scholars and some activists in other environmental movements (Pellow 2014, 2018; Pulido, Kohl, and Cotton 2016). That said, the anti-*racist* commitments of EJ activists and EJ scholars are rarely seen in other environmental politics. They have explicitly lambasted racism within the mainstream environmental movement (Pezzullo and Sandler 2007a; Taylor 2014b), and, as I show throughout this book, EJ advocates within and beyond the state also decry racist ideology within regulatory agencies and its detrimental influence on agencies' EJ reform efforts.

Government Agencies' Efforts to Institutionalize Environmental Justice Principles

In 1993, in response to years of pressure from EJ activists and scholars, U.S. EPA created an Office of Environmental Equity (soon to be renamed the Office of Environmental Justice), and in 1994 President Clinton issued Executive Order 12898 (EO 12898) instructing all federal agencies to integrate EJ principles into regulatory practice (Clinton 1994a). While a few EJ-supportive staff from regulatory agencies helped advocate for the federal government's official endorsements of environmental justice, agencies' EJ efforts are widely understood as prompted largely by EJ advocates. Even EPA's own "Environmental Justice" webpage introducing its EJ efforts situates key moments of federal EJ policies and programs in a timeline of the broader EJ movement (EPA 2017a).

Since the early 1990s, EJ activists and scholars have celebrated the government's official recognition of EJ while expressing considerable skepticism about its EJ efforts. That wariness is well justified, given the neoliberal backlash against environmental regulation and civil rights since the 1980s. Early critics noted that EJ at U.S. EPA was marginalized: situated in a small office and given few resources or authority over the rest of the agency.

Yet agencies' EJ efforts cannot be so easily dismissed these days. As I detail in chapter 2, many environmental regulatory agencies in the United States have started to adopt EJ policies, programs, and practices in response to EJ activism. The U.S. EPA has led such efforts, developing EJ programs and providing EJ guidance to federal, state, and tribal agencies, many of which have started to integrate EJ principles into their own policies, programs, and practices. Agencies undertaking EJ efforts have created formal EJ policies, convened EJ advisory committees, developed EJ trainings for staff, developed public participation guidelines to disseminate information more widely and solicit community input on regulatory decisions, and developed EJ screening tools to identify communities that are environmentally overburdened and socially vulnerable. They hire "EJ staff" who educate coworkers about environmental inequality, propose ways to integrate EJ principles throughout agency practice, and collaborate with coworkers to implement those proposals. Additionally, a few agencies have funded cross-agency and multi-agency projects to reduce cumulative impacts in certain overburdened communities and establish models for systematically reforming regulatory work, created EJ grant programs allocating funds to community-based and tribal organizations, and started to develop EJ protocols for the core regulatory functions of permitting, enforcement, and rulemaking.

EJ advocates inform these processes through agencies' EJ advisory committees and public meetings, and occasionally by being hired to administer EJ programs. Even while advising agencies on EJ reforms and otherwise seeking regulatory protections from environmental harm, EJ activists' stance toward the state is critical and confrontational. Indeed, they often describe their role as *forcing* the state to do things it is not committed to.

Notwithstanding these valuable EJ reform initiatives that reflect years of hard work by EJ-supportive staff and EJ activists who advise them, agencies' EJ efforts still fall far short of key EJ movement principles. Notably, EJ reforms are not institutionalized in ways that would systematically reduce cumulative impacts in overburdened and vulnerable communities or create greater environmental equity across communities. They also lack adequate accountability measures and in some cases may undermine critical EJ advocacy. Agencies' EJ efforts improve environmental conditions in certain cases, create new ways for people in overburdened and marginalized communities to invest more time in the regulatory process, and establish valuable precedent needed to institutionalize EJ reforms throughout regulatory practice. However, agencies' EJ efforts have, at this point, required few substantive concessions from industries that profit off of hazards and little meaningful, systematic change to the regulatory practices that authorize them to do so.

After many years of hard work by agency EJ staff and their EJ-supportive coworkers, agencies' efforts to implement EJ policies still fall far short of the expectations of the advocates who fought for them. Why has this happened? For staff trying to fight for environmental justice from the inside of these agencies, what constraints do they face? This book answers these questions, and in so doing offers new insights into why government agencies fail to keep our most vulnerable communities safe from environmental harms. It also shows how EJ staff and their EJ-supportive colleagues endeavor to surmount these challenges and fight for environmental justice from the inside out.

Other Studies of EJ Policy Implementation

Other environmental justice scholars have contributed important insights into why, despite the hard work of some agency staff, government agencies' EJ efforts fall so short of the principles of the EJ movement that fought for them. Some scholars take a political economic approach, emphasizing that elected officials have neutered EJ programs and restricted their funding due to industry hostility to the new regulatory restrictions those programs might bring (Eady 2003; Faber 2008; Gauna 2015; Gerber 2002; Liévanos 2012; Liévanos, London, and Sze 2011; London, Sze, and Liévanos 2008; Shilling, London, and Liévanos 2009). Such work situates agencies' disappointing progress on EJ within the decades of neoliberal weakening of government protections for the environment, labor, and the poor. Others taking a legal studies approach highlight how court decisions and weak EJ policy undermine agencies' EJ efforts by underspecifying their authority to implement more robust EJ reforms, failing to provide clear instructions for implementation, and directing staff to focus on practices that reflect narrow interpretations of EJ (Cole 1999; Foster 2000; Gauna 2015; Holifield 2004, 2012; Konisky 2015a; Noonan 2015; Yang 2002). Scholars have also attributed agencies' disappointing EJ efforts to technical limitations, such as the inadequacy of EJ analytical techniques that would more accurately identify the most environmentally burdened communities and the full scope of harms they face (Eady 2003; Gauna 2015; Holifield 2012, 2014; Payne-Sturges et al. 2012; Shadbegian and Wolverton 2015).

This scholarship informs my own analysis. Indeed, all staff I interviewed identified these factors—limited resources, regulatory authority, and analytical tools—as constraints to EJ policy implementation. This set of explanations was so consistent that I refer to it as "the standard narrative" about why agencies' EJ efforts fall short of meeting EJ advocates' principles. In chapter 3, I detail these claims and show how these factors most certainly stymie agencies' progress on EJ. Yet I also provide evidence that agencies could nevertheless do more to support environmental justice—and thus that something else is going on. That is, while the standard narrative is not an inaccurate story about agencies' EJ efforts, it also is not a complete one. In this book, I show that the slow progress of environmental regulatory agencies' EJ efforts *also* stems from elements of regulatory workplace culture: practices through which agency staff, in responding to proposed EJ reforms, express their ideas about how things are done and should be done within these organizations. Drawing on popular notions of agencies' goals, practices, and effectiveness, some staff reject proposed EJ reforms. At the same time, due to conflicting ideas about the best ways to pursue environmental justice, some agency staff promote "EJ" in principle but do so in ways that deviate from traditional tenets of the EJ movement. While the standard narrative suggests that the slow pace of agencies' EJ efforts stems from factors beyond the control of agency staff, I show in this book that staff bear some responsibility for these outcomes. I also show how agencies' EJ staff and their EJ-supportive peers work to confront and circumvent these constraints, though their marginalized and subordinated status makes this difficult.

Organization Theory: Institutional Logics and Resistance to Change

This book provides fresh insights into why environmental regulatory agencies, as a group of organizations, have institutionalized few substantive EJ reforms to regulatory practice in response to social movement pressure despite, in many cases, formal policy commitments to those social movement principles. Organization theorists' studies of other organizational contexts provide useful insights into such outcomes.

Like other organizations, environmental regulatory agencies are shaped by the organizational fields within which they are situated. Organizational fields are comprised of networks of actors that interact with organizations (including from industry, the state, and social movements), as well as *institutional logics*—widespread cognitive understandings of how things *are* done and normative positions about how things *should* function (Davis et al. 2005; DiMaggio and Powell 1983; Friedland and Alford 1991; Meyer and Rowan 1977; Scott 2014). Organizations often face *competing* institutional logics—"fragmented and contending institutional pressures," which present ongoing tensions and challenges for organizations (Scott 2014, 182; see also Greenwood et al. 2011; Pache and Santos 2010, 2013). For example, social movement demands for regulatory and policy change often conflict with industry expectations as well as bureaucrats' own ideas about the government's roles and responsibilities. Scholars have investigated and categorized organizations' responses to such seemingly incompatible expectations (Greenwood et al. 2011; Pache and Santos 2010, 2013). Some organizations respond by symbolically legitimizing some demands—such as those of a social movement—without implementing substantive changes to the organization's activities. In such cases, the organization's practices have become *decoupled* from those formally declared commitments—such that the organization has effectively coopted them to manage external challengers (Gamson 1975; Hallett 2010; Meyer and Rowan 1977; Pache and Santos 2013; Selznick 1966). In other cases, organizations respond by refusing to change at all, resulting in *organizational inertia*.

Scholars have identified the *mechanisms* that contribute to this decoupling and inertia (Campbell 2005; Scott 2014, 151–156). For example, scholars explain that state capacity limitations, such as funding and political autonomy, mediate the extent to which organizations institutionalize social movement demands that conflict with other institutional logics (Bonastia 2000; Kellogg 2011; Liévanos 2012; Rogers-Dillon and Skrentny 1999; Skocpol 1985; Skrentny 1998; Zald et al. 2005). Such reform efforts are also shaped by the extent to which key agency representatives express support for movement principles (Jenness and Grattet 2001, 131; Shilling, London, and Liévanos 2009; Zald, Morrill, and Rao 2005) and institute surveillance and sanctions to compel compliance (Zald, Morrill, and Rao 2005; Kellogg 2011). Scholars also observe that organizations' responses to competing logics can be shaped by internal disagreement among its own members, who often hold differing interpretations of the organization's purposes and goals (Alvesson 2011; Binder 2007; Espeland 1998; Greenwood et al. 2011; Hallett and Ventresca 2006; Kellogg 2011; Pache and Santos 2010, 2013). Anne-Claire Pache and Felipe Santos (2010, 2013) thus encourage scholars to treat organizations not as "unitary actors developing strategic responses to outside pressures," but instead as "complex entities composed of various groups promoting different values, goals, and interests ... [and which] play an important role in interpreting and enacting the institutional demands exerted on organizations" (2010, 456, 459).

In particular, while some organization members respond to institutional pressures by endorsing organizational changes, other organization members successfully resist them. This resistance to change gets enacted not only by elites, but also through *everyday interactions among staff*. Thus, identifying the mechanisms producing organizational inertia includes taking a *constructionist approach*—identifying the discursive and other interactive processes among organization members through which they define what the organization does and should do, and tracing the effects of these practices (Phillips and Hardy 2002; Schwalbe et al. 2000). In everyday interactions as well as reports and other objects, organization members continually maintain and defend claims about what the organization's purpose, goals, identity, priorities, and practices are and should be and ward off competing ideas (Alvesson and Robertson 2016; Binder 2007; Burke 2018; Espeland 1998; Fernandez 2015; Kenny, Whittle, and Willmott 2016; Kreiner and Murphy 2016; Lawrence 2008; Pratt et al. 2016). As Alvesson (2011) and Scott (2014) explain, organization members interactively make sense of and maintain these meanings through direct assertions about the organization's mission, identity, and priorities, but also in ways that are only partially verbalized—such as through stories, classification, labels, jargon, gestures, signals, humor, and rumors. Moreover, these interactive dynamics play out on unequal terrain—the ability of organization members to successfully enforce or resist calls for change depends on their relative power within the organization and how widespread their ideas are among organization members (Greenwood et al. 2011; Pache and Santos 2011).

This Book's Argument and Theoretical Contributions

As I detail in chapter 2, the practices of environmental regulatory agencies with formal EJ policies are largely decoupled from their formal EJ commitments, while other agencies display complete organizational inertia in the face of calls for regulatory reform from EJ activists and the concerted efforts of EJ-supportive staff within them. Other EJ scholars have shown that these outcomes stem in part from *material* elements of agencies' organizational fields that are beyond the control of agency staff—resource constraints and political economic pressure, uncertain legal authority to implement EJ reforms, and underdeveloped analytical tools. In this book, I follow the constructionist approach of organizational discourse studies and build on a long line of constructionist scholarship in environmental sociology[3] to offer a new, additional explanation for the disappointing progress of environmental regulatory agencies' EJ reforms.

Drawing on extensive interviews with agency staff and observations of agency meetings, I show that environmental regulatory agencies' EJ efforts are undermined not only by material constraints outside the control of agency staff but also by ways in which staff, when responding to proposed EJ reforms, strive to defend what they think the goals and priorities should be of the regulatory organizations they work for and to which they feel very committed. That is, I show that *cultural* elements of agencies' organizational fields—specifically, institutional logics about environmental regulatory agencies' goals, priorities, and effectiveness—produce disagreement among staff about which proposed EJ reforms (if any) are appropriate and compel some staff to engage in practices that undermine agencies' EJ reforms. Some staff outright reject proposed EJ reforms, such as by verbally disparaging them as irreconcilable with the organization's identity, claiming that environmental inequalities are not serious, ignoring EJ staff members' recommendations, and in some cases even bullying EJ staff because of their EJ work. Through these everyday discursive and other practices, some staff define "environmental justice"—the fight against racial and other forms of environmental inequality—as outside the scope of what these organizations do. This resistance has transcended changes in elected officials and their varying degrees of support for EJ reforms. In conjunction with the material constraints other scholars have demonstrated, these cultural practices stymie the efforts of agencies' EJ staff and their EJ-supportive coworkers. These practices and the beliefs that motivate them constitute part of the structures of oppression that produce environmental injustice in the first place. Some are unique to regulatory agencies. Others are not; notably, this study provides a lens to examine how racial ideologies and ideas of justice pervasive in U.S. culture play out within these organizations in ways that limit the prospects for reforms designed to reduce racial environmental inequality.

To be sure, these practices are not done by all staff. However, they are common enough to undermine the efforts of agencies' EJ staff. Because EJ staff are few in number and possess minimal authority within their organizations, they are unable to *require* the institutionalization of EJ principles that conflict with dominant institutional logics. Instead, they must educate their colleagues about EJ, try to convince them that EJ reforms are worth their support and cooperation, and negotiate EJ reforms their colleagues will accept. Some bureaucrats become supportive of EJ staff members and the reforms they propose. However, others do not, and I show in chapters 4, 5, and 6 how their resistance to EJ undermines the efforts of EJ staff and contributes to organizational inertia—the continuation of regulatory practice that fails to protect America's most vulnerable and environmentally burdened communities. Moreover, I show in chapter 7 how some EJ-supportive staff themselves unwittingly weaken their own EJ programs by operationalizing "EJ" in ways that deviate from longstanding priorities of the EJ movement.

My findings strengthen the scholarship on EJ policy implementation by showing that agencies' disappointing progress on EJ reforms stems not only from hostile acts of conservative political elites, industry pressure to deregulate, and other factors scholars have rightly noted, but also from everyday practices through which some staff define how these institutions should best protect public health and the environment. In this book, I focus on these elements of regulatory workplace culture because they have received little attention in the scholarship to date. Making greater progress on EJ reforms within environmental regulatory agencies will require more resources, clarification and perhaps expansion of various regulatory authorities, more robust EJ analytical tools, endorsement by leadership, and other factors that other scholars have rightly noted. But it will also require changing these agencies' organizational culture so that staff and leadership treat EJ as *central* to what these organizations do, and so that they define EJ in ways that align with longstanding EJ movement principles.

By providing a rare glimpse inside these agencies, this book augments scholarship illuminating U.S. environmental regulatory agency culture (Espeland 1998; Fortmann 1990; Harrison 2011; Langston 1995, 2010; Mintz 2012; Pautz and Rinfret 2011, 2014; Rinfret and Pautz 2013; Robertson 2010; Taylor 1984). These studies—as well as this book—help us understand that, in many cases, state institutions' failures to curtail environmental degradation stem in part from the ways bureaucrats within them strive to do what they think best serves the agency's mission. More broadly, these findings show that scholars trying to explain environmentally problematic government practices should attend to popular ideas among government agency staff, how they act on them, and other internal dynamics within government agencies—dynamics that often transcend political administrations.

Yet this book is not only a story about constraint. Throughout, I also identify ways in which EJ staff and their small but growing network of colleagues supportive of EJ reforms work to circumvent those constraints, in other cases directly challenge them, and in the process make EJ part of their agency's organizational identity. Although they are members of environmental regulatory agencies, many also identify as part of the EJ movement or at least as strong supporters of it. They can thus be understood as activists working within the agencies, trying to change them from the inside out, akin to the "insider activists" and "tempered radicals" striving to change organization practice in accordance with movement principles in other contexts (Banaszak 2005; Espeland 1998; Katzenstein 1999; King and Pearce 2010; Meyerson and Scully 1995; Santoro and McGuire 1997; Soule 2012). They also constitute a subset of "expert activists" or "shadow mobilization"—formally trained experts working to support EJ movements (Frickel 2004a,b; Frickel, Torcasso, and Anders 2015). Throughout the book, I identify the discursive and other mechanisms through which EJ staff and their EJ-supportive colleagues attempt to challenge their coworkers' resistance to EJ, redefine their agencies' goals, reevaluate how effectively they have been met, and in turn build further support for proposed EJ reforms among the ranks of agency staff.

Research Approach and Methods

This book addresses the following questions: Why do government agencies allow environmental inequalities to persist? Why do they have such a hard time improving environmental conditions in our nation's most overburdened and vulnerable communities? I study agencies' EJ efforts as a case through which to help answer these questions, as environmental justice is explicitly, fundamentally about ameliorating these problems. Thus, I ask: Why, despite the commitments and accomplishments of agencies' EJ staff, have their EJ programs, policies, and practices done so little to improve conditions in the most environmentally burdened communities and to reduce environmental inequalities among communities? My first interviews with EJ staff indicated that other scholars' explanations for the slow pace of EJ programs, while not inaccurate, are incomplete, as EJ staff emphasized to me that they face resistance not only from conservative elected officials and industry but also from some of their own coworkers. Thus, to strengthen our understandings of why government agencies have not protected our most overburdened and vulnerable communities, I illuminate the experiences of staff who lead and advocate for EJ reforms to regulatory practice, and in particular I focus on their interactions with coworkers who resist these efforts.

The title of this book is a nod to Luke Cole and Sheila Foster's excellent early overview of the EJ movement, *From the Ground Up* (2001). Their title references their focus on grassroots activists' perspectives on environmental injustice. As Cole and Foster explain: "[G]rassroots struggles are a window into the social relations and processes that underlie distributive outcomes. A view from the ground (or the field) allows us to see the many dimensions of power struggles, the relationships of actors within these struggles, and the role of the regulatory and legal framework in structuring those relationships" (10, 12). My book examines a parallel struggle—that of agency EJ staff and their EJ-supportive colleagues, who work from marginalized positions within their own organizations to pursue environmental justice.

I wanted to understand the challenges EJ-supportive staff face in trying to promote EJ reforms within their organizations. To do so, I conducted confidential, semi-structured interviews with staff from environmental regulatory agencies and ethnographic observation at agency meetings in the United States. Ethnographic observation and interviews enabled me to identify how different staff define their responsibilities and agency identity, how they define what "EJ" means, how staff react to proposed EJ reforms, and which practices EJ-supportive staff employ to pursue environmental justice in light of the constraints they face. The semi-structured nature of the interviews allowed me to pursue certain themes of interest, my participants to narrate and interpret their experiences, and us to develop the rapport necessary to discuss politically controversial issues. Confidential interviews and internal (i.e., not public) meetings give staff the space to express beliefs they do not (and cannot) express in formal agency documents or public events.

Central to this book are interviews I conducted from 2011 to 2019 with 89 current and former agency representatives. Most of my interview participants have worked at their agency for at least 15 years. About half of these are or were EJ staff who administered agency EJ programs. I interviewed nearly all of the EJ staff at my study sites, which enabled me to gain rich, robust insights into the experience of staff advocating for EJ reforms. The majority of these individuals are persons of color, which appears to reflect the broader population of agencies' EJ staff. The other half were not formally assigned to work on "EJ" programs; their sentiments about EJ reforms varied from enthusiasm to ambivalence to contempt, some participated in their agency's EJ efforts as their time and interests allowed, and most of these individuals are white, as are most staff in environmental regulatory agencies. I asked my interview participants to describe their current and past involvement with agency EJ efforts, which EJ reforms (if any) they view as important and which they disagree with, which challenges agency EJ efforts have faced, how staff react to proposed EJ reforms, and whether and how those reactions have changed over time. For my interviews with EJ staff, I also asked how coworkers' reactions influence the implementation of EJ reforms, and to describe the strategies they use to persevere in their EJ efforts despite the constraints they face. The interviews with other (non-EJ) staff enabled me to corroborate and augment EJ staff members' accounts and to glean a broader set of perspectives on EJ reforms.

Interview participants included representatives from U.S. EPA (including EPA headquarters, eight of its regional offices, and one other satellite office), U.S. Department of Justice, U.S. Department of the Interior, seven state environmental regulatory agencies (California Environmental Protection Agency, Colorado Department of Public Health and Environment, Connecticut Department of Energy and Environmental Protection, Minnesota Pollution Control Agency, New York State Department of Environmental Conservation, Oregon Department of Environmental Quality, and Rhode Island Department of Environmental Management), and city or county agencies in California, Colorado, and Missouri. To account for variation among agencies' progress on EJ policy implementation, I included agencies with the most longstanding and advanced EJ efforts (notably, U.S. EPA, California, and New York) and others with less substantial EJ reforms and programs. My study sites also vary in the number of designated EJ staff, their geographic region in the United States, and whether they have a formal EJ policy endorsed by agency leadership or the legislature. Including state-level agencies was important, as they hold primary responsible for enforcing much federal environmental law and have considerable discretion with how they do so. Notwithstanding the variation among these study sites and their improvements over time, all agencies' EJ efforts still fall short of EJ advocates' expectations (as I detail in chapter 2). Thus, the multi-sited study design enabled me to identify conditions that transcend this diverse array of institutions. Where exceptions exist, I note them and identify the factors that help to explain them.

I also observed numerous agency meetings relating to their EJ efforts. These included public meetings: informational sessions about EJ grant programs, EJ advisory committee meetings, a public participation event about an EJ controversy, and various other agency-convened EJ webinars, workshops, and conference calls. These ranged from 90 minutes to two full days. These helped me meet and recruit interview participants, observe how staff talk to EJ advocates, and observe how EJ advocates advise agencies on what their EJ efforts should entail. My observations also included internal (not public) agency EJ-related meetings. These included four internal EJ planning meetings, and one internal EJ training session for staff. These lasted from one to two hours, and each included about 15 to 30 agency staff. These internal meetings were especially valuable, as they allowed me to observe how bureaucrats react to and characterize EJ reforms. Whereas in public meetings bureaucrats tend to present a united front and be very circumspect, in internal meetings they debated the merits of proposals and defended competing perspectives.

I analyzed my interview transcripts, fieldnotes, published scholarship, and other documents for what they revealed about constraints to regulatory agencies' EJ efforts and techniques through which EJ-supportive staff strive to circumvent or confront those constraints. Throughout the book, I have endeavored to be clear about how much I can generalize from my data. In some cases, I have sufficient evidence that an element of regulatory culture is fairly widespread. Notably, I interviewed such a large portion of all EJ staff in the United States, and their accounts have so much in common, that I feel confident making claims about the experiences of EJ staff in U.S. environmental regulatory agencies. Additionally, my own findings and other scholarship alike indicate that environmental regulatory agency staff tend to identify as public servants and environmental stewards, take great pride in their work, and often make sacrifices for their jobs. In contrast, some of the practices and beliefs I describe—including those relating to racism and racial inequality—have not been studied by other scholars in the context of environmental regulatory agencies. Thus, while extant scholarship shows that these beliefs are widespread in U.S. society and my own data allow me to confidently state that these practices widely affect EJ staff, I am unable to specify how widely held these ideas are by staff in general.

I also interviewed 50 representatives of EJ activist organizations, both to better understand what they feel agencies' EJ efforts should entail and to evaluate how well agencies' EJ grant programs meet the needs of grantees and other EJ activists. The activists I interviewed are diverse in racial/ethnic identity and located in California, Colorado, Georgia, Maryland, Massachusetts,

Minnesota, New York, Oregon, Pennsylvania, Puerto Rico, Rhode Island, and Washington, DC.

I acknowledge that some individuals do not fit neatly into one category of "scholar," "bureaucrat," or "activist." Some of my research participants identify as activists working within the state, some activists and bureaucrats publish academic scholarship, and some individuals traverse all three fields.

Most of the staff I interviewed at all agencies expressed acute, repeated concerns about confidentiality, as did some of the activists. I started all interviews by briefly describing my research project and my confidentiality protections—notably, that I would not identify any of my research participants in conversation, written communication, or publications. Most asked numerous questions about the confidentiality protections, often at several points in our interview, and how I would characterize their identity in my writing. While some insisted that I could quote them freely and use their name, most spoke only on condition of confidentiality—and some made clear that I should not let anyone know they had talked with me at all. Agency staff were most worried that their own supervisors or colleagues would learn that they were critically commenting about the organization's progress on EJ, how colleagues react to proposed EJ reforms, and industry pressure on agency decision-making. I used a multi-sited study design to make it difficult for my readers to guess the organizational affiliation of any participant who I quote. I also use pseudonyms and obscure identifying characteristics of all research participants—including the organization they work for, the state or region they work within, and sometimes even their gender and/or racial identity. I have not shared any research participant's identity with other participants except when given permission to do so.

The staff interviews and observations of internal agency meetings constitute the heart of my data collection and enable this book's unique insights into the challenges facing EJ staff and their EJ-supportive colleagues. They were also hard won. Government agencies are notoriously closed institutions under the best of circumstances, and in this case I conducted my research during a time in which environmental regulation and civil rights protections alike are under political attack. Fortunately, I had largely completed interviews with federal agency staff before the new Trump administration restricted staff members' abilities to speak with researchers. In the appendix, I elaborate on my research methods.

Key Terms

Among EJ advocates, scholars, journalists, and bureaucrats, the terms "EJ community" and "community with EJ concerns" are commonly used shorthand for communities that are environmentally overburdened and disproportionately vulnerable (or "susceptible") to the effects of exposure to those hazards because of racism, sexism, poverty, linguistic isolation, and/or other factors. However, these terms can be confusing, as sometimes they are used to refer specifically to those communities that have politically organized to fight those hazards. I therefore use the phrase "overburdened and vulnerable communities" because my focus is on policies pertaining to all communities characterized by a significant degree of hazard and susceptibility to harm from exposure to that hazard, rather than only communities politically mobilizing for change.

"Overburdened" populations are those that are disproportionately subjected to multiple environmental stressors, which can include contaminated water, air pollution, risk of flooding and other harm from disasters, unsafe housing conditions, workplace hazards, dangerous street traffic, lack of safe play spaces, threats to Indigenous people's subsistence and cultural resources, and inability to access fresh, nutritious, affordable, and culturally appropriate food. "Vulnerable" populations are those that are more susceptible to the adverse effects of exposure to environmental harms (Cutter, Boruff, and Shirley 2003; EPA 2017k, 10–19; NEJAC 2014; Solomon et al. 2016). These include groups that public health experts widely regard as physiologically vulnerable—children, the elderly, pregnant women, and individuals with asthma or compromised immune systems. They also include members of working-class, racially marginalized, immigrant, linguistically isolated, and Native American communities, whose abilities to withstand and recover from environmental harms are compromised by racist biases and violence, exclusion from medical and other social services, fear of interacting with law enforcement, and other social factors (see NJDEP EJAC 2009, 18).

Environmental regulatory agencies are arranged hierarchically, with lower and mid-level staff reporting to "managers," who report to "senior management" (which includes political appointees and senior-level "career" managers). I use the term "staff" generically to refer to any agency representative; I specify some individuals as "managers" when that (more powerful) status is relevant to the discussion. I characterize as "EJ staff" those tasked with leading their agencies' EJ reform efforts; they are very few in number and usually have little authority. I refer to other agency representatives as "other staff," "colleagues," "coworkers," or "bureaucrats"; these catch-all terms refer to staff of all ranks, both career and politically appointed individuals, and any degree of support for EJ reforms (some are strongly supportive, others ambivalent, and others staunchly opposed). Where I use the term "bureaucrat," following Lipsky (1980) and others, I do so non-pejoratively.

I use the phrase "elements of regulatory workplace culture" (or "elements of regulatory culture") to refer to the combination of narrative interactions among staff (which I describe in chapter 4), other interactive dynamics among staff (chapter 5), staff beliefs about their agency's responsibilities and the relationship of proposed EJ reforms to them (chapter 6), and EJ staff members' own definitions of key EJ principles (chapter 7).

The Scope of This Book

To manage the length of this book, I have bounded its scope in several ways. First, I focus on *state and federal agencies' EJ efforts in the United States* and the experiences of their staff. This book does not elaborate the significant ways in which *municipal* decision-making can produce or prevent environmental inequalities. As leading EJ scholars have long demonstrated, discriminatory zoning policies can allow hazardous facilities to become clustered in low-income and racially marginalized communities (Bullard 1990; Bullard et al 2007; Taylor 2014a). That said, through the course of this research, I have interviewed and observed some municipal public health and environment decision-makers. None of their narratives deviated from what I found among state and federal regulators. Thus, I include some of those data in this book. Given that these findings are influenced by the unique historical and current political, cultural, and legal contexts of the United States, other research is needed to investigate the shape of agencies' EJ efforts in other countries (see Bulkeley and Walker 2005; Scandrett 2007) and the factors constraining them.

Second, I focus on environmental regulatory agencies' efforts *formally designated as "environmental justice."* Government agencies have other programs not characterized as "EJ" per se that can improve material conditions in overburdened and vulnerable communities. These include agencies' valuable efforts to remediate lead, mold, and pest infestations in public housing and schools. However, research demonstrating that environmental inequalities have persisted over time (Ard 2015) indicates that such programs are not sufficient. Environmental justice requires that government agencies make environmental equity and the reduction of cumulative impacts in overburdened and vulnerable communities an explicit agency *policy*—rather than leaving it to the whims of uncoordinated special programs. Focusing on agencies' "EJ" efforts enables me to examine whether and how an agency is formally prioritizing these goals.

Third, I focus on *environmental regulatory agencies* instead of other types of government agencies. To be sure, EJ advocates are concerned about a wide range of problems facing their communities—such as accessible and affordable public transportation and healthy food—that are the purview of other types of government agencies. Those organizations thus have important roles to play in institutionalizing environmental justice, and some have started to do so (e.g., DOT 2017, USDA 2015). I focus on environmental regulatory agencies like U.S. EPA because remediating hazards in overburdened, vulnerable communities has always been the leading goal of EJ advocacy, and environmental regulatory agencies have the broadest-reaching control over the hazards to which overburdened and vulnerable communities are exposed.

Fourth, I focus on *elements of environmental regulatory culture*. Other scholars have rightly noted that material factors constrain environmental regulatory agencies' progress on EJ reforms. I elaborate and honor these explanations in chapter 3, and then I focus the rest of the book on cultural explanations precisely because they also matter and have received almost no attention by other scholars. I am unable to specify the *relative* importance of these various constraints. They all matter, and making meaningful progress on EJ reforms will require addressing all of them.

Fifth, I *recommend general EJ reforms to environmental regulatory agency practice* (in chapter 8). I do not specify precisely how to roll them out. Agency staff need this guidance, but it is beyond the scope of this book. Additionally, environmental justice requires reforms that extend beyond the purview of environmental regulatory agencies. EJ advocates have rightly insisted that environmental inequalities are just one symptom of state-sanctioned inequality and racist oppression, which manifest also in realms of health care, labor markets, workplaces, food and nutrition, law enforcement, and education. Justice thus requires policies to redistribute wealth more equitably (e.g., through more progressive income tax structures, higher corporate taxes, higher minimum wages, stronger protections for organized labor, universal health care, and equitable public education), policies to democratize decision-making (e.g., campaign finance reform and fighting voter suppression), as well as policies, regulatory practices, and cultural change to combat racism and other forms of oppression. In short, EJ requires changing the structures that currently give some groups much greater opportunities than others—environmental and otherwise. I write this book as one contribution to this greater cause, and with the hope that it provides insights into how bureaucrats might help to support the broad goal of justice.

Organization of This Book

In chapter 2, I describe agencies' EJ efforts to date, and I specify key ways in which they are essentially decoupled from longstanding EJ movement principles and fail to meet the needs of overburdened and vulnerable communities.

In chapter 3, I address the typical explanations offered by scholars and agency representatives alike for the slow pace of government agencies' EJ efforts: that agencies possess *insufficient resources* to implement proposed EJ reforms; that environmental laws do not grant government agencies the *regulatory authority* to implement some of the EJ reforms proposed by EJ staff; and that agencies' efforts to institutionalize EJ tenets into regulatory practices are hindered by *technical factors* such as insufficient data and underdeveloped EJ analysis techniques. I show that these material elements of agencies' organizational fields indeed condition agencies' EJ efforts, yet I also establish that these explanations do not fully explain agencies' disappointing progress on EJ and thus argue that additional explanations are needed.

In chapters 4 through 7, I showcase my data from interviews with agency staff and observations of agency meetings to demonstrate that environmental regulatory agencies' poor progress on EJ reforms stems also from *aspects of regulatory workplace culture*—ways that bureaucrats respond to EJ staff and interact about proposed EJ reforms. In chapter 4, I describe *discursive mechanisms through which some staff resist proposed EJ reforms*. I show how bureaucrats make claims in everyday workplace interactions—including about their organizations' identity and the scope of racial inequalities—that defend existing regulatory practice and delegitimize proposed EJ reforms. In chapter 5, I describe *other mechanisms through which some staff undermine proposed EJ reforms*—such as ignoring EJ staff and the practices they recommend—and I show how these practices undermine the efforts of

EJ staff. While chapters 4 and 5 identify mechanisms through which staff express resistance to change, chapter 6 offers *explanations* for that resistance to proposed EJ reforms, including uncertainty about how to apply EJ principles, bureaucrats' lack of experience in overburdened and vulnerable communities, as well as institutional logics that cast EJ reforms as inappropriate and unnecessary. In each of chapters 4 through 6, I also showcase how EJ staff and their EJ-supportive colleagues respond to these elements of regulatory workplace culture. Informed by EJ activists, they design and implement EJ reforms and strive to build support for them among their coworkers. Through their practices, EJ-supportive staff brandish a set of institutional logics that are new to environmental regulatory agencies, challenge claims about the effectiveness of regulatory practices, and assert the need to prioritize environmental improvements in America's most overburdened and vulnerable communities.

In chapter 7, I focus my attention on EJ staff themselves, showing that some of the decoupling of agencies' EJ efforts from longstanding priorities of the EJ movement also stems from the ways some EJ staff define "EJ" and apply their ideas. I demonstrate competing claims among EJ staff— such as about the best mechanism for achieving social change—to explain why some EJ staff design EJ programs that deviate from longstanding EJ movement principles. I explain that these conflicts among EJ staff reflect competing institutional logics within U.S. politics in general and the U.S. environmental justice movement in particular.

In chapter 8, I conclude by summarizing my arguments about the importance of agencies' EJ efforts for combatting environmental inequalities that pose grave risks to human health, my critical evaluation of agencies' EJ efforts to date, and my explanations for the slow pace of agencies' EJ reforms. To foster conversation about what *justice* requires of the next environmental regulatory regime, I conclude with numerous recommendations for strengthening the process and progress of EJ policy implementation within environmental regulatory agencies.

2 Government Agencies' Environmental Justice Efforts: Review and Critical Assessment

I have been working with communities even before the term environmental justice existed. Nowadays, unlike when I started doing this work, agencies, many
of them, have diverse staff. Some of them do multi-lingual public notices. They
actually have hearings in communities where they come and smile and have
translation. But what hasn't changed is that, in 99.9 percent of the situations,
they still ignore the facts, violate environmental justice, stab communities in the
back, and issue permits to polluters, no matter what.
—Barry, EJ activist

Many offices have made progress [on environmental justice], but it's all relative.
It's not light-years of progress. It's more like six inches of progress.
—Government agency EJ staff person

In this chapter, I describe and critically evaluate state and federal environmental regulatory agencies' policies, programs, and practices formally designated as "environmental justice." As I will show, some have started to
implement valuable EJ efforts that reflect the hard work and commitments
of agencies' EJ staff and others who support them. However, they fall short
of EJ principles in numerous important respects.

Agencies' Key EJ Efforts to Date

In response to pressure from EJ advocates, some environmental regulatory
agencies over the past 20 years in the United States have started to adopt EJ
policies, programs, and practices.

EJ Policies

EO 12898 directs each federal agency to make EJ part of its mission by reducing environmental problems disproportionately harming low-income and minority communities.[1] In a subsequent memorandum, President Clinton specified that the legal authority of EO 12898 is based in the National Environmental Policy Act and Title VI of the Civil Rights Act. Notably, to strengthen federal enforcement of Title VI of the Civil Rights Act, the memorandum directs agencies to ensure that recipients of federal funding (including state and local governments) do not discriminate on the basis of race, color, or national origin or disparately impact people along those lines (Clinton 1994b).

EPA subsequently developed the following definition of EJ:[2]

> Environmental justice is the fair treatment and meaningful involvement of all people regardless of race, color, national origin, or income, with respect to the development, implementation, and enforcement of environmental laws, regulations, and policies. EPA has this goal for all communities and persons across this nation. It will be achieved when everyone enjoys the same degree of protection from environmental and health hazards, and equal access to the decision-making process to have a healthy environment in which to live, learn, and work. (EPA 2017a)

Just as the EJ movement has fought both for more equitable environmental outcomes and more democratic decision-making processes, this definition entails distributive elements ("fair treatment" and "same degree of protection from environmental and health hazards") and procedural ones ("meaningful involvement" and "equal access to the decision-making process"). EPA also recently formally established the links between these principles and its policies for working with tribes and Indigenous peoples (EPA 2014). Other federal agencies have also developed their own EJ definitions and policies.

Some states have formally committed to integrating EJ principles into one or more areas of agency practice via executive order, legislative policy, strategic plan, and/or administrative order. These include California, Colorado, Connecticut, Hawaii, Illinois, Indiana, Maryland, Massachusetts, Minnesota, New Hampshire, New Jersey, New Mexico, New York, Oregon, Pennsylvania, Rhode Island, South Carolina, and West Virginia. Nearly all of these adopt language from EO 12898 and EPA's definition. Because agencies' environmental laws and policies have not historically included any language about environmental inequalities, formal EJ policies legitimize EJ principles and proposed EJ reforms to agency practice.

EJ Staff

Agencies' EJ efforts are led by "EJ staff," who propose EJ policies, programs, and reforms to regulatory practice, and solicit feedback about and support for those proposals from coworkers, managers, and agency leadership. They are primary contacts for communities concerned about environmental regulation, and they help concerned residents navigate government agencies and connect with agency staff who can assist them. Ultimately, all staff should do EJ through their daily work. In the meantime, EJ staff lead the process of designing EJ reforms to colleagues' work practices.

EJ staff members' efforts are shaped by their limited resources and subordinated structural position within the agencies. EJ staff are few in number—out of hundreds or thousands of employees in any agency, only one or a few are formally assigned to EJ efforts. U.S. EPA's EJ program is by far the largest, with approximately 20 staff in its Office of Environmental Justice in Washington DC and an additional few "EJ coordinators" throughout headquarters and at each of its 10 regional offices (out of 15,000 employees). EJ staff receive few resources with which to conduct their work and generally have little to no authority over other staff. Thus, they cannot impose reforms; instead, they must educate their colleagues about the scope, forms, and roots of environmental inequality and convince coworkers that EJ reforms deserve their cooperation. EJ staff also ask other staff to help design, test, and implement EJ reforms and programs, with some doing so more extensively than others.

Public Meetings and Advisory Committees

EJ staff hold public meetings and hearings to solicit input on their proposed EJ reforms and programs. Some states convene EJ advisory committees (e.g., Michigan Environmental Justice Work Group Report 2018) that typically include representatives from EJ organizations, tribes, academia, industry, and local government. The National Environmental Justice Advisory Council (NEJAC) serves this function for U.S. EPA and has provided extensive written recommendations for how the agency can better support environmental justice. These range from general recommendations about increasing public participation and working with tribes, to specific guidance on integrating EJ principles into agency efforts to prevent chemical plant disasters, reduce air emissions associated with goods movement, and bolster natural disaster preparedness (EPA 2017h).

Peer Learning within and across Agencies

EJ staff at EPA's headquarters and regional offices provide EJ guidance to other federal agencies, state agencies, and tribal governments. Federal agencies share proposed EJ reforms through the Interagency Working Group on Environmental Justice (EJ IWG). In the past, EPA helped fund states' and tribes' EJ reform development efforts through its States and Tribal EJ Cooperative Agreements grants program (EPA 2009a). EPA also periodically hosts All States Environmental Justice conference calls (one in the western United States and another in the eastern United States) for EJ staff from EPA, state agencies, and local agencies. As of late 2018, EPA EJ staff are developing webinars to train states on designing specific EJ reforms. Additionally, EPA and states participate in The Environmental Council on States (ECOS), which occasionally addresses EJ policy reform proposals (notably, see ECOS 2017). Some agencies convene quarterly or monthly internal EJ steering committees comprised of representatives from various agency units.

Some agencies offer EJ trainings to educate staff about the scope and roots of environmental inequalities, build support among staff for EJ reforms, and identify practices through which staff can ensure that future agency actions account for and, ideally, reduce the unequal nature of environmental hazards. Some EJ trainings are administered to teams of workers by EJ staff trained to guide group conversation and learning, but most are administered as optional, online tutorials for individual bureaucrats to complete as their time permits. The task of training staff is a monumental one, given that there are approximately fifteen thousand staff at EPA, about the same at the Department of Energy, and tens of thousands more across other environment-related agencies.

Identifying Overburdened and Vulnerable Communities

To help target their EJ efforts, agencies use EJ screening tools that identify communities that are environmentally overburdened and vulnerable to those hazards (Holifield 2012, 2014; Lewis and Bennett 2013; Payne-Sturges et al. 2012; Shadbegian and Wolverton 2015).

Some agencies have used such tools to conduct extra public engagement within overburdened and vulnerable communities. For example, Connecticut's Department of Energy and Environmental Protection (CDEEP) has published a list of "EJ Communities" defined by various socioeconomic status criteria (CDEEP 2017a). Per statute, the agency requires certain types of hazardous industries seeking to locate or expand facilities in those communities to do extra public engagement (CDEEP 2017b). As another example, California law specifies that at least 25 percent of the proceeds from the state's greenhouse gas cap-and-trade program must fund projects that improve environmental conditions in socially and environmentally "disadvantaged communities." CalEPA uses its EJ screening tool, CalEnviroScreen, to identify areas eligible for those grant funds.[3]

EJ Projects

Some state and federal agencies have participated in place-based EJ projects (sometimes called "EJ pilot projects") to improve environmental conditions in overburdened, vulnerable communities (Bruno and Jepson 2018; Lashley 2016; Liévanos, London, and Sze 2011; London, Sze, and Liévanos 2008). Through these projects, agencies can develop and test practices for increasing public participation in regulatory decision-making, conduct environmental monitoring in innovative ways, collaborate more effectively with other agencies, and build capacity for change among residents. In some cases, agencies have been able to document concrete, measured reduction of environmental harm (e.g., see EPA 2018d, 18). Some projects also demonstrate how redevelopment can serve the community's interests and needs (i.e., not simply those of developers), such as by providing green jobs and constructing health clinics, public transit, affordable housing, or other infrastructure (NEJAC 1996). EJ staff emphasize that these projects set valuable precedent—providing models for how to do regulatory work differently. For instance, efforts to develop more environmentally just general plan processes in National City and Jurupa Valley, California, paved the way for a 2016 law that requires all California cities and counties to incorporate EJ concerns into their general plans (Senate Bill 1000) (CLI 2016). EJ staff also emphasize that EJ projects help create inspirational changes that can legitimize proposed EJ reforms among staff. Agencies' reports that describe their progress in supporting EJ principles tend to showcase such projects (e.g., see EPA 2018d).

Some other agency programs that fund or govern environmental cleanup and community revitalization projects, while not called "EJ" explicitly, have policy language that encourages such projects to be conducted in overburdened and vulnerable communities. For example, many agencies allow companies that have violated environmental laws to offset part of their penalties with a Supplemental Environmental Project (SEP) that improves public health and/or the environment beyond what existing law requires. A few agencies—including in California, Colorado, Illinois, Massachusetts, Missouri, Oregon, and Virginia—encourage violators to do SEPs in overburdened and vulnerable communities (Bonorris 2010; California 2015). Some agencies, including in Colorado and Illinois, have encouraged EJ advocates to submit ideas for potential SEPs to agency staff, who collect these suggestions and share them with violators interested in discussing a SEP in their settlement negotiations.

EJ Grant Programs

EJ advocates lobbied for government agencies to create dedicated EJ grant programs to help address the gap in funding for small-scale, grassroots EJ organizations (Brulle and Jenkins 2005; Faber and McCarthy 2001; Hansen 2012). A few government agencies in the United States have "Environmental Justice" grant programs that provide funding to community-based, non-profit organizations and tribes for nearly any type of project that improves environmental conditions in overburdened and vulnerable communities (Harrison 2015, 2016; London, Sze, and Liévanos 2008; Vajjhala 2010). These are the California Environmental Protection Agency (CalEPA) Environmental Justice Small Grants Program (118 grants awarded from 2005 to 2016), New York EJ Community Impact Grant Program (145 grants from 2006 to 2017), U.S. EPA Environmental Justice Small Grants Program (1,421 grants from 1994 to 2017), and U.S. EPA Environmental Justice Collaborative Problem-Solving (CPS) Cooperative Agreement Program (61 grants from 2003 to 2016). Most of these programs' grants have been between $15,000 and $50,000, though EPA CPS awards range from $100,000 to $120,000. The City of San Francisco's Environmental Justice Grants Program allocated 55 grants from 2001 until its end in 2010. Program administrators recruit reviewers from within the agency representing different areas of technical expertise, who score proposals per program requirements (description of project objectives, work plan, and detailed budget).

A few additional agencies offer issue-specific "EJ" grant funding opportunities to grassroots organizations (e.g., Massachusetts' Urban Forestry EJ Pilot Grant Program provided funding for organizations planting trees in urban areas). Additionally, National Institute of Environmental Health Science's (NIEHS) former Environmental Justice Partnerships for

Communication Grant Program funded collaborations between expert scientists and community organizations to research environmental hazards disproportionately burdening vulnerable populations.

Agencies' EJ grant programs help sustain organizations and coalitions that are often overlooked by foundations and other funders. Funded projects help inform bureaucrats and decision-makers about grassroots EJ organizations and issues facing overburdened and vulnerable communities, when state actors may otherwise only be familiar with the concerns and work of the most prominent environmental organizations. Some EJ grant programs create partnerships among grassroots organizations and other actors. EPA staff have especially lauded its grant programs that feature its "collaborative problem-solving" model (including the CPS program) for helping grantees to continue solving problems after the funding ends (e.g., King 2012; Lee 2005).

Agencies also fund EJ organizations and local government agencies' EJ work through programs not called "EJ" per se and whose greater resources enable their funded projects to significantly impact public health and the environment. For example, EJ advocates widely hailed EPA's former Community Action for a Renewed Environment (CARE) grant program (EPA 2017d; King 2012), EPA's former Community-University Partnership (CUP) grant program (EPA 1998a), EPA's Brownfields Redevelopment grant program (EPA 2017e), NIEHS's Research to Action grant program (NIEHS 2017), Housing and Urban Development's (HUD) former Sustainable Communities Initiative (HUD 2017), Technical Assistance Grants offered through EPA's Superfund and other programs (EPA 2017f), and EPA's Urban Waters Small Grants program (EPA 2018f). California's new Community Air Grants program also supports EJ organizations (ARB 2018).

EJ Reforms to Core Regulatory Practice

Arguably the most important form of EJ policy implementation is the systematic integration of EJ principles into the core regulatory decision-making practices through which agencies govern environmental conditions: rulemaking, permitting, and enforcement. Whereas EJ grant programs and other EJ projects improve environmental conditions at specific sites as funding allows and can be done by a relatively small number of staff, integrating EJ principles into core regulatory practice could reduce environmental inequalities and democratize decision-making through every regulatory decision and across each agency's geographic jurisdiction, and they require the cooperation of most agency staff.

These efforts accelerated in the Obama administration when EPA Administrator Lisa Jackson's senior advisor on EJ prioritized the development of guidance documents for integrating EJ principles into core regulatory functions. These guidance documents have focused on two objectives: creating more opportunities for public engagement, and integrating EJ analysis into regulatory decision-making. "EJ analysis" can include using EJ screening tools to identify communities that have the greatest environmental burdens and social vulnerabilities, assessing how a regulatory decision might disproportionately burden some groups over others, and/or doing a cumulative impact assessment to identify how all of a community's hazards and vulnerabilities together impact human health. The federal government's guidance documents on integrating EJ analysis into environmental review required under the National Environmental Policy Act is an early and prominent example of such materials, which were further developed in 2016 (CEQ 1997; EPA 1998b; EJ IWG 2016; see also CalEPA 2010). Subsequent guidance documents identify how other environmental laws and regulations authorize federal agencies to implement specific EJ reforms, drawing on analyses such as those in EPA's EJ Legal Tools report (EPA 2011b). I will briefly note how agencies have sought to integrate EJ into three key specific areas of core regulatory work: rulemaking, permitting, and enforcement. This work is very nascent. With the exception of guidelines for increasing public participation, agencies are still debating what specific changes to staff practices are required for EJ.

Rulemaking   Rulemaking is the process through which environmental regulatory agencies translate laws into enforceable regulations (or "rules"). Regulations set air and water quality standards and specify permissible production and waste management practices. Agencies regularly introduce new rules and revise existing rules, processes called "rulemaking." Decisions about which rulemaking to attempt in any given year are driven by many factors, including the current administration's priorities, court decisions, resources, other agencies' regulatory decisions, and pressure from the legislature, industry, environmental organizations, and other stakeholders about what the agency's priorities should be. To develop or revise rules, rulemaking staff (or "rulewriters") consider various social, economic, and ecological costs and benefits of each rule option. There are no hard and fast requirements about how to rank these considerations. EJ advocates have long argued that industry's disproportionate influence over the rulemaking process has led to weak environmental rules.

The most robust agency effort to integrate EJ principles into the rulemaking process is EPA's set of final guidance documents issued in 2015 and 2016 (EPA 2015a; EPA 2016a; Shadbegian and Wolverton 2015). These authorize and encourage EPA rulewriting staff to consider, in addition to other factors, potential "EJ concerns"—how a rule might create, exacerbate, or ameliorate disproportionate and adverse impacts on vulnerable communities. The documents specify points in the federal rulemaking process at which such considerations can be made, techniques for identifying and assessing these potential EJ concerns, how to decide which rules are highest priority for EJ analyses, and opportunities for increasing public involvement in the rule development process.

Federal agencies have increasingly considered EJ in their rulemaking analyses. EPA economists report that, whereas EJ analyses were conducted in fewer than two EPA rules per year between 1995 and 2009, they were conducted for more than 20 EPA rules per year from 2010 to 2012 (Shadbegian and Wolverton 2015, 117–118). Some EPA rulewriting staff told me that nearly all "major" new rules include EJ analyses (though others and EJ advocates characterize most of these as fairly superficial).

In Colorado, the Department of Public Health and the Environment (CDPHE) Health Equity and Environmental Justice staff got the department to adopt a new EJ analysis requirement into its "Regulatory Efficiency Review" policy in 2016. The new language specifies that staff must "[d]etermine if the regulation has health equity and environmental justice implications" and, if so, "identify if regulatory implementation practices can be changed, if the regulation needs to be revised, or if changes to statute/federal regulation are needed to address the health equity and environmental justice implications" (CDPHE 2016).

Permitting Permitting is the process through which regulated entities apply for permission to pollute. Environmental regulatory agencies develop legally enforceable permits for each regulated pollution source. A regulated entity submits a permit application; agency staff then review those applications for concordance with existing laws and develop a draft permit that undergoes internal and sometimes external review. Very rarely, agencies deny permit applications. EJ advocates criticize permitting processes for being overly influenced by regulated entities and insist that communities deserve greater ability to influence permit decisions. Indeed, some agencies only inform the public after the permit has been issued. EJ advocates also argue that permits need stronger permit conditions to reduce the environmental hazards to which overburdened communities are exposed. One EJ advocate asserted several times to me that "[p]ermitting is the holy grail of integrating EJ into regulatory practice," underscoring the important role permits play in shaping a community's environmental conditions.

To date, agencies' efforts to integrate EJ principles into permitting have focused on increasing community involvement in permit decision-making processes. EPA, other federal agencies, a handful of state agencies, and the Environmental Council of the States have created guidelines that encourage permitting staff to create more opportunities for public comment on draft permits for facilities in overburdened and vulnerable areas, advertise those comment opportunities in ways likely reach potentially affected community members, hold public hearings at times and locations accessible to community members, and present relevant background information in language accessible to broad audiences (i.e., without dense technical jargon, and in languages other than English where appropriate) (ECOS 2017; EPA 2006, 2011a, 2013a, 2016b; IEPA 2018; MPCA 2015; ODEQ 1997). EPA encourages permit applicants to conduct enhanced outreach with residents and EJ advocates when permits affect overburdened and vulnerable communities (EPA 2013a). Laws in Connecticut and New York require those seeking permits for certain types of major new facilities and facility expansions in low-income communities to do extra public engagement (CDEEP 2017a; NYSDEC 2003). New York policy further requires the state's Department of Environmental Conservation (NYSDEC) to facilitate alternative dispute resolution between permit applicants and the public to help resolve any conflicts that emerge in the permit review process (NYSDEC 2003). Additionally, a few agencies have offered training sessions to help community members and their advocates better understand the permitting process and how to participate in it most effectively (MPCA 2017; EPA 2018d, 24).

A few agencies require that staff conduct EJ analyses when reviewing permit applications for facilities in and near overburdened and vulnerable communities (e.g., NYSDEC 2003; Massachusetts 2002, 2017; MPCA 2018). Notably, California Senate Bill 673 (2015) formalized this goal for CalEPA's Department of Toxic Substances Control, instructing its staff to consider the vulnerability of nearby populations, as well as the facility's regulatory compliance history, when reviewing permit applications for hazardous waste facilities (CLI 2015). During the Obama administration, U.S. EPA EJ staff developed guidance documents for conducting and applying EJ analyses during permit review (EPA 2016b, 17). Their goal, pending leadership approval to continue this work, is to help states adapt this guidance to their own regulations and programs.

Enforcement Enforcement refers to the processes through which environmental regulatory agencies monitor regulated actors' compliance with regulations and permit conditions and use education, warnings, and penalties to enforce environmental law. In addition to the fact that hazardous facilities are clustered in working-class and racially marginalized communities, research has shown that regulatory enforcement has been less stringent in those areas (Konisky and Reenock 2015). Government agencies could integrate EJ principles into enforcement by prioritizing and increasing the frequency of inspections in overburdened and vulnerable communities, holding regulatory violators in those areas accountable to the greatest extent possible, informing communities of regulatory violations, correcting violations in ways that benefit the community, and prioritizing cleanup of contaminated sites in those areas.

Several agencies promise to increase regulatory enforcement in overburdened and vulnerable communities (EPA 2016b; Massachusetts 2002, 2017; MPCA 2015, 7–8). EPA's Office of Enforcement and Compliance Assurance (OECA) has reportedly developed internal guidance documents directing staff to consider the vulnerability of populations surrounding regulated sites and industries when setting enforcement priorities and all other steps of regulatory enforcement. New York Commissioner Policy 29 directs the New York State Department of Environmental Conservation (NYSDEC) to conduct supplemental inspections in facilities suspected of being out of compliance in "potential environmental justice areas" (NYSDEC 2003, 5). NYSDEC has done this through its Operation ECO-Quality program (for a similar effort in California, see CalEPA n.d., 2015; DTSC 2016).

Critically Assessing Agencies' EJ Efforts

Some states have *none* of the valuable accomplishments I have listed—no EJ policy, EJ staff, EJ advisory committee, staff trainings, or EJ grant programs, and certainly no semblance of formal EJ reforms to core regulatory practice. Of those that do, their EJ staff emphasize that they and their EJ-supportive colleagues work hard to design EJ reforms, and their agencies' EJ track records have improved over time. That said, all agencies' EJ efforts are limited in certain key respects.

Inadequate Efforts to Reduce Cumulative Impacts and Environmental Inequalities

Agencies' place-based EJ projects improve conditions in many overburdened and vulnerable communities and constitute models that agencies can use for crafting broader reforms. However, agencies have made little progress on institutionalizing EJ reforms to core regulatory practice in ways that would systematically, broadly reduce cumulative environmental impacts in overburdened communities and make environmental conditions more equitable across communities. Agencies' EJ reforms to core regulatory work have focused on increasing public participation: getting more information to the public about regulatory decisions and providing more opportunities for the public to comment. These are important improvements upon existing regulatory practice from which communities have historically been excluded, and some staff have put countless hours into developing and advocating for these reforms. However, EJ advocates and residents feel that agencies largely ignore the input they provide through EJ advisory committees and public hearings (Lashley 2016; Liévanos 2012; London, Sze, and Liévanos 2008).

Although EPA staff increasingly consider EJ when developing new and revised rules, those efforts are still the exception rather than the norm. Policy analyst Douglas Noonan recently observed that, aside from a few EPA-reported rules that relate to EJ, "Other instances of the EPA exercising discretion in incorporating environmental justice into its rulemaking are few and far between" (Noonan 2015, 101). Earlier studies reached similar conclusions; indeed, Banzhaf (2011, 5–6) concluded that the EPA's regulatory impact assessments include "perfunctory, pro forma assertions that it is not creating or exacerbating an environmental injustice" lacking substantiating evidence (see also GAO 2005; Vajjhala, Van Epps, and Szambelan 2008). One EPA rulewriter told me in 2018 that EJ analyses are rarely done and that managers "never" use EJ analyses to shape the final rule. EPA's guidance documents on rulemaking say that rulewriting staff "can" and "should" conduct EJ analyses to "consider EJ" during the development of new or revised regulations, but not that they *must* do so, despite the fact that doing so is required under the National Environmental Policy Act. Moreover, agency decision-makers are under no obligation to ensure that that the final rule improves material conditions in overburdened and vulnerable communities and reduces environmental inequalities. EJ advocates lament that very little of any final rule has reflected EJ concerns.

Agencies' EJ guidance documents for permitting have similarly focused on increasing ways for communities to learn about and comment on pending permit applications. The policies directing agencies to conduct EJ analyses during the permitting process (those of California, Massachusetts, and New York, and for the federal NEPA process, all described previously) do not instruct the agencies about what to do with the "consideration" of EJ. NEJAC has criticized the nonbinding nature of EPA's guidances on integrating EJ into permitting, noting that the implementation of EPA's suggestions is "dependent upon the discretion and self-imposed commitment of EPA's leadership" (NEJAC 2013a, 4). Legal scholar Eileen Gauna notes that EPA permit writers have regularly ignored the agency's recommended EJ practices, doing thin EJ analyses if they do them at all, and that few permits have been amended or halted on EJ grounds (Gauna 2015; see also Foster 2008; NAPA 2001). Alyse Bertenthal (2018) shows that courts have been complicit in this, as they have deemed adequate even extremely brief references to EJ issues in agencies' permitting decisions and not challenged agencies' decisions.

EPA's guidance documents on integrating EJ into core regulatory work, which took years to develop, are a significant accomplishment. That said, ultimately their value is in their implementation. One EPA staff person told me in 2018 that these guidance documents are still "not implemented in any significant way," and the extent that they are implemented is "more as a result of happenstance than something that is methodical and systematic."

Scholars have raised similar concerns in the realm of enforcement. While EPA's enforcement staff might "consider" EJ throughout the enforcement lifecycle, scholars show that the enforcement of major federal environmental laws has not increased in low-income and racially marginalized communities since EO 12898 (Konisky 2009; Konisky and Reenock 2015). EPA staff were unable to provide me with any concrete evidence that enforcement priorities have shifted toward overburdened and vulnerable communities.

EPA's progress on enforcing Title VI of the 1964 Civil Rights Act is among the most glaring examples of an agency's failure to enforce EJ-related law. Under Title VI, private actors can file administrative complaints with federal agencies about federally funded activities or decisions that are discriminatory in intent or effect along lines of race, color, or national origin. Where federal agencies find that their funding recipients are out of Title VI compliance, the federal agency can negotiate a voluntary Title VI compliance agreement with the funded entity, terminate the funding, or refer the case to the Department of Justice for litigation. EPA has failed to adequately investigate Title VI violation claims, many of which have languished at EPA for over a decade. EPA accepted few Title VI complaints for investigation, rejecting most for not meeting minor procedural specifications (Cole 1999; Deloitte Consulting 2011; Engelman Lado 2017, 88–90; S. Foster 2000; Gauna 2015; Gordon and Harley 2005, 160; LoPresti 2013; Mank 2008; Matthew 2017). Only twice has EPA reached a formal finding of discrimination, and these two cases were badly mishandled. In the first, where EPA after many years found that California pesticide laws allowed Latino school children to be disproportionately exposed to harmful soil fumigants, EPA reached a settlement agreement with California's Department of Pesticide Regulation without involving the citizen complainants in those deliberations, and the terms of that settlement provided no remedies or protections for schoolchildren.[4] In the other case, EPA took two decades to determine that Michigan's Department of Environmental Quality discriminated against black community residents concerned about the permitting of an incinerator in Flint, and EPA only issued nonbinding recommendations and failed to pursue the case further (Engelman Lado 2017, 85). Other Title VI cases have been settled out of court through alternative dispute resolution, but their settlements have focused on procedural fixes rather than improving substantive environmental conditions in disproportionately burdened communities.

Legal scholar Marianne Engelman Lado emphasizes that EPA has failed to enforce Title VI in other ways. Federal agencies can initiate "compliance reviews" to evaluate the extent to which state agencies and other federal funding recipients are complying with Title VI. EPA has initiated a Title VI compliance review only *once*, whereas some other federal agencies do this regularly (Engelman Lado 2017, 50, 52). EPA could also require the entities it funds to develop and submit a Title VI compliance plan as a condition of receiving federal funding (see also Lazarus 1993). While other agencies have done so, EPA has not (Engelman Lado 2017, 68–69, 73). Some EPA insiders disagree that EPA could withhold funding from a state regulatory agency, noting that EPA could not afford to take over a state agency and that any threat to do so would instigate retaliation from that state's political elites (see also Gauna 2015, 98). Yet EPA could use Title VI compliance reviews and compliance plans to constructively help states and other federal funding recipients design much-needed, systematic civil rights reforms.

Numerous investigations, including a scathing and widely circulated 2016 report by the U.S. Commission on Civil Rights, have lambasted the agency's Title VI track record (U.S. CCR 2016; CPI 2015). Shortly after that report was released, the EPA's NEJAC addressed the issue at its meeting, where EJ advocate Vernice Miller-Travis stridently excoriated the EPA for its failure to enforce Title VI. Her comments, delivered with anger and punctuated by pounding her fist on the table, underscored the significance of Title VI and EPA's failure to enforce it:

> The only statutory ground that environmental justice stands on is the Civil Rights Act of 1964. It is the piece of law in statute that undergirds environmental justice. The Executive Order is *not a law*. It does not have the force of law, and it does not supersede any existing law passed by Congress and signed by the President. The Executive Order is a great thing, but if the next president decides that they do not like the Executive Order, the Executive Order is *history*. So, if you are *not* enforcing the Civil Rights Act, you are *not* moving the environmental justice agenda. It is the thing upon which environmental justice stands.[5]

Staff often attribute EPA's Title VI failures to the management of the office that handles Title VI complaints. Several noted that past management directed staff to use any administrative grounds possible to reject Title VI complaints, that none of the office's staff had any particular interest or experience in civil rights law, and that some were assigned to work there after having done poorly in other jobs within the agency. EPA staff also emphasize that the office started to change under the leadership of Lilian Dorka, appointed in 2016, who, as one staff person noted, was "the first person with a practical understanding of Civil Rights law" at the EPA. In late 2016, EPA vowed to strengthen its enforcement of Title VI, issued a new strategic plan and investigation manual for its staff, initiated alternative dispute resolution in several unresolved cases, moved Title VI enforcement into its Office of General Council, and conducted outreach with many states about civil rights law compliance (Buford 2017a; EPA 2018d, 39; Matthew 2017). Whether these efforts work remains to be seen.

Undermining EJ Activists' Pursuit of Stronger Environmental Protections

Additionally, some agencies' EJ efforts have been criticized as undermining EJ activists' pursuit of stronger environmental protections. Some EJ advocates and scholars argue that agencies' EJ advisory committees and other public engagement efforts neuter EJ advocacy by keeping EJ activists busy attending meetings and playing nice with state actors rather than challenging them (Holifield 2004). At the same time, industry actors participating in some agencies' EJ advisory committees have rebuked EJ advocate participants' key principles, thereby neutering the committees' recommendations and leaving EJ advocates feeling they had wasted their time (Holifield 2004; Kohl 2016; Liévanos 2012; Liévanos, London, and Sze 2011; London, Sze, and Liévanos 2008; NEJAC 2011).

Some EJ advocates have raised related concerns about agencies' EJ grant programs. Their stringent application requirements leave some EJ advocates concerned that the grant programs favor professionalization and thus marginalize the most grassroots-based of organizations—those for whom the grant programs were originally designed to fund and who need grant resources the most. Additionally, federal and some state agency policies prohibit staff from providing tailored advice about grant programs to any prospective applicants (e.g., EPA 2015b, 15). While reportedly designed to ensure that agency staff treat all applicants equally, it undermines inexperienced grassroots organizations that struggle to compete with more experienced and well-funded organizations. Moreover, some EJ advocates argue that agency EJ grant programs discipline and neuter EJ organizations by compelling them to court the agencies, stay busy preparing applications, and compete with each other, rather than collectively challenging the state for stronger environmental regulations and enforcement.

My analysis of agencies' EJ grant programs indicates that they might undermine EJ advocates' pursuit of stronger regulatory protections in two additional ways. First, agencies' EJ grant programs may channel EJ organizations away from their longstanding pursuit of change through regulatory and policy reforms and instead toward individualized mechanisms of change (Harrison 2015, 2016).[6] Most EJ grant programs' requests for applications (RFAs) implicitly discourage applicants from proposing projects that pursue environmental change through regulatory or policy mechanisms. Where the San Francisco and New York RFAs list examples of eligible projects, most entail individual behavior modification ("teach local residents and school children about the nutritional and public health benefits of growing and eating fresh produce") and market-based change ("promote purchase of environmentally preferred products and the use of less toxic consumer goods"); none include policy reform, regulatory enforcement, or increasing public participation in regulatory decision-making processes (NYSDEC 2011, 6; San Francisco 2010, 9). U.S. EPA's program documents encourage industry-friendly collaborations. Notably, its CPS program documents promote collaborations "with various stakeholders such as communities, industry, academic institutions, and others" (EPA 2008, 1). EPA proclaims: "When multiple stakeholders work together, they create a collective vision that reflects mutually beneficial goals for all parties" (EPA 2008, 3). Similarly, the U.S. EPA EJ Small Grants RFA specifies that proposals "should include strategies for ... building consensus and ... should demonstrate collaboration with other stakeholders," including industry and government agencies (EPA 2013b, 3–4). Certainly, partnerships can help organizations combine forces to achieve their shared goals (Lee 2005; King 2012; Mock 2014). That said, grant program documents that emphasize collaboration with industry implicitly discourage organizations from proposing activities industry actors would reject, such as advocating for stronger environmental regulations or increased enforcement.

The New York program further discourages regulatory reform projects by requiring that funded projects align with the strategic priorities of the Regional Economic Development Council. Applicants must get their local Regional Development Council to verify that the proposed project is consistent with the council's strategic plan or describe "the economic benefits of the proposed project" (NYSDEC 2016, 12). However, these councils are comprised largely of industry representatives (e.g., NYCREDC 2011, 2), and their strategic plans imply that they would not support projects that would threaten business interests. For example, the first page of the New York City Regional Economic Development Council's recent strategic plan executive summary states that "Entrepreneurial business formation is hampered by a complex regulatory environment," and that the council's plan "is focused on accelerating economic growth" and "seeks to reinforce the prominent industries and large institutions that anchor the city economy" (NYCREDC 2011, 4). Applications that do not include this endorsement or description automatically lose points—in some cases, enough to make the difference between getting funded or not. Such requirements surely discourage applicants from proposing activities that would upset local industry.

Most programs' funded *projects* also deviate from EJ advocates' prioritized model of change. Of the 1,082 funded projects whose description specified a mechanism of change, only 33 percent (352) included actions that hold the state accountable for improving environmental conditions (e.g., organizing residents to participate in regulatory or land-use planning events, or pressing agencies for basic municipal services, stronger environmental regulations, or enforcement of existing laws). Two programs had especially low rates of such projects: San Francisco at 11 percent (6 of 53 projects) and New York at 12 percent (13 of 106 projects). The remaining projects sought change only through nonregulatory means, typically through urging individual residents to modify their own lifestyles (e.g., reducing consumption of fish from contaminated rivers, growing one's own produce, increasing physical activity, or recycling household waste). Others encourage local industry to voluntarily reduce emissions (e.g., educating truck drivers about diesel idling). Others sought change by providing goods or services (e.g., solar panels or energy audits) at a reduced cost. Only California EPA's grant program differs from the others in this regard. CalEPA's RFA explicitly encourages projects aimed at regulatory and policy reform and increasing public participation in environmental decision-making processes, which are featured in its RFA's stated program goals and example projects (CalEPA 2013, 1, 4). Additionally, 72 percent of its funded projects (67 of 93) pursue change through regulatory and policy mechanisms. In chapters 3 and 7, I offer two explanations for why this program differs from other agencies' EJ grant programs.

To be clear, these nonregulatory projects are not antithetical to EJ. Also, the grant programs allocate more resources into vulnerable and overburdened communities for many valuable activities. However, these funding patterns signal which kinds of projects are most likely to get funded and thereby channel organizations into proposing and conducting such work. Although government grants are not the primary source of EJ organizations' funding, they do comprise a significant portion of it and thus help shape organizations' practices and priorities.[7]

Also, "collaborative" agreements between residents and industry can undermine organizing efforts. Although the EPA Collaborative Problem Solving (CPS) program RFAs list various possible stakeholders that could be involved in collaborative partnerships, and several EPA EJ grant program staff asserted that projects need not include *all* relevant stakeholders, multiple CPS grant recipients told me that they felt pressured by EPA to reach consensus with industry in ways that undermined their own goals. One grantee who proposed to help his community address its concerns about multiple polluting facilities said that EPA required their project "to be totally collaborative." He lamented that because industry actors in the collaboration rejected most activities residents and activists proposed, they only did activities "that didn't upset industry." They addressed indoor air quality, smoking, and diesel bus routes—which he considered "the lowest common denominator"—and were unable to tackle "the big issues" that mattered most to residents. He feels that the project undermined his future organizing prospects, as many residents felt frustrated with his organization for pursuing a limited array of activities.[8]

Additionally, the programs' discursive emphasis on and predominance of projects relying on residents and industry actors to voluntarily improve environmental conditions imply that EJ does not require stronger regulatory and policy protections and that residents and industry actors can and should handle those responsibilities. This message about what "EJ" means and requires gets taken up by agency staff, who look to EJ programs to learn about EJ and how they could apply its principles into their own work.

Scholars Tianna Bruno and Wendy Jepson (2018) reached similar conclusions in their assessment of EPA's Environmental Justice Showcase Communities (EJSC) program. For example, they detail how one EJSC project denied that the industrial air and water pollution residents were most concerned about reach harmful levels and focused on teaching residents to care for their own health by changing their household cleaning practices. The authors conclude that "the EJSC programme does not seek to curb, reform, or facilitate environmental regulation. Rather, the EJSC programme activities and priorities focus on decollectivising environmental justice claims and subordinating programme interventions to interests of market-based actors. ... EJSC programme advanced a vision of environmental justice counter to the core ideals of EJ progressive politics ... [and] aligns more with the success and comfort of industry rather than the livelihood, health, and safety of the communities under the burdens of industrial emissions" (278, 285, 289).

Second, agencies' EJ grant programs undermine EJ advocates' pursuit of stronger environmental restrictions on environmental harms by increasingly emphasizing and funding projects that substantively focus on boosting environmental amenities without reducing environmental hazards. While all of the programs' RFAs allow a wide range of projects in terms of their substantive foci, some of the programs' documents emphasize activities not geared to hazard reduction. Both the New York and San Francisco programs' RFAs encourage community gardens, nutrition education, parks and trails, and energy efficiency, scarcely mentioning projects that substantially reduce hazards like air and water pollution (NYSDEC 2011, 6; San Francisco 2010, 9). Additionally, the New York program for several years dedicated a certain percentage of its EJ grant funding to "Green Gems" grants that funded projects relating to "parks, open space, community gardens, or green infrastructure" (NYSDEC 2015).

Most projects funded by these programs align with the EJ movement's substantive focus on hazard reduction, with 83 percent of the funded projects (1,267 of 1,533) committed to reducing one or more hazards to health or community (e.g., monitoring air or water for contaminants, collecting other data on toxic "hot spots," educating subsistence fisherfolk about PCB-contaminated fish, constructing sanitation systems, and improving drinking-water purification and/or storage systems), often in addition to fostering environmental amenities. Only the San Francisco program deviates in this regard: just 22 percent of its projects (12 of 54) include activities that reduce environmental hazards in any meaningful way.

However, for nearly all of the programs, the portion of funded projects dedicated to hazard reduction has declined over time. The New York program's projects dedicated to hazard reduction dropped from 92 percent in the first two funding cycles (12 of 13) to 45 percent in the last two cycles (23 of 51). U.S. EPA's CPS projects dedicated to hazard reduction dropped from 95 percent (38 of 40) in its first two cycles to 65 percent in its latest two cycles (13 of 20). U.S. EPA's Small Grants projects dedicated to hazard reduction dropped from 91 percent in the first four cycles (351 of 387) to 75 percent in the last four cycles (117 of 155). The San Francisco program's projects dedicated to hazard reduction dropped from 30 percent in the first few funding cycles (8 of 27) to 15 percent in the most recent four funding cycles (4 of 27). Only the CalEPA program differs from the others in this regard, with its portion of projects dedicated to hazard reduction increasing from 91 percent in the first three cycles (39 of 43) to 93 percent in the latter three cycles (56 of 60).

Most agency EJ grant programs are moving away from hazard reduction and increasingly funding projects that develop and maintain community gardens, farmers markets, parks, and trails; plant trees; install alternative energy infrastructure or energy-efficient appliances; establish recycling programs; conduct ecological restoration; or educate youth about nutrition, cooking, exercise, or wildlife. Such projects are not, in principle, inconsistent with EJ, and many of these projects provide tangible gains relatively quickly and with comparatively little strife. EJ activists have long framed EJ as including hazard reduction *and* the provision of environmental amenities. The problem is that, in the grant programs, these other projects are replacing, rather than augmenting, those focused on hazard reduction. The focus on urban greening—and decline of attention to hazards—is made further problematic by the fact that so much greening happens on top of existing hazards without remediating them (Frickel and Elliott 2018).

Conclusion

To date, many environmental regulatory agencies have engaged in valuable efforts to support environmental justice. Yet justice requires that much more be done to ensure that all communities are afforded the same degrees of environmental protection. Twenty-five years have passed since President Clinton signed EO 12898, and state and federal agencies have, by all accounts, made little headway in institutionalizing EJ throughout regulatory practice. Most states have few or no formal EJ efforts. Those that do have increased public participation in regulatory decision-making procedures but done little to systematically reduce hazards in overburdened communities and foster environmental equity across communities. Some agency EJ efforts may even undermine EJ advocates' pursuit of stronger environmental protections.

In chapter 8, I recommend numerous ways agencies can support environmental justice: strengthening basic EJ infrastructure (EJ policies, EJ staff, and EJ trainings for other employees); more meaningfully fostering public participation so that communities can influence regulatory decisions; integrating EJ reforms in core regulatory practice that would systematically reduce cumulative impacts in overburdened and vulnerable communities and achieve greater environmental equity across communities; conducting targeted, agency-wide and cross-agency improvements in overburdened and vulnerable communities; strengthening EJ grant programs to support critical EJ organizations working to influence regulatory practice;

and developing robust accountability measures to ensure that agencies meet these goals. To be clear, I do not mean to imply that such changes are easy. Changing regulatory practice is always difficult and slow, and the most robust and important EJ reforms are unprecedented and not obvious to staff. Reforming agency practice in line with EJ principles will require considerable collaboration and deliberation.

Why has it been so hard for agencies to accomplish these goals? To make progress on institutionalizing EJ principles into regulatory practice, we need to identify and confront the factors that have constrained agencies' EJ efforts to date. The rest of this book turns to this task—to unpacking the factors that thwart the efforts of EJ staff, even those working in agencies with EJ policies and EJ-supportive leadership. I will explain why, even under the best of circumstances, agencies' EJ efforts leave so much to be desired. I first turn to the set of factors agency representatives consistently identify to explain the slow pace of their agencies' EJ efforts: limited resources, regulatory authority, and analytical tools. Because this set of explanations is made so unfailingly, I call this the "standard narrative." As I will show, the standard narrative is not unwarranted; the constraints it highlights present significant obstacles to agency staff striving to implement EJ reforms. However, it also obscures as much as it reveals and does not fully explain agencies' disappointing progress on environmental justice. I then turn to the heart of the book, showing that agencies' EJ efforts are constrained by elements of regulatory culture—pushback from coworkers who see EJ reforms as antithetical to their organization's identity (chapters 4–6), as well as the fact that some EJ staff define "environmental justice" in ways that deviate from longstanding EJ movement principles (chapter 7).

3 "It Is Out of Our Hands": The Standard Narrative

Introduction

Staff leading agencies' EJ programs and reforms express significant frustration and disappointment with their slow progress. In our interviews, EJ staff and other staff alike explain that EJ policy implementation is constrained by material factors—especially limited resources, regulatory authority, and analytical tools—*that are beyond the control of agency staff*. I characterize this as the *standard narrative*, as all of my participants referenced one or all of these factors, and they align with scholars' explanations for the disappointing pace of agencies' EJ efforts. In this chapter, I describe how the limited nature of resources, regulatory authority, and analytical tools, as well as a few other factors beyond staff members' control, most certainly undermine the prospects for EJ reforms at environmental regulatory agencies. Yet, I also argue that there are good reasons to question how *fully* these factors determine agencies' EJ efforts. I argue that, despite these constraints, agencies could still do more to institutionalize EJ principles into regulatory practice. This will set the stage for the rest of this book, where I demonstrate that other dynamics—internal to agencies and within the control of agency staff—stymie agencies' EJ programs and practices as well.

Resources

Agency staff widely attributed the slow pace of their organizations' EJ efforts in part to *resource limitations*. Without funding, staff cannot conduct outreach in communities to be affected by regulatory decisions. It also means having only a few EJ staff, and that each of them, to be able to design EJ reforms other staff will regard as reasonable, must understand the full range of activities that the agency does—an extraordinary task for one person to accomplish. Moreover, few staff know how to design reforms to existing regulatory practice, and most feel overburdened with other tasks; dwindling resources leave staff feeling unable to do the crucial work of collaboratively designing actual EJ reforms to existing practice.

Many bureaucrats asserted that they do not have enough staff or time to implement the reforms EJ staff recommend. As Gary, a manager in one agency's permitting division, stated in our interview: "We just can't magically take on the EJ program with all of the extra pieces that's needed just with our permit engineers. We are going to need more people. We have one person. How much can one person do? … We can *look like* we're doing it, or we can do it to a certain point. But we can't *do* it." Staff in permitting and rulemaking explained that their responsibilities are so time-consuming and bound by strict deadlines that they cannot imagine how they can also do EJ analysis and extra community engagement. Sue, a rulewriter at EPA, described how consent decrees (court-ordered deadlines) and other restrictions mitigate against doing EJ analysis: "If you have a consent decree, and you have to get out a rule in nine months or something like that, OMB [Office of Management and Budget] takes three months of that, so you have six months to get a rule out. Basically, you have two weeks to write it, and 5,000 other people need to read it and comment on it for the next five months.... If we are only given seven or eight months to get a proposal out, you can be sure that we are not going to try to use anything new, we are not going to actually go out and try to get any more data." In the context of a general contraction of staff and other resources, bureaucrats see EJ reforms as pulling already-overworked staff away from core regulatory functions and adding work. As Paul, an EJ staff person, explained: "It's robbing Peter to pay Paul. If we have three staff [in the EJ office], that's three fewer staff that Enforcement has to go out and do inspections and reduce emissions."

Additionally, because resources are increasingly scarce within these agencies, staff are required to defend the value of every activity to justify current funding; however, the value of EJ practices is difficult to measure in agencies' quantitative metrics. Carol noted that staff are required to document the "ROI" (return on investment) of their activities. As for EJ activities designed to help community members "have a really meaningful voice in the decisions in their communities, … it is really hard to articulate the ROI. And so it is hard for them to *account* for that work against their measure of

accomplishments that they have to produce." Her coworker Paul characterized "the mission" of EJ staff as "ephemeral," which makes their accomplishments difficult to quantify and thus their funding difficult to justify:

> In EJ, if I say we have increased the capacity of this community to address its own
> environmental problems—which to me is the most meaningful thing I can say
> about what I've done—somebody says, "Okay, what does that mean? How do
> you count it?" ... In the short term, I have no answer for that....What we find
> ourselves doing is constantly scrutinized and questioned—"What are you really
> doing?"—and it is really kind of hard to pin down....When everything of value
> has to be quantified and monetized and converted into a cost-benefit analysis, it
> leaves out a lot of the issues that are very important in EJ.

Carol and Paul both used the term "ROI" without defining it. (I asked them
to define it for me.) The fact that "ROI" and "cost-benefit analysis" are in
their everyday lexicon indicates that the pressure to quantitatively justify
their tasks is pervasive.

Many staff attribute these resource constraints to industry, which pressures agencies to focus their resources on approving industry requests. In a
context in which elected and appointed officials cater to powerful industry interests, staff are wary of participating in EJ reforms that might invite
controversy. For example, one permitting manager asserted that "we don't
have the resources" to implement EJ staff members' recommended reforms.
She explained that the agency "has received a lot of scrutiny, including
political scrutiny over not issuing permits fast enough to keep up with the
speed of business," pressure that "is coming from the governor directly." In
this context, the notion of doing anything that would slow down the permit preview process, such as EJ analysis or extra community engagement,
strikes staff as politically impossible: "We have been asked to do more and
more and more and more with less, to where at this point we are probably
missing things, the things that we are obligated to do. And then asking us
to do more, it is not going to be received well." Other staff at her agency
echoed these concerns. Kate explained that industries waiting for permits
"start calling and complaining. Some of them go up the chain all the way
to the governor, and they are just constantly calling mid-level managers
like, 'Where's my permit? I can't construct!' Or, 'I can't operate without
my permit. Where is it?' With sources calling and pressuring the mid-
managers—managers don't want to have their boss get a call—so they are
like, 'Issue the permit. Get it done!'" Permitting staff feel *personally* pressured

by industry, elected officials, and managers to approve permits quickly. To be clear, some staff did not make these claims. Given that publicly stating such ideas could jeopardize one's job and perhaps career, it is impossible to know exactly how widespread these sentiments are.

Some EJ staff explained that antiregulatory pressure from industry and political elites supporting its interests compels EJ staff to proactively minimize and tame their EJ efforts to protect the resources allocated to them. In 2018, EPA EJ staff told me that, to keep the Office of Environmental Justice from being defunded, the EJ reforms that are most controversial because they are designed to systematically increase scrutiny of regulated entities—integrating EJ principles into rulemaking and permitting—would "probably be on pause" for a couple of years. As one noted, "We don't want to create more problems for EJ in the long run.... If this is what some of them [politically appointed leaders] associate EJ with, that might mean the end of the whole thing." Additionally, EJ staff acknowledge that EJ organizations need more funding but explain that keeping EJ grants small helps protect EJ grant programs from conservative elites who would oppose these programs otherwise. Margaret explained, "We also need to reduce evidence of expenditures.... If they can't say that we are a waste of money, then they will need to find a different target." In an interview I conducted with Margaret and one of her EJ coworkers, one stated that "conservative" legislators "are always looking for ways to eliminate these programs. They go after EJ grants, they go after _____ [the agency's EJ advisory committee], they try to dismantle the _____ [agency's other EJ programs]." Margaret and her coworker explained how, as a result of this pressure, EJ staff tame their EJ programs to avoid raising the ire of hostile elites. I asked whether this hostility has increased in recent years. Both replied, "Oh yeah!" emphatically and in unison, looked at each other, and then laughed briefly, although the mood was not particularly jovial.

Other evidence supports these claims. Agencies have always devoted few resources toward their EJ programs (Konisky 2015a; Ozymy and Jarrell 2017). Many agencies devote zero funding to EJ. Those that do fund EJ efforts have only one or a few EJ staff tasked with developing EJ reforms for the entire agency. When I first met with staff at the Colorado Department of Public Health and Environment, the agency's one EJ staff person was tasked with spending 5 percent of her time on EJ efforts—just two hours per week. U.S. EPA's Office of Environmental Justice (OEJ) is by far the most well-funded government agency EJ program in the United States; its annual appropriated budget has averaged about $5 million in recent years, which amounts to just 0.06 percent of the EPA's budget (EPA 2018a).[1]

Republican legislators have introduced many bills over the years to defund the federal government's EJ programs (Buford 2017b). EPA's EJ efforts accelerated most substantially when the Obama administration's first EPA administrator, Lisa Jackson, put EJ on the agency's priorities and infused it with resources (Konisky 2015b, 247). Prospects look dim under the Trump administration. Although OEJ appears to be protected and agency staff suspect that it would look "outright racist" to eliminate the office, its operating resources remain uncertain. Moreover, the Trump administration's initial threat to cut OEJ's budget marked EJ as controversial and something other offices now do not want to align themselves with. Several EPA staff said in early 2018 that they feel they cannot discuss "environmental justice" with their colleagues, much less try to implement proposed EJ reforms, because of the administration's early suggestion that it would cut OEJ's funding.

Some EJ grant programs have been defunded entirely (notably, EPA's former CARE program), while in other cases agencies have received funding to offer EJ grant programs only sporadically (as is the case for NYSDEC's EJ Community Impacts Grant Program). Budget cuts can halt EJ advisory committee meetings, thereby constraining staff members' understandings of communities' concerns and stalling the advisory committees' abilities to craft documents guiding agencies' EJ efforts. Leadership also uses budget cuts to disband intra-agency and interagency EJ committees, key networks that EJ-supportive staff use to share and develop concrete EJ reforms to regulatory practice. Sometimes agencies gut such groups only partially, where the shell of the committee remains but its most influential members stop participating. One example is the federal Interagency Working Group on Environmental Justice (EJ IWG). As originally developed by the Clinton administration, the EJ IWG included senior officials who had the power to marshal resources and tools to support EJ in all federal agencies. However, according to EPA staff, agencies' senior management stopped participating after just a year or two, which caused the accountability and resources for doing EJ to plummet. Other scholars have noted that limited funding has truncated the reach of EJ pilot projects (Liévanos, London, and Sze 2011), left California EPA unable to implement the comprehensive vision of EJ endorsed in its strategic plan (London, Sze, and Liévanos 2008), and rendered the CALFED EJ advisory committee unable to investigate and document the environmental inequalities it was concerned about (Shilling, London, and Liévanos 2009).

Agencies have faced resource cuts across the board, thereby requiring remaining staff to do more with less. Conservative legislators intent on reducing regulatory restrictions on industry affairs have cut U.S. EPA's budget nearly every year for the past 25 years when measured in real dollars (adjusted for inflation) (Slesinger 2014). Budget cuts and internal funding reallocations disrupt entire lines of work within agencies, and their repercussions are far greater than their dollar amounts suggest. They halt the collection of data that staff rely on to evaluate the safety of facilities and the adequacy of environmental standards; curtail site visits for enforcement and community engagement; force agencies to rely on regulated entities' self-reported data about emissions and regulatory compliance; prevent staff from collaborating within and across agencies on innovative initiatives; and force staff from defunded programs into jobs for which they have little to no experience. All of these people, data, networks, and other forms of resources are necessary to run programs like agencies' EJ efforts. Additionally, when funding is tight and declining, staff are unable to accomplish all of their responsibilities and thus will, quite reasonably, reject changes that might increase their workload. Such is the case with EJ reforms like EJ analyses and extra community engagement; especially while reforms are being proposed, drafted, and piloted, they will require some additional effort by agency staff. When staff are overworked and overwhelmed, taking on any new responsibilities can seem like too much to ask.

Challenging the Narrative about Resources and EJ

Certainly, resource limitations impose constraints on the scope and pace of agencies' EJ efforts. Yet EJ staff also argue that many EJ reforms do not necessarily require significant resources, agencies can implement many of them, and doing them will become more streamlined with practice.

Tanya, who has led the development of draft EJ reforms for permit review, emphasized that permitting staff could do sufficient EJ analysis in just a few hours and, therefore, they can do these much more frequently: "They hear 'EJ analysis,' and they think, 'Oh, I have to spend all these days on it.' No. It, all in all, is maybe a half day, tops, *if* you find something.... It's not really that much added work!" Similarly, Martin asserted that some staff "see it [EJ analysis] as an add-on": something to do after doing the rest of one's analysis, and maybe requiring that they go change the work they have already done. If staff instead consider EJ during the course of their work, "then it is not that much more expensive, and it could be saving time because then you don't have to go back" and revise what is already done.

Other EJ staff note that the time required to do EJ analysis declines with practice. For example, after describing how court-ordered deadlines make rulewriters feel unable to do EJ analyses, Elizabeth said she pushes her coworkers to do EJ analysis regularly so that the process becomes more efficient: "part of the regulatory impact analysis and not a secondary analysis that we have to do." Other EJ staff explained that they are developing triage-type guidelines that rulemaking and permitting staff can use to quickly determine which rules and permits need particularly robust, in-depth EJ analyses and which others do not.

These assertions raise important questions about just how resource-intensive agencies' proposed EJ reforms are. In some cases, we know already that EJ reforms are not particularly time-consuming, such as with prioritizing inspections for facilities in overburdened and vulnerable communities. In other cases, proposed EJ reforms have barely been put to the test in any agency, so we do not know how time-consuming they are. Conducting EJ analysis for permit applications and proposed rules is characterized as labor-intensive by some and quite simple and straightforward by others—the jury is out, and more practice is needed.

Additionally, discussions about the resources consumed by agencies' EJ efforts should acknowledge that EJ staff are forced to spend considerable time in decidedly unproductive conversations with coworkers. Specifically, as I will show in chapter 4, some coworkers demand that EJ staff repeatedly defend the *merits* of EJ reforms—including whether environmental inequalities even exist and warrant agency attention. This is time that could more productively be spent collaboratively developing concrete, practicable reforms to regulatory practice that would meaningfully address those well-documented inequalities.

Regulatory Authority: Laws, Executive Orders, Regulations, and Policies

Another constraint to agencies' EJ efforts is concern that various EJ reforms are not authorized under existing law. Many staff noted that industry actors threaten to sue agencies for doing anything not explicitly mandated by law—and often follow through on those threats. Specifically, most staff referenced the threat of being sued for taking actions that could be construed as violating the "arbitrary and capricious" standard of the federal Administrative Procedure Act (APA),[2] which specifies that agency decisions must be based on and logically stemming from relevant factors. As Angela stated:

> Every regulator, their biggest fear in the world is a lawyer suing them for being arbitrary and capricious about some sort of reg. I mean, it is what drives every word that goes into a document.…There is a business community that is making absolutely sure that you don't do one more thing than that regulation requires you to do. It may be nice to get that stream up to this standard. But, the law doesn't say that you have to, so don't you dare do that because I'll sue you if you do.…We are not in the business of saying no. We are in the business of saying yes.

To underscore her point about how common lawsuits are, Angela listed off all of the highest-level managers in her agency and noted that they are all attorneys. Indeed, many staff emphasized that one of the largest groups of staff in their agency—and those who hold considerable power—are attorneys. These attorneys' responsibilities include not only bringing legal actions against those who violate environmental law but also, and perhaps more importantly, defending the agency against industry lawsuits of "regulatory overreach."

My interview with Steve illustrated how EPA's attorneys used concerns about regulatory authority to neuter one of the agency's most ambitious EJ efforts: integrating EJ into the permitting process. Steve first described how EJ and permitting staff who had developed ideas for reforming the permit review process to improve environmental conditions in overburdened and vulnerable communities were convened into a formal work group by Obama administration leadership: "At the start, it was like, great, let's pull best practices together and let's build in some sections of the Clean Air Act that have never been applied, and let's get that out there and let's build it into our permitting.… In our first many months of meeting, we had a really great table set with everything we had all been talking about for the previous 10 years or so." However, the agency's attorneys gutted those efforts, claiming they could be challenged in court. As a result, the workgroup was cornered into making recommendations for industry "best practices" for engaging with communities (EPA 2013a). Steve's disappointment was clear:

> We spent the next four years coming up with very tame, lame procedures.…At the end of the day, we have not had any effect on the process to the extent that

our permitters are willing to impose requirements based solely on EJ considerations. ... [The attorneys] wore us down, basically saying, the logic was, "Well, this
stuff's pretty tricky. ... Probably the way forward here is to get some friends in the
industrial side of things who are *willing* to be innovative." That is why what you
saw in 2013 was a list of best practices. By that time, we had fallen into a mode
of, "Well, let's just look for friends [in industry] who are willing to do good stuff
and we'll give merit badges or something." Obviously, we were not coming from
a regulatory approach. Not even a very serious policy approach. We were coming
from a moral suasion approach. ... It has been a long, downhill slide. The high
point was at the start of the initiative in 2011, and ever since then, everything we
tried to put on the table got watered down, shrunk, and doesn't really have a lot
of meaning now.

Concerns about industry lawsuits lead powerful agency members to whittle
EJ reforms into "tame and lame" recommendations that do little to improve
conditions in overburdened and vulnerable communities.

Given industry actors' capacity to sue agencies and history of doing so,
staff feel tremendous pressure to not do anything that would provoke regulated entities to challenge their decision-making processes. This includes EJ
reforms that are, by all measures, very minor. For example, Patricia, a
permit writer who has helped develop EJ reform proposals, described how,
to enhance outreach, she and her coworkers suggested sending postcards
announcing the public comment period for a draft permit to community
members who had previously submitted comments about a different facility's
permit application. "The facility said: ... 'Using that mailing list is beyond
your authority. ... We are going to sue you.' ... We ended up not doing it then.
Because we were like, you know what, maybe we are already on rocky ground
here. ... We didn't want to rock the boat." What is notable is that such a minor
proposal is considered "rocking the boat." Patricia elaborated that industry
lawsuits absorb considerable agency resources, the agency lacks sufficient
resources to fulfill its responsibilities, and it needs to have a good (economy-
supportive) reputation to maintain its funding from the legislature.

Industry pressure to not regulate makes many staff dismiss EJ reforms as
unrealistic. Some have decided that the only thing they can do to improve
conditions in overburdened communities is to ask industry actors if they
would be willing to *voluntarily* improve some element of the local environment. For example, Stacy lamented: "Our statute that gives _____ [the agency]
its authority is very broad, and we cite that on occasion. It is basically, impose
the necessary requirements to protect human health and the environment.

But then the flip side is that we also have rules that say, if permittee meets these criteria, we are obligated to issue them a permit, and one of those criteria is that they meet the rules and the regulations. So theoretically, if we impose something that was more strict, I think one could argue that we are being arbitrary or capricious.... [Therefore] it all comes down to voluntary actions." In a context in which regulations and statutes convey mixed messages and in which industry aggressively challenges regulatory authority, staff defer to the option that industry will not fight: asking industry actors if they would voluntarily do things to benefit surrounding communities. While beneficial, this is a remarkably thin interpretation of EJ reforms.

Some staff are afraid to attempt even this narrow type of EJ reform. For instance, Patricia expressed fear of even asking facilities in overburdened communities to voluntarily conduct enhanced public outreach about proposed permit renewals or modifications in overburdened and vulnerable areas. She noted: "If they challenge you, you would have to be like [*shifts into a soft, meek voice and physically cowers*], 'Well, I will talk to my supervisor.' Or back down.'" Other staff view industry actors as so unwilling to do anything more than is explicitly required by statute that even these industry-friendly negotiations, in their minds, waste precious agency resources. As Gary, a manager in permitting, stated:

> Nobody [in industry] wants to really go any further if they do not have to.... Some people [industry representatives] just flat out say, "If you can't show me, in law, where you can make me do this, I'm not doing anything, and I don't care." We've got a couple facilities right now in _____ [city name], basically [they say], "You can come and get me if you think you can, but you can't. And I'm not going to do anything, and I don't care what these people in these neighborhoods say at all." They basically have said that, flat out. There are other people who are willing to at least try and do more, but the "more" never really gets to the point where we are driving down their [emissions] limits to levels that are below what they are now probably.

To be sure, some regulated entities do more to protect the environment and meet community interests than statute requires of them. However, agency staff conveyed that such examples are the exception rather than the norm. Through lawsuits, pressuring elected and appointed officials, and rejecting EJ staff proposals, industry effectively conveys to agency staff that it will do little more than is unambiguously required by law. Such pressure undermines agencies' progress on EJ, as staff see proposed EJ reforms as inviting lawsuits or otherwise futile.

The history of environmental law is one of lawsuits and associated court rulings that have interpreted federal environmental statutes in increasingly narrow ways and constrained what agencies can do under those statutes' authority. While various actors sue agencies, industry, with its deep financial resources, has the ability to instigate and sustain lengthy and expensive lawsuits to a much greater degree than environmental organizations or community groups. As such, environmental legal battles have largely served industry's interests.

Scholars have detailed how industry and political elites serving its interests get industry actors into agency leadership positions, where they directly overturn rules to restrict agencies' formal regulatory authority (Brown 2007; Cordner 2016; Davidson and Frickel 2004; Downey 2015; Faber 2008, 2018; Freudenburg and Gramling 1994; Harvey 2005; Langston 2010; Mintz 2012; Nash 2006; O'Brien 2000; Raffensperger and Tickner 1999; Schnaiberg and Gould 1994; Tickner 2003; UCS 2008, 2018, 2019; Vogel 2012; Whiteside 2006). Scholars have detailed how agencies' EJ efforts reflect industry interests because industry actors define agencies' regulatory authority in highly circumscribed and industry-supportive ways (Liévanos 2012, 495).

Agencies' EJ efforts are particularly vulnerable to industry pressure because they are not backed by unambiguous law. Most agencies have no EJ law, policy, executive order, or other mandate. EJ mandates that do exist are generally of weaker legal status than environmental statutes, and the environmental statutes like the Clean Air Act and Clean Water Act focus on reducing aggregate levels of pollution, not increasing environmental equity (Noonan 2015). Executive orders cannot contradict constitutional or statute law. Also, while agencies can be sued for failing to act on legislation, there is no formal mechanism for external stakeholders to induce agencies to comply with executive orders or internal policy statements (Konisky 2015a; Noonan 2015). Additionally, whereas statutes *require* federal agencies to reduce aggregate pollution levels, the National Environmental Policy Act and EO 12898 only direct federal agencies to *consider* EJ concerns during regulatory practice (Konisky 2015a; Noonan 2015). Since the early 1990s, various Democratic legislators have authored bills to bolster the authority of EJ programs and policies, but none have been put to a floor vote (Konisky 2015a, 35–36, 41).

Key court decisions have narrowed the extent to which communities can hold EPA and other federal agencies accountable for enforcing Title VI of the Civil Rights Act (Engelman Lado 2017; Gordon and Harley 2005; Gross and

Stretesky 2015; Mank 2008). Notably, in 2001 the U.S. Supreme Court ruled in *Alexander v. Sandoval* that citizens can sue recipients of federal funding for violating Title VI of the Civil Rights Act only in circumstances of *intentional discrimination*. Instead, most cases of racial environmental injustice constitute *racially disparate impact* (i.e., lacking evidence that federally funded entities engaged in discriminatory *intent*). For disparate impact cases, *Sandoval* established that communities can only bring administrative complaints (i.e., not lawsuits) against the agency. The problem with administrative complaints is that their resolution is left to the priorities and resources of the agencies. As noted in chapter 2, U.S. EPA has, by all accounts, failed in its handling of Title VI complaints and only once initiated a compliance review to ensure that an agency it funds is complying with Title VI.

Another decision that set a highly problematic precedent for Title VI enforcement at U.S. EPA was its 1998 decision on a Title VI complaint known as *Select Steel* (Cole 1999; Engelman Lado 2017; S. Foster 2000; Mank 2008; Matthew 2017). The complaint, filed by EJ advocates against Michigan Department of Environmental Quality (MDEQ) for permitting the Select Steel Corporation of America to build a steel "mini-mill" in Flint, Michigan, alleged that the facility would have a disparate impact on the largely low-income, black community already burdened by many environmental hazards. The first Title VI administrative complaint that EPA decided on its merits, EPA dismissed it on the grounds that the anticipated emissions would not violate the National Ambient Air Quality Standards (NAAQS) for ozone and lead. That is, EPA decided that the permit created no disparate impact because it purportedly posed "no adverse effect," measured in terms of compliance with NAAQS. This particular element of the *Select Steel* decision has come to be known as the "rebuttable presumption" that compliance with environmental health-based thresholds (like NAAQS) invalidates Title VI complaints' allegations of adverse impact.

Select Steel has been heavily criticized by environmental justice and civil rights advocates. Some of the major criticisms are that significant health damage can occur at levels below NAAQS levels; the EPA did not assess the *cumulative* harm posed by all hazards but instead only the impact of each individual pollutant against its relevant health standard; compliance with NAAQS and state air toxics standards does not preclude the risk of industrial accidents; the investigation should have acknowledged additional pathways and stressors harming residents' health; and EPA ignored the existence of toxic hot spots in which pollutants exist at high enough levels to cause adverse health effects even when the broader region overall meets the standard. Additionally, as Cole (1999) points out, Flint was not even in attainment with NAAQS for ozone at or after the time of the complaint and investigation. Moreover, as Dayna Matthew (2017) has argued, the logic EPA used in the *Select Steel* decision ignores the heart of civil rights law: disparity. Matthew argues: "All other agencies and courts enforce disparate impact claims under Title VI by identifying and addressing disparity. The EPA, in contrast, analyzes Title VI disparate impact claims by focusing on adversity. 'Disparate impact' goes to the issue of equality, while 'adversity' refers to physically measurable standards of pollution, without regard to the extent of the harm communities bear in relation to one another" (Matthew 2017, 6).

Despite these and other criticisms, *Select Steel* set a powerful precedent, and EPA has used the ruling's logic to dismiss the majority of Title VI complaints it has investigated (Engelman Lado 2017; Foster 2018; Mank 2008, 43; Matthew 2017, 6). Scholars note that powerful industry interests pressured EPA into the *Select Steel* decision (Cole 1999; Mank 2008, 41).

Staff members' abilities to implement proposed EJ reforms are constrained by other state and federal environmental statutes, executive orders, and mandates. For example, many federal environmental statutes leave considerable discretion to the states. This helps explain why EPA has made EJ recommendations to the states, rather than imposing requirements that could more meaningfully improve conditions in overburdened communities. The Trump administration is further deepening this deference to states through its strategic prioritization of "cooperative federalism" (EPA 2018b).

Additionally, numerous laws and policies require that new rules pass a cost-benefit test, which often weakens rules in general and precludes EJ concerns in particular (Konisky 2015a, 43–44). Benefits of regulatory controls on pollution (e.g., prevented deaths and illnesses, improved ecosystem functioning, maintained biodiversity, and reduced environmental inequality) are largely difficult or impossible to calculate. In contrast, costs of regulatory restrictions (e.g., potential lost jobs and profits) are much easier to quantify. Also, industry regularly overestimates the costs of regulations by tenfold or more. In some cases, agencies' requirements to evaluate the economic impacts of proposed regulations *prohibit* consideration of social impacts (e.g., CRS 2016). Additionally, some laws impose time limits on agencies' review of permit applications, which restrict staff members' abilities to conduct extra analysis or outreach for applications pertaining to facilities located in overburdened and vulnerable communities.

Challenging the Narrative about Regulatory Authority and EJ

That said, as legal scholars have shown, existing law does authorize many EJ reforms that are rarely implemented (ELI 2001; Engelman Lado 2017; S. Foster 2000, 2008; Guzy 2000; Lazarus 1996; Lazarus and Tai 1999; NAPA 2001; Shadbegian and Wolverton 2015). EPA's EJ Legal Tools document identifies how federal environmental statutes authorize agencies to implement various EJ reforms throughout agency practice (EPA 2011b). EPA's general council at the time, Scott Fulton, characterized "our environmental laws" as "replete with opportunities" to practice EJ in EPA's rulemaking and permitting activities (Fulton 2012, 5). Scholars note that EPA's authority to reform agency practice in line with EJ principles does not "only" rest in EO 12898 but also in statutes (including the National Environmental Policy Act, the Civil Rights Act, and others), and that EPA regulations prohibit both intentional discrimination and unintended discriminatory effects (e.g., EPA 2011b, 94).

Notably, whereas some permitting staff assert that the demographic characteristics of surrounding communities cannot influence how staff treat a given permit application, scholars show otherwise (ELI 2001; S. Foster 2000; Foster 2008, 233–234, 315–316; Gauna 2015; Gordon and Harley 2005, 161; Lazarus and Tai 1999; NAPA 2001). EPA's Environmental Appeals Board (EAB) has held multiple times that, when evidence shows that a hazardous waste facility or a new major source of air pollution might have a disproportionate impact on a low-income community or community of color, permitting agencies can conduct extra EJ analysis, conduct extra public outreach, and include permit conditions that prevent such impacts (S. Foster 2000; Foster 2008, 233–234, 315–316; Gauna 2015; Rechtschaffen, Gauna, and O'Neill 2009, 249–259; Gordon and Harley 2005; Lazarus and Tai 1999). In its 1995 decision *In re Chemical Waste Management of Indiana, Inc.*, the EAB reasoned that "if the nature of the facility and its proximity to the community would make it impossible to craft a set of permit terms that would adequately protect the health and environment of such populations, the agency would have the authority to deny the permit" (S. Foster 2000). In this decision, the EAB directed permitting staff to take "a more refined look" when there is a "superficially plausible" claim that a permit would create a disparate impact on the surrounding community (Gauna 2015, 61–62). In subsequent decisions, the EAB reached the same conclusion about these authorities under various environmental statutes. Indeed, there is precedent that agencies *should* do so as a matter of course, as EAB has sent a permit back for review because the permitting agency did not do an EJ analysis in response to public concerns (Gauna 2015, 63; Gordon and Harley 2005, 161).

Additionally, precedent that mitigates against proposed EJ reforms can be superseded. Notably, under the Obama administration, EPA made progress on abandoning the *Select Steel* rebuttable presumption standard for determining Title VI cases. In 2013, EPA quietly issued what has come to be known as the "adversity" white paper, which states that the agency will no longer presume that compliance with environmental standards (like NAAQS) precludes the existence of adverse impacts and other violations of Title VI of the Civil Rights Act (EPA 2013c). In January 2017, EPA issued part of its new External Civil Rights Compliance Office Compliance Toolkit, which specifies the agency's new approach to processing Title VI complaints and appears to withdraw the *Select Steel* standard for determining adversity (EPA 2017j).

Although acknowledging that statutes limit their work in certain ways, EJ staff frame regulatory authority to do EJ reforms as more expansive than is commonly claimed and as deserving reinterpretation. Stacy, a permitting engineer who plays a lead role in her agency's EJ efforts, noted, "For as much as the regulations are prescriptive, there is also still a lot of area for interpretation and argument." Malcolm asserted, "There are a lot of ways that legal language can be interpreted. And how much latitude there is, is open to interpretation. So, it is how much you want to do it." They and other EJ staff frame agencies' progress on EJ policy implementation as constrained not so much by statutes but by current interpretations of them and bureaucrats' willingness to fight for new understandings of them.

Indeed, staff have effectively searched for and found the authority needed to implement EJ reforms after being told that such reforms were prohibited by law. One notable example pertains to EPA's recent revision of the Petroleum Refinery Rule. Community members and EJ advocates have long pressed agencies to more aggressively restrict dangerous petroleum refinery practices (such as flaring) and require air monitors along their fencelines (perimeters) to track their emissions, recommendations that industry has vociferously fought. Two EPA staff described to me how they took the communities' concerns and requests seriously, determined that EPA data substantiated those concerns, and found the authority needed to strengthen regulations controlling fugitive emissions, create new rules for flaring operations, and add fenceline monitoring requirements into the newly revised regulations. Although the new regulations were not as substantial as EJ and other environmental advocates had hoped, fenceline monitoring valuably enables the agency to "ground truth" its emissions data that it uses to construct new rules for the industry and permit conditions for individual facilities. The rulewriting staff I interviewed noted that EPA's Office of General Counsel (OGC) explicitly stated that the agency did *not* have the authority to require fenceline monitoring. However, "we did figure out a way to do it within the confines of the Clean Air Act." She and her coworkers persisted—they had to "push this thing day and night for, I would say, six years solid." Despite strident pushback from industry and after debating with EPA's attorneys, she and her coworkers got that requirement into the rule revision. Her coworker explained that they were able to strengthen the regulation because they sought out the necessary regulatory authority: they had a "willingness to explore where we could use the authority." She asserted that EPA's EJ Legal Tools document will help "move this work along" and that the agency is in the "growth stages" of using its authority to support environmental justice. This example demonstrates that "authority" to do something is not immutable, and that staff can contest and redefine it.

Heather, who helped draft her agency's guidelines for integrating EJ principles into the rulemaking process, stated that they made progress in doing so because some managers were willing to question the accepted boundaries of regulatory authority.

> **Heather:** I and several other colleagues had come up with this idea actually very close to when I first started at the agency and then it kind of died. It wasn't the right time, because our political [appointee] left and she was the one who was really interested in it. And then we tried pitching it to another person, and they said, "Oh, this seems legally very problematic, just another place for us to get sued" and wasn't interested. So, it wasn't until the beginning of this administration, where there was a larger movement towards doing something....
>
> **JH:** But not, to your knowledge, any formal expansion of the authority around EJ?
>
> **Heather:** No....They just made a different calculation about what the risks were and decided to go forward.

That is, Heather and her coworkers made progress on integrating EJ principles into regulatory practice by contesting other bureaucrats' claims about the limits of their regulatory authority.

Others argued that existing regulatory authority need not determine an agency's progress on EJ, as they are helping to draft new regulations authorizing staff to implement proposed EJ reforms. For instance, Elise noted that she is "working directly with permit project managers, for example, trying to identify the gaps where we can make some regulatory changes." Getting regulations in place that authorize staff to do EJ reforms, even if not *mandating* staff do so, valuably disrupts claims by managers, agency attorneys, and industry actors that staff are prohibited from doing such practices.

In sum, bureaucrats' abilities to implement proposed EJ reforms are constrained in certain respects by statutes, executive orders, and regulations. Environmental regulatory agencies require further legal analysis specifying their authorities to implement various proposed EJ reforms. Additionally, where regulatory authority to implement important EJ reforms is lacking, legislative action or executive orders will be needed to create it. That said, as I have shown here, considerable evidence suggests that agencies have *more* authority to integrate EJ principles into regulatory practice than the standard narrative conveys. "Regulatory authority" is stretchy and open to contestation—it is something that agency staff have been able to help redefine. Moreover, even where laws supporting EJ are limited, the regulatory actions they authorize are not regularly implemented by staff. A clear example of this is the rarity with which EPA permitting and rulemaking staff follow their obligation under the National Environmental Policy Act to "consider" EJ implications of their decisions, as I showed in chapter 2. For all of these reasons, we cannot attribute agencies' limited progress on EJ solely to issues of regulatory authority.

Analytical Tools

Staff also explain that they need better analytic tools to determine how regulatory decisions may affect environmental inequalities. In this book, I characterize such tools generally as "EJ analysis." EJ analysis can include what is often called *equity analysis*, a determination of whether a regulatory action (rule, permit, program, or project) may exacerbate, maintain, or reduce existing inequalities across population groups (EPA 2016a,b, 23–26, 2016c; NEJAC 2004, 2010; NRC 2009; Nweke et al 2011).

Robust equity analyses require *cumulative impact assessment*, which would identify the environmental hazards facing those to be affected by the regulatory decision, the vulnerabilities that exacerbate the effects of exposure to those hazards (e.g., psychosocial stress, age, and lack of access to health care), and how these various environmental and social stressors together affect human health. EPA proposed a cumulative impact assessment framework in 2003 (EPA 2003), and various cumulative-impact analysis methodologies are being developed (CalEPA 2010; Solomon et al. 2016). Some are designed to identify how a regulatory decision like a proposed policy or permit contributes to communities' other environmental stressors and vulnerabilities. Others, called *EJ screening tools*, translate cumulative impact assessment results into easy-to-use formats that indicate areas that are most environmentally burdened and socially vulnerable (Holifield 2014; Lewis and Bennett 2013; NEJAC 2010; Payne-Sturges et al. 2012; Scammell, Montague, and Raffensperger 2014). They use geographic information systems (GIS) mapping technologies to integrate data on environmental hazards and social vulnerability in a semi-quantitative manner. They often give each geographic unit (e.g., each census tract) a cumulative impact score, which enables users to visually identify areas of greatest cumulative impact. Staff could use EJ screening tools to allocate resources (e.g., for conducting more robust EJ analyses or prioritizing enforcement inspections). EPA's EJSCREEN data mapping and screening tool and CalEPA's CalEnviroScreen are two of the most recently developed EJ tools for presenting and analyzing data (CalEPA 2017a; EPA 2017b).

It is important to note that equity and cumulative impact assessments differ from standard environmental regulatory impact analyses (Brown 2007; Nash 2006; O'Brien 2000; Raffensperger and Tickner 1999; Senier et al. 2017; Tesh 2001; Tickner 2003; Vogel 2012; Whiteside 2006). Typically, regulatory impact assessments estimate the aggregated benefits and costs of a proposed regulatory decision, and not how those benefits and costs would be distributed within society. Additionally, standard regulatory assessments evaluate the risks posed by a single environmental hazard, in isolation from the other existing hazards and social vulnerabilities; when assessed in this way, each stressor might appear inconsequential, even though together they may significantly harm human health. Scammell, Montague, and Raffensperger (2014) explain that standard regulatory impact assessment "is based on the tacit (and incorrect) assumption that ecosystems and human populations can tolerate an endless accumulation of innumerable 'acceptable' insults" (103). By ignoring the additive and synergistic effects of various stressors, standard regulatory analytic practice underestimates the full scope of environmental harm and environmental inequality.

Environmental regulatory agency staff often attribute their agency's slow progress on EJ policy implementation to constraints they face in trying to conduct EJ analysis. Many staff emphasize that EJ analysis is hindered by extensive data gaps, including the dearth of scientific data about facilities' actual emissions, people's exposures to any given hazard, how various social vulnerabilities affect our bodies' responses to those exposures, and varying physiological consequences of exposure to combinations of hazards. Staff lament that data for many hazards are available only at broad geographical scales (e.g., county or state), and thus EJ analyses do not reveal some localized overburdened and vulnerable spots within regions that are otherwise relatively well-off. Also, some hazards data are guarded by regulated entities. While communities are rightly concerned about the interactive effects of pollutants, food insecurity, crime, and other factors, analysis that could fully integrate these variables is, as Tom asserted, "25 years away."

Stacy explained that the uncertainties in EJ analysis undermine her confidence in using those analyses to shape the content of regulatory decisions. Specifically, in discussing the prospects for using cumulative impact assessment to impose stronger permit conditions on facilities in environmentally overburdened and vulnerable areas, she stated: "I don't know that we feel confident enough in turning that qualitative [cumulative impact] analysis into true quantitative permit limit.... [Although] we are able to take measurements down to very small levels, we don't know what that means. We don't know how these things interact." Regulated entities will fight any decision based on analysis that is not watertight.

Some rulemaking staff argued that EJ analysis results should be presented in quantitative terms so that they can be integrated into the analysis specifying the regulation's net cost or benefit. Decision-makers pay particular attention to analyses that aggregate the costs and benefits of a regulatory decision into one common metric (typically, dollars). To be sure, regulations do not require that staff monetize all impacts of a regulatory decision, and many staff and others do not like the idea of doing so because important EJ concerns are difficult or impossible to monetize (e.g., quality of life, stress, suffering, and noise and light pollution) and thus are incommensurable.[3] But, as Heather explained, "benefit-cost analysis gets the most bandwidth" with decision-makers. When staff expect that a decision will disproportionately burden marginalized groups, "if you can express that in monetary terms, you are more likely that it will get incorporated" into the final regulatory decision. Some staff are helping to develop quantitative environmental inequity indices so that EJ issues can be factored into the cost-benefit analysis for regulatory decisions (Maguire and Sheriff 2011).

Staff also are uncertain how to make decisions based on EJ analyses. Although regulators can do rudimentary EJ analyses, the question remains about how to decide whether the results signify outcomes that are adverse and unequal. As Dan stated, EJ analysis "is difficult to do, because it is as much a political definition as a scientific one. What is 'disproportionate'? ... What threshold constitutes an environmental 'burden'?" In some cases, scientists have thresholds that specify the point at which a particular chemical poses a problematically adverse risk (notably, for cancer). However, there is no objective point at which the cumulative impacts affecting a population are sufficiently harmful or unequal to justify any given regulatory action. Additionally, staff wonder how they should weigh the results of their EJ analysis relative to other factors they must consider, such as the decision's impacts on sustainability, or its economic impacts on industry.

Additionally, these analytical limitations hindering agencies' EJ efforts are exacerbated by the fact that those working to develop EJ analytical techniques are isolated from each other. Ryan, who helped develop his agency's EJ screening tool, lamented that "there is no community of practice": staff within and across agencies developing EJ analytical tools "don't necessarily talk to each other." He noted, moreover, that there is no professional network of researchers developing EJ analyses for use in environmental regulatory agencies that could promote best practices and consistent protocol.

Bureaucrats' concerns about the limits of existing analytical tools needed to more fully support agencies' EJ efforts echo those raised by scholars, who strive to develop better tools and specify how to apply them in the context of statute-bound regulatory decision-making (Baden, Noonan, and Turaga 2007; Banzhaf 2011; Bullard et al. 2007; Chakraborty, Maantay, and Brender 2011; Chakraborty 2018; Couch and Coles 2011; Gauna 2015; Holifield 2012, 2014; Liévanos 2018; Maantay and Maroko 2018; Mennis and Heckert 2018; Mohai and Saha 2015; Mohai, Pellow, and Roberts 2009a;

Morello-Frosch et al. 2011; Nweke 2011; Nweke et al 2011; O'Neill 2000; Payne-Sturges et al. 2012; Scammell, Montague, and Raffensperger 2014; Senier et al. 2017; Sexton and Linder 2011, 2018; Shadbegian and Wolverton 2015; Solomon et al. 2016).

Currently, in most cases, analysts simply cannot do quantitative cumulative impact assessments that account for the full array of stressors affecting communities. Scholars have highlighted that there is a considerable amount of "undone science" pertaining to the scope of environmental hazards and people's exposures to them (Frickel and Elliott 2018; Hess 2016). For example, air pollution monitoring generates data about the concentration of a few pollutants in large regional airsheds, thereby providing few insights into the location of toxic hot spots. Often, monitoring is not conducted in areas likely to be overburdened and vulnerable to the effects of exposure to those pollutants. Many toxic air pollutants are rarely monitored at all, such as airborne agricultural pesticides. When monitoring is done, researchers often have a difficult time determining the sources of toxins detected. Polluting facilities' emissions data are generally estimates based on the type and size of facility, rather than actual monitoring. Due to these various data constraints, researchers use residential proximity to hazardous sources of pollution as proxies for exposure; such estimates do not specify people's actual exposures to hazards. Additionally, Frickel and Elliott's (2018) research highlights the need to account for *past* industrial practices whose toxic legacies are largely unaccounted for and obscured by urban development.

The science of pollutants' toxicity, in which researchers examine how exposure to certain amounts of a particular pollutant affects laboratory animals, is also similarly characterized by widespread data constraints. Researchers disagree about how to design such studies so that the duration and timing of exposures best reflect what humans will experience, about which animals to use, and about which endpoints or symptoms to monitor. Such toxicological studies do not illuminate the full array of health outcomes from exposure to any given chemical. For example, scientists cannot accurately observe in animals the full array of effects of chemical exposures (such as pain, anxiety, fear, distrust, and anger), and short-lived laboratory animals do not experience human bodies' full range of diseases that take many years to manifest (such as various forms of cancer). Toxicological studies examine the apparent health effects of exposure through a certain route of exposure (e.g., dermal or dietary) but not others. Very little toxicological research examines how the effects of exposure to environmental stressors (singularly or in combination) vary by race, age, and other demographic factors. Additionally, very few studies have been done on the health effects of chemical mixtures, or how environmental and other factors combine in ways that affect health. It is difficult to imagine how researchers could quantify a community's vulnerability to the effects of exposure to environmental hazards. For instance, how might researchers calculate the degree to which food insecurity, racist violence and other forms of discrimination, and housing market risks affect a community's vulnerability to the effects of exposure to environmental harms? We know these factors affect health, but we do not know how to quantify those factors individually or together.

Challenging the Narrative about Analytical Tools and EJ

Although EJ analysis tools and the protocol for using them in the regulatory context require further development, agencies' EJ reform efforts can proceed despite these challenges. Many EJ-supportive staff emphasized to me that agencies currently have enough data and sufficiently robust tools to conduct EJ analysis during regulatory decision-making processes, such as targeting enforcement investigations in overburdened and vulnerable communities and identifying the EJ impacts of proposed rules, standards, or facility expansions.

Even some who detailed the limitations of current EJ analytical tools nonetheless emphasize that agencies *can* start using those tools now to improve environmental conditions in overburdened and vulnerable communities. As Tom stated, "There is a lot we can do with what we know now, even if we don't have the best cumulative impact analysis." One rulewriter who has participated in his agency's efforts to integrate EJ analysis into rulemaking acknowledged that they do not have the ability to fully calculate human susceptibility to harm from exposure to environmental hazards. However, as he explained, substantial scientific evidence shows that susceptibility factors consistently correlate with race and income. As a result, he and his colleagues can use racial and income demographic data as proxies for susceptibility. He stated that these "baby steps" toward calculating susceptibility are adequate for now. He also noted that data constraints are not always as absolute as staff claim: "People say, 'We don't have the data,'" but the issue is often not that they don't exist but that they are expensive, or that integrating them is a "headache, a lot of work. ... We can always estimate."

Indeed, EPA has asserted multiple times that cumulative impact assessment, notwithstanding current limitations, is feasible now in many circumstances and becoming increasingly robust (EPA n.d., 2003). While regulatory agency staff cannot do EJ analyses that fully characterize all existing environmental impacts and social vulnerabilities, they *can* do rudimentary but functional EJ analyses that will undoubtedly improve regulatory decision-making over current practice.

Moreover, EJ analytical tools are constantly being improved, and there are numerous ways agencies can strengthen their EJ analytical processes (EPA 2016b, 23–26; Solomon et al. 2016). Agency staff are among those developing such tools, which will help ensure that they are applicable in regulatory decision-making contexts (Maguire and Sheriff 2011; Nweke 2011; Nweke et al. 2011; Shadbegian and Wolverton 2015).

Other External Factors Shaping Agencies' EJ Efforts

Some of my research participants and scholars who have observed agencies' EJ efforts occasionally identify other factors beyond the control of agency staff that shape agencies' progress on EJ reforms. I note these briefly here.

Leadership Priorities

Numerous staff asserted that, given EJ staff members' lack of authority over other staff, their abilities to implement proposed EJ reforms are hindered when politically appointed leaders do not formally designate EJ as an agency priority. Martin, an EJ staff person, explained that managers and other career staff will not implement EJ reforms unless political appointees endorse EJ, attend EJ planning meetings, instruct staff to implement proposed EJ reforms, and monitor staff progress on doing so. Martin stated that this is a function of "will, not resources" and that "[p]eople inside the government listen to and care about the administration's priorities. These things matter."

Some staff emphasize this constraint by identifying exceptions that prove the rule: top leadership who *do* actively endorse EJ principles. Many EJ-supportive staff applauded Obama administration EPA leadership, especially Administrator Lisa Jackson, for legitimizing environmental justice efforts within EPA. Heather, who has helped design her agency's EJ reforms to the rulemaking process, explained that progress on EJ "does not happen unless you have someone at the very top who communicates that it is a priority. ... If, at the end of the day, it is not important to the person making decisions and they are going to ignore that anyway, then that is not where you are going to invest your time and energy." Heather explained that she is capitalizing on the current administration's support for EJ by institutionalizing EJ analysis into rulewriters' everyday work processes: "Trying to get it into the normal workings of the agency is so important, because then it will be less likely to be subject to all of those political changes, which we can't control." That is, leadership support for EJ can enable staff to implement EJ reforms that will (hopefully) persist through subsequent administrations less supportive of EJ principles.

Kim, who helped her agency's enforcement office integrate EJ reforms throughout its practice, stated that they are "way ahead of other offices" principally because the office's top official insisted that managers design and implement these EJ reforms. This official created an EJ committee comprised of all of the office's top managers, met with the committee monthly, required managers to report on their progress, and required each division to appoint an EJ coordinator to work with the agency's principal EJ staff. Kim asserted, this "pushing" by top leadership is "super important" and the EJ reforms "would not have happened otherwise."

Yet, while support of politically appointed leadership fosters progress on EJ reforms, it isn't enough. Numerous staff I interviewed lamented that, although the top leaders in their agency endorse EJ reforms, staff and managers still rarely implement them. Even agencies with robust, explicit support for EJ from their appointed officials—such as U.S. EPA in the Obama administration, and Minnesota's Pollution Control Agency under Commissioner John Linc Stine—still have made only minimal progress on EJ reforms relative to what they could achieve. Meaningfully reforming agency practice according to EJ principles requires not only that leaders endorse the concept of EJ but also that managers and other staff implement EJ reforms.

"Silos of Excellence": Lack of Regulatory Coordination

EJ-supportive staff, advocates, and scholars also emphasize that agencies' limited progress on EJ reforms stems from the lack of coordination within and between agencies. Within agencies, offices regulating air pollution, water pollution, and hazardous waste are isolated from each other, which presents an institutional barrier to evaluating and addressing cumulative impacts created by many different hazards. Additionally, in many cases,

EJ is treated as another area of regulatory work separate from air, water, and other "core programs." As Andrew, who worked in rulemaking at EPA, explained: "The tongue-in-cheek phrase was 'silos of excellence.' ... [EPA is a] horizontally totally unintegrated organization. EJ is in another silo somewhere else, and we don't have any way through the walls."

This "siloed" nature of environmental regulation also includes the lack of coordination across agencies. U.S. EPA's EJ staff at headquarters are charged with coordinating the EJ work of its regional office staff, who are responsible for helping state agencies' EJ efforts. Some guidance and coordination occur, but insufficiently. Some state agency EJ staff developing their own EJ guidance documents (such as integrating EJ analyses into the permitting process) told me that they have not been able to get EPA to share its draft documents with them, leaving them to reinvent the wheel rather than building on what other agencies have done.

Environmental Justice Policy Advocacy

Some staff also noted that their progress on EJ reforms is conditioned in part by whether EJ and civil rights advocacy compels legislators to pass EJ policy. Numerous EJ staff identified California as a leading example of how this can strengthen an agency's progress on EJ reforms. The state's strong EJ movement has devoted considerable effort toward state-level policy change (Perkins 2015). The California legislature has, in response, passed numerous laws specifying EJ reforms that public agencies must implement, due in part to its prominent and growing Latino caucus that has been broadly supportive of civil rights reforms. EJ advocacy can help strengthen agencies' EJ efforts informally as well. Activists demanding EJ reforms to regulatory practice and applauding agencies' EJ reform efforts can provide the external pressure and encouragement needed to legitimize EJ reforms. That said, in most cases, EJ advocacy is not strong enough relative to industry to compel agency leaders and elected officials to endorse EJ reforms.

Mainstream Environmental Advocacy

Finally, some staff noted that the priorities and practices of mainstream environmental organizations often limit the extent to which agencies support environmental justice. Although some of the "big green" mainstream environmental organizations today support EJ more than they have in the past, their regulatory work still focuses on holding agencies accountable for protecting wilderness areas and meeting aggregate air pollution standards and does little to demand agencies comply with the Civil Rights Act or EO 12898. Moreover, they still often engage in practices that undermine the prospects for EJ reforms at environmental regulatory agencies. For example, Joan noted that a prominent mainstream environmental organization criticized her agency for its recent EJ reform efforts: "The Sierra Club, when environmental justice is brought up, has said, 'You are detracting from the environmental cause.'"

Conclusion

Agency staff clearly convey that agencies' abilities to address environmental inequalities are limited by resources, regulatory authority, analytical tools, and other material factors. I call this the *standard narrative* because some element of it was expressed by each of my research participants and because it coheres with EJ scholars' explanations for agencies' disappointing progress on EJ reforms. The central message in the standard narrative is that EJ is out of their hands—that it is limited by factors *beyond the control of agency staff.*

I do not dispute that these factors matter. To the contrary, I have shown that they matter very much. Agencies will need more resources to fulfill all of their responsibilities, including their EJ reform efforts. There is much work to be done to clarify the legal authority agencies possess to implement proposed EJ reforms, and certainly some EJ reforms will require that legislatures create additional authority for agencies to implement them. Furthermore, analytical advancements will help agencies do their EJ work more robustly. Other factors matter too, including explicit support from leadership and pressure from social movements.

Yet, we should question how *fully* the standard narrative explains agencies' slow progress on EJ policy implementation. Notably, the standard narrative implies that agencies *cannot* do more to support environmental justice—that asking more of these agencies is unrealistic. However, in this chapter I provided evidence that agencies do have sufficient resources, regulatory authority, and analytical tools to implement EJ reforms *to a greater extent* than they have to date. They can use tools that are currently available, have the authority to do EJ analysis in designing rules and permit conditions (as well as other heretofore unimplemented EJ reforms), and have the resources to do many if not most of the reforms EJ-supportive staff and EJ advocates recommend.

We should question how fully the standard narrative explains agencies' progress on EJ. While it reveals some significant constraints to agencies' EJ efforts, it obscures others. I show in the coming chapters that, even if we were to resolve the issues associated with these factors beyond the control of agency staff, there are other forces internal to agencies that will need to be addressed for agencies to reform regulatory practice in line with EJ principles. Staff bear some responsibility for the extent to which agencies integrate EJ principles into regulatory practice. My point is not that resources, laws, and data gaps don't matter. Rather, my point is that we need to look further to fully understand the challenges facing efforts to institutionalize EJ principles into regulatory practice. I focus on certain elements of regulatory culture, showing in chapters 4, 5, and 6 that bureaucrats reject EJ reforms as contradicting their organization's identity and responsibilities, and then turning in chapter 7 to the fact that even some staff highly supportive of EJ reforms define "EJ" in ways that deviate from longstanding EJ movement principles and design EJ programs accordingly.

4 "We Do Ecology, Not Sociology": Staff Narratives That Undermine EJ

We are pushing against something that does not want to be disturbed.
—Janine, an EJ-supportive, government agency staff person

You are pushing against a brick wall in every single direction. Internally with staff at the state agency, I felt like, with a lot of people, I was pushing against a brick wall all day just to move it a centimeter.
—Mary, government agency EJ staff person

Cultural Resistance to Environmental Justice

In my interviews with agency staff about the challenges facing their agency's EJ efforts, they all first identified one or more of the factors beyond their control that I described in chapter 3: limited resources, regulatory authority, and/or analytical tools. In particular, they lament that staff across the agencies are regularly asked to do more with less, under heightened scrutiny and criticism.

That said, at every agency in my study, including those whose leadership has explicitly endorsed EJ principles, nearly all of the staff I interviewed who help implement their agency's EJ efforts described facing resistance to EJ from some of their own coworkers now and in the past. EJ staff at every agency in my study described their EJ work as always having been "a battle" or a "struggle." For example, Michael, who has helped propose EJ reforms in his agency for many years, stated that "[m]any offices are absolutely hostile to the notion of EJ." Barbara stated, "Lots of folks at _____ [this agency] think that we should not be doing EJ." Penny described her EJ work as "isolating" and that she and the other EJ staff in her agency "face a lot of resistance" from other staff. Nicky summed up her years of experience as an EJ staff person at multiple agencies this way: "It's just this total resistance." An EJ staff person at EPA noted that "even when the wind was at our backs, like it was in the Obama administration," getting staff to implement EJ reforms "is like pulling teeth. With the exception of only a few people, no one here is excited about EJ." EJ staff and their EJ-supportive colleagues conveyed that they are deeply frustrated by the cultural constraints to EJ. The EJ staff I interviewed have been doing this work for many years, some for over two decades. They described this pushback against EJ and colleagues' failure to make a good-faith effort to integrate EJ into regulatory practice as longstanding, transcending political administrations, exhausting, and disheartening.

I asked EJ staff and their EJ-supportive coworkers to explain for me what gave them these impressions: things their colleagues have said or otherwise done that undermine EJ reforms to regulatory practice. Additionally, in my interviews with staff and observations of agency meetings, I documented ways that bureaucrats discursively challenged or otherwise undermined EJ staff and the reforms they propose. As organizational theorists have noted, organizational inertia in the face of pressures for change from social movements and other actors in the organizational field is something that requires *work* (Lawrence 2008). This resistance to change is frequently hard to see, as it is often conducted by non-elite organization members in everyday interactions. In this chapter and in chapter 5, I identify those everyday practices through which environmental regulatory agency staff resist proposed EJ reforms.

In this chapter, I show that environmental regulatory agency staff promoting EJ reforms experience a working environment in which organization members are allowed to *discursively* challenge EJ reforms. I make this case by identifying how bureaucrats, with each other and with me, vocally contest and delegitimize proposed EJ reforms, and I specify the work this pushback accomplishes.

The narratives I will showcase are often directed toward EJ principles in general. Where they are levied against a specific EJ reform proposal, I indicate that in the text. EJ staff did not want to name colleagues engaging in these practices; instead, they focused our conversation on the discourses they found troubling. As I discuss in the appendix, my data do not allow me to determine how widespread these narratives are. However, EJ staff and their EJ-supportive coworkers report that they face these kinds of claims regularly enough that they undermine efforts to integrate EJ principles into regulatory practice, and they rarely mentioned managers or other staff challenging these narratives.

In making these arguments, I employ a constructionist approach to analyzing discourse of environmental regulatory agency staff. The words, phrases, stories, and other elements of narrative expression that we use to characterize people, things, events, and phenomena do a lot of work—they shape our understanding of how things *are*, as well as how things should be. Rather than seeing language as an objective description of the world around us, I am interested in how the particular language we use *constructs* our understanding of how the world is. Thus, I examine how staff debate the merits of proposed EJ reforms with each other and with me—how they negotiate and define what kinds of reforms (if any) are reasonable—and identify the consequences of those interactions for the institutionalization of EJ principles into regulatory practice. In this chapter, I showcase how some staff reject proposed EJ reforms, identify what makes these claims persuasive and problematic, and specify the forms of power the various speakers wield. I conclude by identifying how EJ-supportive staff circumvent and confront colleagues' narrative pushback against EJ.

Casting EJ as Conflicting with the Agency's Identity

Many EJ staff stated that their EJ reforms are stymied by colleagues' assertions that EJ proposals conflict with the *identity* of the organization. Organization members make claims about the organization's identity and "who we are" to ward off calls for change (Alvesson 2011; Kenny, Whittle, and Willmott 2016; Kreiner and Murphy 2016; Lawrence 2008; Pratt et al. 2016; Scott 2014). I draw on scholarship that takes a process-oriented, social constructivist approach to organizational identity that shows how it is a "never ending 'work-in-progress'" (Pratt et al. 2016, 11): a continual, interactive, narrative, and behavioral process through which organization members strive to defend the organization's status quo.

In some cases, such claims are quite general. For example, Steve told me that a manager in his agency's air pollution division said to him, "There is serious stuff we are doing, like protecting air. And then there is this peripheral stuff: EJ, Title VI." Staff often frame EJ as contrary to the agency's identity by characterizing EJ as a fleeting "fad" or "trend"—and one they do not regard highly. At agencies whose politically appointed leadership endorses EJ, staff sometimes dismissively characterize proposed EJ reforms as "just the politics du jour"—as something that will fade with the next administration. Penny, who was only a few months into her EJ staff position at the time of our interview, told me that her coworkers had already characterized EJ as "a trend" and said to her, "As soon as the executive leaves, it will be back to business as usual." Some also say, "'How much time do you have again?,' reminding you that you are appointed and you are probably going to be out in a year, and they will still be here." Such accounts echo scholars' observations that organization members often resist change through "condescending reactions that trivialize the proposal for change" (Fernandez 2015, 385; see also Burke 2018, 132). Similarly, Elise told me that some of her colleagues are "resistant," "describing EJ as a 'fad' or a 'trend' ... [or] 'flavor of the month'" in casual conversation. Esther said that some of her coworkers would say about EJ: "It is a boutique program: it's here today, it's gone tomorrow." These narratives diminish EJ reforms as marginal to the agency's "true" work. So too does the argument, made many staff, that EJ practices are only the purview of EJ staff and not the responsibility of other agency members.

Disciplinary Training

Other EJ staff described how some colleagues define EJ as inconsistent with what the agency is and does by drawing disciplinary boundaries between EJ staff and the rest of the agency. In separate interviews, two staff at one agency noted that someone wrote a (now famous) memo to an EJ staff person rejecting their report about racial environmental inequality by asserting, "[This agency] does ecology, not sociology." Esther described to me how she would implore permit writers and rulewriting staff, "You have got to look at the demographics, you have got to look at the impact [of permits and rules] on these communities," to which they would respond, "We don't do sociological work." Such narratives dismiss EJ analysis as beyond the bounds of what their organization does. Drawing these distinctions among staff is a rhetorical technique called "boundary work." Gieryn (1999) showed that scientists actively draw boundaries between "scientific" and "non-scientific" knowledge to continually reestablish their intellectual authority. Such narratives echo the boundaries between "science" and "politics" that other scholars have observed scientists use to cast EJ politics beyond the realm of an organization's responsibility (Holifield 2004; Ottinger 2013).

I observed staff employ this boundary work. For example, I attended an EJ training for a team of staff. The training included a short video describing some roots of environmental inequalities; the video presented data on racial wealth inequality and argued that it stems not from an individual's work ethic but largely from racism, unequal funding for public education, and other social structural factors. Immediately following the video, the team's manager, Bob, angrily and stridently instructed the EJ staff leading the training to "be careful," proclaiming "there aren't any data to back up those stats" shown in the video and asserting, twice, "You're talking to scientists." Framing content as unsubstantiated carries a lot of weight in environmental regulatory agencies that identify as science-based organizations. By asserting his professional status as a "scientist" and implying that the video content was unscientific, Bob authorized himself to discredit the video, despite the fact that the material on EJ was beyond his realm of expertise. Additionally, as the senior person in the room, he implicitly authorized his staff to challenge or ignore the EJ training material and made it difficult for them to defend it. Managers' practices matter considerably, because they have the power to require their staff implement EJ reforms—and the discretion to not do so.

Expertise

EJ-supportive staff described colleagues using other forms of boundary work to dismiss EJ reforms. Notably, some staff frame community engagement practices as violating their agency's identity as an organization within which decisions are made by professional experts with advanced academic training. For example, Janine described trying to get engineers and scientists in her agency to take seriously input from residents who are not formally trained as experts. She said that they push back, saying, "Why should I solicit input from the public when I was hired to make these decisions myself?" Such narratives frame residents as lacking the sufficient expertise to provide legitimate input into regulatory decisions. Elizabeth noted that some colleagues disparage community engagement by saying that community activism undermines proper environmental reforms. To illustrate, she said that "a manager" lambasted community engagement: "This is a quote, 'Don't these people know that this is the most important rule that the agency is putting out this year and we have to protect this rule?' ... That was one line out of a probably 20-minute tirade." Such claims frame community input as obstructing, rather than strengthening, environmental protections. My interview with Jackie, an EJ staff member, indicated that her coworkers convey their lack of regard for community input through how they characterize the task of translating regulatory documents into publicly accessible language. They say dismissively, "'Oh, I'm going to take these documents, I have got to dumb them down.' ... We hear that, 'Oh you've got to dumb that down,' which is so insulting. No, you don't have to 'dumb it down.' You just need to translate it in a way that meets your target audience ... in terms they can identify with."

Similarly, Sara described how her coworker Tim, a manager who voluntarily joined the internal group of staff representing and leading EJ efforts in the agency, rejected EJ staff members' calls for community engagement in a recent proposed regulation. Tim would declare: "It is a very high-level technical regulation. They [the community] probably won't understand it. They probably won't understand the need for it. They probably don't have any experience in engineering or science. So, what are they going to tell us about this regulation that would make us change it?" Such narratives establish that the agency's decisions should only be made by formally trained experts and thus that public input has no role in regulatory decision-making. Sara further lamented that some coworkers dismiss EJ advocates' input as unreasonable: "The other thing that I hear a lot is, 'Well, they always ask us for things that we can't do. Why do we talk to community members anyway? They just want us to move ____ [an oil refinery]. They just want us to re-route ____ [a freeway]. We can't do that, so why are we talking to them?'" Many bureaucrats have made similar comments to me. To be sure, communities often *do* want the facilities moved or other outcomes that might exceed an agency's authority. Yet this narrative problematically frames community input as *only* unreasonable—that community members cannot productively contribute to regulatory decision-making.

Other scholars have shown that scientists, regulatory officials, and industry actors draw boundaries that cast EJ and other community activists as unscientific, uneducated, irrational, "emotional," or otherwise lacking legitimacy (Allen 2003, 2004; Bell 2016; Brown 2007; DiChiro 1998; Espeland 1998; Harrison 2011; Kimura 2016; Kurtz 2007; Ottinger 2013). Much of this delegitimization is gendered. Conversational norms in government settings afford deference and respect to certain (white, male) ways of speaking and foster disparagement of people who use other styles of talk; elites often dismiss women activists as "hysterical" or "irrational"; and activists are often denigrated for failing to comply with dominant gender norms (e.g., notions that women should focus on mothering and be "polite" rather than angry, and that men should support local industry and be "tough" in the face of environmental hazards). These scholars have shown that residents can contribute valuable observational data of illnesses and pollution and suggest new explanations for illness clusters. Elites' boundary work undermines the legitimacy of community members and EJ staff to participate in regulatory decision-making, and it marginalizes their concerns about environmental hazards.

Bureaucratic Neutrality

In many cases, staff undermine EJ staff members or the reforms they propose, or both, by asserting that they violate the agency's need to be neutral. Bureaucratic neutrality is a key norm within government agencies. Staff invoke it regularly, framing their organization as a neutral actor that uses science to make correct and unbiased decisions and withstands inevitable criticism from all stakeholders. Staff members' pushback against EJ reforms invokes bureaucratic neutrality in various ways.

For example, in cases where EJ-supportive staff members' recommendations reflect those of community members, some coworkers dismiss those staff by casting their agreement with EJ activists as violating the agency's commitment to bureaucratic neutrality. In my interview with Paula, she did this when she disparaged her agency's EJ staff as biased for agreeing with EJ activists in a contested rulemaking decision. She described how EJ activists had criticized a recently revised regulation that she had helped work on: "It was still the same canned, 'Okay, you still suck, _____ [name of agency].'" She characterized her agency's EJ staff as mindlessly following those activists:

> Our EJ guys in our EJ office were calling us up saying, "This sucks." ... They didn't bother listening to us, either. They were purely blowing with the wind. _____ [a particular EJ activist] requested meetings with all the high-ups in _____ [the agency] and blah, blah, blah, and came and said all these things. ... [At a key moment very late in the process, the lead EJ staff person] said, "Oh, this [regulation] is weak." He didn't know anything about it. He was just talking to _____ [the EJ activist]. ... They were all kind of like one coalition. They all seemed to speak with the same voice. If one person was going to say, "This sucks," we didn't hear any countering opinion. Everybody was like, "Yeah, he's right. This sucks." Everything was fine until the head guy gets a phone call from the head guy on the outside or whatever and then it's all bad.

Paula derides the activists' opinions by characterizing them as using "the same canned" criticisms of the agency. By claiming that the agency's EJ staff had no objections to the regulation language until one phone call from one activist, she is able to denigrate EJ staff as puppets controlled by activists ("purely blowing with the wind") and not listening to reasonable scientists. These framings unilaterally dismiss their objections as unfounded and biased. Additionally, she grossly misrepresents EJ activists' access to and control over regulatory decision-making—the suggestion that EJ activists can demand meetings with high-level regulatory officials ("the high-ups") does not match EJ activists' experiences.

In other cases, bureaucrats invoke claims of bureaucratic neutrality by denigrating EJ staff who had prior experience in EJ activist organizations. These narratives frame the agency as comprised of disinterested servants dedicated to serving "the public" and, in contrast, EJ activists as exploiting the public for biased, partisan, or otherwise non-neutral ends. For instance, Elise, who previously had worked for EJ organizations, told me that "a high-level manager" in her agency disparaged her as a "professional activist":

> She described how she knows that I used to be a *professional activist*. And she was referencing another group of people in a community that were *professional activists* and making a very clear distinction between *professional activists* and community....In spending decades in this work, she had become pretty jaded about activists ... and saw them working at odds with community members who *she* is trying to help....Her perspective on that has certainly permeated her leadership in her division. Very clear boundaries and lines [are] drawn between community members who are living near a project [hazardous site], and the professional activists who don't have the true interests of the community in mind and have their own agenda.

Importantly, this manager holds considerable authority and conveys to her subordinates her disdain for EJ advocates. Certainly, some activists do not faithfully represent the interests of the communities they claim to defend. However, many EJ advocacy organizations work hard to avoid this problem. Also, decisions by government agencies and industry actors rarely serve the interests of marginalized communities. Yet industry and state actors often use this narrative of "outside agitators" or "outside activists" to delegitimize environmental activist organizations (Lerner 2005; Ottinger 2013; Pellow 2004).

Staff often reject the core EJ principle that staff should direct extra resources to communities whose demographic characteristics render them disproportionately vulnerable to the effects of exposure to hazards, arguing that such practice violates the agency's commitment to treating industry actors fairly. For example, Richard was active in his agency's EJ efforts but stridently opposed most of the EJ reform proposals. In our interview, I asked him to explain his opposition. He said that the proposed EJ reforms violate the agency's responsibility to ensure a "level playing field" for industry: "It would be very unfair of any government agency to go out to this area and say, just because you [facility] are in an industrial area, and just because there is a socioeconomic problem, if you will call it a problem, whereby the poor have to live in your area because that is all they can afford—We can't enforce a stricter set of standards on them based on [compared to] somebody [another facility] that is not in that area. Because that does not create a level playing field, from a business standpoint. [It is] unethical, in my opinion, for us to do something like that." He disparaged as unfair the proposals that the agency make an extra effort to reduce environmental hazards in low-income communities, communities of color, or environmentally overburdened communities, because they would require concessions from polluters in those areas and not others. Throughout our interview, he reiterated this insistence that the agency must maintain a "level playing field" for industry and thus should not take community context into account when determining a facility's permit conditions, identifying enforcement priorities, or other regulatory work. In his opinion, doing so would violate this aspect of his agency's identity. I attended multiple EJ meetings at his agency and personally observed him and others stridently reject all but the most minimal proposed EJ reforms by proclaiming the need to "maintain a level playing field" for industry. EJ-supportive staff there told me that such denouncements have stymied their efforts to design and implement EJ programs. Staff, like Richard, who lack formal authority over EJ staff can nonetheless undermine proposed EJ reforms by stonewalling, especially because agencies usually develop EJ reforms through consensus-based decision-making.

Similarly, many staff insist that using demographic data to determine communities' vulnerabilities to harm from exposure to environmental hazards violates agencies' commitment to treating all *communities* equally. Paul, an EJ staff person, described how staff rebuke his proposed EJ programs: "They say, 'I already do EJ. I give everybody the same opportunity....We treat everyone equally.'" I observed staff use this narrative to reject proposed EJ reforms. For example, Tim insisted that proposed EJ reforms are "unnecessary" because "we are doing the same thing for people regardless of who they are and where they live."

Often, this pushback explicitly asserts that the *race-conscious* nature of EJ reforms violates their organization's neutrality. At all organizations in my study, much of the discursive resistance to EJ that I witnessed and was told about focused on the fact that proposed EJ reforms explicitly identify and seek to reduce, among other things, *racial* environmental inequalities. For example, Elizabeth stated that "some staff and managers" disparage proposed EJ reforms by characterizing them as "reverse racism. [They say,] 'Why should those communities of color get this extra treatment? We need to protect that middle-class white community, too.'" Neutrality, which is important in government agencies, means ignoring racial inequality.

Such statements reflect dominant racial ideology in the United States today. Bonilla-Silva (2014), Lipsitz (1995), Omi and Winant (2015), and other contemporary race scholars show that popular "colorblind" narratives like "I don't see race," and "post-racial" claims that success comes from hard work and hardships from one's own failings rather than racism or government policies, frame racism as limited to conscious prejudice and located in the past rather than as an ongoing systemic phenomenon. Such "colorblind" narratives assert a commitment to abstract liberalist notions of racial equality while, at the same time, ignoring the "racialized social system" in which industry practices, social democratic government reforms, and neoliberal regulatory rollback have systematically, disproportionately afforded material resources to whites (Bonilla-Silva 2014). These narratives recast race-conscious civil rights policies (such as affirmative action programs and agencies' EJ reforms) as "reverse racism"—unfairly discriminating against and taking resources away from whites. Importantly, scholars show that people wield these narratives "even when they are well-meaning and intend to be non-racist," thereby "debunking the idea that racial reproduction rests on intentional, malevolent, or politically conservative white actors" (Mueller 2017, 221).

Building on scholarship showing that government institutions, including their staff, play key roles in producing and policing racial categories and racial meanings (Bonilla-Silva 2014; Goldberg 2002; Kurtz 2009; Lipsitz 1995; Mascarenhas 2016; Moore and Bell 2017; Omi and Winant 2015; Park and Pellow 2004; Pellow 2018; Pulido 2000, 2015; Richter 2017; Taylor 2014a), my findings demonstrate how some environmental regulatory agency staff use colorblind and post-racial narratives to reject EJ reforms as violating their commitment to bureaucratic neutrality, in turn bolstering a regulatory system that has disproportionately protected whites. Wendy Moore and Joyce Bell (2017) explain that people widely appeal to impartiality and neutrality to preclude acknowledgement that government institutions have ignored and reinforced racial inequality and to reject calls for institutional reforms that would reduce those inequalities: "Color-blind racist discourse ... often takes place through an espoused commitment to 'abstract liberalist' discursive tenets, which profess rhetorical commitment to equality of opportunity and, at the same time, minimize the contemporary relevance of the history of explicit racial oppression as well as contemporary institutional and structural mechanisms that perpetuate racial inequality" (101; see also Evans and Moore 2015).

Bureaucrats' pushback against EJ reforms illustrates this work that colorblind narratives do. One EJ staff person who has led video-guided EJ trainings for staff showed me the following anonymous feedback submitted by a coworker, who used colorblind arguments to reject as unfair the EJ training and other proposed EJ reforms designed to reduce racial environmental inequalities:

> The whole idea of this thing is based on a lie. There are many people that I have spoken to about this training that fundamentally disagree with what EJ purports to do. In the minds of many common sense folk this is nothing but propaganda. The lady in the video basically eludes that everything we do is racist, whether that's in the work environment, during our leisure time, or just as individuals. Not true at all....The training also concludes that when in doubt just blame a white person for your life circumstances if they are bad. I think that is the most racist thing I've seen in a long time. What I would change would [be] to have this training be taken out of the department. Having it be mandatory is the type of social engineering BS that the department and country does not want. It's Hitler-eske [sic]....Working hard and getting ahead in life is color-blind and not racist, just like the vast vast majority of people in this country.

By stating unequivocally that "the department and country" are "not racist," this staff member frames the EJ training and proposed EJ reforms that acknowledge racial inequalities as themselves "racist" and thus unjust. Rather, justice requires being "color-blind."

Key here is the fact that bureaucracies and their staff are expected to be neutral. Thus, even though these organizations' procedures have disproportionately benefitted whites, organization members reject EJ reforms as violating the guiding principle of bureaucracy itself: impartiality. Race-conscious policies like EJ reforms are confusing to many staff and something to defend their organization against. Accordingly, staff can critically portray those promoting EJ reforms as biased or selfish, or both. Numerous EJ staff told me that colleagues vaguely disparage EJ reforms as unjustifiably trying to hoard resources for a particular group of racial minorities. For instance, Peter recounted that coworkers derided elected officials advocating EJ policies as doing so "for their own political purposes … for getting and maintaining the support of their constituents." Similarly, Peter said they accused him of using EJ as a way to "self-promote" and "opportunistically" look after his own self interests. Such narratives delegitimize EJ reforms as unwarranted and those who promote them as self-serving.

There are numerous variations of this narrative. Some staff invoke norms of bureaucratic neutrality to delegitimize EJ reforms by claiming that discrimination can happen to anyone and thus that EJ reforms giving "special treatment" to racially marginalized communities are unfair. Richard, a white man, used this narrative in our interview. He unapologetically explained to me that he proactively got involved in—and "put his heart into"—his agency's EJ planning efforts to enforce his belief that attending to race and racial inequalities is patently unfair and violates his agency's norm of bureaucratic neutrality:

> You want somebody to really put their heart into something? Give them a say in it.…Somebody could have lived it. *I* lived it, to be honest with you. I'll give you a brief story. I was an undergraduate, I'm a white male, right? And I walked into a [government agency] office and I put in an application for employment. And the lady sitting who accepted my application looked at me, and she said this, and I'll never forget it, what, 25 years ago or whenever it was. She said, "I'll accept your application, but I don't think you're going to get called back, because they are looking for a woman or a minority." And I just remember thinking to myself, do you realize what you just said to me is *discrimination*? Which wraps itself back into EJ: race, right? [*Voice rises*] … To have somebody look me in the eye and say that to me, it went straight to my soul, and I have *not* forgotten it to this day. Because I was qualified. I was eligible. I never got a call. That was *just as much discriminatory* as somebody who encountered this daily based on their race, religion, et cetera. So. You don't have to be of a certain classification, if you will, to experience this. I think it happens across the board. Coming back to your question earlier about why I am involved in EJ, I think a level playing field for everybody is very important. This isn't just about one group.…This is America. We all need to be equal, regardless, period, end of story.

By asserting that discrimination happens to everyone, Richard can deny actually existing racial inequalities, and he actively shapes the EJ planning process to make the agency's EJ efforts be as thin as possible. By wielding a strident commitment to neutrality, he legitimizes his efforts as part of a broadly embraced element of organization identity. Richard's comment reflects the racial narratives that are institutionalized in U.S. society. As Teeger (2015) explains: "Drawing on ideas of individualism and meritocracy, adherents to colorblindness resist acknowledging the racist structuring of society. As a result, they actively oppose race-conscious policies aimed at redressing these inequities, allowing the status quo of racial inequality to continue unfettered" (1177). Richard's efforts matter. He vocally frames EJ reforms as "reverse discrimination" that violate agency identity to rationalize making his agency's EJ reforms *voluntary* rather than required. As I observed at one of his agency's EJ planning meetings, as he reiterated in our interview, and as his colleagues confirmed, he vocally insists that the agency should make EJ a *suggestion*—a voluntary practice that staff can do if they so choose—and not mandatory. Given the various material and cultural constraints against EJ reforms, staff are unlikely to implement them unless they are mandated. Moreover, in his organization, EJ reforms are based on consensus; thus, even one person is able to limit what the agency's EJ reforms will be.

EJ-supportive staff emphasize that not all of their colleagues push back against EJ reforms in this way. However, colorblindness, being institutionalized throughout U.S. society, constitutes a discursive resource *anyone can* draw on to protect "a racially unequal status quo from challenge" (Teeger 2015, 1177). In this case, staff deploy these narratives to defend the way they do their work.

EJ-supportive staff also explained that colleagues rarely express such beliefs beyond the setting of a private conversation. For example, Elizabeth, quoted earlier, noted, "I have heard people make these kinds of statements in meetings and in one-on-one conversations, [but] behind closed doors, people will be much more frank than in a meeting." I asked her to recommend a colleague who asserts that EJ reforms constitute reverse racism and would discuss those concerns with me. She paused, considered a few possibilities, and decided she couldn't: "They know to avoid saying those things to you." Elizabeth's account characterizes her workplace as one in which colleagues use colorblind narratives to discredit proposed EJ reforms, but that they would rarely express these ideas in settings researchers could observe. EJ staff at other agencies made this same point to me. Thus, what makes Richard's statement so striking is not only that he explains that he waters down his agency's EJ efforts because he feels that one affirmative action-type decision wronged him decades ago, but also that he said it *to me*, an outside researcher (a sociologist!) he had just met. Elizabeth's point is that other staff deploy such narratives but would not do so with me. Thus, EJ staff members' accounts of their coworkers' shop talk provide crucial insights into constraints facing EJ reforms, as their experiences cannot usually be observed by outside researchers.

Chana Teeger (2015) observes that colorblindness enables people to reconcile the dilemmas entailed in explicitly confronting racial inequality. In the case of environmental regulatory agencies, EJ reforms offend staff members' identities as neutral public stewards and ask them to do new tasks at a time when agencies' authority and resources are under attack, in turn making staff defensive and producing conflict in staff meetings. I observed even EJ-supportive staff use colorblind narratives to resolve tensions inherent in discussions about environmental injustice. For example, this occurred in a meeting I attended in which about twenty representatives from across one agency came together with EJ staff to develop EJ reform proposals. About thirty minutes of the meeting was dedicated to a presentation and discussion about a recent local controversy in which the agency discovered an underground plume of a toxic contaminant within what was characterized as a "low-income EJ area." A white male staff person gave a presentation about the issue. He noted that, after the agency announced its water monitoring findings about the high concentrations of the contaminant in local drinking water and advised the community to drink bottled water, community members were very upset, asking when government agencies would clean up the contamination and who would provide the bottled water. He concluded by stating that all of the agencies involved feel that they do not have the resources to pay for remediation or bottled water, and then he casually noted, offhandedly, "Everybody wants a handout." The group proceeded to discuss the issue, asking the presenter technical questions about the case, which most of them appeared to have not known about until this meeting. One of the EJ staff members in the room, a white woman who has helped lead the EJ efforts at her agency for several years, commented to the group: "The politics and language would be different if this happened in ____ [a nearby predominantly white, relatively wealthy community]. We wouldn't say, 'They are looking for a handout.'" Conversation paused. Her comment established agencies as active participants in the production of environmental inequalities. This is an uncomfortable assertion for staff of organizations tasked with being impartial. The group resolved this discomfort by retreating to colorblind claims that the agency would not unwittingly treat some communities differently than others. The presenter disagreed with her, saying "It would be the same" and defensively repeating that the agency would treat any community in the same way. Several other meeting participants also quickly denounced her suggestion that agency members could be implicitly, unconsciously biased against working-class communities. No one came to her defense, agreed with her, challenged those who disagreed with her, or asked her to explain her comment. In my fieldnotes, I wrote that several "pushed back against her, seemed quite defensive of the department." Notably, this pushback even came from Norah, another (white) EJ staff person in the room, who asserted that differences among communities in how their environmental issues are resolved stem *not* from differential treatment by the agency but instead from the fact that wealthier, white communities have the resources to scientifically document their problems. Certainly, Norah's latter point is valid—an agency is more likely to take action on environmental issues when scientific documentation substantiates the problem, and wealthier communities have more resources to recruit such scientific assistance. Yet Norah and the others foreclosed racially conscious discussion and learning about how agencies serve white, relatively wealthy communities better than others and ways agency practice could be reformed to redress this inequality. This group leads the agency's EJ efforts and is thus the space most likely to support critical reflection; indeed, Kellogg (2009) has shown that creating teams of reform-oriented staff is essential for instituting organizational change in other contexts. These snapshots of staff interaction illustrate techniques through which people maintain the ideologies of post-racism and colorblindness in ways that reconstruct ignorance about and mystify solutions to contemporary mechanisms of racial inequality (as Mueller 2017, Teeger 2015, and others have done in other contexts).

In other cases, staff reject proposed EJ reforms by asserting that the colorblind interpretation of neutrality is codified in law, such that agencies cannot lawfully take into account communities' racial and other demographic characteristics. For example, Nicky, who worked at multiple government agencies, elaborated that some coworkers stridently rejected many proposed EJ reforms by asserting that taking race into account would violate the law, even after top agency attorneys vouched for the legality of the reforms she was proposing. Specifically, the attorneys clarified that agencies' decisions cannot be based "*solely* on race," and thus that EJ analyses can take community racial characteristics into account—along with other pertinent variables, such as air quality, truck traffic, and asthma rates—to target enforcement efforts, allocate grants, and other practices. Nevertheless, "When you have any of those conversations [about proposed EJ reforms], you will always find some white person will say, 'We can't do that, because the law says we can't do that.' ... One of the most challenging things in all of the meetings we were having was someone would always bring up this thing, 'We can't do that. We can't base anything on race.'" Notably, "always," "in *all* of the meetings," Nicky had to spend time addressing this discursive rejection of proposed EJ reforms, despite the fact that those reforms were approved by top agency attorneys. I witnessed this myself at her former organization. One of her former colleagues, Dan, a white man, said during my interview with him that he and "a lot" of his coworkers feel strongly that his agency should not take communities' racial characteristics into account at all: "The biggest thing I would change would be ... to have the state definition—the official definition—of what an 'environmental justice community' is to be based on the actual conditions on the ground, rather than the demographics, rather than the poverty and the race composition. ... I always try to make this argument, and a lot of the other people were, too." To explain, he insisted repeatedly that the agency was prohibited by law from taking communities' racial characteristics into account during regulatory efforts. "It's illegal to use race as the sole criteria for government policy." Yet, in reviewing his agency's EJ programs and policies, I found no evidence that any of its EJ decisions "use race as the sole criteria," nor did EJ staff at his agency indicate to me that they thought they should be. Having to spend so much time debating this point stymied the ability of Nicky and other EJ staff to make progress on integrating EJ into regulatory practice. Moreover, bureaucrats make discursive commitments to race neutrality and formal equality to defend existing regulatory practice that supports and ignores racially unequal protections from environmental harm.

Prejudiced Disparagement

Some staff delegitimize EJ programs by using prejudiced arguments that working-class communities, those of color in particular, are undeserving of government assistance. For example, Rose told me that, when she first proposed an EJ grant program to fund community-based organizations working to reduce environmental hazards, "Inside the agency, they started screaming and hollering: 'Are you crazy? ….They don't know how to do paperwork.…They'll be out buying cars and televisions.'" This pushback, rooted in a stereotype of low-income people as irresponsible, was so severe that Rose had to implement unprecedented restrictions on how the grants could be spent. Additionally, this motivated her to keep the grants small in size. She recalled deciding, "To keep people off my back, I'm going to make sure that that the money isn't a lot. Maybe about $20,000, $25,000—no more than that. I didn't want to go beyond that. Because I knew the oversight was going to be terrible."

I witnessed staff discursively wield racist prejudice along with postracial narratives to disparage proposed EJ reforms. In my interview with Dan, he expressed considerable criticism of his agency's EJ efforts. When I asked how he would change them if he could, he responded that he would remove discussion of race from the agency's EJ policy and not take a community's racial composition into account when doing its regulatory work. He explained that he opposes race-conscious EJ programs and reforms largely because communities of color do not deserve assistance from government agencies:

> Community of color and poverty don't correlate the way they used to.…South Asian communities [have] incomes that would blow mine out of the water. They are making two or three times what I'm making, their average income. Under _____ [the agency's] definition, they still qualify as environmental justice communities, because they are communities of color. They are living in McMansions there, but they still qualify as communities of color—people aren't white for the most part—and so they're still called EJ communities. I don't think that should be the case. I don't think environmental justice should be targeted towards communities that can pretty much take care of themselves and don't need our help.…The latest wave of immigrants into _____ [this region] is Russians. Under the criteria, they are white. They are impoverished, they are fleeing political oppression, they are fleeing terrible conditions back in Russia. They come here, they're in really hard shape. Really having a tough time of it. And they aren't

people of color. So, it's difficult to have them covered under the EJ policy....One of the directors of the EJ office asked me this question one time: "Why on earth would anyone want to live in an EJ community?" My answer was, "Because you get all these extra benefits from the government." ... Your community can win a bunch of money from the government. You can get a big infusion of cash from the government, in addition to other help from the government if you qualify as an EJ community....So that's why I think the definition of environmental justice community should be more refined and based on the actual conditions, targeted towards the communities that really do need the help and really are dealing with environmental burdens, really are dealing with health burdens, really are dealing with food deserts and that kind of thing. And not because the majority of the people there don't happen to have whatever qualifies as white skin.

Dan frames his agency's EJ programs as giving undeserving communities of color tremendous cash while whites (here, Russian immigrants) are unfairly excluded. Dan's assertion that communities benefitting from the state's EJ efforts do not actually have environmental problems is inaccurate—those grants are eligible only for projects reducing risks in communities facing multiple environmental harms. Additionally, his characterization of the grants as large sums of cash also is untrue. They are capped at $50,000 (and many were less than $10,000) and are allocated as reimbursements for actually accrued expenses for the proposed project detailed in their application. Also, his claim that projects serving poor white communities would be excluded from the grant program is untrue—like all other agency EJ grant programs, it allocates funds to organizations improving environmental conditions in racial minority *and/or low-income* communities. Dan's comments frame racial inequalities as a thing of the past and communities of color as undeserving, and thus race-conscious government EJ programs as unjust and violating the organization's commitment to neutrality. He regularly tried to shape the EJ program to accord with his beliefs. However, to do so, as we saw earlier, he used a seemingly innocuous, objective, and indisputable argument: that agencies are prohibited by law from basing decisions on race.

Dan's discourse matters. He worked in his agency's EJ grant program for several years and thus was likely regarded by coworkers unfamiliar with EJ as a reasonable spokesperson about what EJ requires. Accordingly, his discursive efforts to restrict his agency's EJ efforts—to strip them of attention to race—likely influenced colleagues' understandings of which agency EJ efforts are reasonable. While he is the only *EJ* staff person I met who expressed such views, whites commonly employ such narratives to delegitimize policies and programs that would extend government resources to communities of color long excluded from them.

The pushback Rose described and Dan stridently wields reflect classist and racist prejudice that are widespread in U.S. society. Dan's account evokes the racist and sexist narrative that poor black women are lazy "welfare queens" who refrain from working to live on government largess, which conservatives widely use to delegitimize welfare programs and other government assistance to the poor. People also use these narratives to disparage community activists fighting for stronger environmental protections. For example, one news article (Milman 2017) described EJ activists' fight against a landfill that polluted local drinking water: "What followed was a 10-year legal battle that finally forced the authorities to address the pollution and connect households to a clean water supply. 'Even then, some of the white people in the town said we were just some n*****s looking for money,' a resident who fought against the landfill said."[1]

On another occasion, I observed staff use such narratives in ways that delegitimized potential EJ reforms and other government assistance for working-class communities. I was invited to a quarterly meeting of about twenty-five county-level public health and environment officials to tell them about my research project and ask for their comments. Although the group does not regularly discuss "environmental justice" per se, the person who invited me felt that the group members do work that is highly relevant to environmental inequalities and thus that they would be interested in learning about my research. After introducing them to environmental inequalities and basic EJ principles, I asked what they thought agencies' EJ efforts should entail. As in my one-on-one interviews with staff, this group's responses were varied, and they insisted that agencies' abilities to address environmental inequalities are constrained by regulatory authority and dwindling resources. Yet some also scoffed at the idea of providing extra state resources to low-income communities—and low-income Native American and immigrant communities in particular—by asserting that community members would squander those investments. To illustrate, here is an excerpt of the discussion as I recorded it in my fieldnotes:

Person A [white man]: "Low-income populations seem to make the worst choices." They don't make much money, but then they buy "cigarettes and booze. Inappropriate choices!"

Person B [white man]: We should get "the WIC ladies" to give you a presentation. "It is a ridiculous waste of money we are throwing at food stamps. They're buying *frozen dinners!*"

Person C [white woman]: *"Ice cream!!"*

Person B: "They can buy all that stuff now. To me, *that's* an injustice. Our government programs are creating the problem."

Person A: He ranted about "program abuse"—"alcohol abuse" among Native Americans, "who learn that the more kids you have, the more money they can get from the government and that it's easier to get a check from the government than get a job." The system is "easy to abuse."

All of these individuals have leadership roles in county public health agencies and thus decide whether their subordinates take inequalities seriously. Because their organizations have not been formally tasked with developing EJ reforms and programs that provide extra assistance to working class and racially marginalized communities, the extent to which they do so will be limited by these officials' racist discursive work that cast those communities' residents as irresponsible.

Dismissing Concerns about Environmental Inequalities

Some bureaucrats challenge EJ proposals by dismissing concerns about environmental inequalities. Anne told me that, in the EJ meetings attended by representatives from the various departments, "We spent *months* just trying to convince some folks that inequity existed and was real." Scott, an EJ staff person at a different agency, said that his colleagues express a lot of "skepticism that this is an issue at all." Jamie noted that, when he first started working on his agency's EJ efforts, managers would belittle EJ concerns: "I remember very vividly people saying that environmental equity, and then it became environmental justice, was not a real issue. That there was no way that in our country that these types of things could actually be happening. That these folks were exaggerating the impacts that were happening inside their communities."

Although Jamie stated that this is less common today, many EJ staff in his organization and others told me that some colleagues still reject proposed EJ reforms by downplaying the severity of environmental inequalities. Nicky, an EJ staff person who recently worked with Jamie, told me that other staff used this narrative to reject her proposed EJ reforms. "One of the first things that I did when I got there was I had all these meetings [about EJ]. And you just heard this complete resistance: 'Why do we have to do that? Things are so different. The world is better.'" Tom, also an EJ staff person, told me in our interview that this claim "comes up a lot: 'We are improving things for everyone.' I have to have this argument all of the time." The problem with his colleagues' arguments is that they ignore and diminish the highly unequal distribution of environmental hazards. Although not necessarily intending to undermine EJ proposals, such claims effectively do by framing them as unnecessary.

Common sayings within environmental regulatory agencies, even when not made about EJ reforms per se, do similar work. Notably, in my own interactions with environmental regulatory agency staff, they regularly invoke their agency's mission statement, asserting "We protect public health and the environment." They do so in ways that imply both aspiration (this is what we *aim* to accomplish) and fact (this is what we *do* accomplish). Consistently restating this establishes that existing organizational practice is effective and forecloses conversation about ways it could be improved.

Linda, an EJ staff person, told me that coworkers rejected EJ reform proposals by explicitly asserting that agency rules effectively protect public health and the environment. For example, they argue that, as long as industry actors are meeting their permit requirements, the agency is protecting all people. Her colleague Sara emphasized this same point. For example, she described how Tim, the manager who volunteered to help steer the agency's EJ efforts, used this argument to disparage proposed EJ policy as unnecessary. In one case, Tim was livid about the agency's new public participation policy that adds requirements over and above the agency's (rather vague) EJ policy:

> He was furious about it.... He said, "We have staff who spend thousands of hours putting together a community meeting where no community shows up. Is that because of a lack of methodology on our part or strategy on our part? No. (*voice rises*) That's because the community trusts us to do our job."* ... To say that that means we are doing a great job and people trust us I think is a little bit of a jump. He was *really* enraged about this [public participation] policy! [He said,] "This is exactly why I hate this stuff. I thought we agreed on this comprehensive [EJ] policy. I read it, and the reason I signed on to it is because you were leaving flexibility, and there was going to be a guidance document, but it wasn't going to be heavy-handed and tell us what we have to do."

Tim's claim that the agency effectively does its job casts proposed public engagement rules as unnecessary. Tim corroborated this in an email to me, rejecting the new EJ rules by asserting that current regulations are sufficient: "We know (and believe) that our regulatory programs, when properly complied with, will protect people and the environment." In an interview with me, Tim characterized community engagement as a waste of time and proposed EJ reforms as "zealous," "impractical," "unrealistic," and "unnecessary." He told me that he consistently says these things in the agency's EJ group meetings that he volunteered to participate in. His colleagues have told me that he vocally contests their proposals, that he vows to fight any EJ proposals that are not optional, that he will ignore the recommended EJ practices himself, and that he will support other staff who ignore them. Tim's claims matter: he was often the highest-ranking person in the agency-wide EJ group, thus functioning as a de facto gatekeeper. Other committee members may have felt persuaded to defer to his opinion, and he can instruct his own staff to not implement proposed EJ reforms. Indeed, the agency's EJ policy is still only a set of voluntary guidances. Sara explained: "We intentionally had to make the policy broad and flexible to get it passed. It was the only way it was going to happen." Yet this flexibility also means that staff can ignore the policy's recommendations.

My interview with Lucy, a senior manager and attorney, provided another example of high-level staff using this narrative to delegitimize and neuter their agencies' EJ efforts. Lucy asserted confidently, "We *do not need* a statute directing us to protect environmental justice or to advance environmental justice, because protecting human health applies to everybody." She asserted repeatedly that communities' concerns about toxic hot spots are "usually" unwarranted. To make this case, she used a hypothetical scenario of a facility that, to comply with regulations, must keep its air emissions below "seven" units (e.g., parts per billion): "Seven is probably the right number in real life, because we protect human health....But how can we help the community *feel* safer? By letting them know what's out there. They may see that there is actually a problem, or [*voice rises*] *they may see it's actually okay!* That the facility can be trusted. They actually are usually at five, or *four!, which is usually the case.*...So then they'll see that things are actually okay." Lucy asserts that regulatory standards are properly set to protect public health and thus that proposed EJ reforms that would increase restrictions on hazardous activities in overburdened communities are unnecessary, despite extensive evidence of human exposure to harmful levels of environmental chemicals (Morello-Frosch et al. 2011; WHO 2016b) and critiques of existing environmental regulatory standards (Blais and Wagner 2008; Brown 2007; Cordner 2015; Vogel 2012).

Additionally, although she acknowledges that monitoring could show that the facility's emissions exceed a regulatory standard, she insists that this is unlikely—despite evidence that facilities often violate regulatory standards (EPA 2016e). She exuberantly elaborated that the "real problem" is that residents and industry don't "trust each other" and just need to talk: "The businesses are as afraid of the communities as the communities are afraid of them. We can see you guys just want the same thing! Can you just talk to each other? ... [*Gleefully*] *Communicate communicate communicate communicate!* It's the answer to so many things! ... Those kinds of good neighbor principles [are] what we are *strongly* encouraging facilities to adopt. ... Let's get to the problem *where it actually is*." Claiming that residents and industry simply need to communicate erases environmental inequalities, and she used these framings to dismiss EJ staff members' and EJ advocates' calls for stronger regulations in overburdened communities. Through these rhetorical practices, Lucy defines increased public outreach as the only legitimate EJ reform to regulatory practice and all other proposed EJ reforms as unwarranted. She referenced an agency EJ document advocating more communication between permitted facilities and concerned community members, stating, "That's what I talk from. That's where my passion is. I really don't think law is the answer." In contrast, EJ staff and advocates view increased public participation as an *initial* step in EJ policy implementation, but that meaningfully doing EJ requires the agency to promulgate stronger regulations and impose stronger permit conditions on facilities in overburdened areas. Lucy related that she voluntarily joined the agency's EJ efforts and that she regularly makes these arguments. EJ efforts are vulnerable to such manipulation, because EJ staff accept the participation of anyone interested to maximize staff involvement in under-resourced EJ efforts. Given her powerful position, Lucy can authorize or terminate EJ programs in ways that EJ staff cannot. Indeed, EJ staff in her agency who had been developing protocol for integrating EJ into permitting related to me that her office undermined their efforts, eliminating their recommended reforms that would have imposed stronger permit conditions on facilities in overburdened communities and insisting that the reforms be limited to "best practice" public participation suggestions for regulated entities.

My interview with Gary, a senior manager at a state agency, reveals how bureaucrats appeal to scientific certainty to frame current regulatory practice as effective, dismiss community members' concerns about the environmental hazards posed by facilities, and cast proposed EJ reforms as unnecessary. I asked him what he thought his agency could do to support EJ, in light of its regulatory constraints. Gary replied that EJ and other community organizations are wrong to be concerned about the safety of industrial facilities in their state. He claimed that, in terms of air pollution in his state, "the real issues" are from mobile sources, which are regulated not by his agency but by federal agencies, and that the stationary sources his agency regulates do not pose risks to public health:

> It doesn't matter what we do [in] permitting—we can ratchet stuff down to the lowest level in the world, but you still have that existing situation [of air pollution from mobile sources]....You have to be out there identifying what the real issues are....A lot of this is really from something totally other than the facility we're talking about. What they're doing, we model it, we'll do all these other things, and find out that it's not causing a problem....They are well controlled....It gets back to, again, good information. Information that's not based on what we *think*, but information that's based on *science*....It's like people don't believe science. Science is not going to change their emotion on how they feel about something.

He reinforced his argument that residents are driven by "emotions" rather than "science" and are concerned about facilities that *seem* scary but are actually harmless by relating the following hypothetical case: "You're a coffee maker [roaster]. Well, it smells. Maybe at first it smelled okay. But if you smell it every day, every hour of the day, it gets to be a little tiring. But there's nothing in that smell that's going to harm you." Gary's argument is persuasive in large part because he insists that the regulatory science definitively shows that facilities' emissions are below levels of scientific concern. Indeed, bureaucrats commonly defend their data as comprehensive and their methods as fully capable of identifying the "true" extent of pollution. Yet, these claims about scientific certainty are unfounded in many ways. Regulatory standards are often not met, and evidence that regions are generally in compliance with standards like the National Ambient Air Quality Standards obscures the fact that smaller areas within them are out of compliance. Additionally, agencies conduct relatively little monitoring for most pollutants. Regulatory benchmarks ("safe" concentrations of chemicals in air, water, or food) do not exist for many chemicals and scenarios. Moreover, regulatory benchmarks are constructed on incomplete data: for any given pollutant, toxicological research has been conducted on only a small subset of possible health effects; innumerable assumptions are made about how to translate those findings to the wide array of human bodies and lifestyles; and those studies examine singular chemicals rather than the mixtures to which humans are actually exposed. Ignoring the limitations of existing regulatory science, Gary definitively asserts that the agency effectively controls facilities' hazards and thus that community members concerned about them are misinformed. Gary's emphatic claims matter: as a leading manager at his agency, he has the authority to decide how his office will define and integrate EJ principles into its work. He noted several times that he insists on these arguments to the agency's EJ staff, refusing to implement their suggested EJ reforms.

Other scholars have also documented state actors discursively creating scientific certainty where it does not exist to dismiss calls for stronger environmental regulations. For example, in her study of conflict over hazardous facilities along the Mississippi River in Louisiana, Barbara Allen (2004, 64, 135–137) shows that the state's governor and state regulatory officials responded to working-class, racially marginalized residents' concerns about pollution from petrochemical facilities by asserting that environmental regulation is effective, and that the problem is that people are poor and lead unhealthy lifestyles (e.g., drinking, smoking, poor diets). These framings push responsibility for residents' illnesses onto residents themselves and declare that environmental inequalities do not exist.[2]

In some cases, staff diminish concerns about environmental inequality by asserting that racism is a thing of the past and thus race-conscious EJ reforms are unnecessary. For example, Brian, an EJ staff person, told me that, in meetings and hallway conversations, some of his white colleagues disparage his EJ reform efforts:

> The bureaucrats say, "Oh, and EJ's important now again.... Here we go again." ...
> We have so many of these people who've been around here for years.... Layer after layer of people who are just gatekeepers and do not think that racism exists [or that the] color of your skin has anything to do with anything, that that's all back in the '60s, [that] we shouldn't be worried about that stuff, and you should speak English. Not in leadership, but in the ranks, and the ranks control a lot of stuff. They call themselves the "we-bes": "We be here before you; we be here after you." ... They say, "We'll wait out this administration. We'll wait out the legislators. Let's just wait them out. They're going to be turned out in a year. We'll just punt it."

Such assertions trivialize EJ reforms as a recurring fad, and also as obsolete because racism is no longer salient. All of these accounts convey that EJ-supportive staff have to spend precious time debating the existence of racial inequality, which stymies their progress on EJ reforms. Furthermore, Brian's account depicts staff proudly declaring they will refuse to implement EJ reforms to regulatory practice and implies that such behavior is acceptable and longstanding. Such post-racial narratives reflect dominant racial discourse in U.S. society, which casts racial inequality as something of the past and thus delegitimizes calls for race-conscious government policy (Omi and Winant 2015).

In other cases, staff dismiss the severity of environmental inequalities by using racist stereotypes that attribute health inequalities to cultural behavioral choices and erase their connection to environmental inequalities. For example, an EJ advocate told me about a public meeting in which a state government agency representative pushed back against the activists' calls for stronger regulation of local environmental hazards by using racist stereotypes that blame residents of color for their own health problems. She recounted: "We actually had a health official stand up and say that a lot of the reason communities were having these impacts was personal choices. He talked about the 'gumbo factor' and the 'chile factor': black people eat too much gumbo, which is bad for your health, and Latinos eat too many 'chiles,' which are bad for your health." These racist stereotypes cast health inequalities as a function of unhealthy cultural norms, making residents— not polluters clustered in their communities—responsible for their own illnesses. In turn, it casts EJ reforms to environmental regulatory practice as unwarranted. This particular narrative is especially effective in the "post-racial" context, given that its stereotypes appear innocuously friendly rather than fueled by racial animus.

"We Already Do EJ"

Some staff verbally reject proposed EJ reforms by asserting that existing regulatory practice is already consistent with EJ principles. For instance, in a long discussion about the various ways her colleagues disparage proposed EJ reforms, Sara told me that one of the most common claims she faces from EJ-resistant colleagues is that they say, in regard to various EJ proposals, "We don't need to do any more, because we already do it."

I observed staff use this narrative to reject proposed EJ reforms. For example, Paula asserted in our interview that EJ analysis "is almost an inherent consideration anyway." During the staff EJ training, I observed Bob use this narrative to vocally dismiss all but the most limited EJ reforms. After we watched and discussed the EJ training video, the facilitator asked the group to suggest how they could apply the video's lessons to their own work. Immediately, Bob, the senior manager in the room, asserted, "We already do it," explaining that they meet with regulated actors at their business site rather than requiring them to travel to the agency's main office and that they hire bilingual interpreters when meeting with regulated actors who are not native English speakers. Bob's assertion indicates to his staff that they can ignore the training because it does not apply to them. The EJ staff person asked for others' suggestions. None disputed Bob's point, and most reiterated it. For example, Bill asserted, "We are an organization that already does this work. We just need to acknowledge our successes." One person noted that he sometimes allows Spanish-speaking people to use an interpreter to take a necessary test required for compliance with a particular regulation—implying that doing so only *sometimes* is consistent with EJ principles and thus adequate. Another concluded that others' responses indicate that he does not need to develop additional ways to support EJ: "I guess I do it, because we do it."

Claiming that "we already do EJ" is problematic in part because agencies rarely perform the practices EJ staff advocate—such as taking community members' input seriously, conducting EJ analysis for every proposed permit application and new regulation, and ensuring regulatory decisions do not exacerbate environmental inequality. Additionally, this narrative forecloses discussion about new ways staff could support EJ. These discursive techniques—narrowly defining what EJ requires and proclaiming that staff already do these practices—are especially effective when wielded by managers, who use their authority within the agency to tell their subordinates which EJ proposals (if any) they need to implement.

Staff also claim that the agency already contributes to environmentally just *outcomes*. For example, Nicky described how her coworkers assert that their hazardous site cleanup work inherently meets EJ principles and thus that going "one step further" (e.g., doing EJ analysis of various cleanup options) is unnecessary: "When you talk about EJ, they also argue that … because most of the contaminated sites are located in low-income communities or communities of color, you *are* practicing and advocating for EJ. So, there is no need to go one step further." Rulewriting staff similarly reject her proposal that they do EJ analysis to determine how a new rule or rule revision would affect environmental inequalities. They say, "Who has the worst air quality? So if I am changing my regs [regulations] for particulate matter, ... then I *am* working for environmental justice. ... My work already incorporates environmental justice by its pure nature. ... We are protecting everybody. And by protecting everybody, we are protecting the most vulnerable." This framing obscures the fact that, although these agencies have reduced some environmental hazards, many others remain unregulated, environmental inequalities and associated health disparities persist, and agencies could be doing more to reduce them.

Furthermore, the claim that environmental regulations necessarily benefit the most-burdened communities is refuted by evidence that regulations can unintentionally increase environmental inequalities. For example, regulatory innovations fostering urban greening efforts such as the development of bike paths and green spaces often lead to gentrification: fueling housing prices and otherwise reinforcing environmental privileges for elites at the expense of other residents (Gould and Lewis 2017). As another example, scholars have shown that California's carbon cap-and-trade system designed to reduce greenhouse gas emissions will worsen emissions disparities by race and ethnicity (London et al. 2013; Pastor et al. 2013).

"Our Hands Are Tied": The Standard Narrative as Resistance to EJ Reforms

Some EJ-supportive staff noted that coworkers invoke limited regulatory authority and resources in ways that prematurely end discussion about proposed EJ reforms. For example, after Sara lamented coworkers' "outright resistance" to proposed EJ reforms, I asked what forms that resistance takes. She responded: "Just the number of times that people just say, 'Well, we don't have regulatory authority to do that.' That's the end of the conversation. That's it. 'That would require regulatory change.' Period. So that just stops everything in its tracks. ... People do this a lot. 'We really want to help, but our hands are tied.'" [*She puts an apologetic look on her face and holds her hands out as if they were tied together.*] She elaborated that, when managers and agency leaders make this claim, it ends the conversation regardless of whether the claim has merit. They do not suggest revisiting their interpretation of regulatory authority or proposing regulatory or legislative reforms to expand their authority. Rather, they cast existing interpretations of authority as uncontestable and proposed EJ reforms as impossible.

Nicky asserted that her coworkers use claims about limited resources to justify their lack of participation in proposed EJ reform activities but then privately reveal that their objection to EJ stems from other factors. "Behind closed doors, they can talk to their buddies and be like, 'This is bullshit. I'm not doing this EJ stuff.' But of course to their managers they are like, 'Hey, I'm busy. I'm doing my work. Who has time for this?'" Ryan said that, when his colleagues say they do not have the data necessary to do an EJ analysis, "sometimes it is an excuse." In chapter 6, I discuss what else may be motivating staff to reject EJ reforms.

Certainly, resources and regulatory authority pose limits on what staff can do. That said, what Sara, Nicky, Ryan, and other EJ-supportive staff convey is that they feel that colleagues often use the standard narrative in ways that end discussion about EJ reforms before that silencing is warranted. Such discursive work marks proposed EJ reforms as undoable and discourages staff from creatively deliberating how to support environmental justice within existing constraints.

Body Language

Some bureaucrats silently challenge the legitimacy of EJ staff and the reforms they propose through their body language in meetings. Linda noted that middle managers at her agency "do a lot of eye rolling at meetings" about EJ, effectively signaling to other meeting participants their disregard for proposed EJ reforms. Tanya commented that staff in some of her agency's offices respond to EJ discussion with "'Ugh.' [*Rolls her eyes, with a grimace.*] ... People rolling their eyes." Peter said some senior-level managers "would look at me with a look of disgust when I would bring up EJ issues."

At internal agency EJ meetings, I observed body language that sent similar signals. For example, in the EJ training in which the manager, Bob, protested content that he found "unscientific," my fieldnotes reveal how other participants physically displayed disrespect for the training: "Attention was really wavering throughout and the group seemed only moderately engaged—lots of yawning, staring off into space, one person fell asleep, and two stepped out of the room briefly." Additionally, at an EJ planning meeting of three EJ staff and about a dozen of their coworkers, I noted that one of the coworkers "sat at the corner and typed on her cell phone the entire time, holding it up in front of her face, not trying to hide it at all," and that "many folks sat back, using their cell phones as if they weren't really in the conversation."

Staff Strategies for Managing Colleagues' Narratives That Undermine EJ

EJ staff and their EJ-supportive colleagues engage in various practices that challenge these narratives and legitimize EJ reforms to regulatory practice.

First, to disrupt coworkers' characterizations of environmental inequalities as insignificant, EJ staff and their EJ-supportive colleagues use EJ mapping tools and statistics in staff trainings to illustrate the scope of environmental inequalities. For example, frustrated with coworkers claiming that environmental inequalities are not serious, Nicky recalled to me that she got the staff revising a particular regulation to create EJ maps plotting the facilities regulated by this rule and the demographic composition of the surrounding communities: "They found out that certain facilities were 50 percent more likely to be in Latino neighborhoods. ... It walked the conversation back to a space of data, and we were able to have a conversation about the fact that these facilities are disproportionately sited, and therefore impacting at higher amounts, Latino populations. ... The whole point of that was, I don't want you to tell me that disparities or disproportionality doesn't exist." By showing the disproportionate concentration of hazards in communities of color, the maps silenced coworkers' discursive pushback—and allowed her to move forward with more constructive conversations about *how* (rather than *whether*) to write rules that reduce racial environmental inequalities.

Anne similarly hailed EJ maps for getting colleagues—especially those who identify as scientists—to acknowledge the existence of environmental inequalities: "Because I'm a statistician, I always fall back to the data and the evidence. And I just feel like if I beat you over the head with the evidence enough times, eventually you are going to go [and agree that environmental inequalities deserve regulatory attention]. And that's the good thing about them being scientists, because they can also recognize that you know [what the data indicate]." Several of Anne's colleagues told me that her map presentations transformed their thinking. Jane noted that it helped her see the value of increased enforcement efforts in overburdened communities. "That opened my eyes and helped me see things somewhat differently. That it wasn't just somebody trying to say that I wasn't doing my job good enough. ... I remember coming out of that [thinking] that one practical solution would be that we could try harder to target inspections in those areas." EJ maps can help staff witness the uneven landscape of cumulative impacts and consider how their own work relates to it. As such, these maps function similarly to the engineering drawings and other "workplace artifacts" that Beth Bechky (2003) shows can help solve problems across professional boundaries within organizations.

That said, Nicky also explained that some coworkers' resistance to the race-conscious nature of EJ analysis was so strident that she felt she had to take race out of the conversation entirely in order to get them to discuss environmental inequality. "In every agency" she worked at as an EJ staff person, "I got so much pushback on race, that I felt like the fight for me is really about reducing pollution and improving people's health. I was able to step back from the argument of, 'I want you to say race with me,' because I was able to say, ... 'We are going to target refineries that are the most polluting.' Once we got to that, I knew we were going to end up where I wanted to end up when I was talking about race. So I focused on the solution and the outcome more than what we're calling it." She managed colleagues' resistance to explicitly discussing *racial* inequalities by focusing on the most *environmentally burdened* communities. Yet, doing so obscures the fact that racism, poverty, and other demographic factors increase some communities' vulnerabilities to harm from exposure to environmental hazards.

Second, to combat colleagues' disparagements of community input, some EJ-supportive staff advise members of the public how to give input that is likely to influence regulatory decisions. Some EJ staff have organized training sessions about the public input processes for permits and rules, suggesting ways to craft effective input. Some also advise concerned community members about how to collect their own data to share with the agencies (i.e., keeping a journal of alarms or flares at the local oil refinery).

Third, to bolster support for EJ among their colleagues, many EJ-supportive staff tell "success stories" about particularly transformative EJ projects their agency has helped foster. They do so at agency meetings, in interviews with researchers and journalists, in blog posts, in their own publications, and in official agency reports. Certain stories are retold quite frequently. Perhaps the most widely recounted is the case of ReGenesis in Spartanburg, South Carolina, which recruited over $3 million in government grants and other investments and cleaned up a hazardous waste site, constructed health clinics, trained and employed local residents, attracted businesses, built affordable housing and sports facilities, rerouted a major roadway to integrate neighborhoods that had been previously divided, and more (EPA 2009b; Fields 2014; Lee 2005). Staff telling this story foreground that the project produced this extraordinary array of outcomes, started with a $25,000 U.S. EPA EJ Small Grant, and was led by Harold Mitchell, a charismatic individual with a friendly disposition. The message is clear: EJ is a positive, productive, win-win endeavor.

One former EPA EJ staff person, Jim, explained that the agency tells Mitchell's story so frequently because Mitchell "demonstrated the seriousness of it without upsetting the people as agitators. He doesn't threaten." While Mitchell's "non-threatening" approach makes his story compelling, his circumstances were not as representative of other environmental justice cases as is often implied. Many overburdened and vulnerable communities struggle to reduce the impacts of industries that are still operating and highly resistant to reducing their hazardous practices, and to get agencies to clean up contamination that is very difficult and expensive to remediate. The process of achieving environmental justice will, more often than not, be highly contentious, because not all actors will win. Thus, generalizing from one particularly positive case obscures the structural constraints that prevent those good outcomes from happening more often. Jamie, an EJ staff person, acknowledged these limitations while explaining why he nevertheless continues to showcase Spartanburg and other inspiring examples of change in overburdened and vulnerable communities:

> For years, we [staff advocating for EJ reforms] battled with them [other staff]. And then we said well, wait a minute. Instead of continuing to try and push them and they're not doing it, what we'll do is we'll go around the process. We'll show folks what real engagement looks like, and the benefits that come out of doing engagement....By no means do I think that Harold [Mitchell] is a model that works everywhere all the time....Everybody is not going to always be a good neighbor. And every project is not going to be successful. But I think we can get enough that we can start to show positive movement....Let's get some wins so that other people want to jump in and be a part of the process....Some people naturally want to be a part of it. Other people want to see that it's safe to get in.

Although these "success stories" do not reflect most communities' experiences fighting for environmental justice, staff advocating for EJ reforms use them as one strategy for deflecting coworkers' narratives that disparage EJ reforms. They assert that these stories inspire colleagues to view EJ as productive, in turn building support for EJ reforms among staff.

Fourth, and most broadly, EJ-supportive staff frame EJ as central to, rather than inconsistent with, the agency's identity. For example, Mustafa Ali helped lead U.S. EPA's EJ efforts until early 2017, when he publicly resigned in protest of the incoming Trump administration. In the press coverage about his resignation, Ali defined the agency's mission precisely in terms of EJ: "If you are at the EPA, remember that your job is about protecting the health and the environment of folks. ... [S]tay focused on the most vulnerable communities and making sure that we are doing everything in our power to help improve their lives and to stand up against injustice in whatever form or fashion that may present itself. When we raised our right hand, that oath that we took was to make sure that we were doing those things" (Paris et al. 2017, 75).[3]

Others implicitly frame EJ reforms as part of agency identity by making justice a regular part of work discussions. For instance, Anne noted that, a few years ago in a meeting, "I said, 'I am just making a public commitment that I will not go to a meeting—I do not care what it's about—without bringing up issues of justice. I am going to do that.' And I do. And people are like [*lowers her voice to a whisper*], 'Here she comes!' But I don't care. I don't care if it's a budget meeting. I don't care if we are talking about computers. I don't care what we are talking about. We have to keep it front of mind, top of mind. Otherwise it does not happen."

Others do so by challenging coworkers' characterizations of what it means for their organization to be neutral or impartial. For example, I attended a meeting in which staff debated doing more stringent permit review for facilities in vulnerable and overburdened communities. After Tim rejected this proposed EJ reform by repeatedly insisting that the agency needs to "maintain a level playing field" for industry, several staff advocating for EJ reforms pushed back against him by recasting EJ reforms as crucial for, rather than contradicting, neutrality and fairness. For instance, Jennifer retorted, "There hasn't been a level playing field [for communities], which is where EJ comes in to play."

Conclusion

EJ staff and their colleagues who support them describe working in an environment in which they struggle against not only external challenges but also internal resistance from coworkers. Staff frame EJ reforms as conflicting with the agency's identity in various ways. Much of this pushback invokes colorblind racial ideology pervasive in U.S. society, casting the race-conscious nature of EJ reforms as violating bureaucrats' requirements to be impartial. Staff also dismiss EJ reforms by disparaging working-class and racially marginalized communities as undeserving of government assistance, minimizing environmental inequalities, claiming agencies' decision-making processes already align with EJ principles, and insisting that limited resources and regulatory authority preclude discussion about proposed EJ reforms. EJ staff described this discursive pushback as a regular part of their jobs, and they rarely mentioned instances of management stepping in to censor such narratives. My own observations of staff substantiate their claims, as I observed coworkers use one or more of these narratives in every meeting I attended and every interview I conducted. These narratives constitute part of the structures of oppression that produce environmental injustice.

EJ staff typically characterized these narratives as directed toward EJ principles in general, though sometimes they noted specific EJ proposals that their colleagues resisted. Most conversation about EJ in these agencies still focuses on public participation. Thus, considerable staff pushback pertains to what are, by all measures, relatively basic, low-stakes EJ reforms—the ones that require few or no concessions from industry. Tom, a long-time EJ staff person, made this point when he said to me that there is "a lot of resistance" to EJ among staff, and "There is a conversation going on, articulating 'What is EJ?' … It just focuses on public participation. We don't even talk about what 'fair treatment' means." That is, staff pushback is not even largely levied against more robust possible EJ reforms that would directly reduce material environmental inequalities.

To be sure, EJ staff also emphasize that not all of their colleagues engage in these practices, that many express concern about EJ issues, and that some are very supportive of EJ reforms. Rather than generalize about *all* staff, EJ staff emphasized that *some* colleagues cast EJ reforms as discordant with regulatory practice and derail the efforts of EJ staff. While I honor that, I want to emphasize that many of the narratives staff use to disparage EJ reforms are *institutionalized*—so widespread and taken for granted in these agencies and in U.S. society that *anyone can* invoke them, and that in doing so they undermine proposed EJ reforms. Such is the case with the insistence that government agencies "be colorblind" and associated dominant interpretations of bureaucratic neutrality, which staff often invoke to defend existing regulatory practice and preclude conversation about how to reform regulatory practice to reduce environmental inequalities.

EJ staff and their EJ-supportive coworkers use various strategies for confronting and defusing these narratives. They use EJ maps and other devices to show that racial environmental inequalities are real and significant, advise community members how to give persuasive input into regulatory decisions, tell stories about inspiring cases of transformative improvements in overburdened and vulnerable communities, and frame EJ as consistent with the agency's identity and mission.

These findings suggest that we need to think critically about the standard narrative about the factors that shape and constrain agencies' EJ efforts—to consider what it obscures. Agencies' EJ efforts are hindered by factors outside the control of agency staff: limited resources, political economic pressure, unclear legal authority, and underdeveloped analytical tools. Yet this chapter shows that staff themselves also play a role in the slow pace of agencies' EJ efforts. EJ staff work in an environment in which coworkers can and do discursively challenge and delegitimize proposed EJ reforms, in turn effectively stymying them. As I show in the next chapter, bureaucrats resist proposed EJ reforms in other ways as well.

5 Other Ways Bureaucrats Undermine Proposed EJ Reforms

I am very proud of the work that I have done in environmental justice. ... I had support of my supervisor and implied support of executive management, tried to further the agency's EJ efforts and focus our resources towards protecting underserved communities, and had some successes with that. But it came at a cost. ... My efforts to request actions of staff or implement new initiatives or methods of doing things were treated as inappropriate and insubordination. ... The cost to my career within this organization has been very high.

—Peter, government agency EJ staff person

Introduction

In every interview with me, EJ staff acknowledge that some colleagues support EJ principles, discuss ways the agency could better support the needs of overburdened and vulnerable communities, and work hard with EJ staff to try to implement EJ programs and reforms. Yet EJ staff and those who support them also lament that other coworkers undermine their EJ efforts. In addition to the discursive resistance described in the previous chapter, I show in this chapter additional everyday practices through which staff undermine agencies' progress on EJ reforms. These findings further demonstrate how organizational inertia in the face of EJ reform efforts stems not only from external factors, but also from interactive dynamics among staff, some of which might initially appear inconsequential.

Ignoring Recommended EJ Reforms

Where agency leadership has publicly endorsed EJ, it may be unacceptable for staff to vocally oppose that directive in the ways described in chapter 4. Yet bureaucrats undermine EJ reforms in subtler ways. Notably, they can and do *ignore* EJ staff members and the practices they recommended. *All* of the EJ staff I interviewed described getting their coworkers to implement recommended EJ reforms as a perpetual battle. Janine lamented that, in her agency, "EJ policy is ignored by most people." Sara recounted that one manager at her agency told her, "If this policy goes through, we will just ignore it. I don't agree [with this policy], and we aren't going to do it, and you can't make us do it." Judy said that coworkers refused to implement her recommended EJ reforms, saying "I can wait you out" and "All I have to do is wait this out." EJ staff emphasize that they cannot force their coworkers to implement proposed EJ reforms. As Linda said, "I am on the bottom of the food chain. I don't have the ability to make anyone do anything." Thus, bureaucrats can quietly resist recommended EJ reforms by ignoring them.

EJ staff acknowledge that, in meetings about proposed EJ reforms, many coworkers nod and ask constructive questions, but most never implement EJ reforms. For example, Elise noted, "In meetings, I will often experience a lot of head nodding. 'Yes, yes, that makes sense. And yes, I could do that.' But then, when it gets back to implementing, … [they] go back to their desk and are like, 'I am absolutely not doing that.'" Her own staff overhear people saying such things and report this to her. After several years in her job, she has seen few staff implement EJ reforms. Such behavior is a common form of staff resistance to organizational change in other contexts as well. Fernandez (2015) characterizes it as "pseudo-agreement": "promises to change followed by inaction and the use of ambiguous language to give the impression that one will comply without true intent to do so" (385).

To illustrate, EJ staff described many examples of coworkers ignoring and refusing to implement proposed EJ reforms. For instance, Anne told me about how one of her coworkers refused to comply with a very basic EJ reform—translating regulations into other languages when appropriate, such as when business owners are not proficient in English. This coworker was tasked with developing regulatory compliance self-inspection guidelines for owners of dry-cleaning facilities. Anne met with her to develop a strategy for these guidelines that would be consistent with EJ principles. "I said, 'Well, what do you think the real problem is? What do you think the root of it [their noncompliance with regulations] is?' She said, 'It's they're Vietnamese. They don't speak our language.' ... [I said,] 'Have you ever thought about translating your materials into another language?' [She replied,] 'Why would I do that? English is our language.' ... Everybody knew about her, and they let her continue in that vein." Anne's point is that this coworker ignored a very basic EJ reform, and that no coworkers insisted she get the regulations translated or otherwise held her accountable for this basic EJ practice.

Managers often ignore EJ when setting budget priorities, allocating little funding to EJ practices. As Jackie noted, "Middle management controls the purse strings and the FTE. The heads of the agencies or the political appointees can use that [EJ] as their platform, but they don't allocate resources or FTE to it. ... Middle managers are saying, we will wait you [politically appointed leaders] out, because you only have four years." Here, "FTE" (short for "full-time employee") is a unit of work time (40 person-hours) and a reference to which tasks managers instruct staff to devote their time to. Even when political appointees endorse EJ in principle, mid-level managers still often decide to not allocate resources to EJ work. Shilling, London, and Liévanos (2009) describe how, in California, CALFED management refused to fund its EJ advisory committee's request for resources to conduct research on key EJ issues, despite CALFED's plentiful budget (702). As one of the EJ advisory committee's members lamented, "At every single turn, every opportunity they had to advocate in the budget process for money to fund this, they didn't" (700).

Staff also resist EJ reforms by ignoring EJ staff members' calls to diversify staff and management. Organizational theorists have noted that recruiting new members from existing networks—rather than diversifying those recruitment practices—contributes to organizational inertia (Tolbert 1988). Most EJ staff described their agency's staff as almost exclusively white and middle class or upper middle class and feel that staff who lack personal experience with oppression or overburdened communities are less likely to perceive EJ efforts as necessary or justified (as I elaborate in chapter 6). EJ staff believe that their agencies can find well-qualified people from more diverse backgrounds to fill open positions, are frustrated that management rarely does so, and feel that this stymies progress on EJ reforms.

Another way bureaucrats ignore EJ staff and quietly undermine the prospects for EJ policy implementation is by failing to search for existing regulatory authority that would support EJ reforms. In chapter 3, I described a few examples of staff searching for and finding existing statutory authority that justified strengthening regulatory standards. When I asked EJ staff how common such efforts were, they said that these were the rare exceptions. My interviews with other staff corroborate this. For example, I asked Hank, a recently retired senior manager with 30 years of experience at his agency, to estimate the extent to which staff try to find existing regulatory authority that justifies EJ activities. He replied that only formally designated "EJ staff" do this. This failure to search out the existing regulatory authority that would support EJ initiatives significantly limits the scope of EJ reforms that an agency can accomplish, given that industry is poised to sue agencies for actions that are not authorized by statutory language. EJ-supportive staff acknowledge that this unwillingness is limited by a lack of support from management. As Steve noted, "Individual permitters, heartfelt, sincere, they do not feel they are supported by their management as far as suggesting innovative things like: Why don't we do really extensive monitoring, or why don't we leverage this requirement to account for the uncertainties in air quality models?"

Additionally, EJ staff lament that their coworkers ignore their calls to give communities the time and respect they give to industry actors. Agency staff meet regularly and easily with industry. Patricia, a permit engineer, told me matter-of-factly that "the people that we work with on a more day to day basis are the permittees." Other scholars have shown that environmental regulators value and cultivate close relationships with regulated entities (e.g., Pautz and Rinfret 2014). In contrast, staff rarely meet with community members, do so almost exclusively through formal events like public hearings, and resent having to do so. Refusing to change this imbalance leaves staff well attuned to industry needs and undermines their abilities to adequately understand and address community members' knowledge and concerns.

Checking the Box: Doing EJ Procedures Only Superficially

EJ staff noted that, when coworkers do implement recommended EJ practices, many do so superficially, treating EJ as "a box to check" rather than changing their work practices to reduce environmental inequalities. For example, Cheryl advised me to "definitely include managers" in my interviews: "Ask them how they see their responsibility. ... For a lot of them, it [EJ] is a checking-off-the-box activity." Similarly, Tom said that many staff "do not think about [EJ] until the end of the process, and it is a box to check." Tanya asserted that staff often treat EJ analysis in permitting as "a check of the box." "'Did I look and see if there are any EJ concerns? Check.' And it might be like, 'Oh I looked and there was none,' and they'll put a justification statement, without doing a thorough analysis.... 'Oh, well we looked, and there was nothing. Check.'"

Michael similarly explained that staff and managers undermine EJ policy implementation by claiming to do EJ while not actually changing their practices: "It doesn't matter whether it is a conservative administration or a Democratic administration. When you elevate the issue of EJ ... they will try to point out how they are trying to do something, but what they are doing is so infinitesimally small, it isn't going to have an impact at all.... They are just doing what they always have done." Notably, his statement emphasizes that this form of pushback against EJ transcends political administrations—that it is rooted in regulatory culture rather than something we can attribute solely to elected officials or other external actors.

Sara noted that some staff "resistance" to EJ takes an "A for effort" form. To illustrate, she described how permitting staff tasked with identifying whether permits under review would have any "EJ impacts" (i.e., whether the facilities are located in overburdened and/or vulnerable communities and would exacerbate the communities' environmental burdens) typically decide that the permits do not—but without consulting EJ staff or examining any data. Other staff confirmed this without any sense of misgiving. For example, Sara's coworker Tim, a manager who has fought against EJ reforms in their agency, told me: "It comes down, in my mind, to how zealous they [staff] are about environmental justice. If they are really interested in it, and they really care about it, they are going to factor it into their job. If they're not, they're not.... [Some] people just say, 'Oh well, I will just do the very minimum I need to do and get a checkmark on the box, and I will be done.' ... Some people are going to really get into that, and some people are not. *But that's okay.*" Because staff have discretion about how to do their jobs, they can decide whether or not to do EJ reforms meaningfully. This is particularly true when managers make abundantly clear that staff do not need to follow EJ policies. Tim certainly has, as illustrated by his statement "But that's okay" if staff are not "zealous about" or "into" EJ, as well as by his numerous statements to me and to coworkers that he will not require his staff to follow EJ guidelines.

To be clear, EJ staff acknowledge that some coworkers meaningfully perform EJ practices. Paul, who has worked on his agency's EJ efforts for many years, acknowledged that some managers are supportive of EJ while others implement EJ reforms only superficially: "For some of the managers—all the way up the line—it is, 'We will do whatever we have to do to make this happen.' And for others, it is, 'How do we talk about it in such a way that we don't have to put any resources into it, but it makes it *look as if* we are meeting the need?'"

Numerous EJ-supportive staff used the example of public hearings and other forms of community engagement to describe how coworkers will often do recommended EJ practices only superficially. They lament that coworkers will hold hearings (i.e., about a permit under review, or a regulation being developed) because they are instructed to or rewarded for doing so, but evince no intention of using the public's input to change the permit or rule. My interviews with staff not assigned to lead EJ efforts substantiate these claims and further suggest that this is common. Andrew, a former EPA staff member, told me that his coworkers treated the EJ mandate to solicit more public input on regulatory decisions as a "performative" exercise in "box-checking" and that public input disappears once their points have been summarized in official reports. Similarly, Hank, the recently retired senior enforcement manager, stated without any sense of reservation that nearly everyone in his office viewed EJ as a pointless "box to check" and did required EJ measures (specifically, holding extra public hearings for enforcement cases located in overburdened and vulnerable communities) with no intention of using public comment to change anything about their enforcement plan:

> There was just an attitude ... of people treating the public hearing step as a box to check. ... A public hearing was something they had to put on, they had to endure, and then they had to write a document related to the comments. But I never got much of a sense from a lot of the technical folks that they truly would consider what was said. ... People would say, "'That's just a box I check. They expect me to change what I wrote?!'" It was like, "I put it in the paper. Check. I had a hearing. Check." And you can just tell, talking to them, ... they had no intention of really considering anything.

I asked him how staff convey this. He replied: "Private employee-to-employee grumbling in the way they describe [needing to hold a public hearing in] the upcoming year. ... Just talking amongst themselves." He added that staff comment to each other that, once the hearing is over, they can continue on with their work, and they express sympathy and agreement by rolling their eyes and saying, "Oh yeah." That is, staff undermine agency EJ efforts by doing EJ practices only superficially, and their disparagements of EJ procedures then legitimize such behavior and establish this as reasonable protocol.

Some staff are less dismissive about community engagement events, but treat them as opportunities to explain to the community why their concerns are unwarranted rather than as ways to gain new insights that could strengthen regulatory decisions. For example, Scott, an EJ staff person, said that his coworkers treat community engagement as a way to neuter community members' anger. To his colleagues, "The premise of community engagement is, the more they know, the more they will go along with us." I and other scholars (e.g., Holifield 2004) have observed bureaucrats laud community engagement events as ways to placate and "build trust" with community members, framing the problem not in terms of environmental inequalities but instead in terms of community members' lack of *trust* in the agency. Bureaucrats expressed considerable concerns about how much the public "trusts" the agency—as if the problem is one of optics rather than inadequate regulation.

Some staff made this same point—that coworkers do not use public comment to shape regulatory decisions—by noting that staff only took seriously public comments from actors deemed to be sufficiently "neutral" or "expert." Andrew noted that his coworkers at EPA would only pay attention to input from expert scientists from the National Academy of Sciences and the U.S. Government Accountability Office. Legal scholars Sheila Foster (2000, 16–20; 2008, 300, 303), Luke Cole (1999), and Eileen Gauna (2015) have noted that EPA's Environmental Appeals Board (EAB) consistently defers to EPA permitting staff and ignores the claims of EJ advocates who appeal permit decisions on EJ grounds. EAB superficially reviews the appeals but routinely rejects them *out of hand* by refusing to question permit writers' decisions. As Gauna observes, "The overall effect of this approach is to leave the Board-endorsed 'more refined look' [its authority to consider EJ in permitting] solely in the hands of a permitting official lacking sensitivity to environmental justice concerns, or one otherwise hesitant to require additional protective measures" (2015, 63).

Management Not Holding Staff Accountable for Implementing EJ Reforms

EJ policy implementation is stymied not only by recalcitrant employees refusing to do recommended EJ reforms, but also by managers who treat EJ practices as optional and otherwise fail to integrate EJ into the standards to which they hold their staff accountable. For instance, Teresa, an EJ staff person, noted that her agency recently instituted a policy pledging to involve communities in environmental regulatory decision-making. To help fulfill this policy, she sought to develop, for each region served by her organization, a list of community organizations they could notify about pending regulatory decisions or other outreach activities. She has implored staff for *years* to build these lists, and very few completed this simple request—even in the regional office whose top leader publicly declared his support for the effort. She attributes this failure to managers: "[Staff] weren't hearing from their management, 'This is important ... We want you to start working on it.'" Without the list of contacts, the agency cannot effectively do outreach to those communities, such as conducting trainings about grant opportunities or informing them about upcoming regulatory decisions.

Jamie stated that most managers do not hold their staff accountable for EJ, which undermines EJ efforts at his agency. After noting the need to "mak[e] this [EJ] not just a priority but something where there are significant results that come out of that," he said, "We all know that is going to happen in a limited way at best, unless there are folks who are saying that this is going to have to be a part of your process. ... How else are those well-meaning folks ... in the permitting process" going to be able "to figure out" how to do it "if they are not hearing from their" supervisors "that 'this is something that we really need you to take seriously'?" Without such accountability, "they are going to struggle and they will have to go into that mode of, 'Well, I have to think extremely creatively about how I can do these incremental pieces' instead of the things that you and I know would really make a huge difference."

Others emphasized that the standards to which managers *do* hold staff accountable constrain staff members' abilities to implement EJ reforms. As Nicky explained, staff members' poor progress on doing recommended EJ practices stems in part from "performance reviews, where you have your job description and you have to comply with it. If a permit reviewer is judged or assessed on how many permits he issues, versus public hearings he held, then he is going to focus on his metrics, which is, 'I want a raise, and I'm going to issue a bunch of permits.' ... There isn't accountability—it [EJ] is not in their performance reviews, it's not like every single manager at every staff meeting says, 'Did you complete that EJ analysis?' ... Or, 'Did you go to a meeting?' Or, 'Did you translate your document?'"

Patricia, a permit engineer who works at a different agency, emphasized that she and her coworkers are told that their primary responsibility is to issue permits quickly, and that carefully attending to communities' environmental concerns is not a priority. In their staff meetings, managers go through the list of pending permits and how long each one has been under review, and the permit engineer assigned to each has to explain why it is taking him or her that length of time to evaluate the permit. Moreover, they are rewarded in their performance evaluations for processing permits quickly. Staff are held individually responsible for the permit, so the industry pressure on the agency to speed up the review process becomes that permitting staff member's own personal burden. This makes staff ignore and resent EJ practices.

Jessica and Kate, permitting engineers at another agency, confirmed that they are evaluated in the same way. Each permit engineer is instructed to process a certain number of permits per time period, and if they do not meet their quotas, they can "get put on a corrective action plan." By evaluating staff in terms of how quickly they process permits, managers effectively discourage them from implementing EJ reforms that might slow down the permit review process, such as conducting more thorough EJ analysis, holding public engagement events, and determining how to address the community's concerns. Some staff told me that their manager has reprimanded them for taking the extra time necessary to integrate EJ analysis into their work. In this context, it is no surprise that permitting staff physically shuddered, stuttered, and otherwise panicked when I asked whether they have considered imposing stronger permit conditions on facilities in overburdened communities to reduce environmental inequalities.

Even where top politically appointed officials have publicly endorsed EJ through executive orders and other formal declarations, staff will ignore proposed EJ reforms if their own supervisors have not made EJ a priority. At one agency I visited, the top leader was a vocal champion for EJ reforms. However, managers framed slowing down a permit review process—for EJ analysis or any other reason—as a *failure*. Several staff mentioned a recent case in which a permit applicant retracted the application because the review was taking too long. Gary, who manages that division, has repeatedly expressed—including to me—his anger with that outcome, declaring that the proposed permit was "good" even though engineers on his staff found it problematic. The fact that this singular example of a "failed permit" pervaded conversations in the agency underscores how much pressure managers put on permitting staff to approve permits quickly—and therefore to *not* implement practices that might take extra time or otherwise upset permit applicants. Gary's division is piloting the agency's efforts to integrate EJ into permitting; therefore, his insistence on holding staff accountable for speedy permit processing rather than meaningful EJ review thwarts the prospects for EJ in all of his agency's permitting divisions.

Permitting staff were not the only ones who made this point. Numerous rulemaking staff told me that upper management rewards teams according to whether they get their rules written *on time*, not whether they meaningfully engaged affected communities in the process of developing the rule or crafted a rule that would reduce inequalities. For example, Elizabeth, who works in rulemaking, noted, "Middle management has a hard time, because their responsibility is getting the rules out, and EJ issues are often seen as a hindrance in getting those rules out." Being held accountable for getting rules *approved*, rather than the extent to which new rules and rule revisions reduce environmental inequalities, compels rulewriting staff and managers to skimp on EJ analysis and community engagement processes that take time. Rinfret and Pautz (2013, 120) noted that many state-level environmental enforcement staff are evaluated, in part, on the total number of inspections completed, and some are assessed according to the friendliness of their interactions with regulated entities. These metrics constitute significant disincentives to doing things that will slow down the enforcement process or upset regulated entities.

To some extent, managers use these quantitative standards (such as number of permits or rules approved) to demonstrate their staff members' productivity. They call this practice "bean counting," and characterize it as something they must increasingly do to show political elites that their offices are worth funding. Yet we cannot attribute their use of these quantitative performance metrics only to political economic pressure from antiregulatory elites. Rather, managers of all stripes emphasized that they hold considerable discretion in how they evaluate their staff. When I asked Hank, the senior manager in enforcement, how enforcement staff are evaluated, he responded, "The process is actually quite subjective. It depends on the individual supervisor." Ron, another top manager in enforcement, elaborated in an email to me that managers use discretion when deciding how to evaluate staff: "While it is true that beans were counted each and every year, in my office the number of cases filed by an individual attorney was not the major factor in the annual performance appraisal. . . . I always thought there were simply too many variables to base performance solely on the number of enforcement actions taken. While each attorney (and admin) had a performance agreement outlining critical job elements, I viewed them as guidelines rather than as commandments." That is, managers have control over how they evaluate staff. This sometimes means evaluating staff based on externally imposed "bean-counting" measures and sometimes other metrics they find more meaningful, but rarely means evaluating staff based on whether or how well they implement EJ reforms. In fact, only twice was I told of managers who held their staff accountable for implementing EJ reforms, aside from participating in an EJ training. Thus, the evaluation standards to which managers hold staff accountable—and the fact that EJ principles are not included in those metrics—are choices managers themselves help make and for which they bear some responsibility.

Stonewalling and Excluding EJ Staff from Pertinent Communication

Some bureaucrats undermine EJ staff by excluding them from pertinent meetings, emails, and other communication. This can be subtle. For example, Penny noted that one of the major constraints she faces in trying to integrate EJ principles into regulatory practice is that many of her colleagues do what she calls "clamming up": "Not seeking out your help, not giving you opportunities for input. Just keeping the door closed."

John asserted that managers shut EJ staff out of conversations and investigations in which he feels they should clearly be involved. He told me that EJ staff are "not integrated. [Managers] are not using that expertise." Although "they use my face" to "build cachet with" community groups, they involve him only superficially. During a recent enforcement investigation, he told management that he and other EJ staff "have information that could be germane" to the case. Management rebuffed him, saying, "We will manage this from up here." This exclusion prevents EJ staff—who work more closely with communities than other staff—from being able to elevate community members' concerns in the regulatory proceedings. When I followed up with him in 2018, he asserted that other staff are improving in this regard, but "the point is still true" that EJ staff are often excluded from decisions about which they have knowledge and expertise.

Similarly, Mary lamented that her coworkers "started leaving me out of meetings." At other times, permit engineers would include her in conversations with community members about a controversial facility but insist that she not talk. These tactics undermined her ability to improve communication between community members and the agency.

Elizabeth said that her coworkers undermined her efforts to integrate EJ principles into the rulemaking process through subtle techniques she characterized as "stonewalling," which range from "overt to covert": "There is an issue going on right now with a source that we are exploring [with regard to] some emissions right now and potential impact [on] the community. The technical folks include me in the meetings, but they don't share the materials with me. ...I have to look over somebody else's shoulder to see. ...I don't have access to [draft documents], to be able to put in the community voice. ...Sometimes we don't get the announcements about proposals until there's a comment period, so we miss the opportunity of doing the engagement." She then commented that her agency developed a new major regulation and formed a team to identify how that rule would affect tribes, and yet neither she nor any other EJ staff have been included, despite having requested to join it. She asserted that this was intentional: "This was a middle management decision." Moreover, coworkers then instructed her to communicate the agency's decisions to community members. "I get excluded, and then I have to actually go out and champion whatever is the cause. So, I come back and bring that [community] feedback in [to the agency], then sometimes it's received and sometimes it's not. Again, if it goes against what they want to do, then they get mad at me." By excluding EJ staff from key meetings, not sharing meeting materials with them, giving them only minimal time to comment on major rule revisions, and getting angry at them for bringing community concerns into the decision-making process, bureaucrats treat EJ staff as a tool for legitimizing agency decisions and neutralizing community concern—not to help ensure that community concerns actually shape the content of the rule, permit, compliance investigation, or other regulatory decision.

Monitoring, Disciplining, and Bullying EJ Staff

Organization scholars have shown that one of the ways organization members resist change is by policing other members' interpersonal behavior (Kilduff 1993; Scott 2014, 154), and environmental sociologists have shown that scientists have been sanctioned by peers for challenging standard practice in mainstream environmental institutions (Brown, Kroll-Smith, and Gunter 2000; Cable, Mix, and Hastings 2005; Corburn 2005; Frickel 2004a,b; Frickel, Torcasso, and Anders 2015; K. Moore 2008). EJ staff have described ways some of their coworkers monitor, sanction, and limit their efforts to communicate with and otherwise serve members of overburdened and vulnerable communities concerned about environmental hazards. For example, Mary told me that she and a fellow EJ staff member contacted two local stakeholders who had previously expressed concern about a certain hazardous facility—one an elected official and the other an aide to another elected official—to let them know that the agency would soon be reviewing the facility's air pollution permit and to describe what the permit process would entail. Mary told me that managers and other coworkers "had a problem" with this communication with these stakeholders and "made a big deal" about it. One manager reported to Mary's supervisor that Mary and her colleague were "saying too much to some of these stakeholders," although Mary insists they shared only public information. Such surveillance and sanctioning constrain the efforts of EJ staff, because building ongoing relationships with community members (including local elected officials) is an important element of helping actors historically excluded from regulatory decision-making understand the terms of debate and the opportunities for input.

John described how his manager expressed displeasure with how much time John spent with community organizations, telling him "You need to be at your desk" and instructing him to instead spend his time working with agency staff within the main office. John agrees that is important, but so too is working with communities. He asserted that there is a deep "suspicion of communities and community people," and a belief that EJ staff "are not sufficiently controllable" when working with community groups who challenge agency decisions.

Barbara described how management in her agency sanctioned her and other staff who worked closely with community groups by reassigning them into other roles and replacing them with staff who lacked such experience.

When the agency's leadership formally directed all offices to more fully integrate EJ into regulatory programs, managers unsupportive of EJ assigned EJ responsibilities to staff who had no experience with overburdened and vulnerable communities and removed Barbara and other staff who had long-standing experience with those groups away from their EJ activities. Because Barbara said she is well networked with other agencies' EJ staff, I asked if this happened in other agencies. She replied, "Yes, absolutely."

Other EJ staff described how coworkers filed formal grievances against EJ staff and conducted formal investigations of their EJ efforts. For example, in chapter 4 I described how staff at Rose's agency vocally questioned the legitimacy of the EJ grant program she helped spearhead, which gave grants to grassroots community organizations. This wasn't all. Rose related: "After one year of the [EJ grant] program, I had an audit, which is unheard of—a program that's only one year old. This is the kind of audit they do after something has been around for like three years. I was livid. They wanted to see if there were people buying televisions and cars. They found no discrepancy at all." That is, staff treated this grant program with suspicion and subjected it to an unprecedented degree of scrutiny.

Even when finding no wrongdoing, formal investigations can nevertheless undermine EJ programs. Peter described how his coworkers halted some of his EJ efforts by filing a formal civil rights complaint, alleging that an EJ training he and fellow EJ staff administered violated staff members' rights, which prompted the agency's civil rights office to conduct a formal investigation. Notably, although this allegation was ultimately disproven, the investigation halted their EJ trainings indefinitely: the investigation took a long time to complete, and the new management that came in during that time was not ready to restart the trainings. Peter lamented that "the formal investigation shut down the training, which was what the complainant wanted to achieve: sabotage the training. ... The investigation unfortunately severely limited our ability to provide foundational understanding and valuable training to staff, which would have furthered their understanding of EJ and underserved communities." EJ staff must strike while the iron is hot—they get permission to do things like in-person, group EJ trainings only when management is supportive and thus must take advantage of those opportunities when they are available. In this case, by the time the investigation was finally concluded, the new managers did not support the EJ trainings.

Peter also described several instances in which he endeavored to bring enforcement actions against hazardous facilities in low-income, racially marginalized communities. However, Peter's management reported his efforts as improper conduct. In one case, a relatively high-level manager "got wind of this and immediately fired off emails to the director, my manager, [and] the division chief, saying, 'What is _____ [Peter] doing? This is completely outside of his jurisdiction. It is inappropriate. He is doing an unauthorized risk assessment at the site. It needs to be stopped.' I was protecting public health, the environment, and children's health, but management claimed that I was acting beyond my authority. So, I came under investigation by my own department." As with the civil rights complaint, these investigations concluded that Peter had not engaged in any misconduct, and he felt further vindicated when several federal agencies subsequently referenced one of the cases he effectively brought enforcement actions against as an example of inappropriate land use and threats to children's health. Despite being cleared of these charges, Peter asserted that he has been blacklisted for his EJ work: "What this has resulted in is challenges to my career. ... Actual supervisors ... would call out [in meetings] and say, 'You are screwed. You are not ever going to go anywhere in the department. You are blacklisted because of EJ. ... You will never get a promotion here, so you might as well leave.'" He has applied for numerous jobs within the agency for which he is experienced and qualified, but not been selected. His quote at the start of this chapter illustrates how much his colleagues' hostility to EJ personally harmed him. Suspicions like these are, of course, difficult or impossible to prove, and there could be other explanations for his lack of promotion. But his accounts illustrate the practices some bureaucrats use to protest proposed EJ reforms, and the degree to which these efforts can harm EJ staff and their productivity. His coworkers' actions cast race-conscious training and enforcement actions as beyond the scope of the organization's responsibilities, a boundary they actively police.

In a pained conversation with me, Michael explained that he and other EJ staff are *informally bullied* for their EJ work, it is tied to the fact that they are persons of color, and such treatment is difficult to prove:

> There are plenty of examples, ... instances in which I know persons have said that a manager has told them, "Don't work on EJ because that may affect your career." ... People have been called "troublemakers." ... When you have a manager that just says it when you are walking down the hall and you haven't talked to that

manager in weeks....They don't say, "Still causing trouble in that particular project?" No! He just says, "Still causing trouble?" ... They weren't precise when they
said it. That's how most discrimination occurs. That's why you can't prove it. It's
because when someone does something that is discriminatory, they are not trying
to be obvious about it....They don't want to give you an obvious red flag [for you
to] record and document what they did. It could be written off as, "Well, maybe
he didn't mean anything by it." Or, "Maybe you're just interpreting it the wrong
way. I wouldn't think anything of it." Or they'll just get dismissive: "Don't worry
about it. Maybe he was having a bad day." But he said it. Most of the time it has
been in the context of EJ.

He explained that these aggressions undermine EJ policy implementation
by compelling staff who would otherwise champion EJ efforts to find other
assignments in the agency or find other employment: "People leave. It gets
grinding. People burn out....Those who are trying to focus on EJ feel a
pervasive sense of tension, friction, of personalities clashing. Some of those
people have moved on. Some stayed and didn't make any headway. It is
a huge emotional drain." Like Peter, Michael feels that he has been blacklisted in the agency because of his EJ work, being passed up for promotions
to jobs for which he is more than qualified and not receiving raises when
he should. He got visibly upset during this part of our conversation, leaving
me with the impression that he has been worn down by such treatment.

Most of the stories of being bullied and sanctioned came from black EJ
staff (and, to be clear, not all described such experiences). In contrast, most
white EJ staff expressed frustration and disappointment with the slow pace
of their agencies' EJ efforts, but did not describe being personally threatened
or punished for their EJ work (with the exception of Peter, who is white).
These observations suggest that the experience of working on agencies' EJ
efforts varies to some extent along racial lines, where black EJ-supportive
staff experience more hostility than their white colleagues do, and underscore the racialized nature of staff resistance to EJ.

Research in other settings shows that this is part of a broader pattern
whereby, in mostly white institutions whose members stridently identify as
race neutral, staff of color who challenge racial narratives or organization
practices that reproduce racial inequality are disparaged as "overly focused
on race [and] too sensitive" (Evans and Moore 2015, 445; see also W. Moore
2008; Moore and Bell 2017). To avoid sanction and maintain their careers
in such settings, staff of color must endure "both everyday racial micro-
aggressions and dismissive dominant ideologies that deny the relevance of

race and racism" (Evans and Moore 2015, 439). Such disciplining can be indirect, as Michael described, or very explicit. For instance, Joyce, a black EJ-supportive staff person, recounted an incident in which her boss, also a person of color and supportive of EJ reforms, admonished her for simply advocating for greater diversity in their mostly white workplace. Specifically, in a meeting of (white) high-level managers, Joyce suggested the organization do more to diversify staff. Afterward, her boss pulled her aside, got right up in her face, and said, livid, "Don't you *ever* say 'diversity' again." She stared at him and then said, "You mean, don't be the black girl?" And he said, "Yeah." She was not invited to any more of those meetings. Her interpretation of this interaction is that racist stereotypes of people of color as "overly concerned" about race made him feel that even mentioning staff diversity would jeopardize their relationships with white staff. Louwanda Evans and Wendy Moore (2015) explain how such disciplining curbs staff members' abilities to resist racially unequal organization practice: "The ideological and discursive construction of people of color as overly emotional, overly focused on race, too sensitive, etc., means that people of color within the institution are constructed in such a way that their resistance to racist organizational structures or denigrating racist incidents is countered before it occurs" (445). Staff of color in such "white institutional spaces" must, in turn, perform an unequal amount of emotional labor to endure racist practice and refrain from challenging it (Bell 2014; Evans and Moore 2015; W. Moore 2008).

Staff Strategies for Supporting Environmental Justice in This Context

EJ staff have developed various strategies for persevering within this context. First, EJ staff enlist coworkers in developing EJ reforms to regulatory practice. Doing so helps make EJ reforms practicable and increases coworkers' sense of investment in and support for those reforms. EJ staff thus serve as coordinators, mentors, and consultants in the process, not as the only ones involved. Organization scholars have noted that involving organization members in brainstorming reform implementation strategies is an important way to minimize resistance to change (Burke 2018).

Second, many EJ staff focus on working with staff expressing interest in EJ. For instance, Tom described how two economists took the lead on developing guidelines for integrating EJ into rulemaking: They "have really taken this on as their life interest. That's the only time when it is possible to truly advance environmental justice. When those people come along, I find a way to involve them. It doesn't matter if it doesn't fit exactly." Paul similarly noted, "I search out those who are most open to EJ," who have a "heart" that says, "I have a responsibility to protect and prioritize communities that bear a disproportionate burden of environmental hazards." He elaborated: "EJ is not evenly applied across the agency. ... It is the coalition of the willing. ... We are hard rock miners, because we go in and we look for the hearts of people who are willing to work with us and invest their time and take on their own bosses." Elise, who leads the EJ efforts at a different agency, noted that some colleagues ask how they can integrate EJ into their own jobs. She explained that she harnesses this:

> That's where I've been focusing most of my time, is to try to figure out how to get that support for people who really want to learn and figure out how to implement this. ... They want to understand more, and they want to have the tools to be able to carry it out in their jobs. And that's really where I see the space of this program growing. ... There are a lot of places where in the department folks are just resistant to any kind of change whatsoever. And so spending a lot of time and resources on those folks can really prevent or distract from trying to build people who actually do want to move environmental justice forward in government. That's the challenge in general: putting out fires, versus building and organizing internally.

Penny similarly emphasized that she strategically maximizes her limited time by "pinpointing areas where I do have support, and figuring out how to use that. ... Some people are really excited by it. Some people really embrace it as a new way to think about things, new standards we should be keeping in mind. ... [Some] come running to me with issues that they see. Super forthcoming with information, looking for support, looking for input, excited and relieved that there is a person in my position." Some EJ staff bring together these EJ-supportive staff from across the organization into an EJ committee that spearheads the development and implementation of EJ reforms, the type of group Kellogg (2009) showed in other contexts to be crucial for overcoming internal resistance to organization reforms.

However, this can pose problems when those who are most interested define EJ in ways that differ from longstanding EJ tenets and insist that others do so as well. EJ staff often feel that they must accept the assistance of anyone interested, either because having more people on board can have a snowball effect of motivating others to participate, or because those who want to get involved with their agencies' EJ efforts are in positions of authority over EJ staff. One example of the latter is Lucy, the senior manager (described in chapter 4) who insisted that EJ does not require stronger regulations but instead only that communities and industry communicate better with each other. I asked an EJ staff person in Lucy's agency why she was involved in their EJ efforts. He explained that Lucy "had a personal interest in it, so [she] became part of the steering group on EJ."

Third, EJ staff and others who are particularly involved in promoting EJ reforms also noted that they deal with coworkers' hostility and indifference to EJ by mentoring and supporting each other, especially junior colleagues. In so doing, they create what Katzenstein (1999) called "habitats"—safe spaces that activists build within mainstream institutions. For example, Janine noted that she mentors younger colleagues interested in EJ to provide "the nourishment required to go back in on a daily basis and face not just the outside-inside disparities but the inside-inside disparities. How do you manage a boss for whom none of this is on his mind? ... How do you build a career, how do you hold yourself, how do you renew hope in those conditions? ... You have to have sufficient structure in your world that you're not just wandering the desert by yourself." In other words, she mentors EJ-supportive staff to help them learn how to protect their own careers while sustaining their commitments to EJ reforms within a context that is hostile to such work. Elise described her efforts to build informal support networks for EJ activists hired into regulatory agencies. She explained that creating the space for "offline conversations" helps EJ-supportive staff navigate their current jobs and handle coworkers' hostility to EJ. Such networks also help EJ advocates manage another consequence of taking jobs within the state: being shunned as "sell-outs" by other activists. Elise noted, "The loneliness I've been feeling lately is [missing] this connection to EJ allies. I have definitely been able to maintain some relationships with folks in the EJ community, and I have not been able to maintain others. And it can be a very lonely place when you feel that you are not able to bring things to fruition for your EJ allies. ... If you are going into a workplace and a situation where you feel like your values are going to be challenged on a regular basis and that it is going to be an uphill struggle, you want to make sure there's a support network ready for you." Numerous EJ staff at EPA credit Dr. Clarice Gaylord, the first head of EPA's Office of Environmental Justice (then called the Office of Environmental Equity), as having nurtured EJ staff and young staff of color at that agency (e.g., King 2014). Always referring to her respectfully as "Dr. Gaylord," they described how she created safe spaces for staff advocating EJ reforms, and they hailed her commitment to creating a fellowship program through which she recruited students from minority-serving college and universities into EPA, ensuring they had mentors to help them succeed, and fostering in them a commitment to serving overburdened and vulnerable communities.

Fourth, EJ-supportive staff assist EJ reform by strategically positioning themselves within their organization. Some EJ staff noted that, when circumstances became unbearable, they changed jobs within their agencies to work under a manager more supportive of EJ reforms. In contrast, others stay in positions in which they experience mistreatment and frustration because changing jobs would undermine the prospects for EJ reforms to which they feel committed. As Michael recounted, "If I [was] not there to maintain attention to inequality, no one else was going to do it."

Fifth, some staff described that they do EJ reforms *discretely,* such as by not characterizing them as "EJ." Taylor mentioned that coworkers resist "EJ" so much that she has decided to call it something else while essentially doing the same thing. Her fellow EJ staff member, Paul, noted that he does this too and explained why: "We sometimes have to work under the radar, because if it came up to [a] manager's level for consideration of what we do with EJ, the answer more likely than not would be no." One staff person from an EPA regional office said that he uses the same strategy to get state agencies that would otherwise be hostile to EJ reforms to start adopting them: "How do you make progress on EJ in _____ [this region]? I have never used the term 'EJ.' I use the term 'vulnerable communities.'" In other words, these EJ staff figure out how to accomplish their goals in subtle ways.

Sixth, when bureaucrats ignore EJ reforms or do them only superficially, some EJ staff and their EJ-supportive colleagues do their coworkers' EJ tasks for them. Taylor confessed with pride that she "sneaks in" EJ analyses when her colleagues fail to do them. Esther told me that, when her coworkers ignored her guidance documents on integrating EJ into permit review, she assigned one of her own staff to help permit reviewers do the EJ analysis: "You can't just tell people, 'You have to do this.' There's no law. It's an executive order....When you go out and work with other programs, you don't just sit in the meeting. You volunteer to do something. You take on some of the work." Esther did this in part because her agency lacked an EJ statute that unambiguously mandates staff implement these EJ reforms.

Esther's approach was one that few other EJ staff described to me; she was in the unusual position of having enough staff that she could afford to assign someone to this task. She also noted that the person she assigned to work on EJ spent nearly *all* of their time doing so. In another context, organization scholar Katherine Kellogg (2014) found that this practice was crucial to institutionalizing reforms; health care institutions that most successfully implemented certain reforms required by the Affordable Care Act hired new staff to do the new work that doctors and other professional staff refused to do. However, this strategy of picking up coworkers' slack—doing the EJ work when others do not—is not sustainable when agencies' EJ staff are too few in number to do all of that work themselves. Instead, they need to get other staff to integrate EJ reforms into their own daily work.

Seventh, to combat the fact that many coworkers ignore EJ reforms and to boost the status and authority of EJ staff, some EJ-supportive staff press agency leadership to create executive-level EJ staff positions. Leaders at California EPA responded to such requests. They created an executive-level EJ staff position within CalEPA's Department of Toxic Substances Control and, reportedly, are currently developing another in one of CalEPA's other divisions.

Eighth, because some bureaucrats dismiss politically appointed leaders' priorities as fleeting fads (as discussed in chapter 4) and ignore EJ reforms even after top leadership makes EJ an agency priority, EJ-supportive staff press agency leaders and elected officials to formally hold staff accountable for implementing EJ reforms. They pressure upper management and appointed officials to adopt formal agency policies, laws, and/or executive orders instructing staff to implement EJ reforms, add EJ as a responsibility into each staff member's job description, and require every office and each staff member, in annual performance reviews, to specify their EJ goals and how they met them. Jamie explained that he and other EJ-supportive staff use these strategies especially to combat the resistance to EJ exhibited by mid-level managers, who have the power to either undercut or support EJ and who work at the agency for more or less their entire careers: "I usually have a pretty good idea of how not only this structure works here but in a few other places, and as I have conversations—honest conversations—with folks, it's your middle management are the places where we still need to make some progress.... If we don't build that strong criteria or language for those folks who are above who are going to be here throughout the duration, then we are going to only get incremental steps in place." Many other staff supportive of EJ reforms argued that mid-level managers are the least supportive of EJ reforms and thus must be compelled to adopt them and hold their subordinates accountable for implementing them.

Conclusion

In sum, in addition to the discursive pushback described in chapter 4, staff undermine EJ reforms by ignoring them, doing them only superficially, not holding their subordinates accountable for implementing them, excluding EJ staff from pertinent communication, and disciplining and bullying EJ staff. Such practices inhibit development and implementation of EJ reforms, further cast EJ as antithetical to agency identity, and wear down EJ staff, particularly persons of color. In narrating these experiences to me, EJ staff and their colleagues who support them did not assert that all coworkers behave in these ways. Rather, they emphasized that these practices were common enough to derail their EJ efforts. These practices are part of the structures of oppression that create and maintain environmental injustices, and these findings illustrate some ways in which they unfold within government agencies.

There were a few exceptions. Several EJ staff, one at every agency in my study, insisted that coworkers were not particularly resistant to EJ reforms. Some of this divergence could stem from intra-agency variability in leadership support for EJ reforms. Occasionally, offices are headed by managers who advocate for EJ reforms and require their staff to implement them, and in such contexts their staff may not be able to engage in the pushback I described in this chapter and in chapter 4. One example is U.S. EPA's Office of Enforcement and Compliance Assurance (OECA) during the Obama administration; the office's leadership assertively supported and started to implement EJ reforms, and an OECA staff person I interviewed insisted that their coworkers were not resistant to them.

This divergence could also stem from professional and racial identity. Most EJ-supportive staff who downplayed coworkers' resistance to EJ have advanced professional degrees in law, engineering, or economics, and most are white. Their professional status likely invokes respectful treatment from colleagues. Those who are white do not experience the micro-aggressions and other pushback staff of color experience and thus are less likely to sense discrimination and indifference to inequality.

The exceptions could also stem from self-protection. My research participants' acute, repeated concerns about confidentiality suggest that some would be reticent to speak critically of colleagues or otherwise divulge information that could get them into trouble. For example, Robin and Jordan, two EJ staff at one EPA regional office, painted a rosy picture of support for EJ among staff and leadership, noting that top managers are "on board with EJ" and often ask EJ staff, "How can I help out?" Certainly, this description could be true. Yet a few circumstances of our interview could have compelled them to represent their work experiences in such a light: they met with me together, and they had a phone line open during the entire conversation to a contact at EPA headquarters' Office of Environmental Justice who they invited to join our call (but who never materialized). Both of these factors (which they chose) limited their confidentiality. Robin and Jordan seemed tense during the entire interview and answered my questions very succinctly. In contrast, nearly all of my other interview participants elaborated at length about the intra-agency challenges they face in doing their EJ work, and, with only a few exceptions, those interviews were conducted one-on-one in private settings.

EJ staff and their EJ-supportive colleagues employ various strategies for managing or mitigating coworkers' practices that undermine their EJ efforts, including enrolling other staff in developing EJ reforms, focusing on working with staff expressing interest in EJ, mentoring and supporting other EJ-supportive staff, doing EJ discretely, doing coworkers' EJ tasks for them, pressing agency leadership to create executive-level EJ staff positions, and urging agency leadership to adopt formal agency policies, laws, and/or executive orders instructing staff to implement EJ reforms.

EJ-supportive staff members' accounts of experiencing and trying to respond to these forms of pushback from managers and other coworkers complicate typical explanations for agencies' disappointing progress on EJ policy implementation. As with the discursive resistance showcased in chapter 4, these findings indicate that, while EJ reforms are stymied in part by factors beyond the control of agency staff, bureaucrats themselves also play a role in these outcomes through things they say and otherwise do in the workplace. As organization scholars have shown in other contexts, these findings illustrate that organizational inertia takes *work*. It is not inevitable. Instead, it occurs in part because organization members, including those with power over other staff, *push back against* calls for change.

Many EJ staff were eager to suggest explanations for why some colleagues engage in these practices, emphasizing that they see their colleagues not generally as uncaring but as striving to reconcile conflicting ideas about how they should spend their time. In chapter 6, I offer some ways to understand why bureaucrats engage in these practices that undermine agencies' EJ efforts.

6 Explaining Bureaucrats' Resistance to EJ Reforms

Most people here are here because they wanted to make a difference.
—Paula, government agency staff person

They feel like they are doing the right thing and they are protecting the people....
I work at a very white organization....It is a very hard pill for them to swallow,
to get them to think that their decisions were ... part of this racial inequality in
environmental decision-making. They don't accept that, because they do good
for the public.
—Nicky, government agency EJ staff person

Public policy is about priorities and values. It is not just about rules. People's personal beliefs and values determine what they will work on and not work on....It
is a question of will. It is not a question of what can or can't be done.
—Michael, government agency EJ staff person

Introduction

EJ-supportive staff offered many ideas about what might motivate the
practices I detailed in chapters 4 and 5. In this chapter, I present several
explanations for why staff engage in practices that undermine EJ reforms.
These data suggest that bureaucrats' pushback against EJ reforms and EJ
staff stems not only from their concerns about limited resources, regulatory
authority, analytical tools, and other material factors beyond their control
(as discussed in chapter 3), but also from elements of regulatory culture.

My data indicate that some staff pushback against EJ reforms stems from
bureaucrats' ideas about what the goals and priorities of environmental
regulation should be. I draw on other scholars' findings about environmental regulatory culture to substantiate my own data. As I discuss in the

concluding chapter, these findings raise questions about the standards to which we should hold agencies and their staff accountable.

Educational Background and Capacity

In chapter 4, I described how some bureaucrats use boundary work to frame EJ reforms as violating certain aspects of their agency's identity. EJ-supportive staff engage in their own boundary work to explain coworkers' resistance to EJ programs and assert a different vision about what environmental regulatory agencies' priorities should be. For example, they draw boundaries between themselves and other staff along lines of educational background to explain colleagues' pushback against EJ reforms. EJ-supportive staff often noted that most of their colleagues are engineers, economists, and lawyers, who are not trained in environmental inequalities, their structural roots, and how EJ reforms could ameliorate them. In contrast, some noted their own training in critical social sciences to explain their appreciation for EJ analysis and conviction that the state has a responsibility to reduce environmental inequalities. One EPA EJ staff person said, "It is not an easy task for EPA staff to do this. They are scientists, lawyers, wonky kinds of folks." Janine asserted that her coworkers' resistance to EJ stems in large part from the fact that they are not trained to think about inequality: "Look at who is in charge": "Lawyers, lawyers, lawyers, a few scientists, and lawyers are in charge of the environmental work;" the "social science side" is "woefully lacking"; and "business schools are teaching environment in a way that lacks questions about equity." Brian concluded that people who understand "the general framework of environmental justice ... do not really exist in our agency."

EJ-supportive staff also emphasized that staff simply lack the technical capacity to conduct EJ analyses and integrate EJ principles into their work practices. One estimated to me that "2 to 3 percent of the federal government actually gets the idea" of what "environmental justice" means, "most people are not clear what to do," and integrating EJ into regulatory practice "is a skillset that people do not have." Numerous bureaucrats told me that they do not understand EJ principles or how to apply them. One staff person noted that these deficits cut in both directions, observing that staff who best understand EJ concepts like vulnerability—the agency's EJ staff—tend to lack professional training in quantitative regulatory impact assessment, which challenges their efforts to integrate EJ principles into existing regulatory practice.

Personality

Numerous staff explained that coworkers' resistance to EJ reforms stems in part from personality traits. Such comments were made almost exclusively about engineers and scientists, asserting that they went into their fields because they are introverted and thus are uncomfortable with a basic EJ reform: increased engagement with the public. For example, Elizabeth explained that this is one reason staff are reticent to interact with the public: "We have a bunch of scientists and engineers. They just don't work with people well. They'd rather look at numbers and gadgets....A bunch of introverts." Engineers themselves used this narrative. For example, Joan emphasized that community engagement conflicts with her personality and interests: "It is really uncomfortable if you're not somebody who is into networking, making cold calls, or knocking on doors....That's not why I got into engineering." Public engagement events often include residents expressing anger and frustration at regulatory agencies for allowing the environmental hazards they suspect are harming their community. It is hard to be yelled at, especially for staff who feel introverted in the friendliest of circumstances.

These two explanations suggest that staff resistance to EJ can be remedied by filling information gaps and training staff in certain new skills. To be sure, such forms of education are justified. Yet, nearly all EJ-supportive staff assert that coworkers' resistance to EJ reforms stems not only from unfamiliarity with new concepts and practices, but also from *ideological opposition* to EJ reforms. I use the term "ideology" to refer to popular claims that legitimize the status quo, often so taken for granted and institutionalized that we rarely question or even notice them. In the rest of this chapter, I highlight ideological commitments—including ideas about what their organization's identity is and should be—that help explain bureaucrats' resistance to proposed EJ reforms.

Expertise and Discretion

Staff explained that some bureaucrats reject proposed EJ reforms that threaten their sense of professional expertise in several ways. First, EJ-supportive staff assert that community members have valid knowledge about their environments, exposures, and remediation and redevelopment priorities but that few coworkers share this view.[1] Instead, some proposed EJ reforms—such as soliciting public input on regulatory decisions—contradict technocratic standards of professional expertise that prevail among environmental regulators.

I observed other staff leverage such technocratic notions of expertise to deride EJ reforms. In chapter 5, I described how Hank spoke critically about colleagues who dismiss public input made at hearings. He explained that requiring staff to conduct more public outreach threatens their sense of authority. To them, "It's like, well, 'Am I going to let someone from the public write this, or am *I* writing it? It's *my* permit!'" They reject the notion that community members' input is valid data for regulatory decision-making. Interestingly, Hank later engaged in this same boundary work by characterizing much public input at hearings as invalid: "Now, some of what was said was just venting and ranting. You are just giving them a chance to do it. But, if someone came in and said, 'Instead of an incinerator, use a centrification for this ... '" [*trails off*]. Here, Hank characterizes one highly technical suggestion as the only input he would consider reasonable. He then dismissively depicted public hearings: "You get ranters and people dressing up and doing dry ice in a barrel that looks bad, wearing costumes. You know, it's kind of like Mardi Gras, some of those hearings. It shows how much it is a media event rather than reasoned technical discussion. I even think the governor did it after ____ [a toxic waste spill] with the water: 'Here is a sample of the water post-treatment.' Glug glug glug" [*mimics drinking a glass of water*]. Certainly, activists and political officials sometimes use such practices to draw attention to and reframe an issue. What struck me is that he conveyed respect for only a very technical type of public input and disregarded the ways "performances" can raise important moral questions obscured by technical debate. The fact that even someone who has criticized staff for being dismissive of public outreach would then disparage most public input as illegitimate suggests that these notions of expertise are deeply held among staff.

Second, bureaucrats' sense of expertise manifests also in relation to agency EJ staff. Some EJ staff told me that coworkers reject EJ staff telling them how to do their jobs. Sara explained that staff "really hate being told what to do." She elaborated that enforcement staff value being able to decide for themselves whether to write up a regulated entity for a violation, *or* to discuss it informally with them without issuing a citation. They value having full discretion—doing their job as they see fit. This defense of their own expertise and discretion compels them to push back against EJ staff who suggest changes to how they do their jobs.

Third, staff members reject EJ reforms because they feel that staff at higher scales of government, particularly those in Washington, DC, lack the "boots on the ground" expertise to make decisions about how environmental regulation should be conducted. EJ staff in EPA regional offices said that coworkers resist proposed EJ reforms in part because they do not respect mandates from EPA headquarters in Washington DC, where many EJ reforms originate. State and local regulatory officials expressed similar resentment about directives from the federal government. As one EPA regional office EJ staff person said of staff at several western state agencies: "They say, 'We are the wild west. We do our own thing.'" While EJ staff described this sentiment to explain why some bureaucrats reject EJ reforms, I have encountered it broadly among staff at EPA regional offices as well as state and local agencies. For example, retired staff from EPA regional offices complained about having been "micromanaged" by headquarters, characterized headquarters as out of touch with issues "on the ground," and applauded political appointees who deferred to the expertise of regional career staff. As Wayne said, "You always wanted to stay away from the people at headquarters. [Ideally they would] just let you do your job, because they were never going to help." Similarly, Ron praised his regional administrators who "really just let us go"—who gave staff discretion and deferred to their judgment. Staff members' strong sense of their own expertise leads some to reject reforms originating from U.S. EPA headquarters.

Agency Mission: Environmental Conservation and Public Health

Many EJ-supportive staff argued that coworkers resist proposed EJ reforms because they feel those reforms violate the agency's mission. For example, Ryan explained that some of his coworkers "do not feel like it is the mission of the agency or of their office." Agencies' actual mission statements are quite broad. For example, EPA declares: "The mission of EPA is to protect human health and the environment" (EPA 2017g).[2] Yet staff appear to attach meanings to their agency's mission that are narrower than the language itself would suggest—and incompatible with proposed EJ reforms.

Some EJ staff asserted that some coworkers are principally committed to conserving and protecting animals, wild lands, and other aspects of the nonhuman environment, and only secondarily to protecting human health. For example, Elise explained that her coworkers push back against her EJ efforts in part because they "got into environmental protection … to protect the environment," which meant "being conservationists." She acknowledges that many are concerned with "protecting people's health. But there's certainly the stronger conservationist thread, I think, through all these folks."

My interviews with other staff support this claim. Tim, a manager at a different agency who has fought against most proposed EJ reforms, endorses this conservationist commitment: "Who are we in this regulatory agency? … We care about our communities. But we also care about the environment. … If you did a poll around here, I think a lot of people work here to protect the trees, not to protect the people. … There's nothing wrong with that. I'm glad."

I asked Wayne, a retired environmental engineer who had worked in various management positions at EPA for about 30 years, to describe his greatest accomplishments. He elaborated with pride about helping to support a network of watershed protection organizations. His description provided insights into the commitments of EPA leadership: "I got a fair amount of notoriety over this from headquarters. Like, 'Wow, that's cool.' It was good notoriety. … They were intrigued and very supportive. … For a relatively low investment, you could really help some of these groups stay. … I got a gold medal for my watershed work. … EPA gave me the gold medal, an individual gold. … There were 17,000 people at EPA that year, and [only] three people got gold medals." In Wayne's account, upper management supported his efforts to help these resource conservationist organizations by giving him respect, funding, and prestigious accolades. Indeed, he received a top agency award, which are normally given to teams of staff. Compare this experience with those of EJ staff, who did not convey to me any sense that their agency wanted them to help EJ organizations "stay" (survive) and instead have been challenged by coworkers for talking with community-based EJ activists. The striking contrast further supports the assertion that, for many staff and leaders, conserving environmental resources is more central to agency mission than is protecting human health in overburdened communities.

Serving and Protecting Industry

In other cases, EJ staff asserted that some colleagues are hostile to EJ because they are principally concerned with protecting the needs of industry, whose practices would be constrained by some EJ reforms. For example, Scott explained:

> We work a lot with the people we regulate, and we become focused, not exclusively, but we become focused on their needs. A lot of our measures are related to efficiency of things, like processing permits in a timely manner....The consultants, the companies, and the people that we interact with on a day-to-day basis: I think we've become good at meeting the needs of those people. We're focused on them. I think part of the culture shift is, "Oh. Hey. We're doing this for the people, and let's remember that." ... [Some staff] don't view interacting with the public as part of their job....An example of that is that we call a permit a "project," [as in] "I'm working on this project." "This project I'm working on." I'm like, "It's not *your* project. It's *their* project." You know? Call it the facility, the permit....It conveys ownership on our part, [as in] "This is something I am invested in."

Scott's narrative characterizes the "culture" in his agency as one in which staff are committed to serving industry rather than the public. He makes this point by noting that managers evaluate staff based on how quickly permits are processed (which enables permit applicants to continue their operations) instead of public health metrics, staff meet with industry (but not "the people") "on a day-to-day basis," staff view interacting with the public as outside of their responsibilities, and staff refer to permit applications in a way ("my project") that implies a sense of investment in industry rather than a sense of policing. Thus, EJ reforms are antithetical to their commitments, and getting staff to implement them will require a "culture shift." EJ staff also made this point by noting that their own commitments to overburdened and vulnerable communities are shared by few coworkers.

This commitment to industry is also evidenced when bureaucrats discipline EJ staff for meeting with community members. In chapter 5, I described how Mary and her colleague were surveilled and disciplined by coworkers for meeting with two local political leaders concerned about environmental inequalities. Their outreach to concerned community members breached the norm of serving industry.

My interviews with other staff corroborate this explanation. For example, as quoted in chapter 4, Richard explained unapologetically that he fights against

EJ reforms because he sees them as violating his commitment to creating a "level playing field" for industry. He conceptualizes fairness only in terms of equity among industry actors. In contrast, EJ-supportive staff express a commitment to equity among communities in terms of environmental harm. Jane similarly explained why she fights against mandatory EJ reforms. When I asked how her own life experiences shaped her views on EJ, she responded: "My work as an inspector helped a lot. I started off very idealistic: 'I am going to save the world. Industry is evil.' You learn you have to work with them. You start seeing what they have to do to just try and do business." Her compassion for industry actors motivates her resistance to EJ reforms. In my research on pesticide regulation in California, I observed county-level regulatory officials express sympathy for industry actors and disdain for community members who raised concerns about pesticide exposure (Harrison 2011). They characterized industry actors as well intentioned and concerned community members as irrational and unfair, responded to pesticide regulatory violations by giving warning letters rather than fines, and, when they did issue fines, made them as small as possible. Such commitments conflict with EJ reforms, which would increasingly scrutinize and restrict hazardous industry practices.

I am not claiming that "most" regulatory agency staff express a proud allegiance to industry. My data do not allow me to make such generalizations, and my findings and those of other scholars provide only mixed support for such a claim. For example, Lynn, a retired EPA enforcement staff person, expressed considerable sympathy for industry, characterizing regulated entities as reasonable, asserting that "they wanted to do the right thing," proudly describing that she would inform industry actors of their regulatory violations and give them time to fix the problem before deciding whether to report them, and speaking enthusiastically about collaborating with regulated entities to identify profitable pollution-reduction strategies. However, she noted that her embrace of industry-friendly regulatory practices was unpopular and "controversial" among her colleagues, who instead preferred to prosecute regulatory violators and viewed her favored practices as "getting in bed with industry." Similarly, Robertson (2010, 8, 9), drawing on his own experience working at EPA, asserts that EPA staff tend to be committed to a strong environmental regulatory state.

Scholars who have surveyed environmental regulatory agency staff paint a complex picture of regulators' commitments. On the one hand, environmental regulatory enforcement staff report having nonadversarial, cooperative interactions with regulated entities; overwhelmingly feel that industry aims to comply with environmental regulations; and assert that industry is not more concerned with making a profit than protecting the environment (Pautz and Rinfret 2011, 2014). On the other hand, these staff also support current environmental regulations and express ambivalence about the idea of regulating less stringently (Rinfret and Pautz 2013).

Privilege and Perception of Environmental Inequality

Additionally, staff often drew boundaries along lines of life experience to help explain bureaucrats' resistance to EJ reforms. EJ-supportive staff observed that most agency staff are white and from predominantly white, middle- or upper-middle-class neighborhoods. They asserted that these types of privilege make staff perceive environmental and other forms of inequality as not serious and thus EJ reforms as unnecessary. For example, Michael noted, "Many offices at _____ [this agency] are homogeneous in terms of race and the orientation of the staff regarding the realities that real people face. This homogeneous complexion of the _____ [agency's] staff contributes to a problem of groupthink—namely, the groupthink that EJ is irrelevant or not worth people's time."

Many EJ-supportive staff revealed their own personal experience of racial oppression, having a diverse social network, and/or living in environmentally hazardous communities. They speculated that such life experience enables them to understand the severity of environmental inequalities and thus the necessity of EJ reforms. For example, several EPA EJ staff noted that Lisa Jackson, the first EPA administrator under President Obama and who by all measures did more to support EJ than any other EPA administrator, is black, was raised in New Orleans, and rushed across the city to save her own mother, stepfather, and aunt from Hurricane Katrina just before it destroyed her mother's home. Jackson herself explained how her own life experiences affected her work at EPA: "It means that I can sit in a room ... and maybe use my position to hear in a different way folks who don't feel heard" (Cappiello 2010). Other scholars have similarly argued that some bureaucrats' experiences living in overburdened and vulnerable communities motivated their commitment to EJ-type reforms (Engelman Lado 2017, 69 fn95; Kohl 2015, forthcoming).

Jamie specified that one of the major "challenges" facing EJ policy implementation at his agency is the "diversity of experiences" among staff.

He noted that he was raised in an industrially polluted community with high rates of cancer and other diseases linked to environmental toxics, and that many members of his own family died from cancer. He explained how this experience fuels his commitment to EJ reforms, and how his coworkers' antipathy for EJ stems in part from their lack of such experience: "I have also watched a lot of people get sick and die over the years who are waiting for those incremental steps [of EJ reforms] to become more than baby steps, to come at a quicker pace....We bring really smart people in who have no connection to communities. So, therefore, the things they create many times miss what is really going on, on the ground in people's lives." He points to his experience growing up in an overburdened community to explain why he views EJ reforms as *crucial and imperative*. Staff who do not have that experience lack that sense of urgency and make decisions that fail to sufficiently address the conditions people face in overburdened communities.

Neutrality and Colorblindness

Numerous staff—some white and some persons of color—explained that coworkers' pushback against EJ reforms stems from their strong belief that serving the public in an unbiased way requires that government agencies ignore communities' racial and other demographic characteristics. For example, Esther said that pointing out that communities of color, on average, have not been as protected from environmental hazards as white communities would cause her coworkers to bristle, precisely because they take great pride in being neutral. They think, "We protect everyone. We don't care what color they are or what income. We protect everyone. When I do an inspection, I do the best inspection, no matter where that facility is." As a result, they resist proposed EJ reforms that instruct them to consider the demographic characteristics of communities when conducting analyses of pending regulatory decisions. As Jennifer explained, this interpretation of bureaucratic neutrality made colleagues conclude that the EJ reforms she proposed did not apply to them: "People have a desire to think, ... 'I'm not a racist. Since I've never been a racist and never will be, I don't see why I have to think about this.'" Malcolm explained that his coworkers misinterpret any reference to racial inequality as an allegation that individual staff have intentionally discriminated against certain communities: "There seems to be a supposition on the part of some that when you talk about environmental justice, there's an insinuation that someone has done something wrong or that someone has targeted someone." The civil rights complaint a coworker filed against Peter, as discussed in chapter 5, shows that even *becoming familiar* with racial inequality is cause for animosity and resistance.

These findings indicate that bureaucrats' pushback against EJ reforms is motivated in part by a commitment to abstract forms of liberal neutrality, in which race-conscious EJ reforms that try to remedy racial inequality violate what it means for staff members to be impartial. This belief reflects the dominant, "colorblind" racial ideology prevalent throughout contemporary U.S. society: the belief that racial equity requires *not* taking race into consideration (Bonilla-Silva 2014; Lipsitz 1995; Omi and Winant 2015). From this perspective, government agency staff must treat all communities and industry actors equally, without regard to unintentional, institutionally produced racial environmental inequalities. Accordingly, staff push back against EJ reforms that instruct them to direct extra resources (in the form of analysis, outreach, inspections, etc.) to communities whose status as racially marginalized, Native American, and/or working class makes them more vulnerable to the harms of exposure to environmental hazards. This conception of neutrality shores up the environmental advantages that have accrued in white communities and precludes reforms that would extend those protections to communities of color.

I observed staff—all white—use claims about neutrality to reject race-conscious EJ reforms, as I quoted in chapter 4. Tim, a manager who works at the same agency as Jennifer, said that he and other staff oppose EJ reforms because they are committed to being colorblind. When I asked him how receptive staff are to EJ reforms, he responded: "People are not that receptive here. Not because they don't know what it is, but because they *do* know what it is. … A lot of what we do here is remediation of contaminated sites. We are not worried about the color of the skin, or the thickness of the wallet in the house that's next door."

Ryan Holifield similarly found that EPA Region 4 staff "took pains to emphasize that they never based their remedial decisions on the racial, ethnic, or economic composition of the community," in contrast to EJ advocates' assertions that agencies should do more thorough analysis and outreach in working-class and racially marginalized communities because they have historically been underserved by regulatory decision-making processes (Holifield 2004, 293, 295). For instance, he quotes one staff member as defending the neutrality of existing practice by saying, "We select a remedy based on *science*, regardless of who lives around the site. Race does not play a part in my decision" (293). Holifield concludes that, in part because of staff members' insistence on taking a colorblind approach to regulatory decision-making, "the Clinton EPA's approach to environmental justice did not include an effort to engineer a 'fairer' distribution of Superfund risk along lines of race or class" (293).

Racist Prejudice

Some pushback against EJ reforms also stems from racist prejudice. Dan's comments showcased in chapter 4 demonstrate this explanation. While Dan may believe that the law prohibits government agencies from taking communities' racial characteristics into account, his narrative reveals that at least some of his resistance to race-conscious EJ reforms and programs stems from racially prejudiced notions that communities of color unjustifiably hoard government resources.

My interviews with EJ-supportive staff indicate that racist hostility in the workplace undermines agencies' EJ efforts because EJ staff are predominantly persons of color and because EJ efforts explicitly address racial environmental inequalities. For example, one black EJ staff person spent most of our interview describing coworkers' racist hostility toward him throughout multiple decades at U.S. EPA. He described instances of other staff and managers bullying him, physically threatening him, and actively limiting his career opportunities. He noted that, while conducting the antidiscrimination training required of all federal employees, he realized that he has experienced "so many" of the prohibited personnel practices described in the training, practices that are "terrible" and "widespread." Coworkers of color have told him about similar experiences. For example, when he first started working at the agency, a black woman who works there and had known him through his previous job called him and said, "Didn't anyone tell you that EPA is a hard place for a black person to work?" He noted that former EPA staff member Marsha Coleman-Adebayo won a discrimination lawsuit against the agency in 2000 on the grounds of racial and sex discrimination (Coleman-Adebayo 2011), that Congress eventually passed the Notification and Federal Employee Antidiscrimination and Retaliation (No FEAR) Act in 2002 to discourage unlawful discrimination and retaliation against employees, and that, subsequently, many EPA staff of color shared their experiences of discrimination and formed support groups for staff of color. When he tells white colleagues about the discriminatory experiences he and other staff of color have endured at EPA, they express utter surprise, saying, "Here?! Really?! I have such a great experience working here." His account conveys that many staff of color feel beleaguered by racist prejudice at work. Enduring such hostility is painful and pulls them away from their own job responsibilities. He emphasized that this is compounded for EJ staff of color, who sustain hostility not only for being persons of color but also for challenging the agency's role in racial environmental inequalities.

Racist prejudice is also evident when white EJ staff are taken more seriously than EJ staff of color. For example, Jim, a white EJ staff person who worked at EPA for several decades, told me that when *he* would talk about EJ reforms with bureaucrats in his office, they would "take it easier from me" than they did from a particular black EJ staff person he worked with, "because I am white. Whereas, if _____ [the colleague] says it, there is an immediate tension. It's a tense situation of racial issues." Jim asserted that when all or most EJ staff are "minorities," as was the case in his office and often is elsewhere, then other bureaucrats think, "Oh, they are just pushing the black agenda." His comments depict coworkers as feeling that black EJ staff unfairly hoard resources for black people ("just pushing the black agenda"), whereas a white EJ staff person advocating for the same reforms would be taken more seriously. When EJ staff are persons of color, as is widely the case, such attitudes drive dismissiveness that undermine agencies' EJ efforts.

EJ staff of color emphasized that they do not view their current workplace as uniquely hostile in this regard. In response to my question about which factors constrain the EJ reform efforts at his agency, Malcolm, a black EJ staff person, responded by describing forms of racist discrimination. For half of our recorded interview and a full 20 minutes after I turned off the recorder when I thought our interview had ended, he elaborated about various forms of racist oppression he has experienced in his life in workplaces and interactions with police, forms of racist violence against black men in the United States today, how prevalent racial discrimination and bias are in U.S. society, and how his agency is no different from broader society in this regard. He concluded, "It is all the time. All the time. This is every day."

A few EJ staff conveyed their sense that racist prejudice constrains their work by describing management condoning staff members' racist behavior.

For instance, one noted that two senior staff members of California EPA's Department of Toxic Substances Control (DTSC), both white men, were found to have exchanged numerous emails containing racist and other hate speech about coworkers and communities DTSC serves (Bogado 2015; McGreevy 2015). Journalist Aura Bogado (2015) and Penny Newman, an EJ advocate she interviewed and who helped unearth these emails through a public records request, emphasize that most of the hazardous waste sites these bureaucrats are responsible for investigating and addressing are located in communities of color. Bogado and Newman argue that these bureaucrats' bigoted attitudes likely led them to do shoddy work in those communities. Indeed, Newman describes multiple instances in which these two staff concluded that community concerns about hazardous waste were unwarranted, while subsequent investigations by advocates and other agencies showed that contamination levels exceeded levels that government agencies deem safe. My research participant who brought this issue up in our interview noted that DTSC retained these two staff, and feels that the agency's management, by protecting and failing to sufficiently discipline blatantly racist staff, effectively tolerates such discourse and signals to other staff that management does not value efforts (like EJ reforms) designed to identify racial injustice and improve regulatory practice in communities of color.

Recent Federal Employee Viewpoint Survey (FEVS) data indicate that the work experiences of federal agency staff are racially unequal in problematic ways, and that these trends largely hold (and in some cases are heightened) for U.S. EPA employees.[3] With the exception of respondents identified as Asian, racial minority respondents report less favorable views than their white counterparts about how fairly evaluations reflect performance, whether promotions are based on merit, the ability of staff to report suspected regulatory violations without fear of reprisal, support for workforce diversity by supervisors and the agency, how well supervisors work with employees of different backgrounds, the agency's success in achieving its mission, whether their supervisor treats them with respect, and the existence of arbitrary action, personal favoritism, and coercion for partisan political purposes. White employees' attitudes matter because they predominate federal agency workforces. Currently, whites comprise 63 percent of all full-time federal employees (OPM 2017). At EPA, whites comprise 69 percent of all staff and 77 to 85 percent of each managerial or executive leadership rank (EEOC 2018).

Racist prejudice within an environmental regulatory agency undermines its progress on EJ because most staff are white, most EJ staff are persons of color, and EJ staff are tasked with trying to get white coworkers to fight racist outcomes of regulatory practice. Whites' ignorance and denials of such disparities further reinforce them.

Ideas of Justice and Effectiveness

Bureaucrats' pushback against EJ reforms also stems in part from popular notions about the standards to which government agencies should be held and how effectively environmental regulatory agencies meet those ideals.

By all accounts, environmental regulatory agency staff are strongly committed to environmental regulation. All staff I interviewed, of all ranks and varying persuasions about EJ, expressed *pride* in their work and strongly identify as environmental stewards and public servants. They described regulatory violators they helped bring to justice, noted contaminated areas they helped restore to levels in which wildlife could thrive, and showed me newspaper articles celebrating their work at the agency. They related stories about sacrifices and risks they took for their jobs. Many noted working long hours to do their jobs well, and some noted that they sacrificed a higher salary by working for the state instead of industry. Many described, without any sense of regret, enduring intimidation and threats of violence from industry actors unhappy with their work. Some EPA veterans described how, during the early 1980s when President Reagan's first EPA administrator, Anne Gorsuch, eviscerated the agency and disparaged its staff, they and their coworkers exchanged practical jokes, anonymous newsletters, t-shirts, political comics, and other satirical antics to criticize the hostile appointees and maintain morale. Some had kept these items and brought them to our interview, proud of supporting each other and their agency in the face of leadership that was hostile to both EPA and its staff. Together, these stories expressed fighting personally for a cause they feel committed to and proud of.

Staff advocating for EJ reforms acknowledge and respect their coworkers' commitments to environmental protection. For instance, shortly after the 2016 election, I asked one longstanding EPA EJ staff person to share his thoughts about the Trump administration's threats to severely cut EPA funding. He responded: "I am not anxious at all.… EPA is staffed by people who really want to do the right thing, and the changes in administration will not change that.... We are good at turning lemons into lemonade," and staff will find ways to do their work, even surreptitiously, irrespective of budget cuts. Although recent history has proved him wrong in certain respects—the Trump administration has undermined staff members' abilities to regulate—his narrative underscores how deeply EPA staff identify as committed public stewards of the environment.

Some have maintained these commitments after retirement. Some former EPA staff helped form and lead SaveEPA, a nonprofit organization comprised of EPA veterans dedicated to fighting the Trump administration's war on the agency. One showed me a letter to the editor he submitted in protest of the Trump administration's gutting of federal climate change research and policy, as well as a link to a news article in which he was interviewed about his work with SaveEPA. Others noted that they mentor current EPA staff about how to weather the Trump administration's efforts to restrict their work.

Other scholars have found that that environmental regulatory agency staff feel that regulation plays an important role in protecting the environment, and that they persevere in their responsibilities even under leadership hostile to environmental regulation (Mintz 2012; Ozymy and Jarrell 2017; Rhodes 2003, 91–93; Rinfret and Pautz 2013; Robertson 2010). After conducting 190 interviews with EPA staff and working in EPA's enforcement offices for six years, Mintz (2012) asserts that there is a "strong sense of mission among the staff" (227), that staff have a "unity of purpose" (228), that they are "highly motivated and idealistic" (228), and that they are "dedicated, resourceful, capable, and well focused" (202), with many working overtime without pay to get their work done. As Ozymy and Jarrell (2017, 207–208) emphasize: "There is a long-standing culture that values enforcement and pursuing a continual commitment to these programs within the agency, [and] these will likely persist under Trump, even if they receive less funding and administrative support. Career administrators will not step back and let the president 'drain the swamp,' but will engage in hidden actions and other stealth methods of keeping these initiatives going."

However, such depictions leave unspecified what staff think *successful* environmental regulation means. Staff advocating for EJ reforms assert that their agency should be assessed according to how well it improves conditions in the most overburdened and vulnerable communities and otherwise reducing environmental inequalities, and that their agencies have not generally met this standard. In contrast, they recount other staff insisting that good environmental regulation means improving environmental conditions *overall* and asserting that their agencies have generally done so. From this latter perspective, which EJ staff describe as pervasive within their organizations, EJ reforms violate what it means to be effective public servants. In turn, these ideas compel staff to push back against proposed EJ reforms. Nicky's quote at the start of this chapter illustrates this point. She feels that her coworkers resist EJ because they identify as selfless public servants who help *everyone*. Due to this, and aggregate measures showing improvements in many environmental conditions over time, they reject the EJ premise that regulatory practice must be changed.

Other EJ staff asserted that coworkers' resistance to EJ stems in part from this particular conception of what successful environmental regulation means. For example, Kate said: "A lot of people in _____ [this agency], I think the great majority, ... work here because we care about the environment. You just care a lot. [You think,] 'I don't see how this [EJ] fits into what I care about,' and you get frustrated." Narratives that I showcased in chapter 4—notably, that agencies are committed to race-blind neutrality, that environmental inequalities are not serious, and that racism is a thing of the past—legitimize these conceptions of environmental regulatory accomplishment and enable staff to assert that racial environmental inequalities are irrelevant to what good environmental regulation entails.

Other evidence indicates that EJ principles conflict with many staff members' conceptions of agency goals and accomplishments. Aside from EJ staff and those who support them, staff I interviewed were unapologetically silent about or dismissive of EJ, or both, and rarely implement proposed EJ reforms. EJ principles or practices did not appear in their narratives about what they felt proud of or what they thought the agency should be doing. None mentioned that government agencies protect some communities much better than others. When I asked how EJ fit into their work, some shrugged, saying it had nothing to do with their jobs, while others said that it was just a box to check in the course of doing their "real" work.

That is, some bureaucrats' resistance to EJ reforms stems in part from the same factor that motivates staff to denounce hostile budget cuts by conservative elites: both challenge a system they feel is effective, they are proud of, they are committed to, and which they feel is fair. Identifying as effective environmental stewards cuts in multiple directions. It compels staff to make sacrifices for their work, persevere under adverse circumstances, and defend their organization from attack by antiregulatory elites—but also to reject EJ reforms as unnecessary and antithetical to the agency's mission.

Bureaucrats' accounts of their agency's accomplishments, and EJ-supportive staff members' accounts of their agencies' shortcomings, together reveal competing notions of how government agencies should be assessed. EJ staff and EJ activists argue that agencies should be measured according to *egalitarian* principles. In this context, egalitarianism posits that government agencies should reduce inequalities among communities and devote a disproportionate share of resources toward helping communities that are most burdened with environmental problems and most vulnerable to their effects. EJ-supportive staff make exactly these recommendations and argue that agencies should be judged according to reductions in environmental inequalities and declining rates of environment-related illness in the most burdened communities.[4]

In contrast, other staff often conceptualize their agency's goals and accomplishments in *utilitarian* terms. Utilitarianism posits that the responsibility of government agencies is to ensure the greatest good for the greatest number of people. Scholars have long shown that utilitarian ideals dominate U.S. environmental law, regulations, and regulatory culture, as well as mainstream environmentalism (Bryner 2002; Espeland 1998; Harrison 2011, 2014; Harvey 1996; Low and Gleeson 1998; Shrader-Frechette 2002). Environmental regulatory agency staff frequently express this idea by measuring their agency's accomplishments in terms aggregated across the population, such as reductions in air pollution across a major region. In our conversations, staff often recite their organization's mission statement— "We protect public health and the environment"—as an *accomplishment*, not only an aspiration. Such narratives foreclose conversation about environmental inequality that persists despite those accomplishments—about the fact that these agencies have not protected public health and the environment of all communities. A utilitarian perspective about what government agencies should accomplish justifies defending their organization as effective and warding off calls for change. The utilitarian ideal is reified through agency reports that invariably celebrate pollution reduction measured in aggregate terms and devote little if any space to "EJ" activities, agency budgets that allocate paltry resources to EJ activities, and employees' job descriptions that are silent about environmental inequality.

EJ staff explained how this fuels pushback against EJ reform proposals. Edward, an agency's EJ staff person, told me that agencies and policymakers reject EJ reforms precisely because they assess regulatory agencies according to utilitarian principles: "These [agencies] are somewhat resistant to taking EJ on board to the degree that we and EJ organizations would like them to. ... Policymakers' conception of the greater good is different from those of EJ organizations. Their mandate is to provide cheap reliable power, and they are willing to disproportionately burden certain communities for the benefit of the greater good." As Edward indicates, egalitarian and utilitarian ideals are at odds with each other—while egalitarianism strives to reduce inequalities, utilitarianism defines them as acceptable when achieving greater gains overall. That said, staff and political elites do not publicly proclaim such priorities. Instead, the sacrifice of certain communities for the sake of the "greater good" is conveyed implicitly, such as when staff and elites celebrate aggregated measures of environmental improvement as indicators of environmental regulatory agency success and remain silent about environmental inequality.

Political philosophers call these "political theories of justice," ideas about which principles should guide the design of public institutions. Some bureaucrats resist EJ because they are committed to a utilitarian notion of justice, whereas EJ staff and EJ activists criticize aggregated measures and argue that the state should instead be held to an egalitarian notion of justice. Bureaucrats push back against EJ in part because they are defending their notion of what government agencies should do and how they should be held accountable.

Staff Strategies for Supporting Environmental Justice in This Context

EJ staff use various strategies to help EJ-resistant coworkers learn about EJ issues, care about them, and implement EJ reforms.

First and most directly, EJ staff and their EJ-supportive colleagues help coworkers determine how to apply EJ principles to their own responsibilities and translate them into concrete tasks. Some develop EJ guidance documents specifying how staff should do their everyday work in ways that support EJ principles. Nicky explained: "People needed those tools, they needed that protocol to help them change the way they were thinking of things.... We had to create the maps, we had to create the questions, we had to make sure we had the Limited English Proficiency Guidance in place, we had to make sure the rulewriters knew which questions to ask in every single rule. We worked with the HR [Human Resources] folks to make sure that [they] are asking questions on every single person's review [about] what did they do to incorporate EJ. It just took all these system changes."

To combat coworkers' ideological resistance to EJ reforms, EJ-supportive staff also try to change agency culture so that more staff will feel supportive of and invested in EJ reforms. One mechanism for doing this is offering EJ trainings for staff. Within these, EJ staff educate coworkers about the scope and forms of environmental inequalities, as well as some of their political economic and cultural roots. Many EJ staff press their agency's leadership to authorize in-person trainings for teams and to make them mandatory. EJ-supportive staff emphasized that they view these trainings as crucial for bringing a cultural shift in the agency. Sara explained:

> We all agreed that, at the end of the day, the most important piece of the [EJ] policy was requiring people to take a training and raising people's awareness, because so many people didn't know anything about [EJ]....This was all about culture change, and that a policy, even a really strict policy, wasn't going to do it. We had to get people bought into it....A lot of this stuff ... would require additional legislation, it would require change in regulation....As staff get more savvy with what EJ actually means, I would hope that they would then be looking at the regs [regulations], saying, "You know what? This could be an opportunity for change here," and maybe they take that to their supervisor.

Sara's hope is that by sensitizing staff to the conditions in overburdened and vulnerable communities, the EJ trainings will inspire coworkers to think critically about existing regulatory practice and identify opportunities for the agency to reduce environmental inequalities. This could include staff proposing to leadership new regulations or defining existing regulatory authority in new, expanded ways.

EJ-supportive staff also foster cultural change with coworkers on a one-on-one basis as learning moments arise. For instance, several described teaching coworkers to conceptualize racism beyond the scope of intentional discrimination and acknowledge that their own institutions unintentionally contribute to racially unequal outcomes. Scott recounted how, after a meeting in which someone made a reference to "environmental racism," a manager called Scott into his office and, visibly upset, said, "I have personally been called a racist." Scott explained, "No. What that means is that our institutions are racist," in the sense that people of color do not have the same opportunities as other people and thus that the system is racially unequal. Scott told me, "This was brand new to him," and that he seemed receptive to thinking about EJ reforms as reducing the *unintentionally* unequal nature of government protections.

Others build support for EJ by reminding coworkers that environmental justice refers to the accumulation of environmental hazards in a wide range of communities. While EJ-supportive staff spend considerable time documenting *racial* environmental inequalities to dispel coworkers' postracial narratives, they remind coworkers that environmental problems cluster in other vulnerable communities, too. Numerous EJ-supportive staff told me that they try to strengthen their coworkers' support for EJ reforms by pointing out that "EJ is not only about race." Jamie explained why making this point is valuable:

> You have folks who don't have the desire to deal with communities of color, and assume that EJ is just about communities of color. What I try to make sure they understand is that it is also about low-income white communities, low-income working communities. That often gets lost, but I continue to bring it back up. I share with folks that ... the community I lived in, our family was the only family of color, but we still had a power plant across the street, our well water was contaminated, our community was built on top of a mine, and my best friends, myself, and a number of the other young people in my community, every one of our parents got cancer. Many of them died from cancer. My father had cancer four times, my mother had cancer one time, my brother had cancer. So, I say all that to say that it can happen to your family just as easily. They don't have to be a family of color, because my friends, they were all white, but every one of them had at least one parent who died of cancer. So, when folks only see EJ as a community of color problem, then sometimes you can't see yourself in that equation.

This framing honors a broad array of environmental injustices. However, the implication that some white staff are likely to care more about contaminated white communities than communities of color is troubling.

To further help EJ-resistant coworkers understand environmental injustice and feel motivated to implement EJ reforms, EJ staff find ways for their coworkers to visit overburdened and vulnerable communities and listen to their residents. As EJ mapping exercises do, such visits make coworkers' ignorance about racial environmental inequality difficult to sustain. Martin emphasized that visiting overburdened communities helps staff realize the ineffectiveness of existing regulatory practice, "make an emotional connection" to people within them, and feel compelled to help develop systematic regulatory reforms to redress those problems. Rulewriting staff have told Tom that talking with members of overburdened and vulnerable communities was "really transformative" because it enabled them to "understand and feel the issues people face" and gave them "the space to think creatively about how to address these issues." Elizabeth, a rulewriter, also asserted that "getting people out and actually interacting with folks" from overburdened and vulnerable communities is "one of the most powerful things that we ever do" because "it really does change hearts and the willingness for folks to engage." EJ staff members' interest in getting their coworkers to see their responsibilities in a new light is supported by scholarship that has shown how social movement pressure and community engagement have helped push scientists to negotiate and redefine what proper science entails, what constitutes legitimate knowledge, and what scientists' relationships to communities should be (Epstein 1996; Frickel 2004a; Hess 2007; K. Moore 2008; Ottinger and Cohen 2011).

Additionally, EJ-supportive staff strive to change regulatory culture by advocating for increasing the diversity of staff along lines of racial identity, ethnicity, gender, socioeconomic status, educational background, and experience working with overburdened and vulnerable communities. Increasing staff diversity brings different perspectives to bear on environmental regulatory decision-making. Jamie explained why he advocates for hiring managers who have experience working with overburdened and vulnerable communities: "As we are hiring individuals, one of those areas could be, what has your past experience been in working with communities? What came out of that? ... If we don't build that strong criteria or language for those folks who are above who are going to be here throughout the duration, then we are going to only get incremental steps in place. ... We need individuals who get it. It makes us a stronger and better agency."

Some staff employ additional strategies to foster greater diversity among management. For instance, Rose documented the glass ceiling for women within her agency and then created programs for advancing skilled, qualified women into technical positions. She also established an internship program that recruited students from historically black colleges and universities to work within the agency. Similarly, Sara advocates for her agency to make its college internships paid rather than unpaid, so that they are not only accessible to students who are wealthy enough to work for free.

Finally, some EJ staff described how they foster diversity specifically by recruiting and hiring EJ advocates of color into the agency as fellow "institutional activists" (Santoro and McGuire 1997). Brian explained why he does this: "The thing is to pull as many people in, to not give up on this institution.... We can't just choose to not deal with it and abandon it, because then it would be worse. [We need] to bring in people from outside to start making those changes."

Conclusion

In this chapter, I offered explanations for bureaucrats' behaviors that undermine the institutionalization of EJ principles into regulatory practice. I first discussed how bureaucrats' practices that undercut their agencies' EJ efforts may stem in part from their educational backgrounds that limit their familiarity with EJ issues and personality traits that make them uncomfortable with doing certain EJ practices. I then shifted gears, showing that bureaucrats' resistance to EJ reforms is not simply based in limited information or skills, but is ideological in nature. Specifically, I suggested that some bureaucrats resist EJ reforms and EJ staff because they offend their sense of expertise. Some resistance to EJ reforms is rooted in bureaucrats' principal commitment to environmental conservation, which leads them to view programs focused on human health, including EJ reforms, as not a priority. In other cases, staff members are committed to serving industry, which leads them to perceive community-focused EJ reforms as not part of their jobs or as unfairly burdening industry, or both. Additionally, bureaucrats' relatively privileged life experiences lead some to believe that racial environmental inequalities are not serious enough to warrant EJ reforms. Some staff resist EJ reforms because they interpret bureaucratic neutrality as requiring colorblindness, which leads them to conclude that EJ reforms targeting racial inequalities are unjustified. Additionally, racist prejudice drives some staff to engage in practices that wound, stall, and otherwise wear down staff of color and those who fight for racial justice. These practices also signal to other staff that racial equity is unimportant, either within the workplace or in terms of environmental inequalities. Finally, I explained that some antipathy toward EJ reforms stems from staff members' utilitarian ideas of justice, which lead them to see EJ reforms as irrelevant to what it means for government agencies to do good work. By motivating staff to engage in practices that undermine proposed EJ reforms that would reduce environmental inequalities, these ideologies comprise part of the oppressive structures that both create and reinforce environmental injustice.

EJ staff and their EJ-supportive colleagues engage in various strategies to address these factors. In addition to developing EJ protocols that specify how staff should integrate EJ principles into their everyday work, they also try to change regulatory culture. They conduct EJ trainings and advocate for them to be mandatory; take advantage of other, one-on-one opportunities to help coworkers adopt new perspectives about EJ principles; help coworkers visit overburdened and vulnerable communities and otherwise become more sympathetic to their concerns; and advocate for increasing the diversity of staff across the agency.

The fact that EJ-supportive staff draw boundaries between themselves and other staff along these lines further conveys their sense that elements of regulatory culture constrain EJ policy implementation. This boundary work is also a mechanism through which they reframe what environmental regulation should be about and for. Through speculating about the roots of coworkers' hostility to EJ, EJ-supportive staff implicitly and explicitly assert that environmental regulation should focus on improving environmental conditions in the most vulnerable and overburdened communities and bringing environmental equity across communities.

These explanations variously indicate that EJ principles constitute an external institutional logic that conflicts with dominant logics about organizational identity within environmental regulatory agencies. These are competing ideas about what constitutes acceptable and appropriate regulatory practice.

Bureaucrats' ideas about what their agencies' priorities and practices should be shape their daily work practices—including in ways that undermine EJ reforms—precisely because staff have discretion about how to enforce environmental law and because of the ambiguous status of Title VI of the Civil Rights Act and EO 12898 relative to environmental statutes. In other words, those legal ambiguities mean that members' ideological dispositions can shape the extent to which they implement and support EJ reforms. Therefore, reforming environmental regulatory agencies to support environmental justice will require serious conversations about who these organizations should be serving and to which metrics they should be held accountable. It will require, as emphasized by staff who advocate for EJ reforms, a shift in regulatory *culture*.

Thus far in the book, I have explained the slow pace of agencies' EJ efforts by focusing on the struggles of EJ-supportive staff to get coworkers on board with EJ reforms. In the next chapter, I focus my attention on EJ staff themselves and their own disagreements about how agencies should institutionalize EJ principles. As I will show, some disappointing aspects of agencies' EJ efforts stem from the ways some EJ staff define "environmental justice" and how they design EJ reforms accordingly.

7 EJ Staff Members' Definitions of Environmental Justice

The EJ movement's vision of success: Is that the only one that matters? ... Is it so sacrosanct that that is it, forever? ... There is an evolving understanding of what EJ is.

—Tom, government agency EJ staff person

Introduction

Thus far, I have presented EJ staff as a fairly united group. In this chapter, I complicate this depiction. To further explain the divergence of agencies' EJ efforts from longstanding tenets of EJ advocacy, I highlight variations in how EJ staff define "environmental justice."

Some EJ staff define EJ in ways that align with longstanding movement tenets: as requiring state-mandated restrictions on environmental hazards in overburdened communities, as well as the building of green spaces, renewable energy infrastructure, and other environmental amenities in those areas. However, other EJ staff members' definitions of EJ deviate from the model of social change and substantive areas of focus that have long dominated EJ activism, and they design agency EJ programs accordingly. I demonstrate that these conflicting notions of what EJ requires reflect debates among EJ activists who help advise agency EJ efforts. I argue that agencies' EJ efforts are conditioned in part by how EJ staff demarcate what "EJ" means and how able they feel to implement those ideas in light of competing institutional demands. Although working in contexts not of their own choosing, EJ staff nonetheless influence how well agency EJ programs align with longstanding EJ movement principles.

EJ Programs Deviating from Longstanding EJ Movement Priorities

The interview data I showcase in this chapter come principally from my interviews with EJ staff and EJ advocates about five agency EJ grant programs that allocate funding to community-based and tribal organizations addressing environmental issues in overburdened and vulnerable communities. I analyzed the documents and funded grants of the California Environmental Protection Agency (CalEPA) EJ Small Grants Program, San Francisco EJ Grants Program, New York State EJ Community Impact Grant Program, U.S. Environmental Protection Agency (U.S. EPA) EJ Small Grants Program, and U.S. EPA EJ Collaborative Problem-Solving (CPS) Cooperative Agreement Program.[1] In these interviews, I sought to understand two troubling patterns I discovered about these programs' documents and funding patterns (which I detailed more fully in chapter 2).

First, whereas EJ advocacy has historically focused on securing stronger regulations and other state-guaranteed protections from environmental hazards, most agencies' EJ grant programs do not evince that *model of change*. Most of the grant programs' materials implicitly discourage applicants from proposing projects that pursue environmental change through such mechanisms. They hail projects focusing on individual behavior modification, market-based change, collaboration with industry, and other voluntary, private-sector measures. They include little to no language encouraging projects that pursue change through policy reform, regulatory enforcement, or increasing public participation in government decision-making. Most of the programs' funded projects also deviate from the model of change EJ advocates have historically prioritized. Given these patterns, agencies' EJ grant programs may unwittingly channel EJ organizations away from their longstanding pursuit of change through regulatory and policy reforms and instead toward individualized mechanisms of change.

Second, agencies' EJ grant programs deviate in some ways from the EJ movement's longstanding *substantive emphasis on hazard reduction*. Program materials from two of the programs (New York and San Francisco) showcase projects not geared to hazard reduction (community gardens, nutrition education, parks and trails, and energy efficiency) and scarcely mention projects that reduce hazards like air and water pollution. In addition, for nearly all of the programs, the portion of funded projects that include any substantial attention to reducing environmental hazards has declined over time. As a result, agencies' EJ grant programs are not reducing dangerous environmental hazards to the extent that they could. The focus on urban greening—and decline of attention to hazards—is problematic in part because so much greening happens on top of existing hazards without remediating them (Frickel and Elliott 2018).

This emphasis on industry-friendly, voluntary environmental amenity projects *rather than* securing state-enforced reductions of environmental hazards also appears in other agency EJ efforts. Notably, EPA's Office of Environmental Justice promotes and uses its Collaborative Problem-Solving (CPS) model in not only its CPS EJ grant program but also numerous other capacities. For example, EPA's Region 4 office has run an "EJ Academy" program that uses the CPS model to train residents and members of EJ organizations to "accomplish their communities' environmental improvement goals" through collaborating with industry and other stakeholders (EPA 2016d; Tennessee 2016). Bruno and Jepson (2018) found this pattern in EPA's EJ Showcase Communities grant program as well. EPA staff often showcase organizations using the CPS model to show how nonconfrontational collaboration can transform communities.

These programs and projects are valuable, as they have helped improve conditions in numerous overburdened and vulnerable communities and constitute precedent-setting models for productive collaboration. However, the emphasis on consensus and collaboration with industry implicitly discounts the pursuit of environmental protections through practices that industry "collaborators" would oppose: stronger environmental regulations and increased enforcement. The interests of industry and residents do not fully align, and yet agency documents touting collaborative, consensus-based decision-making obscure those differences.

Although the EJ grant programs and other projects I described here are only one portion of agencies' overall EJ efforts, they serve the important function of helping to educate other staff about what "EJ" means. As Paul noted, "a challenge is engaging our colleagues in a way that sensitizes them to whatever environmental justice is. Grants are one way of doing that." The consistent promotion of industry-friendly, win-win projects focused on boosting amenities in communities leaves a problematic impression that EJ does not require stronger regulatory and policy protections, that residents and industry actors can and should handle those responsibilities, and that EJ requires building parks, gardens, and other environmental amenities *rather than* reducing environmental hazards.

EJ Staff Members' Definitions of EJ and Their Strategic Practices

My interviews with current and former agency EJ staff provide valuable insights into why most of the EJ grant programs and these other EJ efforts deviated from the EJ movement's longstanding primary model of change and substantive areas of focus. These bureaucrats' depictions of the history and evolution of the programs reveal competing characterizations of what EJ means and how agency EJ efforts should be designed to accord with those ideas.

EJ as Principally Requiring Regulatory Protections from Environmental Hazards

Many EJ grant program staff frame EJ as requiring, first and foremost, reducing environmental hazards in overburdened and marginalized communities through regulatory and policy reform and enforcement. They strive to create EJ programs and reform regulatory practice so that their agencies will more effectively restrict environmental hazards in overburdened and vulnerable communities. They acknowledge that EJ requires both reducing hazards in and revitalizing overburdened and vulnerable communities. Tom, who has long played a key role in his agency's EJ efforts, emphasized this: "Environmental justice is really about ... getting rid of the negatives but also bringing in the positives, like transportation and parks.... If you are going to do work that really is going to be transformative, you need to keep doing this in both ways, ... both regulatory and nonregulatory, ... both cleanup and revitalization. EJ walks on two legs. They have to work together."

Other EJ staff emphasize that, although the nonregulatory, amenity-building elements of environmental justice are easier, government agencies must reduce environmental harms. As Michael explained: "The community garden is easy. Focusing on art within a community, that's easy.... While those things are nice, people who are disproportionately burdened by environmental problems, their problems need resources for some more sophisticated issues ... like redlining and incompatible land uses. This is where we need more attention." To be sure, community garden projects are not *easy* in an absolute sense, as they require physical labor and can entail conflict with city leaders intent on utilizing space for capitalist development (Gottlieb and Joshi 2010; Mares and Peña 2010; Schmelzkopf 2002; Smith and Kurtz 2003). Michael's point is that gardens and art installations do not provide the structural changes needed to substantially reduce hazards in overburdened and vulnerable communities.

However, as I described in chapter 3, some EJ staff confessed that the context they work in is hostile to agency EJ programs and to regulatory actions against industry, and thus they frame some of their EJ programs in a nonregulatory, industry-friendly light to protect them from being defunded.

Such practices, although done to protect EJ programs, have problematic consequences. EJ activists I interviewed stated unequivocally that program document language signals to prospective applicants which types of projects are most likely to be funded. Some told me that, when applying for government EJ grants, they do not propose projects that strive to increase environmental enforcement or strengthen regulations, which they do not feel agencies would fund. Others, who focus on regulatory reform, said they do not apply for government EJ grants at all because they assume their work would not be funded.

Jamie, an EJ staff person, lamented that the relatively "easy" projects like community gardens increasingly win grants, while activists' "harder work" of reducing contamination through legislative reform needs more funding: "There is a dire need for dollars ... so that they can do the harder work ... to be able to understand the real serious impacts from some chemicals that might be inside of their community, to be able to deal with proposed legislation." He characterized the "easier" projects—those that build parks and other environmental amenities and pursue change through educational or voluntary initiatives—as valuable complements to but not substitutes for government protections against hazards. Yet he also feels that, were his program to emphasize projects that seek government protections against industrial hazards, regulated entities and political elites might try to defund it.

CalEPA's EJ grant program shows that such pressure does not always prevent EJ staff from designing their programs in line with longstanding movement priorities. CalEPA's EJ grant program documents feature projects aimed at regulatory and policy reform and increasing public participation in environmental decision-making processes to reduce air and water pollution, exposure to pesticides and toxic chemicals, and the cumulative impacts of pollution (CalEPA 2013). Its portion of projects dedicated to hazard reduction is always high and increased from 91 percent in the first three cycles to 100 percent in the latter two cycles. Of its funded projects, 76 percent pursue change through regulatory and policy mechanisms.

Current and former CalEPA EJ grant program staff argued that the program should focus on helping residents of marginalized communities and other EJ advocates reduce environmental hazards in their communities through regulatory and policy reforms. One emphasized that he revised the request for applications (RFA) to explicitly encourage projects focused on hazard reduction. Another stated that the "most effective projects" are those that help community organizations learn how to "affect decision-making processes." Another asserted that EJ "means that we who were trained in the EJ world" play a lead role in making regulatory decisions.

CalEPA EJ staff are not entirely protected from industry pressure their peers at other agencies described. Scholars have shown that industry protection dominates CalEPA's Department of Pesticide Regulation, whose organizational mission entails maintaining the use of pesticides (Liévanos 2012; London, Sze, and Liévanos 2008). Industry actors have helped slash regulatory budgets and neuter some CalEPA EJ efforts (Harrison 2011; Liévanos 2012; London, Sze, and Liévanos 2008; London et al. 2013). However, CalEPA EJ program staff insisted that that they were able to administer the grant program with some autonomy vis-à-vis the rest of the agency. CalEPA EJ staff cited EJ *activists*—not industry—as most influential over their own ideas and the grant program. Their ability to implement a grant program consistent with activists' priorities stems in part from the fact that they share EJ activists' historic understanding of what EJ requires.

The CalEPA EJ grant program leaders' status as political appointees likely helps them defend their principles, whereas other agencies' EJ grant programs are run by career employees understandably concerned with protecting their jobs. Also, CalEPA representatives' ability to craft the grant program according to movement principles is aided by contextual factors like the California legislature's uniquely prominent and rising Latino caucus, the state's demographic transition to a majority people-of-color state, and its strong EJ and racial justice movements increasingly focused on state-level policy change (Perkins 2015). These factors help constitute the institutional environment that conditions who gets appointed, hired, and promoted in agencies, and which kinds of programs are perceived as reasonable. Yet the

San Francisco EJ grant program—which shares CalEPA's political context but diverged sharply from the CalEPA program's model of change and substantive focus—demonstrates that these institutional environmental factors do not fully determine the outcome. Rather, as I will explain, the two California programs' staff defined EJ in divergent ways—and implemented their EJ grant programs to align with those respective visions.

Some of my research participants insisted that administrative rules constrain EJ grant programs' abilities to support projects aimed at regulatory and policy reform. Specifically, state and federal laws restrict government grants from being spent on lobbying or litigation, which many EJ activists use to pursue regulatory and policy reform (CalEPA 2013, 5; EPA 2013b, 14; EPA 2015b, 8; NYSDEC 2011, 8). Additionally, the RFAs require that projects be completed and demonstrate measurable outcomes within one or two years, and most grants are quite small (CalEPA 2013, 3; EPA 2013b, 2, 5; EPA 2015b, 1; NYSDEC 2011, 9; San Francisco 2010, 1). These parameters conflict with the long-term and resource-intensive nature of policy and regulatory reform. These major restrictions and requirements apply to the CalEPA program just like the others, and yet its documents and funding patterns *do* reflect the EJ movement's model of change. Thus, other factors are at work, including, as I will show, competing ideas among EJ staff about what EJ means.

EJ as Nonregulatory Support for Environmental Amenities

My interviews with EJ grant program staff reveal that problematic patterns in agencies' EJ efforts also stem in part from the fact that some bureaucrats define EJ in ways that differ from longstanding movement priorities and design those programs accordingly. These staff expressed a similarly high commitment to EJ policy in general. However, they emphasized that the way to achieve EJ is through nonconfrontational, industry-friendly processes and building environmental amenities *rather than* regulatory restrictions on environmental hazards.

For example, Robert led the design of one of these grant programs and lamented that, when he was tasked with designing the program, EJ advocacy had "a very oppositional frame. It was *always* about stopping something, always about *defending*, about *fighting*. And I really wanted it to be propositional." He asserted that the dominant ("oppositional") approach to EJ activism focused on seeking stronger regulations on hazardous facilities, an approach he characterized as outdated, closed-minded, "limited," "laughable" in the "obvious" nature of its limitations, and lacking solutions. He viewed the grant program as an experimental way to shift EJ activism: "I was thinking about this stuff when we did the grant program in this way. I just knew that something wasn't right and that we did need to identify some level of solutions. ... I think that experiment over time—as I look at it—was the right one." Robert acknowledged that EJ activists balked at how he designed the program: "People didn't like it. ... It didn't go over too well. ... It was amazing the vitriol we received." Despite this reaction from the activist community, he designed the grant program to align with his framing of what EJ should look like. Indeed, nearly all of its funded projects pursue environmental change through charitable service provision, individual behavior modification, and green space construction—using nonregulatory means to build environmental amenities rather than (i.e., not in addition to) using regulatory protections to reduce environmental hazards. As an example of a project that exemplifies "the values that are embedded within the principles of environmental justice," he lauded a local organization that does "crowd sourcing [for] solar panels," which "allows for individual ownership [and] ... for individuals to invest whatever level of resource they want to into something they believe in." His status as a political appointee might explain his sense of freedom to design the program as he wanted despite EJ activists' backlash.

Another example is Edward, whose agency's EJ grant program was one of those that almost exclusively funded projects that boost environmental amenities (rather than reducing environmental hazards) through nonregulatory practices. Edward recounted with pride how he convinced his agency to devote a certain portion of its EJ grant funds specifically to projects that build gardens and parks ("that was my brainchild"). He explained that, whereas EJ activism tries to reduce environmental "burdens," green space projects produce "real benefits." At the time of our interview, he was working to establish a separate grant program devoted strictly to such projects and whose grants would be larger than the maximum amount currently allowed in the agency's "EJ" grants. He framed these environmental amenity projects as uniquely effective and as deserving dedicated funding, and he applied this notion when designing his agencies' grant programs.

Dan also helped run this same agency's EJ grant program for several years. Dan framed urban greening projects as epitomizing EJ, and environmental regulatory reforms as inconsistent with their grant program. He waxed at length throughout our interview about community garden projects, asserting that they enable residents to "overcome" hunger, "increase health of people," "provide cohesion within the community again," "bring contaminants out of the soil," and "help improve asthma and help take lead out of the body." He also claimed that "the crime rate dropped off precipitously" after a garden was built in a particular neighborhood and that "people are taking ownership and pride in their communities again." Certainly, community garden projects can help contribute to some of these ends, and more (Alkon 2014; Alkon and Agyeman 2011; Alkon and Norgaard 2009; Gottlieb and Joshi 2010; Mares and Peña 2010; McClintock 2014; Sbicca 2018; White 2011; Winne 2008). However, what is notable and problematic about Dan's narrative is that he asserts confidently that gardens inherently and uniquely make people healthy and neighborhoods peaceful. When I asked about grant applications that propose to organize residents to participate in regulatory decision-making, he stated that this was not the type of project his agency would fund. Yet his agency's EJ grant program technically allows such projects. His agency's problematic grant-funding patterns dovetail precisely with his and Edward's definitions of what "EJ" entails. Dan explained that he shapes the grant program funding patterns by "educating" his coworkers who review the proposals and select the winners to bring their definition of EJ into line with his own: "They had their own idea of, this is what environmental justice would be....People [staff] were like, 'Well, how is a garden going to benefit environmental justice, [which] is about environmental cleanup?' ... So, I spent a lot of time after that meeting with my reviewers, talking to them, educating them....That was a huge benefit to spreading the EJ message throughout the agency." These coworkers who review grant applications also, in turn, serve as informal EJ point persons in their own divisions, thereby further disseminating Dan's message about what EJ requires.

Susan, who administers another agency's EJ grant program, characterized a longstanding EJ organization as "another confrontation-turned-success story." She explained that the organization, which typically used confrontational tactics to publicly shame regulatory agencies and polluting industry actors, instead used its EJ grant to educate truck drivers about reducing their idling to lower diesel emissions. In Susan's account, "success" means dropping confrontational efforts to achieve regulatory protections and instead encouraging industry actors to voluntarily change their behavior. Her role here was an active one: she recounted to me that "We kept telling" the organization's director that he should propose an educational, nonconfrontational grant project—and so he did, and they funded it.

Pam, who runs one agency's EJ grant program, lauded getting community groups and industry actors to reach "consensus" about how to address the residents' environmental concerns: "Folks are collaborating and partnering. And it's not 'us or them.' It's trying to get everybody to a win-win. ... You want to just try to get a resolution that works for everybody. And so therein lies the whole notion of consensus. ... Everybody wants to live in a healthy environment. And it's trying to move some of the organizations away from communities saying [to industry], '[We want to] just shut you down.' ... Sometimes you have got to help the employer understand, 'Well, this is impacting their health.' ... And they become good neighbors. But, until you can get everybody off the gnashing and clawing ... [trails off]." By framing industry actors as simply unaware of residents' pollution concerns, "success" in terms of pacifying community anger, and all actors as wanting the same thing, Pam casts voluntary agreements as a "win-win" solution and the consensus-oriented grant program as a way to achieve it. Such arguments dovetail with claims by other staff that industry and communities want the same thing and just need to communicate, such as Lucy's arguments showcased in chapter 4.

Barbara Allen observed this same phenomenon in her research on environmental justice conflict in Louisiana's chemical corridor. Allen (2003, 96–114) describes how the Louisiana Department of Environmental Quality's (DEQ) EJ coordinator Janice Dickerson, who identified and worked as an EJ activist before being hired into the agency, insisted that EJ requires collaborating with industry and that the DEQ EJ program should focus on "empowering" residents to solve their own problems. Under Dickerson's watch, the agency's EJ program did nothing to redress chemical plant pollution and instead focused on constructing a playground, trainings residents to better protect themselves during industrial disasters, and setting up panels where residents could voice their concerns. In fact, DEQ EJ program leaders stated explicitly that residents should use the panels as a way to voice grievances "in lieu of litigation" (Ward and Dickerson 1995, 11, cited in Allen 2003, 99). They also boasted that the EJ program's actions have led to "greater understanding between community and industry" (Ward and Dickerson 1995, 12, cited in Allen 2003, 100), casting the problem as one of misunderstanding rather than a long history of industrial accidents and chemical pollution.

These narratives about what EJ requires misleadingly imply that environmental problems are not serious, industry will address communities' concerns voluntarily, and thus regulatory interventions are unnecessary. Yet such claims are often wrong, evinced not only in regulated entities' failures to comply with environmental laws and the large swaths of the United States out of compliance with air and water quality standards, but also industry actors' strident refusals to do more than is required of them. For example, Cindy, a manager of one agency's enforcement division (and someone who expressed very little support for her agency's EJ reform efforts) stated that, in regard to "bringing companies back into compliance: generally speaking, they do not want to do more than they have to. Sometimes they do, but not very often." Staff throughout various agencies emphasized this point to me, which challenges the claim that industry actors participating in collaborative EJ grant projects will voluntarily agree to reduce their emissions and otherwise be significantly better neighbors.

Even some of the EJ staff who comprehensively defined EJ as requiring both regulatory and nonregulatory mechanisms of change, as well as reducing hazards and building environmental amenities, also use some problematic narratives that hail industry-friendly approaches as the best way to pursue EJ. For example, Tom stated, "I wanted to develop a model for" solving problems in a "collaborative" way, and he applied those ideas to designing his agency's EJ grant program and other EJ efforts. He explained his goals: "A lot of the communities themselves are trapped in [thinking that] if you're talking about environmental justice, you're only talking about the regulations, or you're only talking about making the government solve the problem for us....But to a large extent, to really be transformative, you can't rely on anybody else to do it—you have got to do it yourself. Those that have succeeded are doing that." On the one hand, Tom implies that EJ entails both regulatory and nonregulatory approaches (and, to be clear, Tom's other EJ efforts at his agency support both of these). On the other hand, his statement denigrates activists who "rely on" the government to protect them and situates regulatory protections as outside the scope of "really transformative" EJ.

As another example, one longtime EJ staff person emailed me to share a blog post he had written about progress in a conflict between residents and a facility about the facility's extensive history of emitting significant amounts of toxic air pollution (including nearly half of the state's airborne mercury). The blog post noted that the facility agreed to reduce its toxic air emissions. When we met shortly thereafter, I asked how his agency got the facility to agree to reduce its emissions. He briefly replied, "We sued them" for being out of compliance. He then elaborated that, after the lawsuit settlement, he convinced the facility managers to participate in a meeting with the community residents. At the meeting, when the residents spoke about the facility, they were so upset that they cried, and he asserted that "seeing the depth of concern compelled the facility managers to change" their practices. He elaborated that the facility representatives just "didn't realize" what an effect they were having on the community, and he proclaimed that bringing industry actors and residents together "always" has such an effect. Even after acknowledging briefly—in response to my question—that the facility reduced its emissions because the agency sued it, his narrative emphasized the power of nonregulatory communication in compelling the facility representatives to have an epiphany and subsequently change their practices. He focused so fully on this narrative about what leads to material reductions in toxic hazards that he essentially ignored a very different but crucial part of the explanation: the lawsuit.

What I find problematic is the fact that some EJ staff—these agencies' internal spokespersons about what EJ means—use narratives that denigrate or dismiss the pursuit of EJ through stronger environmental regulation and that frame nonregulatory approaches to EJ policy implementation as sufficient and superior to regulatory approaches. These EJ staff members' characterizations of EJ matter. Some designed the grant programs to implement the notion that EJ should emphasize building consensus between activists and industry and to focus on building amenities rather than reducing hazards. Staff tailor their RFAs to highlight "good examples" of EJ projects and describe "successful" grant projects in outreach events and materials, which influence the types of applications they receive. Staff select reviewers to evaluate and rank the applications, and they train their reviewers to understand EJ in certain ways. Some noted that they actively encourage particular organizations to submit proposals. Some design and administer grant application workshops to educate prospective applicants about the program and how to write a strong proposal, and some design and administer training workshops for grant recipients. Some strive to get their agencies' other grant programs to adopt language cohering with their definition of what EJ requires. Moreover, many EJ grant program staff train their colleagues about EJ principles and how the agency can institutionalize them in other areas of regulatory practice, and some train their peers in other agencies about what EJ means. Through all of these means, bureaucrats' specifications of what EJ requires shape program outcomes.

EJ Activists' Definitions of EJ and Influence on Agency EJ Programs

EJ staff members' characterizations about what EJ requires reflect debates among EJ advocates who have sought to shape the design of agencies' EJ reform efforts. To demonstrate this, I draw on my interviews with several dozen leading EJ advocates who helped advise the design of agency EJ efforts, as well as my observations of these and other EJ advocates at EJ advisory committee meetings and other agency events.

The Traditional Approach: EJ Requires Combatting Hazards through Regulatory Controls

Consistent with longstanding EJ movement emphases, approximately half of the EJ activists I interviewed asserted that EJ requires principally reducing environmental hazards through regulatory and policy mechanisms.

For example, Erin, an EJ organization executive director, elaborated that the EJ movement contests mainstream environmentalists' focus on addressing environmental problems through individual behavioral change: "Environmental injustice is not caused by individual behavior. It is caused by people's lack of decision-making and stems from racial inequality and corporate power." Accordingly, her organization pursues EJ through "multiracial organizing to impact local decision-making arenas, state policy reform, increasing civic engagement on a local level, and trying to shift the voter base to be more progressive and supportive of EJ policies on a broader scale." Similarly, Jeff, the executive director of an EJ organization, argued that EJ requires "substantive outcomes" in the form of "direct emission reductions" through "chang[ing] the laws, because they don't protect people of color:" "If the laws as written aren't working for environmental justice communities, then the laws need to be changed." Another example is Sandy, the executive director of a prominent and well-regarded EJ organization whose mission statement emphasizes that their priority is stronger regulations and enforcement of polluting industries. She argued that "authentic" EJ organizations use amenities projects as "an entry point to organizing" for stronger regulations. Additionally, she dismissed as inconsistent with EJ the propensity of some organizations to provide a technical service without organizing community members toward political change: "There's plenty of people who do the lead hazard work that don't ever contact those folks again after they get their houses taken care of."

When I asked about their grant projects that deviate from this priority, many explained that they view them instrumentally—not as ends in themselves, but as ways to motivate and organize residents toward larger campaigns focused on hazard reduction and policy change. For example, Sandy noted that her organization occasionally teaches residents how to mitigate lead hazards and increase energy efficiency in their homes. She explained that such projects help residents come to view pollution reduction—including by industry—as a reasonable expectation: "We started with a household toxics program, which people would view as pretty tame. But ... it is not a big leap to, if you can do it—if you just change out everything under your sink—then what about the company down the street? Think they could do that? Why shouldn't they make that same kind of change?" She said she uses these trainings focused on individual behavior modification to recruit residents for larger campaigns focused on large-scale polluters:

> Some people just want service. They want the light bulbs. They want the lead to be out of their home. But for others, it's a way in. They just aren't going to respond to the knock at the door, saying, "We're all getting together to work on the power plant down the street, are you willing to help us?" ... [But] if one of our organizers is in their home doing the energy education, helping them do a little energy audit, helping them get changes to their home on the lead. ... That's about relationship building. And you don't get that kind of time—you get five minutes at the door, maybe, probably not—and they're sending you on your way. So, if you use it right, then I think you get more yes's than no's.

That is, while her organization's primary objective is regulatory restrictions on hazards in overburdened communities, she uses other types of projects toward achieving that end.

These advocates acknowledge the value of combining regulatory and nonregulatory approaches to improving conditions in overburdened and vulnerable communities, and to both reducing environmental hazards and boosting environmental amenities. However, they emphasize that their priority and the important contribution of the broader EJ movement is the pursuit of regulatory restrictions on environmental hazards that cluster in working-class and racially marginalized communities.

They criticized agency EJ efforts according to this priority. Another EJ organization leader, Monica, argued that "rules and regulations" are "what EJ work is all about. ... The types of activities that an environmental justice organization would be doing" include, principally, "training [communities] on government and regulatory processes." When I asked how she would judge agencies' EJ grant programs, she responded: "Are the projects eventually resulting in actual policy change? Because you have to have the policy change to get the real outcomes." Winston, another leading EJ organization's representative, critiqued agency EJ grant programs on the same grounds: "You often don't get the funding you need to change the systems the government is running."

These EJ advocates have tried to shape agencies' EJ efforts through participating in agency EJ advisory committees, speaking at public hearings, submitting letters, talking with agencies' EJ staff, and, in some cases, going to work for agencies as EJ staff themselves. As I will show, the extent to which agency EJ programs reflect these views is tempered in part by the fact that some other EJ activists advocate a different notion about what EJ requires.

Reframing: Crafting a New Common Sense about What EJ Means
The other half of the EJ activists I interviewed expressed a different, "new common sense" about what EJ means. This new common sense *disparages* the hazard reduction and regulatory approach that have long been the core of EJ advocacy and glorifies other types of activist practice as *sufficient* and *superior to* such efforts. These EJ advocates waxed enthusiastically about their efforts to build gardens, trails, and alternative energy infrastructure through charitable service provision and individual behavioral change, characterizing such work as "proactive" and "propositional," led by the "new guard," effective, and "solutions-oriented."[2] In contrast to the "two legs" perspective exemplified by Tom, many of these activists characterized the practice of fighting toxic industries and pressing for stronger environmental regulations in *pejorative* terms, as "reactive" and "oppositional," led by the "old guard," ineffective, and lacking solutions. Like Robert, quoted earlier, many lauded the movement for "evolving" *away from* the "reactive" pursuit of hazard reduction through regulatory and policy reform and *toward* the construction of environmental amenities through nonregulatory means. By holding leadership roles in their own organizations and regional EJ alliances, they directly shape movement framing. Moreover, by informing—and in some cases directly running—agency EJ programs, these activists shape agencies'

EJ policy implementation efforts. Their disparagements of traditional EJ movement approaches to addressing environmental inequalities legitimize some of the problematic trends I identified in agencies' EJ programs.

These narratives were not limited to EJ activists positioned within the agencies like Robert, quoted earlier in this chapter. Stacy, who heads a statewide "EJ Alliance" and leads discussions about explicitly "reframing" EJ activism among her member organizations, similarly argued that the EJ movement should make a "proactive" turn toward focusing on constructing environmental amenities. Her statements are striking not for the projects she advocates, as they are among the outcomes EJ activists have long supported. Rather, what is remarkable is her implicit *disparagement* of EJ activism focused on reducing hazards through regulatory and policy protections. Her brief references to the need for increased regulatory enforcement were dwarfed by her extensive characterizations of the EJ movement's traditional focus on fighting hazardous industry as outdated and lacking solutions. She argued for EJ activism to be "more sophisticated," "start being more solution-oriented," and "actually create solutions"—"versus just fighting with regulatory agencies about how much they do or don't enforce certain rules." She advocated a "proactive" shift in EJ activism, which she explained means "bringing things in" to communities, including renewable energy systems, green spaces, mixed-use urban development, and green jobs. She presented this "new" approach to EJ as enlightened and innovative compared to older, "reactive" EJ: "A lot of groups have really gone to another level. ... Obviously, those specific site battles are in many ways the foundation and the cornerstone of a lot of EJ work. But ... we are also trying to move away from that particular model of organizing and working. ... We are just really trying to have a different framing on our work. ... A proactive framing around all the things that we're trying to bring into these communities to transform them." She advocates this reframing of EJ because "I got tired of people being passive. ... Somebody has to step up and have some initiative and innovation around environmental justice." Stacy's narratives influence other activists and the broader discourse about what constitutes appropriate "EJ" practice. Her status as a leader in the movement's framing efforts was revealed throughout my fieldwork, as other EJ activists characterized her coalition as playing a key role in advocating the "new" style of EJ. To be clear, my concern is with the *discourse* she used. In fact, her organization's activities include efforts to strengthen environmental regulations. Yet her narrative tells a different story about what EJ requires—one that denigrates the pursuit of regulatory restrictions on environmental hazards as passé and ineffective.

Matt, the executive director of an EJ organization and self-identified EJ leader in his region, employed similar rhetoric. He argued that community organizing to redistribute political power and press for policy change is outdated: "It's not the 1960s Chicago any more.... We need to modernize the Alinsky model." Instead, he hailed the pursuit of change through entrepreneurialism and constructing green spaces as "the new model of EJ." He described a local organization that trains immigrants in small business development and builds parks in immigrant communities as "*the thing when it comes to EJ*" and "*the new model*" of EJ because it "*has a self-perpetuating business model.*" Matt actively informs broader discourse around what EJ means, both among activists and bureaucrats. He helped spearhead the government EJ efforts in his state, including an EJ advisory committee that serves the governor and agencies. U.S. EPA has actively endorsed his approach, presenting Matt's organization with an Environmental Justice National Achievement Award.

Other EJ advocates more explicitly expressed disdain for activism fighting environmental hazards through regulatory and policy protections. When describing her recent focus on river restoration, Katherine noted how her own definition of EJ has changed over time away from "EJ in the traditional format," a term she used to refer to advocacy for state-mandated pollution reduction. She used to engage in such practices but now views them as "passive" and having "no outcome." Katherine emphatically criticized activists demanding the state reduce pollution as foolish and ineffective—as "too busy fighting this phantom they can't identify, rather than going out and saying, 'Hey, let me see what I can do to make this *better.*'" She asserts that she has "evolved" to organizing outdoor activities and getting volunteers to remove garbage and invasive plants, practices she hails as effective and "active": "The tire cleanups: it gets folks in touch with the river.... You feel like you are doing something.... You're going to improve the environment with *active* kinds of initiatives, and that's what we do.... Then, it was fighting people. Now, it's fighting *for* something." That is, she dismisses the "traditional EJ" pursuit of pollution reduction through state protections as "passive" and lacking solutions and instead hails other activities as uniquely able to accomplish change.

While my data do not allow me to determine how pervasive these claims are among EJ activists in general, I can say that they were expressed by many of the prominent EJ activists I interviewed who helped advise the design of agency EJ grant programs. Additionally, several other scholars show that some EJ organizations have moved away from fighting for stronger environmental regulations and in some cases use "new common sense" rhetoric that naturalizes the neoliberal shift in activism (Carter 2016; Ottinger 2013; Perkins 2015).[3]

Reframing "EJ" as not requiring hazard reduction or regulatory reform enables organizations that have historically eschewed the EJ movement to cast themselves as part of it, in turn reinforcing the new common sense about what constitutes "EJ." For example, Chris identifies as an EJ advocate and helps lead a citywide EJ forum, although the organization for which he is the executive director is generally regarded as a mainstream (not EJ) environmental nonprofit. His organization's board of directors insists that the organization focus on expanding access to parks, gardens, trails, energy-efficient household appliances, and other environmental amenities through individual behavioral modification and providing resources and services. The board has historically refused to identify as an "EJ" organization, which it perceived as "out picketing a waste dump." Chris hailed his organization's approach, characterizing "working on the benefits side" as "really solving an EJ problem." Recently, he convinced his board that the organization's work "*is* EJ" by framing their work as "the benefits side of EJ." The board "likes that" framing—and now openly identifies the organization as part of the EJ movement.

Russ, a New York activist who runs a longstanding community garden organization, praised New York's EJ grant program funding patterns by disparaging activism that pursues environmental change through regulatory mechanisms. He asserted that his organization does EJ work, but he distances himself from other EJ advocacy by refusing to use the label—"It is totally EJ work, but we don't call it EJ work"—because, he claims, that phrase would not resonate with community gardeners. Russ's effusive praise for the work of "these people" who work in gardens contrasted strikingly from the dismissive tone with which he described "EJ campaign-type work":

> The people we are working with, they woke up one day, and they decided, "I'm going to do that really hard work of rolling up my sleeves and cleaning out that lot." These people are more practical, more A-B-C-D, more roll-up-your-sleeve

types than the person that goes to City Hall and holds protests and demands that they do something. The people that we work with are a lot more about *doing* something.... One thing that makes these community gardens so attractive is that all of these government programs have come and gone, and people think, here we are still with all these problems.... But when the garden project is done, you can *touch* and *feel* that something has been done, that capacity has been built, that something is better and will keep getting better. But with the campaign-type work, people see that some organization got the money, and then there is nothing to show for it.

His narrative wholly discounts "EJ campaigns" and "government programs" as ineffective and disappointing. In contrast, it frames residents' garden labor as productive, fostering hope, and building capacity. As a result, he hailed the New York EJ grant program for funding the type of EJ work he characterized as so valuable: "That these programs allow for garden projects that weren't serious EJ campaigns is a really good thing.... What's great about these programs is that, even though we don't call our work 'EJ,' we have been able to take advantage of the grants anyway."

Numerous activists insisted to me that *any* project within overburdened and vulnerable communities counts as "EJ." This argument was made to me, for example, by the executive director of a nonprofit organization that recruits children in overburdened and vulnerable communities to pick up trash in their neighborhoods—despite the fact that her organization does no work to reduce serious environmental hazards or democratize environmental regulatory decision-making processes.

The new common sense problematically dismisses the crucial role of strong environmental regulations in providing protections that industry and the public will not and cannot do. These findings raise troubling questions about the future of the EJ movement, particularly whether it will continue to fight for stronger regulatory protections for our nation's most vulnerable communities. Ironically, the new common sense narrative echoes earlier neoliberal rhetoric that EJ advocates so strongly (and rightly) denounced. For example, in the U.S. EPA's Common Sense Initiative during the 1990s, industry representatives, labor unions, and mainstream environmentalists explicitly derided environmental regulations as ineffective and stifling innovation, collectively identified ways to address key environmental problems through voluntary and market-based mechanisms and not through regulation, and framed this neoliberal shift as the "next generation of environmental protection" (EPA 1996). Although EJ advocates rejected this initiative at the time, my findings here suggest that this approach eventually gained traction among some key EJ advocates, who are drifting from longstanding tenets of environmental justice.

To be clear, many EJ leaders reject the new common sense narrative about what EJ requires. For example, after I described my findings to Barry, a prominent EJ leader in our interview, he followed up via email: "I don't think working collaboratively with polluters and government agencies ... is environmental justice at all. And I reject the terminology calling this approach 'new' EJ. That is a sad, sad commentary for those who think fighting polluters and standing in solidarity is passé and 'old guard.'" Framing advocacy for state-mandated pollution reduction as lacking solutions dismisses its outcomes: securing protections against toxins and other hazards. The valorization of entrepreneurial practice and behavioral-based change, and framing EJ as inherent in environmental amenity projects, makes residents responsible for their own contaminated environments, fails to hold industry and the state accountable, and fails to address the serious environmental hazards harming human health.

Although problematic and contested, the new common sense framing about what constitutes good EJ practice shapes agencies' EJ programs. As noted, some activists directly applied this notion of EJ when hired to design agency grant programs. For example, Robert, quoted earlier in this chapter, was an EJ activist before being appointed to lead the design of his agency's EJ grant program, and he intentionally crafted the program to compel the movement to, in his words, "evolve" toward "proactive" practices. Despite the "vitriol" he received for doing so—which signaled how much other EJ activists disagreed with his priorities—he proceeded in his efforts. He continues to advocate this new common sense about EJ. Since departing the agency, Robert has joined a leading and longstanding EJ organization, advocating these ideas in that capacity and within the regional EJ coalition of which his organization is a prominent member.

Other agency staff sympathetic to the movement emphasized that activists shape agency EJ program implementation. Mandy, a representative of one agency's EJ grant program, noted, "We don't promote one thing or another. We look at what the community wants." Brian explained that he revised his agency's EJ grant program RFA according to feedback from EJ activists: "I reached out. I have 100 people.... I just polled them. It's all EJ people. 'These are the goals we are considering. Rank them up.' ... I went with their recommendations." This is not problematic practice—agency EJ efforts *should* heed activist advice. Rather, it shows that agencies' EJ programs are shaped in part by activists' arguments. Indeed, EJ staff described learning from EJ activists through conversation, news stories, academic literature, EJ advisory groups, and grant applications. For example, Dan, the EJ grant program manager I quoted earlier in this chapter for elaborating his enthusiasm for community gardens and framing regulatory reform as inconsistent with his grant program, told me that reading the "EJ literature" and the grant proposals taught him that food access is a "bigger problem in these communities than environmental pollution is." Without a doubt, millions of people in the United States suffer from chronic food insecurity and the many problems it creates. I do not dispute this. What I find striking about Dan's narrative is his reading of these advocates' arguments—namely, that environmental pollution is not an issue the agency needs to prioritize.

Popularizing the New Common Sense

The new common sense is popularized by some charismatic, media-savvy champions of environmental activism in working-class communities of color. Notable are Van Jones, advisor to President Obama on climate change, and Majora Carter, MacArthur Award-winning "eco-entrepreneurship" advocate (TEDxMidwest 2010), who together established the organization Green for All.

In his best-selling book, *The Green Collar Economy* (2008), Jones elaborates Green for All's vision for "solving the two biggest issues facing the country today—the economy and the environment" (back cover). Specifically, he hails green entrepreneurialism and individual behavior modification, and he disparages activism that critically confronts industry and regulatory agencies as "reactive," "oppositional," "negative," "demanding," and lacking solutions. His name came up in many of my interviews with California EJ activists, some even referring to him simply as "Van," indicating their personal familiarity with him given his history of work there. While some expressed misgivings about his advocacy, others valorized it. Many EJ leaders use the same narratives that permeate his writing, giving a cursory nod to regulatory and policy reform (or disparaging it) and emphatically advocating a "new" "proactive," "positive," "solutions-oriented," and "propositional" style of EJ activism that frames regulatory approaches to change and hazard reduction as outdated.

In New York City, Majora Carter founded Sustainable South Bronx "to promote environmental justice" (SSB 2015), won a prestigious MacArthur Foundation award for her advocacy, and was hailed by the *New York Times* as "one of the city's best-known advocates for environmental justice" (December 14, 2008). Placing particular emphasis on exercise, healthy eating, urban agriculture, green entrepreneurialism, and green jobs, she has helped to shape EJ activism and agency programs in that region and legitimize such practices as emblematic of "EJ."

Some scholars repeat and legitimize this narrative. For example, in a study of EJ activism in Los Angeles, Eric Carter (2016) characterizes the "earlier generation" of "reactive" EJ advocacy fighting "hazards as they develop" as "EJ 1.0." He distinguishes this from "EJ 2.0," which is comprised of groups "taking a more proactive approach to restoring nature and producing new environmental 'goods' in the city" and foregrounding diet and exercise education (5). Carter briefly acknowledges, "it is fair to ask whether EJ 2.0 contributes to social and environmental justice goals" (20). However, his characterizations of "the transition from EJ 1.0 to EJ 2.0" and his unsubstantiated assertion that "childhood obesity and its associated health effects, such as diabetes, represent a more persistent and widespread threat to the Latino community than toxins in the environment" (6) disparage activists' fights against hazards as outdated and unnecessary and frame the movement as productively evolving away from such work.[4] Such narratives help popularize the new common sense about what EJ means, thus indirectly legitimizing agency EJ efforts cohering with that new vision.

The popularity of gardens and other urban greening efforts cannot be overstated. Journalists, scholars, and bloggers write innumerable news stories, dissertations, and other reports about them, hailing them as able to solve an extensive array of problems facing working-class, urban communities. Popularizing the new common sense helps determine what is politically possible, shaping the discourse and decision-making of grant program administrators.

I want to be clear about my concern. Community gardens certainly produce some fresh produce in areas that are underserved by grocery stores. Also, like parks, trails, tree plantings, and other environmental amenity projects, they provide new opportunities for play and exercise, create green spaces many residents welcome and value, are often conducted in ways that foster youth leadership development and civic engagement, and can be important sites for enacting and redefining cultural identity (Alkon 2014; Alkon and Agyeman 2011; Alkon and Norgaard 2009; Gottlieb and Joshi 2010; Mares and Peña 2010; McClintock 2014; Sbicca 2018; Washington 2008; White 2011; Winne 2008). Other benefits attributed to them—such as significantly reducing food insecurity and crime—are empirical questions that deserve investigation. However, these projects cannot accomplish everything, and yet they are widely framed as doing so. Significant environmental hazards harm the health of residents in overburdened and vulnerable communities and must be addressed directly. For these protections to be guaranteed for residents, they must be secured through regulatory restrictions on hazardous activities and chemicals. Instead, environmental amenity projects are often promoted with unsubstantiated, sweeping claims that regulatory restrictions on environmental hazards are now *unnecessary*.

Structural Drivers of Neoliberal EJ Advocacy

The shift among some EJ advocates toward a more industry-friendly, nonregulatory version of EJ parallels the neoliberal shift within the broader environmental movement (Faber 2008; Guthman 2008a, 2011; Harrison 2008, 2011, 2014, 2017; Heynen et al. 2007; Lockie 2013; Park and Pellow 2011). As EJ advocates explained to me and as scholars have documented, numerous structural factors compel EJ activists to shift their practices in these ways.

EJ advocacy has long been among the most underfunded social movements in the United States, receiving under 1 percent of all charitable foundation environmental grant funding (Faber and McCarthy 2001, i). In recent years, philanthropic foundations have shifted their environmental funding priorities away from regulatory and policy reform, litigation, and other practices that have long constituted the core of EJ advocacy (Brulle and Jenkins 2005; Faber and McCarthy 2001; Guthman 2008b; Hansen 2012). Thus, activists increasingly engage in the practices that foundations will fund.

Also, advocates have dropped some of their involvement in regulatory and policy reform because accomplishing such goals has become exceedingly difficult in recent decades, as elected officials supporting industry interests have fought environmental regulations (Carter 2016; Perkins 2015). In this context, EJ and other environmental activists feel compelled to pursue environmental improvements through other mechanisms of change. Scholars have documented that EJ advocacy for stronger environmental regulations and policies is made difficult by industry actors' and conservative elected officials' propensity to publicly disparage proposed environmental policies as "job killers." Industry actors use public relations firms and phony "community" or "environmental" organizations to tout industry products as safe and hail the purported benefits they bring to communities (Faber 2008).

Scholars have also shown how neoliberal rollback has undermined community support for advocates critical of industry. For example, Stephanie Malin (2015) shows that neoliberal deregulation compelled working-class, rural, white communities in Utah and Colorado to champion the revival of uranium mining and milling in their areas, and to disparage activists fighting against these facilities that pose grave risks to human health and bring only uneven and temporary economic benefits. As health care, labor protections, and other elements of the social safety net have been eviscerated in recent decades, mining and milling companies build public support by promising jobs and presenting themselves as moral actors providing much-needed social services. Gwen Ottinger (2013) shows how similar dynamics undermined EJ advocacy against petrochemical facilities in Louisiana's Mississippi River corridor. Industry engineers defined the conversation about chemical facility safety in terms of responsible choice—framing themselves as responsible, enterprising individuals who choose to live and work near the plants and framing other residents' health problems as stemming from irresponsible individual behavioral choices like smoking, diet, and exercise. In so doing, they obscure the scientific uncertainties about chemical plant safety. At the same time, regulatory rollback and declining funds for basic social services created among residents a "need to be entrepreneurial" (95)—a need to seek industry investments into basic community development projects and to make their neighborhoods attractive to upwardly mobile prospective home buyers. Many residents thus pushed for a friendly partnership with industry to fund neighborhood beautification projects and rejected EJ activists' criticisms of the town as "unlivable."

The "new common sense" narrative about EJ may reflect not only activists' need to strategically reorient their priorities within the neoliberal political economic context, but also their *internalization* of neoliberal ideas about what good citizenship looks like. In the context of deregulation, industry hostility to environmental regulations, and declining foundation support for advocacy aimed at regulatory reform, scholars have argued that people have come to adopt and internalize neoliberal ideas about what constitutes responsible citizenship. Drawing on social theorist Michel Foucault, they characterize this as neoliberal subjectivity or "governmentality," the increasingly widespread belief that responsibility for care rests not in the public sphere of state-protected rights, but instead in the private sphere in which individuals are responsible for their own well-being (Dean 1999; Guthman 2011; Jessop 2002; Rose 1999). Scholars have demonstrated various ways in which neoliberal governmentality manifests and its problematic implications. For example, numerous scholars demonstrate the rise of neoliberal governmentality in the realm of health politics in general and public concern about obesity in particular (Biltekoff 2013; Bobrow-Strain 2012; DuPuis 2007; Guthman 2011). They show how medical professionals, alternative food advocates, and the public alike have become preoccupied with addressing public health not through stronger environmental regulations and securing the public's right to health care but instead through shaming individuals to be more "responsible" citizens through weight loss, diet reform, exercise, growing their own food, and other individual behavioral changes. They attribute this both to neoliberal political economic pressures and accompanying neoliberal notions of individualized responsible citizenship (as well as classist, sexist, racist, sizeist, and other discriminatory norms). The new common sense about EJ may be an expression of neoliberal subjectivity. In contrast to EJ staff who lamented having to neuter their EJ programs to protect them from hostile attack by industry and conservative elected officials (as I described in chapter 3), Robert and other "new common sense" EJ staff did not convey a sense of conflicting institutional demands. Rather, they appear to conceptualize EJ in ways that align with the ideology pushed by conservative elites and thus feel able to implement EJ policy in line with their beliefs.

Conclusion

I have shown in this chapter that government agencies' EJ efforts are shaped in part by how EJ staff define what "EJ" means. Some EJ staff frame EJ in ways that are consistent with longstanding EJ movement priorities: as requiring the pursuit of regulatory restrictions on environmental hazards, in addition to partnerships with other actors to help build environmental amenities and revitalize overburdened and vulnerable communities. Of these staff, some work in a context that allows them to craft EJ programs that align with this full scope of ideals. Others feel that pressure from industry actors and elected officials hostile to environmental regulations is so great that they cannot always design EJ programs in accord with this notion.

Other EJ staff characterize EJ quite differently: as epitomized by nonregulatory projects that create environmental amenities *instead of* regulatory restrictions on environmental hazards. These staff designed their agencies' EJ grant programs and other EJ efforts accordingly. Because the nonregulatory nature of this definition coheres with the interests of elites who control agencies' resources and priorities, these EJ staff described little resistance putting it into practice.

The notion of EJ wielded by this latter group of EJ staff in part reflects the efforts of some EJ leaders to craft *a new common sense* about what EJ means. These advocates dismiss the pursuit of hazard reduction through regulatory and policy reform as ineffective and outdated, other mechanisms of change and substantive foci as enlightened and uniquely efficacious, and the movement as progressively evolving in these ways. To the dismay of many other EJ advocates, those endorsing the new common sense about EJ strive to change public opinion about what constitutes good EJ practice and to directly shape the design of agency EJ programs. Some influence agency EJ efforts by acquiring EJ staff positions and directly designing EJ programs to accord with this framing of EJ. In other cases, they influence agency EJ staff through expressing this characterization of EJ in their grant applications, publications, and communications with staff. This helps explain why some agencies' EJ grant program outcomes and other EJ efforts reflect this "new common sense" nonregulatory model of change and, increasingly, its substantive focus on amenities rather than hazard reduction.

Numerous factors help explain this shift among some EJ advocates, which parallels the shift occurring in the broader environmental movement. Charitable foundation funding for policy and regulatory reform advocacy has declined substantially. Regulatory and policy reform work has become extremely protracted and costly as antiregulatory elites increasingly control the political process. In the wake of deregulation, some communities feel that they must court industry actors rather than challenge them. Also, some EJ staff and EJ advocates may have internalized neoliberal ideologies. Building on others' findings that EJ advocacy has been pushed in increasingly conservative directions, I have shown how some EJ activists discursively perpetuate that narrowing.

Notwithstanding these structural pressures and the valuable roles that nonregulatory practices and the development of environmental amenities can play in improving conditions in overburdened communities, the so-called new common sense has problematic consequences. Among other things, it disparages the regulatory reforms needed to reduce hazards in overburdened communities, and it misleadingly implies that all environmental problems can be resolved through asking residents to change their own consumption practices or industry actors to simply be better neighbors. These apparent factions within the EJ movement deserve more critical attention. If building parks and gardens and modifying residents' lifestyles are replacing rather than augmenting state-mandated hazard reduction, this discursive shift might signal not an *expansion* of the movement but instead its *derailment* from what distinguished it in important ways from mainstream environmentalism in the first place. As such, its influence on agencies' EJ efforts might pull the latter further away from what is needed most: regulatory restrictions on the numerous environmental hazards that harm the health of residents in America's most overburdened and vulnerable communities, and over which they have little responsibility or power.

8 Conclusion

In the post-2016 era, pushing forward with a civil rights strategy to achieve environmental justice may seem pie-in-the-sky, particularly given reliance on federal agencies for enforcement. Yet this is a long-term fight, one that begins with an understanding that in the environmental context, decision-makers must be accountable for discrimination on the basis of race and ethnicity.
—Marianne Engelman Lado (2017, 94)

Taking Stock

Our environmental laws, regulations, and enforcement have improved air and water quality, reduced the number of deadly industrial accidents, and made food and other products safer for consumers. Their staff widely express dedication to public service and environmental protection. Yet, at the same time, environmental inequalities persist. Racially marginalized, working-class, and Indigenous communities continue to face environmental harms that wealthier, white Americans do not. Many agencies have taken valuable steps toward improving environmental conditions in overburdened and vulnerable communities. Yet, notwithstanding these efforts, substantial evidence shows that environmental justice requires our government's attention now as much as ever before.

We can see both this progress and its shortcomings in agencies' recently announced EJ accomplishments. Take, for example, U.S. EPA's 2018 resolution of a Title VI complaint submitted on behalf of residents sickened by and fed up with hog-farming waste in North Carolina. For over two decades, as hog farms in the southeastern United States have ballooned in size, their operators have stored hog feces in open-air "lagoons" and sprayed the waste onto fields (Hellerstein and Fine 2017). The stomach-turning stench extends for miles and makes being outdoors unbearable for nearby residents, most of whom are low-income persons of color who do not benefit from these facilities. Moreover, the waste spreads pollutants—including antibiotic-resistant bacteria—into the air and local creeks (Hatcher et al. 2017; Wilson et al. 2002; Wing and Wolf 2000). For years, residents, EJ scholars, and journalists researched and documented these hazards and agencies' failure to address them, while industry actors have intimidated and threatened those who challenge their practices (Hellerstein and Fine 2017). In 2014, nonprofit organizations North Carolina Environmental Justice Network (NCEJN), Rural Empowerment Association for Community Help (REACH), and Waterkeeper Alliance, Inc. filed a Title VI administrative complaint with EPA, alleging that North Carolina Department of Environmental Quality (NCDEQ) violated Title VI of the Civil Rights Act by permitting hog farm waste disposal practices that disproportionately harm black, Latino/a, and Native American residents and allowing industry actors to intimidate residents concerned about the waste. In May 2018, the complainants and NCDEQ reached a settlement agreement through U.S. EPA's mediated alternative dispute resolution process, and, in response, U.S. EPA closed the administrative complaint (EPA 2018c). In some ways, this story can be read as an accomplishment. The relatively quick resolution of the complaint demonstrates EPA's promise to speed up its shamefully inactive Title VI complaint resolution process. Some community advocates involved celebrated the agreement. For example, when announcing the agreement at a REACH meeting, co-founder Devon Hall declared, "We should celebrate our victories. Even those that may appear to be small. This is no a small matter here, trust me" (Clabby 2018). But others were less enthusiastic. Resident Elsie Herring, who has long challenged the hog industry's waste disposal practices, observed at that meeting, "Seems like we're doing the same thing over and over again. And there is no resolution" (Clabby 2018). Indeed, the agreement specifies that NCDEQ will monitor air and water quality, conduct EJ analyses, comply with civil rights law, and engage more with residents and EJ advocates. While these actions ultimately may help justify restrictions on hog waste in the future, for now they do nothing to reduce hazards harming these residents' health and quality of life. Such examples illustrate that we need to evaluate agencies' accomplishments in light of their broader context. Hall is absolutely right to celebrate even the small victories, but agencies still need to do much better.

Agencies' declarations about changes in regional air pollution similarly illustrate that their declared progress toward environmental justice can obscure continuing environmental injustices. For example, U.S. EPA's *Environmental Justice FY2017 Progress Report* details many agency efforts to improve conditions in overburdened and vulnerable communities (EPA 2018d). The first accomplishment showcased in EPA's press release about the report—at the top of the report's executive summary, and up front in the main text—is the agency's finding that the proportion of low-income people living in areas that meet National Ambient Air Quality Standards (NAAQS) for particulate matter under 2.5 microns in size (commonly known as PM 2.5) increased from 43 percent in 2006–2008 to 92 percent in 2014–2016 (EPA 2018d, 5, 8–10; EPA 2018e). In other words, a greater percentage of low-income Americans live in areas that meet the regulatory standard for this deadly form of air pollution that contributes to asthma, heart attacks, and other heart and lung diseases. This marks important progress toward environmental justice. The fact that EPA is tracking its progress is laudable, as are EPA regulatory efforts that pushed more regions to comply with NAAQS. Yet the report does not address other ways we might gauge the agency's progress on EJ in relation to PM 2.5. To that point, shortly before EPA announced its report, an article published in the *American Journal of Public Health* (Mikati et al. 2018) showed that people living in poverty and people of color are exposed to considerably higher amounts of PM 2.5 pollution compared to the general population. Notably, it showed that black Americans are exposed to 54 percent more PM 2.5 than the broader population. The authors, all EPA researchers, emphasize these racial disparities: "Disparities for Blacks are more pronounced than are disparities on the basis of poverty status," and "a focus on poverty to the exclusion of race may be insufficient to meet the needs of all burdened populations" (e1, e6). Mikati and colleagues' findings do not contradict those in EPA's report. Rather, they remind us that improving in some metrics in the pursuit of environmental justice does not absolve agencies of the responsibility to track, report on, and improve their progress on others. To meaningfully support environmental justice, much more needs to be done.

The EJ movement has fought to bring environmental injustices like these to light, and many state and federal environmental regulatory agencies have responded by passing EJ policies and developing EJ programs. I write this book in 2018, the 25th anniversary of U.S. EPA's Office of Environmental Justice. Such milestones offer an opportunity to take stock. In these two and a half decades, how well have government agencies institutionalized the principles of the EJ movement? What challenges face such efforts? As I showed in chapter 2, some agencies have done much to support EJ. These accomplishments reflect years of hard work by EJ activists and some agency staff, have undoubtedly improved conditions in some communities, and constitute models for change that can inform efforts to institutionalize EJ reforms throughout agency practice. Yet, taken as a whole, environmental regulatory agencies' EJ efforts nevertheless fall short of meeting key tenets of EJ advocacy. Government decision-making has yet to be restructured in ways that would substantially, systematically reduce environmental inequalities, and major environmental inequalities persist (Bullock, Ard, and Saalman 2018; Konisky 2009; Konisky and Reenock 2015). This book shines new light on why environmental regulatory agencies have displayed this organizational inertia in the face of calls for regulatory reform from EJ activists and the hard work of EJ-supportive staff.

Main Argument and Theoretical Contributions

Like so many other socio-environmental problems, agencies' disappointing progress on EJ reforms is caused by many factors. As other EJ scholars have shown, government agencies' EJ efforts are stymied by *material* elements of agencies' organizational fields that are beyond the control of agency staff and managers: limited resources, regulatory authority, and analytical tools, as well as leaders' priorities that shift with changes in administration. These explanations mirror the "standard narrative" circulating within regulatory agencies. In chapter 3, I showed how these factors hinder the integration of EJ principles into regulatory practice. Yet, I also demonstrated that agencies can do more than they currently are to integrate EJ tenets into regulatory practice. Something else is going on.

Through interviewing and observing agency staff as they discussed potential EJ reforms, I found that the standard narrative is a valid but incomplete set of explanations, and that the slow pace of EJ policy implementation stems also from the ways bureaucrats themselves define their responsibilities and respond to EJ staff members' proposals for change. I showed in this book that *cultural* elements of agencies' organizational fields—specifically, institutional logics about environmental regulatory agencies' goals, priorities, and effectiveness—compel some staff to engage in practices that undermine the efforts of agencies' EJ staff and their EJ-supportive coworkers. The disappointing pace of agencies' EJ efforts stems not only from hostile acts of conservative political elites and industry pressure to deregulate, but also from elements of regulatory culture that transcend changes in leadership.

As I detailed in chapter 4, some staff resist EJ reforms discursively in meetings and private conversations, defining "EJ" as outside the scope of what these institutions are and do. Some staff outright reject proposed EJ reforms as irreconcilable with the agency's identity. In particular, they invoke colorblind racial ideology dominant in U.S. society by asserting that the race-conscious nature of EJ reforms violates what it means for government agencies to be impartial. Staff also disparage EJ reforms by using prejudiced arguments that working-class and racially marginalized communities targeted by EJ programs are undeserving of them, and by asserting that environmental inequalities are not serious, that the agencies' decision-making processes already align with EJ principles, and that limited resources and regulatory authority preclude discussion or implementation of EJ reforms. Throughout, I showed how these various practices undermine the efforts of agencies' EJ staff.

In chapter 5, I detailed how bureaucrats' resistance to EJ reforms manifests in other ways as well. EJ staff asserted that most coworkers ignore EJ staff members' recommendations or implement them only superficially. Staff fail to hold their own subordinates accountable for implementing EJ reforms, exclude EJ staff from pertinent communications, and surveil and restrict EJ staff who work with community groups. Occasionally, bureaucrats formally sanction EJ staff for working to redress environmental injustices and informally bully EJ staff because of their EJ work. Certainly, not all staff engage in these practices I described in chapters 4 and 5. However, enough do to stymie and derail EJ staff.

In chapter 6, I offered numerous explanations for the problematic practices I detailed in the two preceding chapters, highlighting dominant institutional logics within environmental regulatory agencies that compel staff to resist proposed EJ reforms. Specifically, I argued that bureaucrats' resistance to EJ reforms can stem from their primary forms of academic training, common personality traits among staff, ideas about expertise, professional commitments, lack of life experience with oppression and/or environmental harm, beliefs about government neutrality and racial inequality, racist prejudice, and ideas about what justice requires of government institutions. In other words, they resist EJ reforms for a lot of reasons. Among these is the same reason that so many of them resent and even protest the Trump administration: EJ reforms and antiregulatory elites alike challenge and threaten a system that staff feel is effective and that they are proud of and committed to. The point is that this pride cuts in multiple directions: it compels staff to make sacrifices for their work and to persevere under adverse circumstances—but also compels some to reject EJ reforms as violating their organization's identity.

In chapters 4, 5, and 6, I showcased the strategies that EJ staff and their EJ-supportive coworkers use to manage this resistance. Some foster EJ reforms by circumventing those who resist it, cultivating a "coalition of the willing" and often working under the radar. Some directly challenge their coworkers' resistance, such as by vocally framing EJ as consistent with the agency's mission, using EJ maps and other devices to show that racial environmental inequalities are real and significant, and telling stories about inspiring cases of transformative improvements in overburdened and vulnerable communities. These staff seek to change not only daily practices but also their coworkers' sense of organizational identity, through the practices listed previously and also by training coworkers in EJ and other anti-racist principles, forming committees of EJ-supportive staff who can develop EJ reforms, recruiting EJ activists into the agencies, advocating for more diversity in hiring, and supporting junior colleagues who advocate for EJ reforms. They aim to build a culture of support for EJ across their organizations because EJ staff are not numerous enough to do all the work required for institutionalizing EJ. To be sure, some EJ programs can be run by just a few people—agencies' EJ grant programs are a notable example. But other EJ reforms include changing the way agencies' core regulatory work is done and thus require most staff to adjust their daily work practices.

With support from some coworkers, EJ staff are fighting for change *from the inside out*. Tending to identify as part of the EJ movement or at least as strong supporters of it, EJ staff can thus be understood as activists working within these agencies. Like the "insider activists" and "tempered radicals" striving to change organization practice in accordance with movement principles in other contexts (Banaszak 2005; Espeland 1998; Frickel 2004a,b; Katzenstein 1999; Kellogg 2011, 2014; King and Pearce 2010; Meyerson and Scully 1995; Santoro and McGuire 1997; Soule 2012), EJ staff occupy a difficult liminal status. In some ways they are simultaneously bureaucrats and activists. However, they are challenged by their own supervisors and colleagues for being too close to community members, and by some residents for being a member of a government institution that has failed to protect them.

In chapter 7, I shifted my focus to EJ staff themselves, demonstrating that some EJ staff have intentionally designed EJ programs that deviate from longstanding priorities of the EJ movement. On the one hand, many EJ staff define "EJ" as EJ activists have historically done: as requiring regulatory restrictions on environmental hazards. They treat other substantive foci (such as building green spaces and other environmental amenities) and mechanisms of change (such as educating residents about healthy lifestyles and urging industry actors to voluntarily improve their practices) as consistent with EJ but secondary to and unable to replace regulatory restrictions on environmental hazards. They strive to design and implement EJ programs that accord with that vision. On the other hand, some agencies' EJ staff depict what EJ requires in quite different ways. Specifically, they characterize EJ as epitomized by the fostering of environmental amenities through industry-friendly, nonregulatory means, *instead of* regulatory reforms on environmental hazards. I showed that staff wielding such notions designed some of their agencies' EJ grant programs and other EJ efforts to align with this framing of what EJ means and requires. Because the nonregulatory nature of this definition coheres with the ideas of elites who shape the agencies' resources and priorities, EJ staff generally feel empowered to put it into practice. Their claims about EJ reflect the efforts of some EJ leaders influential in the activist and agency arenas to craft *a new common sense* about what EJ means.

In sum, various institutional logics compel staff to resist proposed EJ reforms that align with longstanding EJ movement principles, in turn reinforcing regulatory practice that fails to protect America's most vulnerable and environmentally burdened communities. The standard narrative obscures these elements of regulatory culture, writing them out of the story about what kinds of factors shape regulatory outcomes.

The ideas, discourses, and other practices I described in this book constitute part of the structures of oppression that produce environmental injustice. This book shows how they manifest within government agencies. Some of the cultural dynamics I highlight may be unique to regulatory agencies. Others are not; in particular, this study shows how staff wield racial narratives institutionalized throughout U.S. society in ways that buttress existing organizational practice that more effectively protects white, middle-class, and affluent neighborhoods than communities of color. This is the case even in states regarded as racially progressive. These findings show what kinds of problematic work these racial narratives do and how imperative it is that we call out and challenge such claims.

These elements of regulatory culture function together with the material factors other scholars have emphasized and that I detailed in chapter 3. Bureaucrats' discursive and other practices that undercut EJ staff are acceptable in a context in which agencies are besieged by budget cuts and industry lawsuits, legal experts debate the regulatory authority to implement various proposed EJ reforms, and the analytical tools needed to more definitively identify environmental injustices are still evolving. Given these material contexts, and the fact that EJ staff have little authority over their own coworkers, EJ policy implementation will depend on how committed staff and managers are to EJ principles, how they define them, and whether they hold each other accountable for implementing them. This is exactly why regulatory culture matters, why so many of my research participants kept returning to it in our interviews, and why I focused this book on it.

Of course, the social, economic, and political factors that are beyond the control of agency staff matter, too. For example, California EPA's (CalEPA) EJ efforts are often lauded as more robust than those of other agencies, especially its various legislation mandating particular EJ reforms to planning and permitting practices (as noted in chapter 2). Certain conditions unique to California and outside the control of agency staff have facilitated this, including the fact that the state's strong, vibrant EJ movement pushes for regulatory change, members of EJ activist organizations have taken EJ staff positions within CalEPA, and the legislature has strengthened civil rights and environmental law. Of course, the impact of these new EJ laws is contingent upon what exactly EJ advocates lobby for, which, as chapter 7 illustrates, could take varying directions. Moreover, while laws are important, they are not enough, as my interviews indicate that some CalEPA staff resist implementing them in effective and extremely problematic ways.

While my data do not enable me to specify which of these material and cultural factors matters *most*, this book demonstrates that they *all* matter. My point is that, to institutionalize robust EJ reforms throughout regulatory practice, staff will need not only greater resources, clear regulatory authority to implement those reforms, more advanced analytical tools, and endorsement by agency leadership, but also changes to regulatory culture so that staff throughout the agencies treat environmental justice as central to their work.

To be clear, most EJ staff assert that regulatory culture is slowly changing— that their network of EJ-supportive colleagues has grown over time. For example, John noted that some colleagues, especially younger ones, "are becoming more willing to push the envelope on EJ," and Mandy insisted that "folks are more willing and more accepting" now than in the past. This increasing support for EJ among managers and rank-and-file staff is vitally important to agencies' progress on EJ reforms. That said, my interviews with and observations of staff indicate that staff and managers who implement and vocally defend proposed EJ reforms are still relatively few and far between.

My findings strengthen the scholarship on EJ policy implementation by showing that, to understand agencies' disappointing progress on institutionalizing EJ principles into regulatory practice, we need to address not only the material factors outside the control of agency staff that other scholars have rightly noted, but also the everyday interactions through which some staff resist proposed organizational changes. We need to identify staff members' ideas about how things are done and should be done within environmental regulatory agencies, and how they enact those commitments.

More broadly, these findings show that scholars trying to explain environmentally problematic government practices should attend to popular ideas among government agency staff, how they act on them, and other internal dynamics within government agencies. In so doing, this book augments scholarship providing rare insights into elements of regulatory culture within U.S. environmental agencies (Espeland 1998; Fortmann 1990; Harrison 2011; Langston 1995, 2010; Mintz 2012; Pautz and Rinfret 2011, 2014; Rinfret and Pautz 2013; Robertson 2010; Taylor 1984). More broadly, just as scholars have done within other conventional environmental institutions (Frickel 2004a,b; K. Moore 2008; Scarce 2000), this book shows how norms, common interactions, presumptions, and other aspects of organizational culture can reinforce environmental problems—that organizations' failures to curtail environmental problems stem in part from the ways in which their members strive to do what they think best serves the organization's mission.

These findings also strengthen scholarship showing that modern state institutions construct racial meanings and reinforce racial inequality (Bonilla-Silva 2014; Goldberg 2002; Kurtz 2009; Lipsitz 1995; Mascarenhas 2016; Moore and Bell 2017; Omi and Winant 2015; Park and Pellow 2004; Pellow 2018; Pulido 2000, 2015; Richter 2017; Taylor 2014a). This book does so by demonstrating micro-level interactional dynamics through which bureaucrats' appeals to bureaucratic "neutrality" and impartiality obscure racialized processes and outcomes, reproduce common-sense racist logics, delegitimize their agencies' EJ efforts, and thus reinforce regulatory practice that has long protected whites much better than people of color. In so doing, this book shows why scholars of environmental and other organizations need to attend to racist discourse to fully explain outcomes like organizational inertia in the face of pressure for change from social movements. Such discursive work can undermine the effectiveness of agencies' EJ committees and steering groups, which otherwise constitute precisely the types of teamwork that scholars have shown to be essential for developing organizational change in other contexts (Kellogg 2009).

By showing how government actors' ideas and actions matter, this book shows why environmental sociologists need to "study up." Studies of marginalized communities and grassroots social movements are important, but so too are studies of relatively powerful actors who make decisions that—intentionally or otherwise—buttress injustice and hinder social justice movements from realizing their goals. This book demonstrates that scholars studying the state should heed Mat Coleman's (2016) call for acknowledging the "pervasively uneventful" nature of state power and studying it "as a mode of slow, chronic killing" rather than "catastrophic" exercise. Bureaucrats' narratives and other actions that individually might seem unremarkable contribute to the persistence of environmental inequalities that cause disproportionate illness, suffering, and premature death in low-income communities and communities of color.

In this book, by showcasing the experience of staff advocating for EJ reforms, I have shed new light onto why no environmental regulatory agencies have yet systematically reformed their core regulatory work in accordance with EJ principles. That said, some agencies have been more successful than others at implementing other EJ programs. This raises a question: Which contexts and practices enable some progress on EJ in these agencies? Organizational studies show that certain conditions and practices have enabled other types of organizations to overcome inertia, at least partially and occasionally (Kellogg 2009, 2014). Further research, including ethnographic observation within environmental regulatory agencies, is needed to identify the conditions and practices that most effectively foster meaningful EJ reforms of regulatory practice.

The Current Political Moment: A Silver Lining

Without doubt, the Trump administration has undermined the U.S. EPA, environmental regulation more broadly, civil rights, and other social protections to an unprecedented degree. When I visited EPA headquarters in 2018, I felt struck by staff members' sense of dismay and heartbreak about the changes driven by newly appointed officials: the shuttering of entire EPA offices, rolling back of regulations, disregard for due process, and casting aside of scientific risk assessments that were decades in the making.

Yet we should not give up on the EPA, other federal agencies, or state agencies. Environmental and civil rights organizations are fighting these changes tooth and nail, and many of the Trump administration's regulatory reforms have been held up in court on legal challenges (Bomberg 2017; Carper n.d.; Davenport and Friedman 2018; ELI 2018; Lipton 2017b, 2018). As Elizabeth Bomberg (2017, 956) writes, "Constitutional checks, societal, local and subnational mobilization, combined with the economic trajectory of low carbon energy, could well offset the President's moves to dismantle environmental protection and climate policy and action. In the end, Trump's impact will depend less on what he does, and more on what others do."

In their own ways, agency staff work to defend the rules and programs they feel committed to. EJ staff and others supportive of their efforts within EPA noted strategies they use to keep their EJ efforts alive within hostile contexts like the current administration. Several described how they are framing EJ programs and practices within the parameters of the Trump administration EPA's *Strategic Plan for 2018–2022* (EPA 2018b), noting that two of its stated priorities, cleaning up Superfund sites and improving drinking water infrastructure to reduce lead poisoning, are core EJ issues. Some EJ staff even characterized these priorities as "a real opportunity to support EJ" broadly within the agency, although others were less optimistic, citing the administration's more concerted emphasis on rolling back environmental regulations. Regardless, EJ staff expressed solid resolve to forge ahead with their EJ efforts despite the ominous context. As one mentioned to me, EPA's Office of Environmental Justice often faced hostility from EPA leadership prior to the Obama administration, and "We will find a way to make progress on EJ in this administration, too."

Additionally, other federal agency staff actively resist the current administration's problematic regulatory actions. Some leak information about them to the press, push back against them in their everyday work environments, and even resign publicly in protest. Some participate in organizations that collectively express staff frustrations while protecting individual members from retaliation, such as Save EPA, Rogue EPA, and EPA's employee union, the American Federation of Government Employees Council 238 (Leber 2017). Staff resistance to the current administration demonstrates their commitment to their jobs and willingness to fight for what they see as right. Stories about beleaguered and defiant environmental regulators resisting or persevering under a hostile administration provide hope and illuminate staff commitment to their jobs in ways that typical narratives about bureaucrats do not. EPA staff punctuate this fight by proudly highlighting the agency's mission—"We protect public health and the environment"—in interviews with me, with journalists, and in their own published statements. That said, this discursive circling of the wagons to defend existing regulatory practice has a darker side as well. As I have shown, some staff use this same all-encompassing argument to reject proposed EJ reforms to regulatory practice. This narrative precludes discussion about environmental inequality that persists despite those accomplishments—about who these agencies protect and who they don't. The strident insistence that "We protect public health and the environment" defends agencies from antiregulatory elites, but it also delegitimizes critique from social justice activists inside and outside the agency who rightly challenge these organizations for not protecting all communities equally.

The current administration's attacks on EPA have prompted among the public, nonprofit organizations, and agency staff alike an unprecedented vocal defense of EPA in particular and environmental regulation in general. The current political moment has a silver lining: we have an opportunity to harness that conviction about the need for strong environmental regulation and have a concerted discussion about *what kind of* environmental regulatory state will best serve *all* people in this country, including, notably, those who bear the greatest burden of environmental harms. This discussion must include government agency staff, as environmental justice requires that they defend not only environmental protection in general, but also commit themselves to prioritizing the reduction of environmental inequality. This is the call the EJ movement has made to mainstream environmentalism for decades. It is as important now as ever before.

As we look forward to a new political administration, we have an opportunity to proactively deliberate what is needed to rebuild the federal environmental regulatory state in this country. We cannot return to what was—to a regulatory apparatus that did a decent job of reducing certain environmental hazards overall but allowed unjust environmental inequalities to persist. Instead, justice requires crafting a new environmental regulatory system that takes seriously the notion of protecting all people and prioritizes improving environmental conditions in our most overburdened and vulnerable communities.

This discussion must include explicit debate about what justice requires. In this book, I evaluated government agencies' EJ policy implementation efforts according to EJ advocates' longstanding ideas of justice, which I summarized in the "Key Tenets of Environmental Justice" in chapters 1 and 2. After observing political conflict over environmental justice for two decades, studying EJ scholarship and political philosophers' theories of justice, and deliberating these various principles with my students, friends, and colleagues, I stand by EJ advocates' longstanding notions of what justice requires. That said, I recognize that they are not immutable and must regularly be subject to democratic deliberation in light of actually existing constraints and opportunities. One EJ staff member, after reading my articles about agencies' EJ grant programs (Harrison 2015, 2016), questioned my decision to use historic EJ movement priorities as the grounds for evaluating government EJ programs. As I quoted in the epigraph to chapter 7, Tom asked me: "The EJ movement's vision of success: Is that the only one that matters? … Is the movement priority sufficient? Is it so sacrosanct that that is it, forever?" I stand by my conviction that EJ requires, first and foremost, stronger regulatory restrictions on environmental hazards in the most vulnerable and environmentally burdened communities. Whatever else EJ entails, this is essential, because neither the public nor industry can or will adequately control such hazards. But Tom makes a good point. We need explicit and democratic conversation about what EJ requires, and about the strengths and limitations of various approaches. I offer the following recommendations as a way to foster that conversation. What follows are specific regulatory reforms needed to support environmental justice—a set of proposals for crafting an environmental regulatory state that is not only strong but also *just*.

Recommendations

These recommendations are based on the "Key Tenets of Environmental Justice" that I specified in chapters 1 and 2, which reflect the priorities of EJ advocacy that agencies' EJ efforts aim to honor (EPA 2017a).

Basic Infrastructure to Support EJ

To effectively support environmental justice, agencies need basic EJ infrastructure. Agencies need *strong EJ policies* that establish EJ as an agency priority and specify accountability measures. They need numerous *EJ staff* who develop EJ protocol, manage EJ programs, communicate with community members and other stakeholders, and educate colleagues about EJ principles. Some should be executive-level positions reporting directly to top management and leading a team of staff dedicated to EJ. Agencies should regularly convene *EJ advisory committees*, comprised predominantly of EJ advocates.

Agencies must mandate robust *EJ trainings for staff*. Ideally these will be in-person, multi-hour group trainings led by skilled moderators who facilitate discussions about the roots of environmental inequalities and key EJ tenets, and help participants determine ways they can apply those principles to their own work practices. Because many agency staff have little experience with vulnerable and overburdened communities, agencies should also, as resources allow, *fund site visits* to overburdened communities in which staff learn from residents. Environmental justice also requires that agencies *increase the racial, ethnic, and class diversity of staff* through recruiting, hiring, and promoting people with experiences relevant to EJ.

EJ requires that agencies receive more resources to conduct environmental monitoring and otherwise *fill data gaps* relevant to overburdened and vulnerable communities. For instance, U.S. EPA's EJSCREEN data mapping and screening tool has very little health or environmental data for members of tribes, which renders those issues invisible and underestimated. In addition, agencies must complete egregiously delayed risk assessments for hazardous, widely used chemicals. Agencies must enlist community members to help set research priorities and inform research design, as community members can identify environmental hazards other actors miss, conduct finely scaled monitoring, and advocate for solutions that best address community experiences (Balazs and Morello-Frosch 2013; Brown 2007; Corburn 2005; NEJAC 2014;

Solomon et al 2016). Regulatory agencies must make regulatory data publicly available and accessible via open-source software (Paris et al. 2017, 49–53). Agencies must further develop EJ analytical tools, consult with EJ advocates about how and when to appropriately use them, and integrate them throughout regulatory practice (Holifield 2014; Liévanos 2018; NEJAC 2010).

Regulatory agencies must work collaboratively to develop and hone their EJ reform efforts. In general, EJ requires changes to regulatory practice that are unprecedented and unclear to agency staff. Thus, agencies must collaborate with scholars to develop concrete recommendations for how, exactly, to reform each agency's regulatory practice in accordance with EJ principles.

Improving Public Participation and Outreach

Environmental justice requires that agencies democratize regulatory decision-making so that community members and their advocates influence regulatory process as substantially as industry does. Although some agencies have started to make progress in these ways, there is more to be done (e.g., NEJAC 2013a,b).

Agencies must create more opportunities for public involvement from early stages in decision-making. They should notify relevant stakeholders—including community groups, EJ organizations, and other environmental organizations—at the start of deliberations about permits, rules, major projects, and new programs so that communities have time to learn about the issues and draft input. Agencies should proactively recruit stakeholders to public hearings.

Democratizing decision-making also requires that agencies help make it possible for community members to attend and participate in public meetings, which can be difficult for those who do not speak English as a primary language, take care of children and other family members, hold multiple jobs, commute long distances for work, and/or rely on public transit. Agencies should advertise proposed regulatory actions and events where residents are likely to see and hear them, translate written materials into publicly accessible terminology and other languages when appropriate, provide translation at hearings when needed, provide time for translation at public hearings so that all who sign up to speak receive the same amount of time to voice their opinions, hold meetings in evenings and on weekends, and hold meetings at locations accessible via public transit and familiar to community members.

Agencies should provide resources communities need to be informed participants in the decision-making process, given that communities often lack the technical expertise, time, and other resources needed to stand on equal footing with industry. This includes making agency data publicly available, preparing and posting accessibly written analyses of those data, and responding promptly to reasonable public information requests. Agency staff should try to anticipate and be prepared to address community members' concerns, even those that staff believe are not technically part of the permit or rulemaking process. This includes bringing experts to speak about other hazards, site remediation, and regulation in the area. To meaningfully encourage public participation and foster productive relationships with community members, agency staff also need to admit the government's past wrongdoing and shortcomings.

Democratizing regulatory decision-making processes also requires that community members and EJ advocates can shape the *outcomes* of those processes. This will require that agencies allow qualitative and lay observations, not just quantitative and expert knowledge, to inform regulatory decisions.

Rulemaking and Rules

Agencies should conduct and apply EJ analyses during every rule development to ensure that rules will increase neither environmental inequalities nor cumulative impacts in the most overburdened and vulnerable communities. Additionally, rulemaking staff need guidance on how to weigh the results of EJ analysis relative to the other factors they must consider when evaluating a proposed rule (such as its costs and benefits, impacts on small businesses, etc.). EPA can help states do this by providing more directed guidance and reviving the State-Tribal EJ Cooperative Agreements grants program. Legislative action could facilitate this process by *requiring* agencies to accomplish these ends with specific, concrete mandates.

Many specific new rules or rule revisions would enable agencies to reduce environmental inequalities. For example, EPA could revise its regulatory standards (such as the National Ambient Air Quality Standards [NAAQS] or the attainment standards for Superfund site remediation) both to ensure they reflect the results of new studies and that they protect the health of not only average adults and subpopulations widely regarded as vulnerable, such as children, but also residents in communities facing the greatest cumulative environmental impacts.[1] Additionally, State Implementation Plans for meeting the NAAQS could set more stringent standards to better protect the health of people in air pollution hot spots. Ensuring that pollution standards protect the most vulnerable people requires that agencies account not only for some populations' vulnerabilities to exposure to a particular pollutant in isolation (e.g., an asthmatic individual's exposure to ozone), but also for the vulnerabilities some communities endure by virtue of their exposure to many environmental and social stressors. Admittedly, this is a tall order, and one that science cannot yet fully fulfill (as I elaborated in chapter 3). Thus, agencies need to implement the precautionary principle during the rulemaking process so that rules prevent and reduce known and reasonably anticipated environmental harm rather than allowing harm to continue while we wait for full scientific certainty. Doing so will compel industry to develop and adopt safer technologies.[2]

Regulations should be revised to eliminate ecologically arbitrary and politically motivated distinctions between old and new facilities so that all facilities are required to meet the same standards. Agencies managing cap-and-trade programs must monitor levels of the target pollutant and its accompanying co-pollutants, prevent the transfer of pollution permits into overburdened and vulnerable communities, and ensure that the target pollutant and co-pollutants decrease over time in overburdened communities (London et al. 2013; Pastor et al. 2013). Finally, agencies' enforcement staff should regularly inform rulemaking staff about industries that need stronger regulatory standards (i.e., industries in which environmental monitoring results or other compliance data indicate that emissions exceed levels of concern).

Permitting

In addition to increasing public participation during review of permit applications according to the principles already identified, agencies should explicitly reform the permitting process to improve material conditions in overburdened and vulnerable communities.

When reviewing permit applications for new and modified facilities in overburdened and vulnerable communities, agency staff should conduct an EJ analysis to determine how the proposed activity's costs and benefits would be distributed across the population, whether it would increase existing inequalities among social groups, and the extent to which the proposed activity would exacerbate cumulative impacts in the most overburdened and vulnerable communities. Staff must be authorized to implement the precautionary principle during the permitting process to ensure that permitted activities do not exacerbate known and anticipated environmental harms in overburdened communities, rather than allowing harm to continue while staff wait for full scientific certainty. When these analyses show that a permit would likely increase hazards facing the most overburdened and vulnerable communities above a level of concern, agencies should deny the permit or impose stronger permit conditions—in other words, conditions exceeding other statutory requirements—to *reduce* the cumulative impacts facing the most burdened and vulnerable communities. These stronger permit conditions could require that facilities regularly reduce the hazardous material they store or emit, create buffer zones between hazardous activities and residential populations, adopt more sustainable technologies, reduce noise and truck traffic, regularly monitor their emissions (e.g., quarterly or at least semiannually), and publicly report their emissions and other aspects of compliance with permits in a timely manner. Additionally, permit reviews must evaluate the applicant's regulatory compliance history. If the applicant has a history of noncompliance, the agency should deny the permit or specify how it will ensure the facility's compliance with the new permit. Additionally, agencies must strengthen their permit appeals systems so that communities can appeal permits on EJ grounds (Gauna 2015). NEJAC has recommended these and other EJ reforms to permitting, and specified regulatory authorities that allow them, for over twenty years (Lazarus 1996; NEJAC 2000, 2011, 2013a). California EPA's efforts under Senate Bill 673 are a promising model (CLI 2015; DTSC 2018).

Agencies' permitting staff should be authorized and required to adopt these practices. Presently, no state or federal policies specify that permits *must not* increase hazards in already overburdened communities. Statutory amendment or other legislative action will be required to authorize and mandate some of these reforms and set deadlines that hold agencies accountable. Finally, EPA can help states develop EJ reforms to their permitting processes by providing directed guidance and funding through State-Tribal EJ Cooperative Agreements grants.

Enforcement

Environmental justice requires that agencies be allocated more resources for enforcing environmental law and bringing regulated entities into compliance. Agencies should focus inspections and investigations on facilities in overburdened and vulnerable communities, especially for facilities with a history of noncompliance. Agencies should place more pollution monitoring devices in overburdened areas, track emissions more frequently there, and gauge regulatory compliance not only in terms of average pollution levels but also localized, short-term, but dangerously high spikes in emissions. Agencies should create mechanisms for individuals to report suspected environmental regulatory violations and for agencies to promptly, collaboratively investigate and address those concerns; the Identifying Violations Affecting Neighborhoods (IVAN) reporting and investigation system in California is one model (IVAN 2018).

When agencies find regulatory violations in overburdened and vulnerable communities, they should impose fines rather than warning letters, and those fines must be high enough to discourage noncompliance. During penalty settlement agreements, agencies should encourage EJ-oriented supplemental environmental projects (SEPs) that reduce hazards in the affected community, and the community should have a significant role in SEP design and conduct. For egregious regulatory violations, agencies should revoke the entity's permits. All of these recommendations must be mandated through legislation or agency policy, or both.

EPA's Title VI complaint resolution process has improved in recent years and must continue to do so. The agency must accelerate its review of Title VI complaints, consult with regional office EJ staff on cases about which they are knowledgeable, process its backlog of complaints, refer cases to the Department of Justice for litigation when needed, allow complainants to shape settlement terms, and ensure that complaint resolutions reduce environmental hazards in the affected communities. Additionally, EPA must continue to help states bring their regulatory systems into compliance with civil rights law. EPA's External Civil Rights Compliance Office will need more staff with expertise in civil rights law and the expressed support of leadership.

State and federal attorney general offices and other executive offices should collaborate with environmental regulatory agencies to strengthen and prioritize the enforcement of environmental law in overburdened and vulnerable communities, as California has started to do (Guidi 2018; Hand 2018). Such actors can use the legal system to force government agencies and regulated entities into compliance with environmental and civil rights law.

EJ Projects: Targeted Improvements in Overburdened and Vulnerable Communities

Agencies should commit more resources toward targeted improvements in specific overburdened and vulnerable communities (NEJAC 2004, 2011). Toward this end, agencies should prioritize the remediation of Superfund sites and brownfields in overburdened and vulnerable communities. Yet targeted improvement projects would ideally be more expansive, entailing inclusive, area-wide, multi-agency, multimedia projects designed to reduce the full array of hazards facing areas with high degrees of cumulative impact, build key forms of infrastructure, foster economic development, and otherwise enable communities to thrive. In addition to hazardous site remediation, projects could include enforcement sweeps of hazardous facilities, street repairs and traffic calming measures, creek restoration, storm-water management, tree planting, public housing construction and renovation, and development of sidewalks, parks, playgrounds, health clinics, public transit, and other crucial forms of infrastructure.

Agencies could also direct additional resources into other state and federal programs that reduce environmental hazards disproportionately burdening working-class communities, such as lead abatement programs focused on low-income housing and public schools. Finally, agencies should integrate EJ principles into all grant programs' RFAs and funding criteria.

Other EJ Grants to Community-Based Organizations

Government agencies should create EJ grant programs that fund community-based and tribal organizations addressing EJ issues, and legislators should ensure that these receive consistent and adequate funding. These programs' documents and proposal evaluation criteria should encourage and prioritize funding for projects that focus on reducing environmental hazards and pursue change through regulatory and policy reform (e.g., CalEPA 2013). These grants should not require recipients to collaborate with industry actors. Agencies should also provide community-university partnership grants and technical assistance grants to help community members research and document their grievances in ways that will be taken seriously by decision-makers.

Staff should request EJ advocates' input on EJ grant program RFA language and application evaluation criteria. If possible, applicants should be able to apply for at least $100,000 and to complete projects over multiple years so that grantees can conduct more sophisticated, resource-intensive projects.

Agencies' EJ grant program staff should proactively advertise the grant funding opportunities to organizations that would likely be interested in applying and hold grant-writing training sessions so that less-experienced organizations can successfully compete for the grants and conduct better projects. Although regulations restrict how staff can answer prospective applicants' questions, grant program staff should find ways to do so (e.g., in workshops before the RFA is officially released). Grant program staff should also pay grantees on time, even if their expenditure reports contain minor errors such as improper invoice formatting. Furthermore, grant program staff should check in regularly with grantees to see if they need help with anything, provide technical assistance as needed, help grantees navigate government agencies to address the broader array of issues they face in their community, and advertise other sources of funding to grantees.

Accountability

Some agencies produce polished reports of their EJ efforts, showcasing several (or many) programs or regulatory decisions that benefit overburdened and vulnerable communities (e.g., EPA 2018d). These efforts were hard won by the staff who participated in them, and the reports valuably illustrate to other staff that EJ reforms are practicable and improve communities in tangible ways. Yet, we cannot gauge how meaningfully agencies' EJ efforts contribute to environmental justice without knowing how representative these success stories are of agency practice and the extent to which environmental inequalities are changing over time. For example, EPA's guidance documents on integrating EJ into rulemaking include positive examples of recent cases in which the rulemaking process included EJ analyses and extra outreach to overburdened and vulnerable communities affected by the proposed rule (EPA 2015a, 2016a). Yet EPA does not specify the extent to which EJ analyses and extra outreach are conducted in other rulemakings, how regularly these analyses and community input influence the final rule, or each rule's expected impact on environmental inequalities. Without such evidence, selected anecdotes of valuable accomplishments can only be taken as outliers in a regulatory system that otherwise ignores environmental inequalities.

Agencies must create accountability measures to track their progress on EJ (Goode and Keiner 2003; NEJAC 2011). This includes measuring patterns and trends of demographic inequality in pollution levels, facility emissions, regulatory violations, and health problems related to environmental conditions, and regularly reporting on these. During the Obama admin-istration, EPA started instituting internal EJ data collection mechanisms and reported some of those for the first time in its *Environmental Justice FY 2017 Progress Report* (EPA 2018d). These must be continued and consider-ably elaborated, and agencies' EJ planning documents need to specify goals for which the agency can be held accountable. Accountability also requires putting EJ responsibilities into staff members' job descriptions and perfor-mance evaluations across the agency and bringing action against individual staff who fail in these responsibilities.

Legislators and executive officials should mandate these EJ reforms, pro-grams, and accountability measures in law. EPA could build detailed public participation plans, EJ analysis, and other EJ and Title VI accountability requirements into the Performance Partnership Agreements (PPAs) it devel-ops with states, which specify conditions they must meet to receive federal funding (EPA 2017i). Many states currently have one or two paragraphs on EJ in their PPAs with EPA; these should be expanded substantially.

Conclusion

Reforming regulatory practice is never easy, and EJ reforms constitute changes that are unprecedented and not obvious to staff. Thus, such changes require dedicated research to specify the precise steps through which each agency can reform its regulatory practice in light of actually existing statutory and analytical constraints.

Agency leadership, managers, and other staff cannot accomplish all of these changes on their own. Elected officials must ensure that environmental regulatory agencies consistently have sufficient funding for core regulatory work and EJ reforms needed to strengthen it. Regulatory agencies also require the authority to pursue environmental justice and mandates requiring them to do so. This includes formal directives clarifying existing authority and new statutory authorities where they do not currently exist. EJ advocates should play a central role in helping identify an alternative regulatory and policy framework so that rebuilding the environmental regulatory state does not become a return to the flawed system that came before.

That said, while funding, formal EJ policies, and robust analytical tools are necessary, they are not sufficient. We will also need a cultural shift in these agencies. Meaningfully reforming regulatory practice in line with EJ principles will require that staff, especially those with managerial authority, are on board and committed to the cause. Accomplishing this will require frank deliberations within each environmental regulatory agency about how well it has historically served all communities, what its priorities have effectively been, why progress on EJ policy implementation has been so slow, and how to revise regulatory practice to help it more effectively protect the rights of all people to a safe environment. This latter task—revising regulatory practice—must include acknowledging and confronting the narratives and other interactive dynamics among staff that have undermined the efforts of EJ staff, as well as the ideas that motivate them. Toward that end, I offer this book. My hope is that staff will read it and discuss how to apply my findings within their own work environments.

Regulatory reform is just one step toward a more just and sustainable world. As numerous scholars have demonstrated, capitalism is, by its very nature, inherently exploitative and environmentally destructive (Downey 2015; Faber 2008; Foster 2000; Harvey 2005; Mann 2013; O'Connor 1998; Pellow 2018; Pulido, Kohl, and Cotton 2016; Schnaiberg and Gould 1994). The regulatory reforms I advocate would curtail some of these effects. Of course, environmental regulatory agencies cannot fulfill that task alone. More fully achieving environmental justice requires a state that actually ensures that all people have access to basic material needs, respect, the opportunity to live a meaningful life, and freedom from harm. Achieving an emancipatory future will require new policies reducing wealth inequality and curtailing corporate power, reforming all government institutions to prioritize equity and sustainability, stronger education about inequalities and oppression to build broad social understanding of the need for those reforms and respect for all people, robust social movements that advocate for them, and much more. While this broad array of reforms is beyond the scope of this book, the findings herein constitute part of the conversation.

Appendix: Study Design and Research Methods

This book is what David Pellow and other EJ scholars call "advocacy research" or "critical scholarship"—designed to be "accessible to and in the service of the people we write about, as well as the general public," and to not only build social theory but also help create a more just world (Pellow 2007, 35; see also Bell 2016, 9–10). I encountered the field of environmental justice through my graduate studies in California. My identity as an EJ scholar-activist crystallized during the course of my dissertation research on political conflict over pesticide drift. For that project, I interviewed and spent innumerable hours with pesticide drift activists—people fighting for stronger regulations of toxic agricultural pesticides that move through the air into their homes, schools, playgrounds, and bodies. While many people are harmed by toxic pesticides, those most exposed to pesticide drift are immigrant farm workers and their families. Moreover, poverty, racism, legal status issues, political disenfranchisement, and other factors render them disproportionately vulnerable to the effects of exposure. As pesticide use and drift incidents continued despite the rise of organic food and growing research documenting harms of pesticide exposure, I gained a resolute conviction about the need for stronger regulatory and policy restrictions on environmental hazards.

My commitments have solidified over time as I learn from EJ activists and watch the hazards they endure persist. The trauma of environmental injustice took on new significance for me in 2014, when my friend Teresa DeAnda died. Teresa was a pesticide drift activist—one of the first I interviewed for my dissertation, the one I spent more time with than anyone else for that project, and the one gracing the cover of my book on pesticide drift (Harrison 2011). She was propelled into activism after toxic soil fumigants drifted into her home and neighborhood in 1999, sickening her friends and family. She died too young, in just her mid-50s, from cancer that spread throughout her body. While she was sick and waiting for an organ transplant, far from her family whom she worried about and missed deeply, we exchanged texts and phone calls more than we ever had before. During this time, the fight for environmental justice became less abstract for me, and much more intimate, devastating, and real.

One of the things pesticide regulatory agency staff told me was that while they understood (to varying degrees) EJ activists' frustrations with the government, they wanted people to know that the agencies were developing EJ policies and programs in response to EJ activism. I designed this project to take their request seriously. In this project and book, I honor what agencies are trying to do in the name of environmental justice. I was surprised and grateful to find that many staff leading their agencies' EJ efforts share this commitment, and I honor their efforts to fight for environmental justice from the inside of these organizations. At the same time, while writing this book, I have held in my heart the injustice forced upon Teresa, her family, and so many others living in communities overburdened with environmental hazards, vulnerable to the painful and deadly effects of exposure, and inadequately protected by government institutions. I therefore hold these agencies to the highest standards of environmental justice and evaluate them accordingly.

Study Design

This project contributes to EJ policy implementation scholarship that describes and explains the scope and contours of environmental regulatory agencies' EJ programs, policies, and practices. Whereas other studies have focused on one or two EJ programs within one agency, I sought to characterize the upper bounds of environmental regulatory agencies' EJ efforts in the United States and to explain why agencies have not been able to do more to reform regulatory practice in line with EJ principles. I conducted this research from 2011 to 2019 with Institutional Review Board approval from the University of Colorado-Boulder (#12–0537).[1]

To explain the slow pace of agencies' EJ efforts, other scholars have principally analyzed agency documents. Yet, as Lipsky (1980) and other organizational ethnographers have shown, "street-level bureaucrats" interpret their responsibilities in various ways and exercise some discretion about how to do their work. Accordingly, to understand the outputs of government agencies, we need to go inside them, talk to and observe staff, and learn about their beliefs and practices that shape the prospects for reforms such as those for which EJ advocates have fought. The interactive dynamics among agency staff that I showcase have received no attention in the EJ literature, where scholars instead have focused their explanations on factors outside of the control of agency staff (as I detailed in chapter 3). Indeed, environmental regulatory agencies are often characterized as "black boxes" whose inner workings are invisible to outsiders. I thus designed this study to show how staff negotiate proposed EJ reforms in light of other commitments and responsibilities.

I used a multi-sited study design in which I interviewed and observed current and former representatives from U.S. EPA (including headquarters, eight regional offices, and one other satellite office), U.S. Department of Justice, U.S. Department of the Interior, California Environmental Protection Agency, Colorado Department of Public Health and Environment, Connecticut Department of Energy and Environmental Protection, Minnesota Pollution Control Agency, New York State Department of Environmental Conservation, Oregon Department of Environmental Quality, Rhode Island Department of Environmental Management, and city or county agencies in California, Colorado, and Missouri. To account for variation among agencies' EJ efforts, I purposively included agencies that are regarded as leading the institutionalization of EJ principles (notably, U.S. EPA, New York Department of Environmental Conservation, and California EPA), as well as agencies whose EJ programs are less well developed. The sites vary in terms of the number of appointed EJ staff, their geographic location, and whether they have a formal EJ policy endorsed by agency leadership or the legislature. Including state-level agencies was important, as they hold primary responsible for enforcing much federal environmental law and considerable discretion in doing so.

The multi-sited study design proved essential for protecting the confidentiality of my research participants. As I will elaborate, many agency staff are highly concerned about confidentiality, and their willingness to speak frankly with me hinged on my demonstrated respect for that concern. At any given agency, only a few staff are formally designated as "EJ staff," and in some cases there is only one. If I had studied only one government agency, it would have been impossible to hide the identity of my participants from other members of the organization. Conducting my research at many organizations (and refraining from identifying my participants' institutional affiliation or geographic location when I discuss or write about my findings) enabled me to share their critical accounts without putting them at risk.

I bounded the scope of my study to make it manageable and facilitate reasonable comparison. I focused on state- and federal-level environmental regulatory agencies, as these institutions have similar responsibilities and statutory constraints. Also, I address environmental regulatory agencies' efforts *formally designated as "environmental justice,"* which allows me to examine whether agencies are formally prioritizing EJ reforms. My characterizations do not systematically describe internal variability in any given agency's EJ efforts. Also, due to space constraints, my assessment does not include EJ efforts that are not widely practiced and unrelated to core regulatory work.

While these organizations' EJ efforts vary to some extent, they all fall far short of what they could be. I thus focus on describing and explaining this commonality—their failure to institutionalize EJ principles as robustly as they could. The question of why some agencies have been able to do more than others in the name of EJ would constitute an interesting comparative analysis, would build upon important studies conducted in other organizational contexts, and is one that will need to be addressed in another book.

Although political pressures vary from one agency to another, the experiences of agencies' EJ staff were remarkably consistent across institutional contexts. I thus highlight explanations that transcend these organizations. In the rare cases that agencies differed in terms of the explanatory factors I address in this book, I note those divergences and identify factors that help to explain them.

Describing and Critically Evaluating Agencies' EJ Efforts to Date

To describe the scope of agencies' EJ efforts (presented in the chapter 2 section "Agencies' Key EJ Efforts to Date"), I scoured agencies' websites, tracked agencies' email announcements, reviewed agencies' EJ-related reports, asked agencies' EJ staff for updates not yet available online, and consulted other scholars' characterizations (e.g., Abel, Salazar, and Robert 2015; Bonorris 2010; Targ 2005). I periodically searched for new documents to update my file for each agency. I triangulated among these to identify the most common agency EJ efforts and the most advanced ones.

I assessed how well they meet EJ movement principles (presented in the "Critically Assessing Agencies' EJ Efforts" section of chapter 2). To develop my criteria for the standards to which agencies' EJ efforts should be held, I reviewed EJ scholarship, EJ activists' materials, and my interviews with and observations of EJ advocates. The latter stem from two of my research projects that together span over 15 years. From 2002 to 2010, I interviewed dozens of EJ activists fighting pesticide drift, assisted them with several research tasks, and participated in activist trainings, workshops, conferences, and other events. These activists were located primarily in California, but some were from elsewhere in the United States (including Florida, Washington, North Carolina, and Minnesota; see Harrison 2011a,b, 2014, 2017). From 2011 to 2018, for the project on which this book is based, I interviewed dozens of EJ advocates around the United States about agencies' EJ programs, and I observed EJ activists at government agency EJ events (details of these interviews and observations will follow). Using these various sources, I developed a list of "Key Tenets of Environmental Justice" (presented in chapters 1 and 2) that I used to evaluate agencies' EJ efforts.

Grant Program Description and Evaluation

To more fully characterize and evaluate agencies' EJ grant programs (see chapters 2 and 7), I analyzed documents and funded projects of the agency EJ grant programs that are explicitly called "EJ"; fund community-based, nonprofit organizations and tribes (not university researchers or nontribal government agencies); fund projects to improve environmental conditions in overburdened and vulnerable communities; and are not restricted to a narrow range of issues (e.g., transportation or tree planting). Restricting my investigation to grant programs that provide funds to community- and tribal-based organizations coheres with EJ advocates' calls for more resources to be allocated directly to such organizations. The five programs that meet these criteria were: California Environmental Protection Agency (CalEPA) EJ Small Grants Program, San Francisco EJ Grants Program, New York Department of Environmental Conservation EJ Community Impact Grant Program, U.S. EPA EJ Small Grants Program, and U.S. EPA EJ Collaborative Problem-Solving (CPS) Cooperative Agreement Program.

I described how well the programs' implementation aligns with EJ advocacy in two key dimensions: mechanisms of change and substantive foci. To do so, I analyzed program materials to identify the rules, restrictions, and other language that specify which mechanisms of change each program encourages and discourages: *regulatory and policy protections* (e.g., fighting for stronger environmental regulations, greater enforcement thereof, state provision of key municipal services, and greater opportunities for public participation in regulatory decision-making) or *other mechanisms of change* (e.g., modification of residents' lifestyle behaviors, market-based measures, charitable service provision, or voluntary agreements with industry). I also analyzed those materials to identify which substantive activities the program encourages: *hazard reduction* (e.g., toxic waste cleanup, or potable water provision) or *other substantive foci* (e.g., park development, tree planting, or energy-efficient appliance installation). I found these program's requests for applications (RFAs) and other program documents on agencies' websites.

To determine how well these programs' funded projects align with EJ advocates' model of change and substantive foci, I also analyzed the abstracts of all funded projects (available on agencies' websites) and, when available, the full application narratives (procured through public records requests). These abstracts and other materials identify the proposed activities that the agency judged when determining which projects to fund. They do not indicate the outcome of the project or grantees' broader suite of activities, so I did not evaluate the projects or grantees in those regards. A research assistant and I independently coded each funded project according to whether the project proposed to pursue change *through regulatory and policy protections* (and perhaps other mechanisms) or *only through other mechanisms of change*, and whether the project substantively focused on *hazard reduction* (and perhaps other substantive activities) or *only other substantive activities*. I then calculated frequencies for each program and how its funding patterns have changed over time. I report my findings about the projects' mechanisms of change for the 1,082 projects that specified a mechanism of social change in the materials to which I had access (60 percent of the 1,800 projects funded) and about the projects' substantive foci for the 1,533 projects that specified a substantive focus (85 percent of the 1,800 projects funded).

Fieldwork: Interviews and Observations

To gain fresh insights into the factors that constrain environmental regulatory agencies' EJ efforts, I conducted confidential, qualitative, semi-structured interviews with agency staff and ethnographic observation at agency meetings. Interviews and ethnographic observation help illuminate how staff frame their responsibilities and "environmental justice," how staff react to new programs, variations in these framings and reactions, and the institutional demands that they feel structure their work (Emerson, Fretz, and Shaw 1995).

In interviews, I strive to understand each participant's point of view, even those whose perspectives I feel unsettled by. The semi-structured nature of the interviews allowed me to pursue certain themes of interest while also allowing the participants to interpret their experiences and to draw my attention to the issues they felt are most important. It also allowed me to develop rapport with my participants, which is necessary when discussing politically controversial issues.

Additionally, confidential interviews and internal (i.e., not public) meetings allow staff to express beliefs they do not (and cannot) express in formal agency documents or public events. As I will discuss further, observing internal agency meetings proved especially valuable for seeing how bureaucrats respond to EJ staff members' proposed EJ reforms. That said, as some of my interview participants noted, their coworkers often are more apt to object to proposed reforms in private conversations, such as hallway chats with each other or in confidential interviews with me, than they would in a meeting, especially when leadership has formally endorsed the reforms. Confidential interviews help create that space for expressing dissent. Thus, both interviews and observation of meetings were valuable methods of data collection for this project.

Interviews with Agency Staff

From 2011 to 2019, I conducted confidential interviews with 89 current and former environmental regulatory agency staff. Of these, I characterize 53 as "EJ staff." They lead their agencies' EJ reform efforts, and their EJ responsibilities are a formal part of their job description. The EJ staff I interviewed constitute nearly all EJ staff at my study sites during the period of my study. Thus, this sample of EJ staff and my observations at agency meetings together provide rich, robust insights into the experience of those leading such reforms within these institutions. Additional staff help implement EJ reforms and programs but do not spend a substantial portion of their work time on EJ reforms, so I do not characterize them as "EJ staff."

I characterize as "other staff" the remaining 36 staff I interviewed. They are familiar with their agencies' EJ efforts to some extent, but EJ reforms are not part of their formal job responsibilities. Their support for EJ reforms range from enthusiasm to contempt. This sample of other staff is neither random nor representative of all agency staff in some way. Thus, I do not use these data to make claims about how agency staff in general feel about EJ reforms. Rather, I use these interviews with "other staff" to augment and better understand EJ staff members' accounts about interactions with coworkers about EJ, enrich my understanding of interactive dynamics among staff in relation to EJ reforms, and collect more perspectives on which EJ reforms are possible and under what conditions. Because these other staff constitute just a small fraction of all environmental regulatory agency staff, I cannot make claims about regulatory culture overall based solely on my interviews with them. However, their responses were consistent with claims EJ staff members make about regulatory culture and with the findings of other scholars who study environmental regulatory culture in the United States (Espeland 1998; Mintz 2012; Pautz and Rinfret 2011, 2014; Rinfret and Pautz 2013; Robertson 2010; Taylor 1984).

Although I had largely completed my fieldwork by the end of 2016, I needed to characterize changes unfolding within U.S. EPA during the Trump administration. I approached this task cautiously, as the administration threatened to downsize the U.S. EPA, prohibited employees from talking with journalists, and retaliated against staff who spoke out against the administration (e.g., see Garcia 2017; Lipton and Friedman 2017b; Lipton, Vogel, and Friedman 2018). In 2017, I gleaned insights from media coverage and brief phone correspondence with contacts at EPA. Additionally, I interviewed retired EPA staff who relayed information from their friends still working within the agency. I conducted these interviews as assistance to the newly formed Environmental Data & Governance Initiative (EDGI), a nonprofit organization of scholars and activists documenting and critically challenging the Trump administration's attacks on federal environmental regulation (EDGI 2018). My role in EDGI was to help interview current and former EPA staff about how changes in presidential administrations affected their work over the course of their careers. I conducted multi-hour interviews with seven EPA veteran employees. I asked these veteran regulators about what types of work they did, challenges they faced, strategies they used to persevere in their work, what they found to be their greatest accomplishments, and their perspectives on EJ reforms.

Despite the Trump administration's actions, my access to U.S. EPA remained sufficiently open. In 2018, I asked the director of U.S. EPA's Office of Environmental Justice (OEJ) for permission to visit to learn about the status of the agency's EJ efforts. With his approval, I spent one week in early 2018 interviewing staff within OEJ and elsewhere in the agency, interviews that he helped arrange for me. All but one of the individuals I requested to meet with that week agreed to talk with me. The visit provided invaluable insights into the climate inside EPA at that time and the strategies EJ-supportive staff were using to persevere in their EJ efforts. To gain further updates, I had additional correspondence with several EPA staff in 2018 and 2019.

To recruit staff for interviews, I purposively sampled for variation in institutional affiliation, race, gender, level of authority within the agency, degree of formal involvement in their agency's EJ efforts, and degree of apparent enthusiasm for agency EJ programs (based on coworkers' characterizations). Of the 89 bureaucrats I interviewed, I identified 35 (39 percent) as men and 54 (61 percent) as women. I identified 46 (52 percent) as white, 25 (28 percent) as black, 11 (12 percent) as Latino/a, and 5 (6 percent) as Asian American, and 2 (2 percent) self-identified as Native American. The racial characteristics of my EJ staff interview participants were quite different from those of the other staff I interviewed. Of the 53 EJ staff I interviewed, I identified 19 (36 percent) as white and 34 (64 percent) as persons of color, which appears generally consistent with the broader population of EJ staff. In contrast, of the 36 other staff I interviewed, I identified 27 (75 percent) as white and 9 (25 percent) as persons of color, which is consistent with the fact that most environmental regulatory agency staff are white (EEOC 2018). My participants have had considerable experience at their institutions; at the time of our interview, most worked at environmental regulatory agencies for at least 15 years, and many of those for over 25 years.

I recruited most participants by contacting them directly; in several cases, interview participants recruited coworkers for me to interview. Typically, I first contacted prospective participants via email by describing my research project, the status of my fieldwork, the topics I hoped to cover in our interview, and a brief statement about confidentiality. If they did not reply, I followed up with a second email within a week. In a few cases in which the prospective participant was unresponsive to these emails, I then called them on the phone to request their participation. Sometimes, several calls were needed.

Recruiting interview participants was not easy, and it required persistence. These staff are busy. Also, they have long been instructed to not talk to journalists or researchers, and thus are initially wary. This posed a challenge for me in several ways. Some prospective interview participants initially insisted that I needed to talk instead to the agency spokesperson. Some felt the need to get their manager's permission to meet with me. Some prospective participants engaged in extended, guarded discussion with me about my research project and confidentiality protections before agreeing to meet with me. The exceptions were retired agency staff, who were remarkably unguarded about meeting with me and forthright in their assertions and criticisms. This was especially the case during the Trump administration, as most of the retired U.S. EPA staff I interviewed were politically organized in protest of the administration's attacks on the EPA and thus eager to have my ear. I secured interviews with current staff more easily as the project evolved, in some cases because an interview participant introduced me to a colleague and vouched for me.

I used several techniques to reassure staff concerned about talking with me. I discussed confidentiality issues right up front (as I will elaborate), and many prospective participants seemed reassured that I understood and took seriously their vulnerability. I also emphasized that I wanted to hear about their personal experiences and feelings about EJ policy implementation, to augment the official narrative. This seemed to resonate with staff who generally are required to speak very carefully and in line with formal agency positions. Additionally, as the project went on, I stated how many agency staff I had interviewed, and prospective interview participants often indicated that they felt reassured by my experience interviewing bureaucrats and were curious to hear what I had learned. Although most interview participants were quite guarded initially, we developed excellent rapport through the course of our conversations.

I secured the participation of nearly every agency staff person I contacted for an interview. I failed to interview 11 agency staff whose participation I requested: one did not receive my request because it was intercepted and rejected by the agency's press office; four did not return my calls and emails; and six declined my requests (of these, one said she was unavailable; two said they were not sufficiently experienced in the issues I wanted to discuss; and three said they were not allowed to talk with researchers). I believe that these failed requests do not compromise my findings. I have no reason to suspect that their narratives would contradict my findings, and I succeeded in interviewing multiple representatives of all state and federal agencies in my study.

During the interviews, I asked participants to describe their involvement with agency EJ efforts, which EJ reforms they view as important and which they do not support, which challenges face agency EJ efforts, how their coworkers react to proposed EJ reforms, and how these challenges and interactive dynamics pertaining to EJ have changed over time. For my interviews with EJ staff, I also asked them to describe the strategies they use to persevere in their EJ efforts.

I formally interviewed 24 staff a second time because we were unable to cover all key questions in the first interview. I had follow-up email or phone correspondence with many participants. I spoke annually with four U.S. EPA EJ staff and EJ staff from three state agencies to discuss updates to their agencies' EJ efforts.

My initial interview with each participant lasted from one to two hours and was audio recorded, except for 20 participants who did not give permission to be recorded or of whom I did not request such permission. I conducted the interviews in person whenever possible, as doing so provides rich visual data (e.g., facial expressions and other body language) that help reveal participants' feelings. (I conducted 18 initial interviews by telephone.) For those I interviewed in person, we met at locations chosen by each participant (their office, a meeting room at work, a restaurant, or outdoors). To visit these agencies, one must be invited, show ID to security guards, sign in, go through a metal detector, wear a badge displaying one's visitor status, and be escorted through the buildings. I was rarely allowed to wander halls on my own; at one site, I was even escorted to the bathroom by a security guard, who waited outside the door. Thus, there is a record of every visit I made to each agency. That said, on some occasions, after meeting with my designated contact, I was able to spontaneously meet with another individual. Thus, not all of my interview participants are reflected in my entries in agencies' visitor logs. Also, in some cases, I met with participants outside of the agency, including in some cases far from the building, so that we could meet away from the gaze of coworkers.

I wrote detailed fieldnotes for all interviews and transcribed the recorded interviews.

Observations at Agency Events

I also conducted ethnographic observation at agencies' EJ-related events, which enabled me to see how staff interacted with each other and with EJ advocates about proposed EJ reforms.

Some of these were *public* events, in which I observed how staff formally represented agency EJ policies, how various actors defined "environmental justice," how agency staff responded to various stakeholders, and how EJ activists reacted to staff members' assertions and decisions. These events included nine agency-convened EJ advisory committee meetings (of which I attended five in person and four via teleconference), three public planning meetings about agencies' EJ efforts, one agency-sponsored hearing about an EJ controversy, one informational teleconference about an EJ grant program, several other agency-sponsored EJ teleconferences, and academic conference presentations by eight current and former agency staff about their agencies' EJ efforts. Each of these events lasted from 90 minutes to two full days. Such events were easy for me to access: they are generally announced in advance via email, they are open to the public, and they are free.

In addition, after making several requests, I was granted permission to attend and observe one invite-only EPA training event for the 2014 recipients of EPA's EJ Collaborative Problem-Solving grants, in which, for two full days, EPA staff from headquarters and regional offices gave trainings on grant project administration and helped grantees network with each other to develop strategies and identify best practices. Also, in 2017 I was invited by U.S. EPA Region 9 EJ staff to participate in a two-day workshop in California for agency staff and EJ grant recipients, organized by U.S. EPA, California EPA, and the Bay Area Air Quality Management District. While there, I gave two presentations about my research findings, fielded questions about my work, had one-on-one conversations with agency staff and EJ advocates, observed EJ advocates' presentations, and participated in a field trip through contaminated neighborhoods in Oakland.

For the public events I attended in person, I sat among the other audience members, was able to freely take notes about actors' claims and nonverbal behavior, chatted casually with other attendees before and after the meetings as well as during breaks, and occasionally recruited interview participants. The teleconferences helped me stay current with the agencies' EJ efforts. However, they were less helpful for illuminating interactions among actors, as I was unable to observe body language or audience reactions;

thus, I tried to attend events in person whenever possible. For all of these events, I wrote up extensive fieldnotes afterward.

I was also able to observe several *internal* agency meetings relating to EJ; by "internal," I mean that these were not open to the public. These included four internal EJ planning meetings, and one internal EJ training session for staff. These lasted from one to two hours, and each included about 20 to 30 agency staff. For each, I was the only "outsider" (i.e., not agency staff), and I spent five to 10 minutes introducing myself, my research interests, and my confidentiality protections, as well as fielding questions from participants. I crafted this introduction with assistance and approval from my Institutional Review Board to serve the function of informed consent without taking undo time from the meeting. In two of these internal EJ planning meetings, I was invited by EJ staff to guide discussion; for about 30 to 45 minutes, I invited the group to share their opinions about agency EJ efforts. All of these internal events proved exceptionally valuable to me, as I was able to observe staff debating with each other the merits of various proposed EJ reforms with greater candor than they ever do in public events. Additionally, they enabled me to corroborate many claims EJ staff members had made to me in private interviews, as I witnessed staff using the same forms of pushback EJ staff had recounted to me.

In all of these meetings, I took extensive notes. I always took hand-written notes, both because I can maintain attention to the conversation more effectively that way than when I use a laptop, and because a laptop's clicking sounds and bright screen can be distracting to other participants. Thankfully, public and internal agency meetings alike are situations in which notetaking is reasonable practice. That said, no one takes notes as copious as ethnographic observers want to, and these meetings often generated such rich data that I took notes constantly. Occasionally, a meeting participant would comment about it, expressing a bit of unease about the degree of detail I appeared to be capturing. I learned to defuse such situations with self-deprecating humor. For example, as I wrote in my fieldnotes following an internal agency EJ planning meeting, "[Linda] commented on how I had taken very copious notes, and I replied that I either take very good notes or very terrible notes, not in between, so I just take very thorough notes."

While the internal agency EJ-related meetings yielded valuable data, gaining access to them was difficult. Government agencies are closed institutions in which the public is allowed to see only carefully crafted outputs that hide the degree and nature of disagreement among staff. To gain access to internal meetings, I made numerous requests, crafted lengthy emails explaining my interests and negotiating confidentiality protections, and relied on EJ staff supportive of my project to advocate for my participation. In some cases, EJ staff conveyed to me that their management was resistant to my presence, and in one case I faced that resistance directly. At two of the internal EJ planning meetings I attended, an EJ-resistant manager entered the meeting late, missed my introduction, and, upon noticing me in the meeting, appeared tense and looked over at me repeatedly. Shortly before the second meeting, I informed her via email that I would be attending, and she confronted the EJ staff person who had invited me, angry about my presence and concerned that I would not protect participants' confidentiality. The following excerpt from my fieldnotes helps illustrate the tension involved with my presence at these internal agency meetings. My EJ staff person contact at this agency

> told me that _____ [the manager] called her when she received my email and was angry to learn that "an outsider" had been present at the EJ meeting I attended in December; recall that _____ [the manager] had arrived late and therefore missed my introduction....She said that she would have said things differently if she had known I was there, because some of the things she said are her own personal opinions rather than representing those of the department, and she called the department's press person....I felt very uncomfortable because I knew that _____ [the manager] was angry....She expressed her concerns—she didn't like not being informed at the time that "an outsider" was in the December EJ meeting that I attended and was worried that her words would be misinterpreted as departmental statements.

I talked with this manager immediately after the second meeting in the hallway. I believe that I effectively addressed her concerns, since, in our subsequent private interview, she was very constructive and seemed relaxed. Although her reaction during and after the staff meeting was uncomfortable for me, such experiences illuminated how unable staff feel to express their opinions about their work and revealed everyday practices through which managers and other staff enact organizational closure and resistance to EJ reforms.

Government agencies, corporations, and other elite institutions can be hard to access. However, Alissa Cordner (2016, 236) rightly asks whether researchers request this access as frequently and persistently as they might.

I note the challenges I faced and how I surmounted them to help demystify the process of gaining access to relatively closed, powerful institutions that deserve critical scrutiny.

Interviews with and Observations of EJ Advocates

For this project, I also interviewed EJ advocates across the United States. To evaluate how well agencies' EJ grant programs meet the needs of grantees and other EJ activists, I conducted confidential, semi-structured interviews with 50 grassroots activists. These include 34 representatives from 29 organizations that received government agency EJ grants. Also, to better understand what EJ advocates wanted agencies' EJ efforts to entail, I interviewed an additional 16 representatives of other EJ organizations that had played leading roles in advocating for agencies to adopt EJ policies and programs.

Most of the grantees and other EJ advocates I interviewed were executive directors or held other leadership positions in their organizations. I interviewed some advocates multiple times, had follow-up correspondence with many others, participated in site visits or tours with several, and had informal conversations with numerous others. I sought variation in organization age and size, geographic region, and, for the grantees, change mechanism and substantive focus of their agency EJ grant-funded project(s). Because I wanted to understand activists' roles in EJ policy implementation, I purposively recruited EJ activists who actively advised the design or implementation of agency EJ efforts and are regarded as leading EJ advocates in this work. Therefore, their narratives provide valuable insights into their influence on the design of agency EJ programs. Because these activists are not a representative sample of the entire movement, I am unable to identify how widespread their narratives are among EJ advocates. More research is needed to identify how widespread these discourses and their associated practices are across the EJ movement.

I recruited participants by contacting them directly by email or phone. I conducted the interviews at locations chosen by each participant, except for several interviews conducted by telephone. Each interview lasted from one to two hours and was audio recorded if the participant gave permission. I asked participants to identify agency EJ programs' major accomplishments, limitations, and opportunities for improvement, to describe their involvement in agency EJ efforts, and to reflect on changes in the EJ movement. Initially, I had assumed that all EJ advocates shared my conception of what EJ meant. I was surprised and unsettled when some of my research participants' descriptions of what good EJ policy implementation entails conflicted with my own ideas. From that point, I treated "EJ" not as a given but instead as an object of study, and I showcased these variations and their implications in chapter 7.

The advocates I interviewed were a relatively even mix of men and women, diverse in racial/ethnic identity, and located in California, Colorado, Georgia, Maryland, Massachusetts, Minnesota, New York, Oregon, Pennsylvania, Puerto Rico, Rhode Island, and Washington, DC.

I failed to interview 14 EJ advocates I had contacted: seven did not return my calls and emails, and seven declined my requests (of these, five said they were too busy; one said he was not sufficiently experienced in the issues I wanted to discuss; and one said he would only participate if my publications reveal the identity of all of my interview participants, which I could not do). I believe that these failed requests do not compromise my findings, as I have no reason to suspect that their narratives would contradict my findings.

Additionally, as noted in the previous section, attending agencies' EJ advisory committee meetings, workshops for grantees, and other public events enabled me to observe EJ activists advising government agency staff about what their EJ efforts should entail.

Confidentiality

Most of the agency staff I interviewed expressed considerable concern about confidentiality. Social science research textbooks and courses, as well as university Human Subjects protections trainings, help researchers ensure that publications do not reveal the identity of research participants to study site outsiders (e.g., other scholars). However, my bureaucrat research participants are specifically concerned about what Tolich (2004) calls *internal confidentiality* breaches—the ability of research participants and other organization members to identify research participants in how I discuss and publish my findings. Most agency staff stated that they do not feel that they are authorized to speak critically about their coworkers or agency practices, and they worry that speaking candidly to me could put them at risk of punishment from management. Almost all of the agency staff I interviewed expressed considerable concern about being overheard or about me sharing their statements with their coworkers. I sensed a tremendous degree of social control within these organizations, as staff described being scrutinized and constrained by managers and other coworkers. As one agency EJ staff person said during our interview, "Everything that we are saying here, I have no problem saying. But if I—let's say the _____ [upper management] saw all of that—they would go crazy. You are getting very frank conversation."

Staff members' concerns about confidentiality are understandable. Some staff noted that they have been "burned" by talking with journalists in the past. Bureaucrats and their correspondence are often subpoenaed for legislative and judicial investigations. As scholar Chris Rea has noted based on his research with environmental regulatory agency staff, being investigated is not an abstract concern for his participants; rather, it is a relatively normal part of work life and thus something to reasonably anticipate (Rea 2018). EJ staff members' concerns about retaliation for speaking critically about their coworkers or agency progress on EJ should be understood in light of the fact that many EJ staff feel that they have already been punished for their EJ efforts and otherwise advocating for racial justice within their organizations. For them, the risk of retaliation is based in real experience. These confidentiality concerns have been made more acute in recent years due to the Trump administration's prohibitions against talking with reporters and retaliations against staff who speak critically about politically appointed agency leadership. One EPA staff person noted at the end of our conversation in early 2018, "People around here are scared to death to talk."

While most EJ advocates I interviewed expressed less concern about confidentiality than did the agency staff, they face their own set of vulnerabilities in speaking candidly with researchers. For example, many EJ advocates expect to apply for government agency EJ grants in the future, and thus are reluctant to speak critically about those grant programs for fear of biasing staff who will review their future grant applications. I thus treated them with the same degree of confidentiality as my agency staff research participants.

I take numerous confidentiality protection measures with all of my research participants. I intentionally included many environmental regulatory agencies in my study to provide cover for my research participants who would have been easily identifiable by coworkers if I had only studied one organization. Because some participants were reticent to sign documentation relating to my project, I verbally affirmed my participants' informed consent to participate in the research rather than using written consent forms. I keep all of my research notes and files in a password-protected computer and in a locked office. The only files I share in which participants are identifiable are audio recordings I share with professional transcriptionists who have strict confidentiality agreements and whose file transmission processes use secure encryption. Additionally, during my fieldwork and in my writing, I use discretion in talking about my observations and do not share anyone's comments in ways they could be identified. In my writing, I use pseudonyms. I represent most staff with vague categories of "EJ staff;" "mid-level manager," or "other staff." I generally obscure each participant's institutional affiliation and geographic region because, in many regions, only one state agency has any meaningful EJ programs. Where a participant's personal history, institutional affiliation, gender identity, and/or racial or ethnic identity are relevant to the discussion, I include them only if doing so does not compromise their identity. This is not always possible, and thus I often limit such detail (such as by referring to a participant as a "person of color" rather than, say, "a black woman"). Carefully protecting internal confidentiality requires, unfortunately, that I refrain from sharing many details that some readers would be interested to know about, such as personal experiences that shape a participant's perspectives on EJ, specific aspects of their office or department's institutional history that shape what it can or cannot do to support EJ, or the specific rule or type of permits a given staff person works on. There is no perfect solution to this situation, and I compromise by taking measures that protect my research participants.

At certain points in my writing, I refrain from using a participant's pseudonym, instead referring to them simply as, say, "an EJ staff person." I did this when describing group situations (such as a debate among staff in a meeting) involving one or more individuals whose pseudonym and critical statements I use elsewhere in the book. Doing so prevents the other participants of the group meeting from being able to identify their colleagues elsewhere in the book.

I discuss these confidentiality concerns with my research participants. When recruiting staff and at the start of our interview, I explicitly acknowledge that there are risks associated with sharing controversial or confidential information with a researcher like myself, summarize measures I take to mitigate those risks (as I have described), and invite participants to discuss their concerns with me. Although some researchers downplay confidentiality issues in their correspondence with potential interview participants to avoid unnecessarily alarming them, I found that my participants were already very concerned about confidentiality before I contacted them. Thus, I believe that acknowledging those concerns and how seriously I take discretion aided my recruitment efforts.

In the middle of numerous interviews, staff instructed me to temporarily stop the audio recorder and even to stop my handwritten notetaking, so that they could relate an example that illustrates their point but was too controversial to have recorded. Of course, I honored all such requests. Some participants declined to have our interview audio recorded at all. In such cases, I took detailed handwritten notes. A few staff asked to review any direct quotes I used from my conversations with them, and a few others asked to review anything I write that could possibly identify them. I honored these requests by sharing drafts with these individuals, using their personal (rather than work) email addresses when they so requested, and giving them at least two weeks to reply to me with any suggested edits to the statements of theirs that I used.

Social Position in the Field

Interviews and observations are embodied experiences. As such, my own social position—how others perceive my racial identity, class status, body size, gender, physical ability, and so on, and how much they regard me as an "insider" to their worlds—variously influence my interactions with research participants. Specifically, my status as a white, professional person who is a sociology professor, and neither an environmental regulator nor a grassroots activist, means that my participants received and talked with me in ways that would likely have been different for a researcher of a different social position.

My status as an outsider to regulatory agencies enabled me to ask agency staff to reflect on their work, coworkers, and organizations in ways they are rarely if ever asked to do. Furthermore, being an outsider makes it socially acceptable for me to ask participants to explain what they mean by certain phrases that they tend to take for granted, to describe the minutia of certain work processes, and to recount in detail how an event unfolded.

That said, my status as an outsider to these agencies and as an academic (which many read as "liberal" and judgmental of statements that could be construed as "politically incorrect") probably dissuaded some research participants from sharing with me attitudes they thought I might disapprove of. Specifically, staff who disagree with proposed EJ reforms might be reticent to share those feelings with an EJ scholar, especially when agency leadership has formally endorsed EJ policies. EJ staff told me that their coworkers who have been most resistant to the race-conscious nature of EJ reforms would likely not express that opposition to me. As one EJ staff person said, her coworkers who have used racist claims to reject proposed EJ reforms are "savvy" in the sense that "they know to avoid saying those things to you." This underscores several important points. First, my presence as a researcher in meetings likely tempered some of the discourse staff use. Second, it indicates that, to gain insights into institutions largely closed to outside observers, we need to take staff members' own accounts seriously. They illuminate interactive dynamics among staff that outside researchers may not ever be able to directly witness.

My own status as a white person mitigated this to some extent. I suspect that white staff who used postracial and other racist narratives with me would not have done so with a researcher of color. EJ staff of color told me about racist narratives that their white coworkers had said to other white staff, who in turn recounted those stories back to the EJ staff. They said that coworkers would not say such blatantly racist things to staff of color. For example, Nicky told me, "I happen to be a person of color, so they don't actually say it like that to my face." Thus, my whiteness enabled me to further corroborate some narratives that EJ staff of color have been subjected to directly or have heard about.

With the goal of documenting oppressive dynamics within environmental regulatory agencies and how these undermine the efforts of EJ staff, I asked EJ staff to describe for me things their coworkers said and did that made their work difficult. At the same time, I did not want to press them too hard to discuss things that are upsetting to them. Additionally, notwithstanding how much they feel that such dynamics have shaped their work, they do not necessarily want their professional legacies to be defined by the racist or other oppressive interactions I have documented here. They want to be known for their skills, perseverance, and accomplishments, not their status as, say, a person of color. I acknowledge that, because of my own status as a white, middle-class person with a certain professional class status who has not been subjected to many of the forms of oppression that my participants have, I may not have always navigated that balance with sufficient sensitivity—but I can say that I strove to do so. I sought to honor and document their experiences, while at the same time not suggesting that they needed to prove such experiences to me, not pressuring them too hard to relive those experiences, and not reducing them to those experiences.

My research participants would occasionally, gently, call out how my racial identity shapes some of my assumptions. For instance, in my interview with one EJ staff person who is black, he described his past experiences of white employers treating him as "stupid" during a time in which he was working on an advanced degree in a highly technical field. I responded by saying that I think I would have been fired for speaking back against such treatment. He responded, "Some of us can't afford to talk back." I felt ashamed of losing track of my own privilege. However, I am also grateful for moments like this that have reminded me how much I carry my own white privilege wherever I go, how easily I can forget it even while working to challenge racial injustice, and to consider how the assumptions I make can be shaped by it.

My class status also shaped my fieldwork in multiple regards. My ability to physically present myself in business casual attire and (increasingly over time) use vernacular common among bureaucrats helped to signal my knowledge of and respect for their world and my interest in learning about it from their perspectives. Additionally, my status as a university professor might also have compelled some agency staff (notably, those who see legitimate knowledge as stemming from formal academic training) to give me time that they might not have given to grassroots activists. My status as a *sociology* professor likely cut in multiple directions. In these agencies, as elsewhere in the United States, there is some bias against social sciences as "unscientific" and too "political," which might have dissuaded some research participants from respecting my project enough to speak frankly with me. That said, many participants, especially but not limited to EJ staff and EJ advocates, expressed respect for my sociological training, noting their own undergraduate social science coursework, appreciation for EJ scholarship written by social scientists, and/or good rapport with EJ scholars who have advised agency EJ efforts.

Data Analysis

I analyzed my interview and observational data to determine what my participants thought agencies' EJ efforts could and should entail, why agencies' EJ efforts have failed to meet these standards, and which techniques agencies' EJ staff use to persevere in their EJ responsibilities.

To do this, I read and coded my transcripts and fieldnotes, focusing on what they revealed about *processes* of EJ policy implementation and the *meanings* participants hold that relate to EJ reforms. In particular, I sought to identify what different staff accomplish, intentionally and/or unintentionally, through their discourse with each other and with me. As Alvesson (2011) and Scott (2014) explain, organization members interactively maintain and challenge shared understandings about their organization's responsibilities and identity through direct assertions about its mission and priorities, but also through stories, classification, labels, jargon, gestures, signals, humor, and rumors.

For my interviews with agency staff, some of my analytical codes emerged from the literature, including their claims about ways in which resources, regulatory authority, and analytical tools constrain agencies' EJ efforts. Several themes emerged unexpectedly in interviews with EJ staff: their definitions of what "EJ" means, their categorizations of activist activities, how they design and administer their EJ programs according to those classifications, their stories about colleagues' practices that undermine their EJ efforts, their claims about the associated consequences, the boundaries they drew to distinguish themselves from staff less supportive of EJ and to explain colleagues' pushback against proposed EJ reforms, and the strategies they use to implement EJ reforms within these circumstances. With other staff, several themes emerged unexpectedly, including how they conceptualize their agency's mission and responsibilities, and discursive techniques through which they deride proposed EJ reforms. With the EJ advocate interviews and observations, some of my codes emerged from the literature, including EJ advocates' opinions about agencies' EJ programs, and their theories about why agencies' EJ programs deviate from EJ advocates' historical priorities. Several themes emerged unexpectedly in the interviews with EJ advocates: typologies of EJ activism, which mechanisms of change and substantive foci they assert the movement should prioritize, and how they advised agencies' EJ efforts accordingly.

I analyzed interviews throughout the course of my fieldwork, and I regularly wrote short memos exploring surprising events, contradictions, and other interesting themes. Before writing this book, I shared and received constructive feedback on my preliminary findings through various routes. In interviews, I often would share preliminary findings, asking participants to comment on them. I presented preliminary findings at numerous academic conferences, workshops, and colloquia, and I also gave two invited presentations about my research at one agency-sponsored workshop for agency staff and EJ advocates. At all of these, participants gave me feedback through questions and comments at the event and afterward via email. I published three peer-reviewed academic articles, whose reviewers gave me extensive comments. I also shared some or all of these publications with some research participants along the way and received frank and constructive feedback from several. As I developed my writing and refined my explanations for this book, I re-coded transcripts and fieldnotes, sometimes several times each. I use secondary data as additional insights into the processes at play.

As with any study, exceptions exist to the patterns I highlight in this book. Notably, a few staff insisted to me that their coworkers are supportive of proposed EJ reforms and do not resist them. I carefully considered each of these exceptions and used analytic induction to explain why these staff members' accounts differed from others' and from my own observations. At the end of chapter 5, I explain these exceptions and why I feel they do not compromise my arguments.

Federal Employee Viewpoint Survey Analysis

In chapter 6, I presented a few results from the Federal Employee Viewpoint Survey (FEVS) as additional evidence that the work experiences of government agency staff differ along racial lines. The U.S. Office of Personnel Management periodically administers the survey to measure the degree to which federal employees feel that they are given adequate resources to succeed, that their work is rewarded, that their workplace is fair and engaging, and other measures of employee satisfaction (OPM 2018). Although reports of FEVS results are available online, I wanted to analyze the results in greater detail than those online reports allow.

My graduate student research assistant, Simone Domingue, requested and obtained the 2015 and 2016 survey data from the U.S. Office of Personnel Management. Domingue recoded the raw 2015 data in Stata 14.1, weighted the data using the sample weights provided in the dataset, and conducted a series of bivariate analyses on survey items. She also compiled spreadsheets comparing positive responses for key survey items from published FEVS results for 2015 and 2016, noting statistically significant differences. She assessed how white participants' responses to questions pertaining to fairness and satisfaction compared to responses from participants identified as American Indian or Alaskan Native, Asian, Black or African American, Native Hawaiian or Pacific Islander, or two or more races. She then summarized for me her methods and findings.

Representing the Data

I use pseudonyms throughout this book for all of my research participants. Doing so enables me to protect their confidentiality, and also to direct the reader's attention to common and consequential *narratives and other practices* rather than to the individual people involved. I use the phrase "elements of regulatory culture" to refer to the combination of narrative interactions among staff (chapter 4), other interactive dynamics among staff (chapter 5), staff beliefs about their agency's responsibilities and the relationship of proposed EJ reforms to them (chapter 6), and how EJ staff define key EJ principles (chapter 7).

I have endeavored to be clear throughout the book that I cannot state precisely how widespread all of the narratives, other practices, and beliefs that I describe are within these agencies. That said, because I interviewed the majority of EJ staff at my study sites, my data provide robust insights into the experiences of EJ staff in environmental regulatory agencies. My data indicate that the narratives and other practices pertaining to EJ described in chapters 4 and 5 are widespread and sufficiently frequent that they stymie the progress of EJ reforms. In chapter 6, where I showcase EJ staff members' speculations about what motivates their coworkers to push back against EJ reforms, I draw whenever possible on other scholars' findings to substantiate those claims. In chapter 7, because I interviewed such a large portion of all current EJ staff, I feel confident that the EJ staff narratives I showcase in this chapter are likely prevalent among all EJ staff in the United States.

A book like this does some things that can be unsettling to some of its subjects. To make this complex set of debates and interactions within government agencies legible to a broad audience, I had to omit much nuance and otherwise simplify the complicated worlds of these government organizations. I also challenge the taken-for-granted, standard narrative about why agencies have made limited progress on EJ reforms, by highlighting an additional factor that contributes to that outcome. My goal in doing so is to illuminate the full range of structures that undermine opportunities for change.

While my primary task is to foreground patterns in a complex, messy social world and showcase a few certain themes of interest, at the same time I have a responsibility to honor that complexity and not oversimplify how I characterize my participants. In writing this book from 2017 through 2019, as so many current and former staff expressed outrage at the new Trump administration's attacks on U.S. EPA, it felt increasingly important to me to convey staff members' commitments to environmental regulation. Thus, while I focus here on staff resistance to EJ staff and EJ reforms, I also endeavored to acknowledge that staff identify as public servants and express strong commitments to environmental regulation. I explicitly grapple with that apparent contradiction—staff defend environmental regulation but push back against environmental *justice* reforms—to acknowledge their commitments and avoid flattening them. Relatedly, I strove to convey how respectfully EJ staff honored their colleagues' commitments to environmental regulation, while, at the same time, expressing deep frustration that EJ does not fit into many bureaucrats' vision of good environmental regulation.

Notes

Preface

1. Save EPA and the Environmental Protection Network are two organizations comprised largely of former U.S. EPA staff working to defend the agency from hostile attacks by the Trump administration (EPN 2017; Save EPA 2017).

2. Among other things, I have assisted the Environmental Data & Governance Initiative (EDGI), a collection of academics and nonprofits addressing potential and real threats to science and federal environmental and energy policy (EDGI 2018). EDGI leads federal environmental data-archiving events and monitors and documents changes to federal agencies. My role in EDGI has been relatively minor; I interviewed some former U.S. EPA staff for EDGI and contributed to some EDGI reports and publications (Dillon et al. 2018; Fredrickson et al. 2018; Sellers et al. 2017).

Chapter 1

1. While the preponderance of evidence indicates that environmental hazards tend to be clustered in low-income communities and communities of color, some studies have found otherwise. When noting this variation, scholars reviewing environmental inequality scholarship discuss how research design can obscure environmental inequalities along lines of race and class (Chakraborty, Maantay, and Brender 2011; Chakraborty 2018; Downey 2005; Shadbegian and Wolverton 2015).

2. Some scholars have argued for the need to bring nonhuman nature into our conceptualizations of EJ (e.g., Schlosberg 2007; Pellow 2018), and this is reflected in key EJ movement declarations as well (Principles 1991). I do not include these important issues here, as they have not been a core concern of the EJ advocacy around EJ policy implementation or of agencies' EJ reform efforts, which together constitute the focus of this book.

3. Many environmental sociologists have employed constructionist analysis to explain the persistence of environmental problems and to showcase various actors'

efforts to bring about environmental change (Hannigan 2006). Constructionist analyses illuminate the *intentional* rhetorical strategies of political elites, industry actors, or social movement organizers to legitimize or delegitimize others' environmental concerns, as well as everyday discursive practices through which people unintentionally reproduce environmental problems. Typically, constructionist approaches contextualize and critically evaluate competing narratives in light of other evidence and identify how they serve different actors' interests.

Chapter 2

1. In the United States, the president can issue executive orders to direct the actions of federal agencies and officers. They have the full force of the law, provided they do not violate legislative statute or the Constitution.

2. See Holifield (2012) for a critical assessment of changes in this definition over time.

3. This is per California Senate Bill 535 (2012), passed in response to EJ advocates' concerns that the cap-and-trade program authorized by California's 2006 California Global Warming Solutions Act (Assembly Bill 32 [AB32]) would exacerbate environmental inequalities. For information on the EJ implications of AB32, see London et al. (2013) and Pastor et al. (2013). For information on California SB 535, see CalEPA (2017a, 2019).

4. The settlement required California's Department of Pesticide Regulation to educate farmworkers about pesticide safety and to conduct air monitoring for pesticides—activities the department already does and that do not help those already exposed (CRPE n.d.).

5. I use italics here, as in other quotations from my interviews and observations, to indicate the speaker's emphases.

6. Social movement scholars have observed that charitable foundations have "channeled" NGOs in conservative directions (McCarthy, Britt, and Wolfson 1991).

7. Brulle (2000) found that, whereas government grants constituted only 8.6 percent of funding for all environmental NGOs he surveyed, they constituted 24 percent of funding for EJ organizations (220, 252).

8. For similar cases of consensus-based process undermining EJ advocacy, see Kohl (2016), Ottinger (2013), Pellow (2000), and Pulido, Kohl, and Cotton (2016). See also Daley and Reams (2015), Foster (2002), and Lashley (2016) regarding why collaborations among community members, the state, and industry do not always work well in an EJ context. I return to these issues in chapter 7.

Chapter 3

1. OEJ's budget figures provided by EPA staff.

2. Administrative Procedures Act 5 USC section 706(2)(A).

3. For the rise of and problems with commensuration in environmental regulatory decision-making, see Espeland (1998) and Taylor (1984).

Chapter 4

1. I obscured the offensive word in this quote.

2. Scholars have long documented elites' propensities to blame individuals for their own health problems and dismiss environmental and other structural contributors to disease and suffering (e.g., Brown 2007; Guthman 2011; Levine 1982). Such claims are part of the broader neoliberal narrative that absolves the state and industry for such outcomes.

3. Mustafa Ali appears elsewhere in this book under a pseudonym.

Chapter 6

1. Scholars have shown that EJ activists widely challenge the epistemic authority of scientists (Allen 2003, 2004; Brown 2007; Collins and Evans 2002; Di Chiro 1998; Espeland 1998; Hannigan 2006; Harrison 2011; Hess 2007; Irwin 2001; Jasanoff 1990; Kinchy 2012; Kroll-Smith and Floyd 1997; Kurtz 2007; K. Moore 2008; Ottinger 2013; Tesh 2001; Wynne 1992).

2. Other environmental regulatory agencies' mission statements track close to this. For example, for California EPA, "Our mission is to restore, protect and enhance the environment, to ensure public health, environmental quality and economic vitality" (CalEPA 2017b).

3. Please see the appendix for a few notes about this dataset and the methods used to analyze these data.

4. Egalitarian principles are not the only ideas of justice that EJ staff and other EJ advocates hold. I discuss egalitarianism here because it is a central principle of EJ activism and to illustrate how EJ advocates' conceptions of justice differ from the utilitarianism underlying much environmental law and staff resistance to EJ reforms. EJ advocates' complex conception of justice includes participatory parity and requires that government agencies combat group-based cultural oppression and its consequences (Harrison 2011, 2014; Schlosberg 2007; Walker 2012).

Chapter 7

1. The appendix details why I selected these programs and how I evaluated them.

2. These EJ activists are using "proactive" differently than social movement scholars and EJ advocates have done historically. Notably, Tilly (1978) distinguished "proactive" mobilizations as activists asserting claims to resources they have not previously enjoyed from "reactive" mobilizations as activists responding to loss of resources or power. In the preface to the 1987 United Church of Christ report on environmental inequalities in the United States, Benjamin Chavis asserts that the report's data can enable EJ advocates to be "proactive"—in that it "should be utilized by federal, state and municipal governments to prevent hazardous wastes from becoming an even greater national problem" (UCC 1987, x).

3. These divisions among EJ activists may reflect class divisions within communities of color, such that middle-class activists in EJ organizations reflect the sensibilities of middle-class America more generally. This deserves further investigation.

4. For evidence that contradicts Carter's specific claims about the relative harms posed by obesity versus pollution and a substantial critique of the anti-obesity "healthism" trend in public health advocacy, see Guthman (2011).

Chapter 8

1. Blais and Wagner (2008) note that many federal regulatory standards are decades old, and most have been revised only once or not at all since their inception.

2. Some examples of existing technology-forcing regulations include federal vehicle emissions standards, and limits on pesticide residues on food mandated by the Food Quality Protection Act.

Appendix

1. I interviewed seven retired EPA staff in 2017 for the Environmental Data Governance Initiative in accordance with CU-Boulder's Authorization Agreement with Northeastern University IRB protocol #16-11-34.

References

Abel, Troy D., Debra J. Salazar, and Patricia Robert. 2015. "States of Environmental Justice: Redistributive Politics across the United States, 1993–2004." *Review of Policy Research* 32 (2): 200–225.

Alkon, Alison Hope. 2014. "Food Justice and the Challenge to Neoliberalism." *Gastronomica* 14 (2): 27–40.

Alkon, Alison Hope, and Julian Agyeman, eds. 2011. *Cultivating Food Justice: Race, Class, and Sustainability*. Cambridge, MA: MIT Press.

Alkon, Alison Hope, and Teresa Mares. 2012. "Food Sovereignty in U.S. Food Movements: Radical Visions and Neoliberal Constraints." *Agriculture and Human Values* 29 (3): 347–359.

Alkon, Alison Hope, and Kari Marie Norgaard. 2009. "Breaking the Food Chains: An Investigation of Food Justice Activism." *Sociological Inquiry* 79: 289–305.

Allen, Barbara L. 2003. *Uneasy Alchemy: Citizens and Experts in Louisiana's Chemical Corridor Disputes*. Cambridge, MA: MIT Press.

Allen, Barbara L. 2004. "Shifting Boundary Work: Issues and Tensions in Environmental Health Science in the Case of Grand Bois, Louisiana." *Science as Culture* 13 (4): 429–448.

Allen, Barbara. 2007. "Environmental Justice and Expert Knowledge in the Wake of a Disaster." *Social Studies of Science* 37 (1): 103–110.

Alvesson, Mats. 2011. "Organizational Culture: Meaning, Discourse, and Identity." In *The Handbook of Organizational Culture and Climate*, ed. Neal M. Ashkanasy, Celeste P. M. Wilderom, and Mark F. Peterson, 11–28. Thousand Oaks, CA: SAGE Publications.

Alvesson, Mats, and Maxine Robertson. 2016. "Organizational Identity: A Critique." In *The Oxford Handbook of Organizational Identity*, ed. Michael G. Pratt, Majken Schultz, Blake E. Ashforth, and Davide Ravasi, 160–180. Oxford: Oxford University Press.

Andrews, Richard N. L. 1999. *Managing the Environment, Managing Ourselves*. New Haven: Yale University Press.

ARB. 2018. "Community Air Grants." Air Resources Board. California Environmental Protection Agency. https://ww2.arb.ca.gov/our-work/programs/community-air-protection-program/community-air-grants. Accessed February 28, 2019.

Ard, Kerry. 2015. "Trends in Exposure to Industrial Air Toxins for Different Racial and Socioeconomic Groups: A Spatial and Temporal Examination of Environmental Inequality in the U.S. from 1995 to 2004." *Social Science Research* 53: 375–390.

Ard, Kerry. 2016. "By All Measures: An Examination of the Relationship between Segregation and Health Risk from Air Pollution." *Population and Environment* 38: 1–20.

Auyero, Javier. 2010. "Chuck and Pierre at the Welfare Office." *Sociological Forum* 25 (4): 851–860.

Baden, Brett M., Douglas S. Noonan, and Rama Mohana R. Turaga. 2007. "Scales of Justice: Is There a Geographic Bias in Environmental Equity Analysis?" *Journal of Environmental Planning and Management* 50 (2): 163–185.

Bakker, Karen. 2010. "The Limits of 'Neoliberal Natures': Debating Green Neoliberalism." *Progress in Human Geography* 34: 715–735.

Balazs, Carolina L., and Rachel Morello-Frosch. 2013. "The Three Rs: How Community-Based Participatory Research Strengthens the Rigor, Relevance, and Reach of Science." *Environmental Justice* 6 (1): 9–16.

Banaszak, Lee Ann. 2005. "Inside and Outside the State: Movement Insider Status, Tactics, and Public Policy Achievements." In *Routing the Opposition: Social Movements, Public Policy, and Democracy*, ed. D. S. Meyer, V. Jenness, and H. M. Ingram, 149–176. Minneapolis: University of Minnesota Press.

Banzhaf, H. Spencer. 2011. "Regulatory Impact Analyses of Environmental Justice Effects." *Journal of Land Use and Environmental Law* 27 (1): 1–30.

Bechky, Beth A. 2003. "Object Lessons: Workplace Artifacts as Representations of Occupational Jurisdiction." *American Journal of Sociology* 109 (3): 720–752.

Bell, Joyce M. 2014. *The Black Power Movement and American Social Work*. New York: Columbia University Press.

Bell, Shannon. 2016. *Fighting King Coal: The Challenges to Micromobilization in Central Appalachia*. Cambridge, MA: MIT Press.

Benford, Robert. 2005. "The Half-Life of the Environmental Justice Frame: Innovation, Diffusion, and Stagnation." In *Power, Justice, and the Environment: A Critical Appraisal of the Environmental Justice Movement*, ed. David Naguib Pellow and Robert J. Brulle, 37–53. Cambridge, MA: MIT Press.

Bertenthal, Alyse. 2018. "Environmental Justice in Context: Assumptions, Meanings, and Practices of Environmental Justice in U.S. Courts." *Environmental Justice* 11 (6): 203–207.

Biltekoff, Charlotte. 2013. *Eating Right in America: The Cultural Politics of Food and Health.* Durham, NC: Duke University Press.

Binder, Amy. 2007. "For Love and Money: Organizations' Creative Responses to Multiple Environmental Logics." *Theory and Society* 36: 547–571.

Blais, Lynn E., and Wendy E. Wagner. 2008. "Emerging Science, Adaptive Regulation, and the Problem of Rulemaking Ruts." *Texas Law Review* 86: 1701–1739.

Bobrow-Strain, Aaron. 2012. *White Bread: A Social History of the Store-Bought Loaf.* Boston: Beacon Press.

Bogado, Aura. 2015. "What This California Department's Racist Emails Could Mean for the Communities It's Supposed to Protect." *Grist,* December 23, 2015. https:// grist.org/politics/what-this-california-departments-racist-emails-could-mean-for-the -communities-its-supposed-to-protect/. Accessed March 7, 2019.

Bomberg, Elizabeth. 2017. "Environmental Politics in the Trump Era: An Early Assessment." *Environmental Politics* 26 (5): 956–963.

Bonastia, Chris. 2000. "Why Did Affirmative Action in Housing Fail during the Nixon Era? Exploring the 'Institutional Homes' of Social Policies." *Social Problems* 47: 523–542.

Bonilla-Silva, Eduardo. 2014. *Racism without Racists: Color-Blind Racism and the Persistence of Racial Inequality in America.* 4th ed. Lanham, MD: Rowman and Littlefield.

Bonorris, Steven, ed. 2010. *Environmental Justice for All: A Fifty State Survey of Legislation, Policies and Cases.* 4th ed. Berkeley, CA: Hastings College of the Law.

Brenner, Neil, Jamie Peck, and Nik Theodore. 2010. "Variegated Neoliberalization: Geographies, Modalities, Pathways." *Global Networks* 10 (2): 1–41.

Brown, Phil. 2007. *Toxic Exposures: Contested Illnesses and the Environmental Health Movement.* New York: Columbia University Press.

Brown, Phil, Steve Kroll-Smith, and Valerie J. Gunter. 2000. "Knowledge, Citizens, and Organizations: An Overview of Environments, Disease, and Social Conflict." In *Illness and the Environment: A Reader in Contested Medicine,* ed. Steve Kroll-Smith, Phil Brown, and Valerie J. Gunter, 9–25. New York: NYU Press.

Brulle, Robert J. 2000. *Agency, Democracy, and Nature: The U.S. Environmental Movement from a Critical Theory Perspective.* Cambridge, MA: MIT Press.

Brulle, Robert J., and J. Craig Jenkins. 2005. "Foundations and the Environmental Movement: Priorities, Strategies, and Impact." In *Foundations for Social Change: Critical*

Perspectives on Philanthropy and Popular Movements, ed. Daniel Faber and Deborah McCarthy, 151–173. Philadelphia: Temple University Press.

Bruno, Tianna, and Wendy Jepson. 2018. "Marketisation of Environmental Justice: U.S. EPA Environmental Justice Showcase Communities Project in Port Arthur, Texas." *Local Environment* 23 (3): 276–292.

Bryner, Gary C. 2002. "Assessing Claims of Environmental Justice: Conceptual Frameworks." In *Justice and Natural Resources: Concepts, Strategies, and Applications*, ed. Kathryn M. Mutz, Gary C. Bryner, and Douglas S. Kenney. Washington, DC: Island Press.

Buford, Talia. 2017a. "EPA Works to Remake Troubled Office of Civil Rights." Center for Public Integrity, January 20, 2017. https://www.publicintegrity.org/2017/01/20/20604/epa-works-remake-troubled-office-civil-rights. Accessed March 7, 2019.

Buford, Talia. 2017b. "Has the Moment for Environmental Justice Been Lost?" ProPublica, July 24. https://www.propublica.org/article/has-the-moment-for-environmental-justice-been-lost. Accessed March 7, 2019.

Buford, Talia. 2017c. "What It's Like Inside the Trump Administration's Regulatory Rollback at the EPA." December 18, 2018. https://www.propublica.org/article/inside-trump-regulatory-rollback-epa. Accessed March 7, 2019.

Bulkeley, Harriett, and Gordon Walker. 2005. "Environmental Justice: A New Agenda for the UK." *Local Environment* 10 (4): 329–332.

Bullard, Robert D. 1990. *Dumping in Dixie: Race, Class, and Environmental Quality*. Boulder, CO: Westview Press.

Bullard, Robert. 1992. "Environmental Blackmail in Minority Communities." In *Race and the Incidence of Environmental Hazards*, ed. Bunyan Bryant and Paul Mohai, 82–95. Boulder, CO: Westview Press.

Bullard, Robert D., Paul Mohai, Robin Saha, and Beverly Wright. 2007. *Toxic Wastes and Race at Twenty 1987–2007*. Cleveland, OH: United Church of Christ Justice and Witness Ministries.

Bullock, Clair, Kerry Ard, and Grace Saalman. 2018. "Measuring the Relationship between State Environmental Justice Action and Air Pollution Inequality, 1990–2009." *Review of Policy Research*. DOI: 10.1111/ropr.12292.

Burke, W. Warner. 2018. *Organization Change: Theory and Practice*. Fifth ed. Los Angeles: SAGE Publications.

Cable, Sherry, Tamara Mix, and Donald Hastings. 2005. "Mission Impossible? Environmental Justice Activists' Collaborations with Professional Environmentalists and with Academics." In *Power, Justice, and the Environment*, ed. David N. Pellow and Robert J. Brulle, 55–75. Cambridge, MA: MIT Press.

Cable, Sherry, and Thomas Shriver. 1995. "Production and Extrapolation of Meaning in the Environmental Justice Movement." *Sociological Spectrum* 15 (4): 419–442.

CalEPA. n.d. *Environmental Justice Compliance and Enforcement Working Group: Los Angeles Initiative Report.* Sacramento: California Environmental Protection Agency.

CalEPA. 2010. *Cumulative Impacts: Building a Scientific Foundation.* Office of Environmental Health Hazard Assessment. Sacramento: California Environmental Protection Agency. https://oehha.ca.gov/calenviroscreen/report/cumulative-impacts-building-scientific-foundation-report. Accessed March 3, 2019.

CalEPA. 2013. *Environmental Justice Small Grants Application and Instructions: 2013 Grant Cycle.* Sacramento: California Environmental Protection Agency.

CalEPA. 2015. *Environmental Justice Compliance and Enforcement Working Group: Fresno Initiative Report.* Sacramento: California Environmental Protection Agency.

CalEPA. 2017a. "Using CalEnviroScreen." California Environmental Protection Agency. https://oehha.ca.gov/calenviroscreen/how-use. Accessed July 19, 2017.

CalEPA. 2017b. "CalEPA Mission." California Environmental Protection Agency. https://calepa.ca.gov/about/. Accessed November 28, 2017.

CalEPA. 2019. "Disadvantaged Community Designation (Updated June 2017)." California Environmental Protection Agency. https://oehha.ca.gov/calenviroscreen/sb535. Accessed March 3, 2019.

California. 2015. "Assembly Bill 1071." California Legislative Information. https://leginfo.legislature.ca.gov/faces/billNavClient.xhtml?bill_id=201520160AB1071. Accessed July 22, 2017.

Campbell, Heather E., Laura R. Peck, and Michael K. Tschudi. 2010. "Justice for All? A Cross-Time Analysis of Toxics Release Inventory Facility Location." *Review of Policy Research* 27 (1): 451–458.

Campbell, John L. 2005. "Where Do We Stand? Common Mechanisms in Organizations and Social Movements Research." In *Social Movements and Organization Theory*, ed. Gerald F. Davis, Doug McAdam, W. Richard Scott, and Mayer N. Zald, 41–68. Cambridge: Cambridge University Press.

Capek, Stella M. 1993. "The 'Environmental Justice' Frame: A Conceptual Discussion and an Application." *Social Problems* 40 (1): 5–24.

Cappiello, Dina. 2010. "Hurricane Katrina Propels Lisa Jackson's Justice Quest at EPA." The Associated Press, January 10, 2010. http://www.nola.com/politics/index.ssf/2010/01/hurricane_katrina_propels_lisa.html. Accessed January 31, 2018.

Carper, Tom. N.d. *Rule of Law? Not So Much. Scott Pruitt's Losing Litigation Record at EPA.* United States Senate Committee on Environment and Public Works. https://www.epw

.senate.gov/public/_cache/files/5/c/5c690fc8-1800-4963-896b-4e76995158aa/B0DF8 DBE8E1D27EA12643E177A7EA644.05212018-pruitt-litigation-report.pdf. Accessed June 27, 2018.

Carter, Eric D. 2016. "Environmental Justice 2.0: New Latino Environmentalism in Los Angeles." *Local Environment* 21 (1): 3–23.

CDEEP. 2017a. "Environmental Justice Communities." Connecticut Department of Energy and Environmental Protection. https://www.ct.gov/deep/cwp/view .asp?A=2688&Q=432364. Accessed March 3, 2019.

CDEEP. 2017b. *The Environmental Justice Public Participation Guidelines*. Connecticut Department of Energy and Environmental Protection. http://www.ct.gov/deep/lib/ deep/environmental_justice/EJ_Guid.pdf. Accessed July 3, 2017.

CDPHE. 2016. "Regulatory Efficiency Review." Colorado Department of Public Health and Environment. https://www.colorado.gov/pacific/hcpf/regulatory-effi ciency-review. Accessed March 3, 2019.

Centeno, Miguel A., and Joseph N. Cohen. 2012. "The Arc of Neoliberalism." *Annual Review of Sociology* 38: 317–340.

CEQ. 1997. *Environmental Justice: Guidance under the National Environmental Policy Act*. Council on Environmental Quality. Executive Office of the President. https:// www.epa.gov/environmentaljustice/ceq-environmental-justice-guidance-under- national-environmental-policy-act. Accessed March 3, 2019.

Chakraborty, Jayajit. 2018. "Spatial Representation and Estimation of Environmen- tal Risk: a Review of Analytic Approaches." In *The Routledge Handbook of Environmen- tal Justice*, ed. Ryan Holifield, Jayajit Chakraborty, and Gordon Walker, 175–189. London: Routledge.

Chakraborty, Jayajit, Juliana A. Maantay, and Jean D. Brender. 2011. "Dispropor- tionate Proximity to Environmental Health Hazards: Methods, Models, and Mea- surement." *American Journal of Public Health* 101 (S1): S27–S36.

Ciplet, David, J. Timmons Roberts, and Mizan R. Khan. 2015. *Power in a Warming World: The New Global Politics of Climate Change and the Remaking of Environmental Inequality*. Cambridge, MA: MIT Press.

Clabby, Catherine. 2018. "Agreement, Court Victory Give Hog Farm Critics Cautious Optimism." *North Carolina Health News*. May 14, 2018. https://www.northcarolina healthnews.org/2018/05/14/agreement-court-victory-give-hog-farm-critics-cautious -optimism/. Accessed March 3, 2019.

Clark, Lara P., Dylan B. Millet, and Julian D. Marshall. 2014. "National Patterns in Environmental Injustice and Inequality: Outdoor NO2 Air Pollution in the United States." *PLoS ONE* 9 (4): e94431.

CLI. 2015. "Senate Bill No. 673." California Legislative Information. https://leginfo.leg islature.ca.gov/faces/billTextClient.xhtml?bill_id=201520160SB673. Accessed March 3, 2019.

CLI. 2016. "Senate Bill No. 1000." California Legislative Information. https://leginfo .legislature.ca.gov/faces/billTextClient.xhtml?bill_id=201520160SB1000. Accessed March 3, 2019.

CLI. 2017. "Assembly Bill No. 617." California Legislative Information. https:// leginfo.legislature.ca.gov/faces/billNavClient.xhtml?bill_id=201720180AB617. Accessed March 3, 2019.

Clinton, William Jefferson. 1994a. "Executive Order 12898: Federal Actions to Address Environmental Justice in Minority Populations and Low-Income Populations." Federal Register 59 (32). https://www.archives.gov/files/federal-register/executive-orders /pdf/12898.pdf. Accessed March 3, 2019.

Clinton, William Jefferson. 1994b. "Memorandum on Environmental Justice." https://www.epa.gov/sites/production/files/2015-02/documents/clinton_ memo_12898.pdf. Accessed February 28, 2019.

Cole, Luke. 1999. "Wrong on the Facts, Wrong on the Law: Civil Rights Advocates Excoriate EPA's Most Recent Title VI Misstep." *Environmental Law Review* 29 (12): 10775.

Cole, Luke, and Sheila Foster. 2001. *From the Ground Up: Environmental Racism and the Rise of the Environmental Justice Movement.* New York: NYU Press.

Coleman, Mat. 2016. "State Power in Blue." *Political Geography* 51: 76–86.

Coleman-Adebayo, Marsha. 2011. *No Fear: A Whistleblower's Triumph over Corruption and Retaliation at the EPA.* Chicago, IL: Lawrence Hill Books.

Collins, H. M., and Robert Evans. 2002. "The Third Wave of Science Studies: Studies of Expertise and Experience." *Social Studies of Science* 32 (2): 235–296.

Corburn, Jason. 2005. *Street Science: Community Knowledge and Environmental Health Justice.* Cambridge, MA: MIT Press.

Cordner, Alissa. 2016. *Toxic Safety: Flame Retardants, Chemical Controversies, and Environmental Health.* New York: Columbia University Press.

Couch, Stephen R., and Charlton J. Coles. 2011. "Community Stress, Psychosocial Hazards, and EPA Decision-Making in Communities Impacted by Chronic Technological Disasters." *American Journal of Public Health* 101 (S1): S140–S148.

CPI. 2015. "Environmental Justice, Denied." Center for Public Integrity. https:// www.publicintegrity.org/environment/environmental-justice-denied. Accessed July 26, 2017.

Crowder, Kyle, and Liam Downey. 2010. "Inter-Neighborhood Migration, Race, and Environmental Hazards: Modeling Micro-Level Processes of Environmental Inequality." *American Journal of Sociology* 115 (4): 1110–1149.

CRPE. n.d. *A Right without a Remedy: How the EPA Failed to Protect the Rights of Latino Schoolchildren.* Oakland, CA: The Center on Race, Poverty, and the Environment.

CRS. 2016. Colorado Revised Statutes § 25-7-110.5(4)(e). https://law.justia.com/codes /colorado/2016/title-25/environmental-control/article-7/part-1/section-25-7-110.5/. Accessed February 21, 2018.

Cutter, Susan L., Bryan J. Boruff, and W. Lynn Shirley. 2003. "Social Vulnerability to Environmental Hazards." *Social Science Quarterly* 84 (2): 242–261.

Daley, Dorothy, and Tony Reames. 2015. "Public Participation and Environmental Justice: Access to Federal Decision Making." In *Failed Promises: Evaluating the Federal Government's Response to Environmental Justice*, ed. David M. Konisky, 143–171. Cambridge, MA: MIT Press.

Davenport, Coral. 2017a. "E.P.A. Workers Try to Block Pruitt in Show of Defiance." *New York Times*, February 16, 2017. https://www.nytimes.com/2017/02/16/us/politics /scott-pruitt-environmental-protection-agency.html. Accessed March 7, 2019.

Davenport, Coral. 2017b. "Counseled by Industry, Not Staff, E.P.A. Chief Is Off to a Blazing Start." *New York Times*, July 1, 2017. https://www.nytimes.com/2017/07/01/ us/politics/trump-epa-chief-pruitt-regulations-climate-change.html. Accessed March 18, 2019.

Davenport, Coral. 2018a. "E.P.A. Blocks Obama-Era Clean Water Rule." *New York Times*, January 31, 2018. https://www.nytimes.com/2018/01/31/climate/trump -water-wotus.html. Accessed March 18, 2019.

Davenport, Coral. 2018b. "How Much Has 'Climate Change' Been Scrubbed from Federal Websites? A Lot." *New York Times*, January 10, 2018. https://www.nytimes .com/2018/01/10/climate/climate-change-trump.html. Accessed March 7, 2019.

Davenport, Coral, and Lisa Friedman. 2018. "In His Haste to Roll Back Rules, Scott Pruitt, E.P.A. Chief, Risks His Agenda." *The New York Times,* April 7, 2018. https://www .nytimes.com/2018/04/07/climate/scott-pruitt-epa-rollbacks.html. Accessed March 7, 2019.

Davidson, Debra J., and Scott Frickel. 2004. "Understanding Environmental Governance: A Critical Review." *Organization and Environment* 17 (4): 471–492.

Davis, Gerald F., Doug McAdam, W. Richard Scott, and Mayer N. Zald, eds. 2005. *Social Movements and Organization Theory.* Cambridge: Cambridge University Press.

Dean, Mitchell. 1999. *Governmentality: Power and Rule in Modern Society.* London: SAGE Publications.

Deloitte Consulting. 2011. *Evaluation of the EPA Office of Civil Rights*. March 21, 2011. https://archive.epa.gov/epahome/ocr-statement/web/pdf/epa-ocr_20110321_final report.pdf. Accessed March 3, 2019.

Di Chiro, Giovanna. 1996. "Nature as Community: The Convergence of Environment and Social Justice." In *Uncommon Ground: Rethinking the Human Place in Nature*, ed. William Cronon, 298–320. New York: W. W. Norton.

Di Chiro, Giovanna. 1998. "Environmental Justice from the Grassroots: Reflections on History, Gender, and Expertise." In *The Struggle for Ecological Democracy: Environmental Justice Movements in the United States*, ed. Daniel Faber, 104–136. New York: Guilford Press.

Dillon, Lindsey, Christopher Sellers, Vivian Underhill, Nicholas Shapiro, Jennifer Liss Ohayon, Marianne Sullivan, Phil Brown, Jill Harrison, Sara Wylie, and the "EPA Under Siege" Writing Group. 2018. "The EPA in the Early Trump Administration: Prelude to Regulatory Capture." *American Journal of Public Health* 108 (S2): S89–S94.

DiMaggio, Paul J., and Walter W. Powell. 1983. "The Iron Cage Revisited: Institutional Isomorphism and Collective Rationality in Organizational Fields." *American Sociological Review* 48 (2): 147–160.

DOT. 2017. "Environmental Justice Strategy." U.S. Department of Transportation. https://www.transportation.gov/policy/transportation-policy/environmental -justice-strategy. Accessed February 28, 2019.

Downey, Liam. 2005. "Assessing Environmental Inequality: How the Conclusions We Draw Vary According to the Definitions We Employ." *Sociological Spectrum* 25: 349–369.

Downey, Liam. 2006. "Environmental Racial Inequality in Detroit." *Social Forces* 85: 771–796.

Downey, Liam. 2015. *Inequality, Democracy, and the Environment*. New York: NYU Press.

Downey, Liam, and Brian Hawkins. 2008. "Race, Income, and Environmental Inequality in the United States." *Sociological Perspectives* 51 (4): 759–781.

DTSC. 2016. "Enforcement Priorities Related to Environmental Justice and Health Risk." Letter to Mr. Gidden Kracov, chairman, DTSC Independent Review Panel. May 6, 2016. Sacramento: California Environmental Protection Agency Department of Toxic Substances Control. https://www.dtsc.ca.gov/GetInvolved/ReviewPanel/upload/ DTSC-Report-on-Prioritizing-Enforcement-in-Vulnerable-Communities-in-Compliance -with-AB-1329-P%C3%A9rez-Chapter-598-Statutes-of-2013-May-6-2016.pdf. Accessed March 7, 2019.

DTSC. 2018. "SB 673: Permit Criteria for Community Protection." Sacramento: California Environmental Protection Agency Department of Toxic Substances

Control. https://www.dtsc.ca.gov/HazardousWaste/Permit_Roundtables.cfm#track1. Accessed November 11, 2018.

DuPuis, E. Melanie. 2007. "Angels and Vegetables: A Brief History of Food Advice in America." *Gastronomica* 7 (2): 34–44.

Eady, Veronica. 2003. "Environmental Justice in State Policy Decisions." In *Just Sustainabilities: Development in an Unequal World*, ed. Julian Agyeman, Robert D. Bullard, and Bob Evans, 168–182. Cambridge, MA: MIT Press.

ECOS. 2017. "State Approaches to Community Engagement and Equity Considerations in Permitting." Environmental Council of the States. https://www.ecos.org/wp-content /uploads/2017/02/February-2017-Green-Report-Final-1.pdf. Accessed March 3, 2019.

EDGI. 2018. Environmental Data & Governance Initiative. https://envirodatagov .org/about/. Accessed March 3, 2019.

EEOC. 2018. Environmental Protection Agency (EPA). U.S. Equal Employment Opportunity Commission. https://www.eeoc.gov/federal/reports/fsp2009/epa.cfm. Accessed June 5, 2018.

Eilperin, Juliet, and Darla Cameron. 2018. "How Trump Is Rolling Back Obama's Legacy." *Washington Post*, January 18, 2018. https://www.washingtonpost.com /graphics/politics/trump-rolling-back-obama-rules/?utm_term=.d8934a036247. Accessed March 18, 2019.

EJ IWG. 2016. *Promising Practices for EJ Methodologies in NEPA Reviews*. Federal Environmental Justice Interagency Working Group. https://www.epa.gov/environmental-justice/ej-iwg-promising-practices-ej-methodologies-nepa-reviews. Accessed March 3, 2019.

ELI. 2001. *Opportunities for Advancing Environmental Justice: An Analysis of U.S. EPA Statutory Authorities*. Washington, DC: Environmental Law Institute. https://www .eli.org/research-report/opportunities-advancing-environmental-justice-analysis-us -epa-statutory-authorities. Accessed March 3, 2019.

ELI. 2018. *Environmental Protection in the Trump Era*. Environmental Law Institute. American Bar Association. Spring 2018. https://www.eli.org/eli-press-books/environ-mental-protection-in-the-trump-era. Accessed March 3, 2019.

Emerson, Robert M., Rachel I. Fretz, and Linda L. Shaw. 1995. *Writing Ethnographic Fieldnotes*. Chicago: University of Chicago Press.

Engelman Lado, Marianne. 2017. "Toward Civil Rights Enforcement in the Environmental Justice Context: Step One: Acknowledging the Problem." *Fordham Environmental Law Review* 29: 46–94.

EPA. n.d. *Response to Public Comments on Plan EJ 2014 Strategy and Implementation Plans. Public Comments Received: Jul 2010–Apr 2011*. Washington, DC: U.S. Environmental

Protection Agency. https://www.epa.gov/sites/production/files/2015-02/documents/plan-ej-2011-comments-responses.pdf. Accessed June 19, 2018.

EPA. 1996. *The Common Sense Initiative: A New Generation of Environmental Protection*. EPA document 400-F-95–001. Washington, DC: U.S. Environmental Protection Agency.

EPA. 1998a. *Community/University Partnership (CUP) Grants Program—1995–98*. Environmental Justice Fact Sheet EPA/300-F-97–002R. Washington, DC: U.S. Environmental Protection Agency.

EPA. 1998b. *Final Guidance for Incorporating Environmental Justice Concerns in EPA's NEPA Compliance Analyses*. Washington, DC: U.S. Environmental Protection Agency.

EPA. 2003. *Framework for Cumulative Risk Assessment*. EPA/600/P-02/001F. Office of Research and Development, National Center for Environmental Assessment, Washington Office. Washington, DC: U.S. Environmental Protection Agency.

EPA. 2006. *Title VI Public Involvement Guidance for EPA Assistance Recipients Administering Environmental Permitting Programs (Recipient Guidance)*. Federal Register Notices 71 (54): 14207–14217. Washington, DC: U.S. Environmental Protection Agency.

EPA. 2008. *EPA's Environmental Justice Collaborative Problem-Solving Model*. EPA-300-R-06–002. June. Washington, DC: U.S. Environmental Protection Agency. https://www.epa.gov/environmentaljustice/epas-environmental-justice-collaborative-problem-solving-model. Accessed July 2, 2018.

EPA. 2009a. *State Environmental Justice Cooperative Agreements Fact Sheet*. Washington, DC: U.S. Environmental Protection Agency. October 2009. https://www.epa.gov/sites/production/files/2015-02/documents/fact-sheet-ej-sejca-grants-2009.pdf. Accessed March 7, 2019.

EPA. 2009b. *The ReGenesis Project*. Environmental Justice Achievement Awards. Washington, DC: U.S. Environmental Protection Agency.

EPA. 2011a. *Plan EJ 2014*. September 2011. Washington, DC: U.S. Environmental Protection Agency.

EPA. 2011b. *Plan EJ 2014 Legal Tools*. Office of General Counsel. December 2011. Washington, DC: U.S. Environmental Protection Agency.

EPA 2013a. *EPA Activities to Promote Environmental Justice in the Permit Application Process*. Federal Register 78 (90): 27220–27233. May 9. [Docket ID No. EPA–HQ–OAR–2012–0452; FRL–9811–1]. Washington, DC: U.S. Environmental Protection Agency.

EPA. 2013b. *Environmental Justice Small Grants Program Application Guidance FY 2013*. Washington, DC: U.S. Environmental Protection Agency.

EPA. 2013c. *Title VI of the Civil Rights Act of 1964: Adversity and Compliance with Environmental Health-Based Thresholds.* Draft document. January 24. Washington, DC: U.S. Environmental Protection Agency.

EPA. 2014. *EPA Policy on Environmental Justice for Working with Federally Recognized Tribes and Indigenous Peoples.* July 24, 2014. Washington, DC: U.S. Environmental Protection Agency.

EPA. 2015a. *Guidance on Considering Environmental Justice during the Development of Regulatory Actions.* May 2015. Washington, DC: U.S. Environmental Protection Agency.

EPA. 2015b. *Environmental Justice Collaborative Problem-Solving Cooperative Agreement Program Application Guidance FY 2015.* Washington, DC: U.S. Environmental Protection Agency.

EPA. 2016a. *Technical Guidance for Assessing Environmental Justice in Regulatory Analysis.* June 2016. Washington, DC: U.S. Environmental Protection Agency.

EPA. 2016b. *EJ 2020 Action Agenda: The U.S. EPA's Environmental Justice Strategic Plan for 2016–2020.* Washington, DC: U.S. Environmental Protection Agency.

EPA. 2016c. *Environmental Justice Research Roadmap.* Office of Research and Development. Washington, DC: U.S. Environmental Protection Agency. EPA 601/R-16/006. December 2016. https://www.epa.gov/sites/production/files/2017-01/documents/researchroadmap_environmentaljustice_508_compliant.pdf. Accessed March 7, 2019.

EPA. 2016d. "2016–2017 Environmental Justice Academy." Email announcement. June 17, 2016. Washington, DC: U.S. Environmental Protection Agency.

EPA. 2016e. Enforcement and Compliance History Online (ECHO) Database. https://echo.epa.gov/. Accessed February 28, 2019.

EPA. 2017a. "Environmental Justice." Washington, DC: U.S. Environmental Protection Agency. https://www.epa.gov/environmentaljustice. Accessed August 14, 2017.

EPA. 2017b. "EJSCREEN: Environmental Justice Screening and Mapping Tool." Washington, DC: U.S. Environmental Protection Agency. https://www.epa.gov/ejscreen. Accessed July 13, 2017.

EPA. 2017c. "Progress Cleaning the Air and Improving People's Health." Washington, DC: U.S. Environmental Protection Agency. https://www.epa.gov/clean-air-act-overview/progress-cleaning-air-and-improving-peoples-health#breathe. Accessed September 6, 2017.

EPA. 2017d. "Community Action for a Renewed Environment (CARE) Resources." Washington, DC: U.S. Environmental Protection Agency. https://archive.epa.gov/care/web/html/. Accessed February 28, 2019.

EPA. 2017e. "Brownfields." Washington, DC: U.S. Environmental Protection Agency. https://www.epa.gov/brownfields. Accessed July 19, 2017.

EPA. 2017f. "Technical Assistance Grant (TAG) Program." Washington, DC: U.S. Environmental Protection Agency. https://www.epa.gov/superfund/technical-assistance-grant-tag-program. Accessed July 19, 2017.

EPA. 2017g. "Our Mission and What We Do." Washington, DC: U.S. Environmental Protection Agency. https://www.epa.gov/aboutepa/our-mission-and-what-we-do. Accessed November 17, 2017.

EPA. 2017h. "National Environmental Justice Advisory Council Recommendations." Washington, DC: U.S. Environmental Protection Agency. https://www.epa.gov/environmental-justice/national-environmental-justice-advisory-council-recommendation-reports-0. Accessed August 9, 2017.

EPA. 2017i. "National Environmental Performance Partnership System (NEPPS)." Washington, DC: U.S. Environmental Protection Agency. https://www.epa.gov/ocir/national-environmental-performance-partnership-system-nepps. Accessed August 12, 2017.

EPA. 2017j. *U.S. EPA's External Civil Rights Compliance Office Compliance Toolkit.* January 18. Washington, DC: U.S. Environmental Protection Agency. https://www.epa.gov/sites/production/files/2017-01/documents/toolkit-chapter1-transmittal_letter-faqs.pdf. Accessed March 23, 2018.

EPA. 2017k. *EJSCREEN Environmental Justice Mapping and Screening Tool: EJSCREEN Technical Documentation.* August 2017. Washington, DC: U.S. Environmental Protection Agency. https://www.epa.gov/ejscreen/technical-documentation-ejscreen. Accessed February 28, 2019.

EPA. 2018a. "EPA's Budget and Spending." Washington, DC: U.S. Environmental Protection Agency. https://www.epa.gov/planandbudget/budget. Accessed March 19, 2018.

EPA. 2018b. *FY 2018–2022 EPA Strategic Plan.* Washington, DC: U.S. Environmental Protection Agency. February 12, 2018. https://www.epa.gov/planandbudget/strategicplan. Accessed March 7, 2019.

EPA. 2018c. *Closure of Administrative Complaint.* May 7, 2018. Documents pertaining to EPA File No. 11R-14-R4. Washington, DC: U.S. Environmental Protection Agency. https://www.epa.gov/sites/production/files/2018-05/documents/2018-5-7_ncdeq_reach_closure_letter_per_adr_agreement_11r-14-r4_recipien.pdf. Accessed March 3, 2019.

EPA. 2018d. *Environmental Justice FY 2017 Progress Report.* Washington, DC: U.S. Environmental Protection Agency. https://www.epa.gov/sites/production/files/2018-04

/documents/usepa_fy17_environmental_justice_progress_report.pdf. Accessed May 21, 2018.

EPA. 2018e. "News Release: EPA FY17 Environmental Justice Progress Report Shows Tangible Results for Vulnerable Communities." Washington, DC: U.S. Environmental Protection Agency. April 19, 2018. https://www.epa.gov/newsreleases/epa-fy17-envi ronmental-justice-progress-report-shows-tangible-results-vulnerable. Accessed March 7, 2019.

EPA. 2018f. "Urban Waters Small Grants." Washington, DC: U.S. Environmental Protection Agency. https://www.epa.gov/urbanwaters/urban-waters-small-grants. Accessed May 23, 2018.

EPN. 2017. Environmental Protection Network. https://www.environmentalprotec tionnetwork.org/. Accessed September 1, 2017.

Epstein, Steven. 1996. *Impure Science: AIDS, Activism, and the Politics of Knowledge.* Berkeley: University of California Press.

Espeland, Wendy Nelson. 1998. *The Struggle for Water: Politics, Rationality, and Identity in the American Southwest.* Chicago: University of Chicago Press.

Evans, Louwanda, and Wendy Leo Moore. 2015. "Impossible Burdens: White Institutions, Emotional Labor, and Micro-Resistance." *Social Problems* 62: 439–454.

Faber, Daniel, ed. 1998. *The Struggle for Ecological Democracy: Environmental Justice Movements in the United States.* New York: Guilford Press.

Faber, Daniel. 2008. *Capitalizing on Environmental Injustice: The Polluter-Industrial Complex in the Age of Globalization.* Lanham, MD: Rowman and Littlefield.

Faber, Daniel. 2018. "The Political Economy of Environmental Injustice." In *The Routledge Handbook of Environmental Justice*, ed. Ryan Holifield, Jayajit Chakraborty, and Gordon Walker, 61–73. London: Routledge.

Faber, Daniel R., and Eric J. Krieg. 2002. "Unequal Exposure to Ecological Hazards: Environmental Injustices in the Commonwealth of Massachusetts." *Environmental Health Perspectives* 110 (S2): 277–288.

Faber, Daniel R., and Deborah McCarthy. 2001. *Green of Another Color.* Philanthropy and Environmental Justice Research Project. Boston: Northeastern University.

Faber, Daniel R., and Deborah McCarthy. 2003. "Neo-liberalism, Globalization and the Struggle for Ecological Democracy: Linking Sustainability and Environmental Justice." In *Just Sustainabilities: Development in an Unequal World*, ed. Julian Agyeman, Robert D. Bullard, and Bob Evans, 38–63. Cambridge, MA: MIT Press.

Federman, Adam. 2018. "The Interior Department Is Sidelining Environmental Justice." *The Nation.* November 13. https://www.thenation.com/article/interior

-department-environmental-justice-arctic-drilling-energy-dominance/. Accessed March 7, 2019.

Fernandez, Sergio. 2015. "Understanding and Overcoming Resistance to Organizational Change." In *Handbook of Public Administration*, ed. James L. Perry and Robert K. Christensen, 382–397. San Francisco: Jossey-Bass.

Fields, Timothy, Jr. 2014. "A Dream Realized: Community Driven Revitalization in Spartanburg." *The EPA Blog*. August 26, 2014. https://blog.epa.gov/blog/2014/08/a -dream-realized-community-driven-revitalization-in-spartanburg/. Accessed March 7, 2019.

Flint Water Advisory Task Force. 2016. *Final Report*. March 21, 2016. Office of Governor Rick Snyder, Lansing, MI.

Fortmann, Louise. 1990. "The Role of Professional Norms and Beliefs in the Agency-Client Relations of Natural Resource Bureaucracies." *Natural Resources Journal* 30: 361–380.

Foster, John Bellamy. 2000. *Marx's Ecology: Materialism and Nature*. New York: Monthly Review Press.

Foster, Sheila. 2000. "Meeting the Environmental Justice Challenge: Evolving Norms in Environmental Decisionmaking." *Environmental Law Reporter* 30 (11): 10992.

Foster, Sheila. 2002. "Environmental Justice in an Era of Devolved Collaboration." *Harvard Environmental Law Review* 26: 459–498.

Foster, Sheila R. 2008. "Impact Assessment." In *The Law of Environmental Justice: Theories and Procedures to Address Disproportionate Risks*, ed. Michael B. Gerrard and Sheila R. Foster, 295–340. 2nd ed. Chicago: American Bar Association.

Foster, Sheila R. 2018. "Vulnerability, Equality and Environmental Justice: The Potential and Limits of Law." In *The Routledge Handbook of Environmental Justice*, ed. Ryan Holifield, Jayajit Chakraborty, and Gordon Walker, 136–148. London: Routledge.

Fredrickson, Leif, Christopher Sellers, Lindsey Dillon, Jennifer Liss Ohayon, Nicholas Shapiro, Marianne Sullivan, Stephen Bocking, Phil Brown, Vanessa de la Rosa, Jill Harrison, Sara Johns, Katherine Kulik, Rebecca Lave, Michelle Murphy, Liza Piper, Lauren Richter and Sara Wylie. 2018. "History of U.S. Presidential Assaults on Modern Environmental Health Protection." *American Journal of Public Health* 108 (S2): S95–S103.

Freudenberg, Nicholas, Manuel Pastor, and Barbara Israel. 2011. "Strengthening Community Capacity to Participate in Making Decisions to Reduce Disproportionate Environmental Exposures." *American Journal of Public Health* 101 (S1): S123–S130.

Freudenburg, William R., and Robert Gramling. 1994. "Bureaucratic Slippage and Failures of Agency Vigilance: The Case of the Environmental Studies Program." *Social Problems* 41 (2): 214–239.

Frickel, Scott. 2004a. *Chemical Consequences: Environmental Mutagens, Scientist Activism, and the Rise of Genetic Toxicology*. New Brunswick, NY: Rutgers.

Frickel, Scott. 2004b. "Just Science?: Organizing Scientist Activism in the U.S. Environmental Justice Movement." *Science as Culture* 13 (4): 449–469.

Frickel, Scott, and James R. Elliott. 2018. *Sites Unseen: Uncovering Hidden Hazards in America's Cities*. New York: Russell Sage Foundation.

Frickel, Scott, Rebekah Torcasso, and Annika Anderson. 2015. "The Organization of Expert Activism: Shadow Mobilization in Two Social Movements." *Mobilization* 21 (3): 305–323.

Friedland, Roger, and Robert R. Alford. 1991. "Bringing Society Back In: Symbols, Practices, and Institutional Contradictions." In *The New Institutionalism in Organizational Analysis*, ed. Walter W. Powell and Paul J. DiMaggio, 232–263. Chicago: University of Chicago Press.

Friedman, Lisa, Marina Affo, and Derek Kravitz. 2017. "E.P.A. Officials, Disheartened by Agency's Direction, Are Leaving in Droves." *New York Times*, December 22, 2017. https://www.nytimes.com/2017/12/22/climate/epa-buyouts-pruitt.html. Accessed March 7, 2019.

Fulton, Scott. 2012. "Environmental Justice: Hearing Communities through the Economic Din." Public statement about EJ Legal Tools. February 23, 2012. National Press Club.

Gamson, William A. 1975. *The Strategy of Social Protest*. Homewood, IL: Dorsey Press.

GAO. 2005. *EPA Should Devote More Attention to Environmental Justice When Developing Clean Air Rules*. GAO-05-289. U.S. General Accountability Office. July 2005. https://www.gao.gov/assets/250/247171.pdf. Accessed March 7, 2019.

Garcia, Feliks. 2017. "Donald Trump Bans Environmental Protection Agency Staff from Talking to Press after Suspending All Contracts." *The Independent*, January 24, 2017. https://www.independent.co.uk/news/world/americas/donald-trump-epa-ban-media-blackout-social-media-grants-contracts-latest-a7544276.html. Accessed March 7, 2019.

Gardner, Timothy. 2017. "Nearly 800 Former EPA Officials Oppose Trump Pick for Agency." *Reuters*, February 16, 2017. https://www.reuters.com/article/usa-epa-pruitt-id USL1N1G11GK. Accessed March 7, 2019.

Gauna, Eileen. 2015. "Federal Environmental Justice Policy in Permitting." In *Failed Promises: Evaluating the Federal Government's Response to Environmental Justice*, ed. David M. Konisky, 57–83. Cambridge, MA: MIT Press.

Gerber, Brian J. 2002. "Administering Environmental Justice: Examining the Impact of Executive Order 12898." *Policy and Management Review* 2 (1): 41–61.

Gieryn, Thomas F. 1999. *Cultural Boundaries of Science: Credibility on the Line.* Chicago: University of Chicago Press.

Goldberg, David Theo. 2002. *The Racial State.* Oxford: Blackwell.

Goode, Ann E., and Suellen Keiner. 2003. "Managing for Results to Enhance Government Accountability and Achieve Environmental Justice." *Pace Environmental Law Review* 21: 289–313.

Gordon, Holly D., and Keith I. Harley. 2005. "Environmental Justice and the Legal System." In *Power, Justice, and the Environment: A Critical Appraisal of the Environmental Justice Movement,* ed. David Naguib Pellow and Robert J. Brulle, 153–170. Cambridge, MA: MIT Press.

Gottlieb, Robert. 2005. *Forcing the Spring: The Transformation of the American Environmental Movement.* Rev. ed. Washington, DC: Island Press.

Gottlieb, Robert, and Anupama Joshi. 2010. *Food Justice.* Cambridge, MA: MIT Press.

Gould, Kenneth A., and Tammy L. Lewis. 2017. *Green Gentrification: Urban Sustainability and the Struggle for Environmental Justice.* Abingdon, UK: Routledge.

Grant, Don, Mary Nell Trautner, Liam Downey, and Lisa Thiebaud. 2010. "Bringing the Polluters Back In: Environmental Inequality and the Organization of Chemical Production." *American Sociological Review* 75 (4): 479–504.

Greenwood, Royston, Mia Raynard, Farah Kodeih, Evelyn R. Micelotta, and Michael Lounsbury. 2011. "Institutional Complexity and Organizational Responses." *The Academy of Management Annals* 5 (1): 317–371.

Grineski, Sara E., and Timothy W. Collins. 2018. "Geographic and Social Disparities in Exposure to Air Neurotoxicants at U.S. Public Schools." *Environmental Research* 161: 580–587.

Gross, Elizabeth, and Paul Stretesky. 2015. "Environmental Justice and the Courts." In *Failed Promises: Evaluating the Federal Government's Response to Environmental Justice,* ed. David M. Konisky, 205–231. Cambridge, MA: MIT Press.

Guidi, Ruxandra. 2018. "California Steps Up for Environmental Justice." *High Country News,* March 29, 2018. https://www.hcn.org/articles/letter-from-california-as-the-feds-step-back-california-steps-forward. Accessed March 7, 2019.

Gustin, Georgina. 2017. "Congress Questions Pruitt on Industry's Growing Influence in EPA." *Inside Climate News,* December 7, 2017. https://insideclimatenews.org/news/07122017/scott-pruitt-epa-testimony-congress-hearing-climate-clean-power-plan-red-team-fossil-fuel-lobby. Accessed March 7, 2019.

Guthman, Julie. 2007. "Can't Stomach It: How Michael Pollan et al. Made Me Want to Eat Cheetos." *Gastronomica* 7 (2): 75–79.

Guthman, Julie. 2008a. "Neoliberalism and the Making of Food Politics in California." *Geoforum* 39 (3): 1171–1183.

Guthman, Julie. 2008b. "Thinking Inside the Neoliberal Box: The Micro-Politics of Agro-Food Philanthropy." *Geoforum* 39 (3): 1241–1253.

Guthman, Julie. 2011. *Weighing In: Obesity, Food Justice, and the Limits of Capitalism.* Berkeley: University of California Press.

Guzy, Gary S. 2000. "EPA Statutory and Regulatory Authorities Under Which Environmental Justice Issues May Be Addressed in Permitting." Memo. December 1, 2000. Washington, DC: U.S. Environmental Protection Agency.

Hallett, Tim. 2010. "The Myth Incarnate: Recoupling Processes, Turmoil, and Inhabited Institutions in an Urban Elementary School." *American Sociological Review* 75 (1): 52–74.

Hallett, Tim, and Marc J. Ventresca. 2006. "Inhabited Institutions: Social Interactions and Organizational Forms in Gouldner's Patterns of Industrial Bureaucracy." *Theory and Society* 35: 213–216.

Hand, Mark. 2018. "California's Attorney General Puts Polluters on Notice with New Environmental Justice Unit." *Think Progress*, February 23, 2018. https://think progress.org/california-attorney-general-puts-polluters-on-notice-21f22ee2da89/. Accessed March 7, 2019.

Hannigan, John A. 2006. *Environmental Sociology.* 2nd ed. London: Routledge.

Hansen, Sarah. 2012. *Cultivating the Grassroots: A Winning Approach for Environment and Climate Funders.* Washington, DC: National Committee for Responsible Philanthropy.

Harrison, Jill. 2006. "'Accidents' and Invisibilities: Scaled Discourse and the Naturalization of Regulatory Neglect in California's Pesticide Drift Conflict." *Political Geography* 25 (5): 506–529.

Harrison, Jill. 2008. "Abandoned Bodies and Spaces of Sacrifice: Pesticide Drift Activism and the Contestation of Neoliberal Environmental Politics in California." *Geoforum* 39 (3): 1197–1214.

Harrison, Jill Lindsey. 2011. *Pesticide Drift and the Pursuit of Environmental Justice.* Cambridge, MA: MIT Press.

Harrison, Jill Lindsey. 2014. "Neoliberal Environmental Justice: Mainstream Ideas of Justice in Political Conflict over Agricultural Pesticides in the United States." *Environmental Politics* 23 (4): 650–669.

Harrison, Jill Lindsey. 2015. "Coopted Environmental Justice? Activists' Roles in Shaping EJ Policy Implementation." *Environmental Sociology* 1 (4): 241–255.

Harrison, Jill Lindsey. 2016. "Bureaucrats' Tacit Understandings and Social Movement Policy Implementation: Unpacking the Deviation of Agency Environmental Justice Programs from EJ Movement Priorities." *Social Problems* 63 (4): 534–553.

Harrison, Jill Lindsey. 2017. "'We Do Ecology, Not Sociology': Interactions among Bureaucrats and the Undermining of Regulatory Agencies' Environmental Justice Efforts." *Environmental Sociology* 3 (3): 197–212.

Harvard Law School. 2018. "Regulatory Rollback Tracker." Environmental Law Program. Emmett Clinic Policy Initiative. Harvard Law School, Cambridge, MA. http://environment.law.harvard.edu/policy-initiative/regulatory-rollback-tracker/. Accessed February 1, 2018.

Harvey, David. 1996. *Justice, Nature, and the Geography of Difference*. Malden, MA: Blackwell.

Harvey, David. 2005. *A Brief History of Neoliberalism*. New York: Oxford University Press.

Hatcher, Sarah M., Sarah R. Rhodes, Jill R. Stewart, Ellen Silbergeld, Nora Pisanic, Jesper Larsen, Sharon Jiang, Amanda Krosche, Devon Hall, Karen C. Carroll, and Christopher D. Heaney. 2017. "The Prevalence of Antibiotic-Resistant Staphylococcus Aureus Nasal Carriage among Industrial Hog Operation Workers, Community Residents, and Children Living in their Households: North Carolina, USA." *Environmental Health Perspectives* 125 (4): 560–569.

Hayes, Kelly. 2016. "How to Talk about #NoDAPL: A Native Perspective." *Truthout*, October 28, 2016. http://www.truth-out.org/opinion/item/38165-how-to-talk-about-nodapl-a-native-perspective. Accessed March 7, 2019.

Hellerstein, Erica, and Ken Fine. 2017. "A Million Tons of Feces and an Unbearable Stench: Life Near Industrial Pig Farms." *The Guardian*, September 20, 2017. https://www.theguardian.com/us-news/2017/sep/20/north-carolina-hog-industry-pig-farms. Accessed March 7, 2019.

Henry, Devin. 2017. "Senate Confirms Top Air Regulator at EPA." *The Hill*, November 9, 2017. http://thehill.com/policy/energy-environment/359593-senate-confirms-top-air-regulator-at-epa. Accessed March 7, 2019.

Hess, David J. 2007. *Alternative Pathways in Science and Industry: Activism, Innovation, and the Environment in an Era of Globalization*. Cambridge, MA: MIT Press.

Hess, David J. 2016. *Undone Science: Social Movements, Mobilized Publics, and Industrial Transitions*. Cambridge, MA: MIT Press.

Heynen, Nik, James McCarthy, W. Scott Prudham, and Paul Robbins. 2007. *Neoliberal Environments: False Promises and Unnatural Consequences*. London: Routledge.

Hochschild, Arlie Russell. 2016. *Strangers in Their Own Land: Anger and Mourning on the American Right*. New York: The New Press.

Hofrichter, Richard, ed. 1993. *Toxic Struggles: The Theory and Practice of Environmental Justice*. Philadelphia: New Society Publishers.

Holifield, Ryan. 2004. "Neoliberalism and Environmental Justice in the United States Environmental Protection Agency: Translating Policy into Managerial Practice in Hazardous Waste Remediation." *Geoforum* 35: 285–297.

Holifield, Ryan. 2012. "The Elusive Environmental Justice Area: Three Waves of Policy in the U.S. Environmental Protection Agency." *Environmental Justice* 5 (6): 293–297.

Holifield, Ryan. 2014. "Accounting for Diversity in Environmental Justice Screening Tools: Toward Multiple Indices of Disproportionate Impact." *Environmental Practice* 16: 77–86.

Holifield, Ryan, Jayajit Chakraborty, and Gordon Walker. 2018. *The Routledge Handbook of Environmental Justice*. London: Routledge.

Huber, Matthew T. 2013. *Lifeblood: Oil, Freedom, and the Forces of Capitalism*. Minneapolis: University of Minnesota Press.

HUD. 2017. "Regional Planning Grants and the SCI." U.S. Department of Housing and Urban Development. https://www.hudexchange.info/programs/sci/. Accessed September 27, 2017.

IEPA. 2018. *Environmental Justice Public Participation Policy*. Illinois Environmental Protection Agency. April 20, 2018. https://www2.illinois.gov/epa/topics/environmental-justice/Documents/public-participation-policy.pdf. Accessed March 3, 2019.

Ingraham, Christopher. 2017. "Flint's Lead-Poisoned Water Had a 'Horrifyingly Large' Effect on Fetal Deaths, Study Finds." *Washington Post,* September 21, 2017. https://www.washingtonpost.com/news/wonk/wp/2017/09/21/flints-lead-poisoned-water-had-a-horrifyingly-large-effect-on-fetal-deaths-study-finds/?noredirect=on&utm_term=.55daa9d75621. Accessed March 7, 2019.

Irwin, Alan. 2001. *Sociology and the Environment: A Critical Introduction to Society, Nature, and Knowledge*. Malden, MA: Blackwell.

IVAN. 2018. "Identifying Violations Affecting Neighborhoods: Environmental Justice Monitoring and Reporting Network." https://ivanonline.org/. Accessed May 25, 2018.

Jasanoff, Sheila. 1990. *The Fifth Branch: Science Advisors as Policymakers*. Cambridge, MA: Harvard University Press.

Jenness, Valerie, and Ryken Grattet. 2001. *Making Hate a Crime: From Social Movement to Law Enforcement*. New York: Russell Sage Foundation.

Jessop, Bob. 2002. "Neoliberalism and Urban Governance: A State Theoretical Perspective." *Antipode* 34 (3): 452–472.

Jones, Van. 2008. *The Green Collar Economy: How One Solution Can Fix Our Two Biggest Problems*. New York: HarperOne.

Jorgenson, Andrew K., and Brett Clark. 2012. "Are the Economy and the Environment Decoupling? A Comparative International Study, 1960–2005." *American Journal of Sociology* 118: 1–44.

Katzenstein, Mary Fainsod. 1999. *Faithful and Fearless: Moving Feminist Protest inside the Church and Military*. Princeton, NJ: Princeton University Press.

Kellogg, Katherine C. 2009. "Operating Room: Relational Spaces and Microinstitutional Change in Surgery." *American Journal of Sociology* 115 (3): 657–711.

Kellogg, Katherine C. 2011. "Hot Lights and Cold Steel: Cultural and Political Toolkits for Practice Change in Surgery." *Organization Science* 22 (2): 482–502.

Kellogg, Katherine C. 2014. "Brokerage Professions and Implementing Reform in an Age of Experts." *American Sociological Review* 79 (5): 912–941.

Kenny, Kate, Andrea Whittle, and Hugh Willmott. 2016. "Organizational Identity: The Significance of Power and Politics." In *The Oxford Handbook of Organizational Identity*, ed. Michael G. Pratt, Majken Schultz, Blake E. Ashforth, and Davide Ravasi, 140–159. Oxford: Oxford University Press.

Kimura, Aya Hirata. 2016. *Radiation Brain Moms and Citizen Scientists: The Gender Politics of Food Contamination after Fukushima*. Durham, NC: Duke University Press.

Kinchy, Abby. 2012. *Seeds, Science, and Struggle: The Global Politics of Transgenic Crops*. Cambridge, MA: MIT Press.

King, Brayden G, and Nicholas A. Pearce. 2010. "The Contentiousness of Markets: Politics, Social Movements, and Institutional Change in Markets." *Annual Review of Sociology* 36: 249–267.

King, Marva. 2012. "Collaboration Program Effectiveness: Comparing Two Community Partnership Programs." Unpublished doctoral dissertation. Fairfax, VA: George Mason University.

King, Marva. 2014. "Who's Your Environmental Justice Shero?" *The EPA Blog*. U.S. Environmental Protection Agency. March 19, 2014. https://blog.epa.gov/blog/2014/03/whos-your-ej-shero/. Accessed March 7, 2019.

Kohl, Ellen. 2015. "'People Think We're EPA, We Can Do Whatever We Have the Will to Do:' Negotiating Expectations of Environmental Justice Policies." Paper presented at the Annual Meeting of the Association of American Geographers, Chicago. April 2015.

Kohl, Ellen. 2016. "The Performance of Environmental Justice: The Environmental Protection Agency's Collaborative Problem Solving Model as Cooption." Paper presented at the Annual Meeting of the Association of American Geographers, San Francisco. April 2016.

Kohl, Ellen. Forthcoming. "'When I Take Off My EPA Hat': Using Intersectional Theories to Examine Environmental Justice Governance." *The Professional Geographer.*

Konisky, David M. 2009. "The Limited Effects of Federal Environmental Justice Policy on State Enforcement." *Policy Studies Journal* 37 (3): 475–496.

Konisky, David M. 2015a. "The Federal Government's Response to Environmental Inequality." In *Failed Promises: Evaluating the Federal Government's Response to Environmental Justice,* ed. David M. Konisky, 29–56. Cambridge, MA: MIT Press.

Konisky, David M. 2015b. "Federal Environmental Justice Policy: Lessons Learned." In *Failed Promises: Evaluating the Federal Government's Response to Environmental Justice,* ed. David M. Konisky, 233–257. Cambridge, MA: MIT Press.

Konisky, David M., and Christopher Reenock. 2015. "Evaluating Fairness in Environmental Regulatory Enforcement." In *Failed Promises: Evaluating the Federal Government's Response to Environmental Justice,* ed. David M. Konisky, 173–203. Cambridge, MA: MIT Press.

Konisky, David M., and Tyler S. Schario. 2010. "Examining Environmental Justice in Facility-Level Regulatory Enforcement." *Social Science Quarterly* 91 (3): 835–855.

Kreiner, Glen E., and Chad Murphy. 2016. "Organizational Identity Work." In *The Oxford Handbook of Organizational Identity,* ed. Michael G. Pratt, Majken Schultz, Blake E. Ashforth, and Davide Ravasi, 276–293. Oxford: Oxford University Press.

Kroll-Smith, Steve, and H. Hugh Floyd. 1997. *Bodies in Protest: Environmental Illness and the Struggle over Medical Knowledge.* New York: NYU Press.

Kuehn, Robert R. 1996. "The Environmental Justice Implications of Quantitative Risk Assessment." *University of Illinois Law Review* 103: 116–139.

Kurtz, Hilda. 2007. "Gender and Environmental Justice in Louisiana: Blurring the Boundaries of Public and Private Spheres." *Gender, Place, and Culture* 14 (4): 409–426.

Kurtz, Hilda. 2009. "Acknowledging the Racial State: An Agenda for Environmental Justice Research." *Antipode* 41 (4): 684–704.

Langston, Nancy. 1995. *Forest Dreams, Forest Nightmares: The Paradox of Old Growth in the Inland West.* Seattle: University of Washington Press.

Langston, Nancy. 2010. *Toxic Bodies: Hormone Disruptors and the Legacy of DES.* New Haven, CT: Yale University Press.

Lashley, Sarah E. 2016. "Pursuing Justice for All: Collaborative Problem-Solving in the Environmental Justice Context." *Environmental Justice* 9 (6): 188–194.

Lawrence, Thomas B. 2008. "Power, Institutions and Organizations." In *The Sage Handbook of Organizational Institutionalism*, ed. Royston Greenwood, Christine Oliver, Roy Suddaby, and Kerstin Sahlin, 170–197. Los Angeles: SAGE Publications.

Layzer, Judith. 2012. *Open for Business: Conservatives' Opposition to Environmental Regulation*. Cambridge, MA: MIT Press.

Lazarus, Richard. 1993. "Pursuing 'Environmental Justice': The Distributional Effects of Environmental Protection." *Northwest Urban Law Review* 87 (3): 787–857.

Lazarus, Richard J. 1996. "Draft Memorandum on Incorporating Environmental Justice into EPA Permitting Authority." July 18, 1996. Washington, DC: National Environmental Justice Advisory Committee.

Lazarus, Richard J., and Stephanie Tai. 1999. "Integrating Environmental Justice into EPA Permitting Authority." *Ecology Law Quarterly* 26: 617–678.

Leber, Rebecca. 2017. "Meet the One EPA Employee Unafraid to Call Out Scott Pruitt." *Mother Jones*, September 28, 2017. https://www.motherjones.com/environ ment/2017/09/meet-the-one-epa-employee-unafraid-to-call-out-scott-pruitt/. Accessed March 7, 2019.

Leber, Rebecca. 2018. "This Might Be Scott Pruitt's Most Destructive Move Yet." *Mother Jones*. April 24. https://www.motherjones.com/environment/2018/04/this-might-be-scott-pruitts-most-destructive-move-yet/. Accessed May 14, 2018.

Lee, Charles. 2005. "Collaborative Models to Achieve Environmental Justice and Healthy Communities." In *Power, Justice, and the Environment: A Critical Appraisal of the Environmental Justice Movement*, ed. David Naguib Pellow and Robert J. Brulle, 37–53. Cambridge, MA: MIT Press.

Lerner, Steve. 2005. *Diamond*. Cambridge, MA: MIT Press.

Levine, Adeline Gordon. 1982. *Love Canal: Science, Politics, and People*. Lexington, MA: Lexington Books.

Lewis, Tonya, and Sean Bennett. 2013. "Environmental Justice, the Demographic Threshold, and the Exclusion Factor: Are Benefits Reaching Communities at Risk?" *Environmental Justice* 6: 213–218.

Liévanos, Raoul S. 2012. "Certainty, Fairness, and Balance: State Resonance and Environmental Justice Policy Implementation." *Sociological Forum* 27 (2): 481–503.

Liévanos, Raoul S. 2015. "Race, Deprivation, and Immigrant Isolation: The Spatial Demography of Air-Toxic Clusters in the Continental United States." *Social Science Research* 54: 50–67.

Liévanos, Raoul S. 2018. "Retooling CalEnviroScreen: Cumulative Pollution Burden and Race-Based Environmental Health Vulnerabilities in California." *International Journal of Environmental Research and Public Health* 15 (4): 762.

Liévanos, Raoul S., and Christine Horne. 2017. "Unequal Resilience: The Duration of Electricity Outages." *Energy Policy* 108: 201–211.

Liévanos, Raoul S., Jonathan K. London, and Julie Sze. 2011. "Uneven Transformations and Environmental Justice: Regulatory Science, Street Science, and Pesticide Regulation in California." In *Technoscience and Environmental Justice: Expert Cultures in a Grassroots Movement*, ed. Gwen Ottinger and Benjamin R. Cohen, 201–228. Cambridge, MA: MIT Press.

Lipsitz, George. 1995. "The Possessive Investment in Whiteness: Racialized Social Democracy and the 'White' Problem in American Studies." *American Quarterly* 47 (3): 369–387.

Lipsitz, George. 2011. *How Racism Takes Place*. Philadelphia: Temple University Press.

Lipsky, Michael. 1980. *Street-Level Bureaucracy: Dilemmas of the Individual in Public Services*. New York: Russell Sage Foundation.

Lipton, Eric. 2017a. "Why Has the E.P.A. Shifted on Toxic Chemicals? An Industry Insider Helps Call the Shots." *The New York Times*, October 21, 2017. https://www.nytimes.com/2017/10/21/us/trump-epa-chemicals-regulations.html. Accessed March 7, 2019.

Lipton, Eric. 2017b. "Courts Thwart Administration's Effort to Rescind Obama-Era Environmental Regulations." *The New York Times*, October 6, 2017. https://www.nytimes.com/2017/10/06/climate/trump-administration-environmental-regulations.html. Accessed March 7, 2019.

Lipton, Eric. 2018. "Court Orders E.P.A. to Ban Chlorpyrifos, Pesticide Tied to Children's Health Problems." *The New York Times*, August 9, 2018. https://www.nytimes.com/2018/08/09/us/politics/chlorpyrifos-pesticide-ban-epa-court.html. Accessed March 7, 2019.

Lipton, Eric, and Lisa Friedman. 2017a. "E.P.A. Chief's Calendar: A Stream of Industry Meetings and Trips Home." *The New York Times*, October 3, 2017. https://www.nytimes.com/2017/10/03/us/politics/epa-scott-pruitt-calendar-industries-coal-oil-environmentalists.html. Accessed March 7, 2019.

Lipton, Eric, and Lisa Friedman. 2017b. "E.P.A. Employees Spoke Out. Then Came Scrutiny of Their Email." *The New York Times*, December 17, 2017. https://www.nytimes.com/2017/12/17/us/politics/epa-pruitt-media-monitoring.html. Accessed March 7, 2019.

Lipton, Eric, Kenneth P. Vogel, and Lisa Friedman. 2018. "E.P.A. Officials Sidelined after Questioning Scott Pruitt." *The New York Times*, April 5, 2018. https://www.nytimes.com/2018/04/05/business/epa-officials-questioned-scott-pruitt.html. Accessed March 7, 2019.

Lockie, Stewart. 2013. "Neoliberalism by Design." In *Routledge International Handbook of Social and Environmental Change*, ed. Stewart Lockie, David A. Sonnenfeld, and Dana R. Fisher, 70–80. Abingdon, UK: Routledge.

London, Jonathan, Alex Karner, Julie Sze, Dana Rowan, Gerardo Gambirazzio, and Deb Niemeier. 2013. "Racing Climate Change: Collaboration and Conflict in California's Global Climate Change Policy Arena." *Global Environmental Change* 23: 791–799.

London, Jonathan K., Julie Sze, and Raoul S. Liévanos. 2008. "Problems, Promise, Progress, and Perils: Critical Reflections on Environmental Justice Policy Implementation in California." *UCLA Journal of Environmental Law & Policy* 26 (2): 255–289.

LoPresti, Tony. 2013. "Realizing the Promise of Environmental Civil Rights: The Renewed Effort to Enforce Title VI of the Civil Rights Act of 1964." *Administrative Law Review* 65 (4): 757–819.

Low, Nicholas, and Brendan Gleeson. 1998. *Justice, Society, and Nature: An Exploration of Political Ecology.* London: Routledge.

Maantay, Juliana, and Andrew Maroko. 2018. "Assessing Population at Risk: Areal Interpolation and Dasymetric Mapping." In *The Routledge Handbook of Environmental Justice*, ed. Ryan Holifield, Jayajit Chakraborty, and Gordon Walker, 190–206. London: Routledge.

Maguire, Kelly, and Glenn Sheriff. 2011. "Comparing Distributions of Environmental Outcomes for Regulatory Environmental Justice Analysis." *International Journal of Environmental Research and Public Health* 8: 1707–1726.

Malin, Stephanie. 2015. *The Price of Nuclear Power: Uranium Communities and Environmental Justice.* New Brunswick, NJ: Rutgers University Press.

Maniates, Michael F. 2001. "Individualization: Plant a Tree, Buy a Bike, Save the World?" *Global Environmental Politics* 1 (3): 31–52.

Mank, Bradford C. 2008. "Title VI." In *The Law of Environmental Justice: Theories and Procedures to Address Disproportionate Risks*, ed. Michael B. Gerrard and Sheila R. Foster, 23–65. 2nd ed. Chicago: American Bar Association.

Mann, Geoff. 2013. *Disassembly Required: A Field Guide to Actually Existing Capitalism.* Edinburgh: AK Press.

Mares, Teresa M., and Devon G. Peña. 2010. "Urban Agriculture in the Making of Insurgent Spaces in Los Angeles and Seattle." In *Insurgent Public Space: Guerrilla Urbanism and the Remaking of Contemporary Cities*, ed. Jeffrey Hou, 241–254. New York: Routledge.

Mascarenhas, Michael. 2012. *Where the Waters Divide: Neoliberalism, White Privilege, and Environmental Racism in Canada.* Lanham, MD: Lexington Books.

Mascarenhas, Michael J. 2016. "Where the Waters Divide: Neoliberal Racism, White Privilege and Environmental Injustice." *Race, Gender, and Class* 23 (3/4): 6–25.

Massachusetts. 2002. "Environmental Justice Policy of the Executive Office of Environmental Affairs." Commonwealth of Massachusetts. https://www.mass.gov/files/documents/2017/11/29/ej%20policy%202002.pdf. Accessed March 3, 2019.

Massachusetts. 2017. "Environmental Justice Policy of the Executive Office of Energy and Environmental Affairs." Commonwealth of Massachusetts. https://www.mass.gov/files/documents/2017/11/29/2017-environmental-justice-policy_0.pdf. Accessed March 3, 2019.

Matthew, Dayna Bowen. 2017. *How the New Administration Could Bring a New Day to the EPA's Title VI Enforcement.* Congressional Black Caucus Foundation. https://www.brookings.edu/research/how-the-new-administration-could-bring-a-new-day-to-the-epas-title-vi-enforcement/. Accessed March 3, 2019.

McCarthy, James. 2005. "Devolution in the Woods: Community Forestry as Hybrid Neoliberalism." *Environment and Planning A* 37: 995–1014.

McCarthy, James, and Scott Prudham. 2004. "Neoliberal Nature and the Nature of Neoliberalism." *Geoforum* 35 (3): 275–283.

McCarthy, John D., David W. Britt, and Mark Wolfson. 1991. "The Institutional Channeling of Social Movements by the State in the United States." *Research in Social Movements, Conflicts, and Change* 13: 45–76.

McClintock, Nathan. 2014. "Radical, Reformist, and Garden-Variety Neoliberal: Coming to Terms with Urban Agriculture's Contradictions." *Local Environment* 19 (2): 147–171.

McGreevy, Patrick. 2015. "Toxics Agency Chief Condemns Racially Charged Emails." *Los Angeles Times,* December 9, 2015. http://www.latimes.com/politics/la-me-pc-toxics-agency-chief-condemns-racially-charged-emails-20151209-story.html. Accessed March 7, 2019.

McKenna, Phil. 2017. "Chief Environmental Justice Official at EPA Resigns, With Plea to Pruitt to Protect Vulnerable Communities." *Inside Climate News,* March 9, 2017. https://insideclimatenews.org/news/09032017/epa-environmental-justice-mustafa-ali-flint-water-crisis-dakota-access-pipeline-trump-scott-pruitt. Accessed March 7, 2019.

Mennis, Jeremy, and Megan Heckert. 2018. "Application of Spatial Statistical Techniques." In *The Routledge Handbook of Environmental Justice,* ed. Ryan Holifield, Jayajit Chakraborty, and Gordon Walker, 207–221. London: Routledge.

Meyer, John W., and Brian Rowan. 1977. "Institutionalized Organizations: Formal Structure as Myth and Ceremony." *American Journal of Sociology* 83 (2): 340–363.

Meyerson, Debra E., and Maureen A. Scully. 1995. "Tempered Radicalism and the Politics of Ambivalence and Change." *Organization Science* 6 (5): 585–600.

Michigan Civil Rights Commission. 2017. *The Flint Water Crisis: Systemic Racism through the Lens of Flint.* Report of the Michigan Civil Rights Commission. February 17, 2017. http://www.michigan.gov/documents/mdcr/VFlintCrisisRep-F-Edited3-13-17_554317_7 .pdf. Accessed March 7, 2019.

Michigan Environmental Justice Work Group. 2018. *Environmental Justice Work Group Report: Michigan as a Global Leader in Environmental Justice.* Michigan Environmental Justice Work Group. March 2018. https://www.michigan.gov/documents/snyder /Environmental_Justice_Work_Group_Report_616102_7.pdf. Accessed March 7, 2019.

Mikati, Ihab, Adam F. Benson, Thomas J. Luben, Jason D. Sacks, and Jennifer Richmond-Bryant. 2018. "Disparities in Distribution of Particulate Matter Emission Sources by Race and Poverty Status." *American Journal of Public Health* 108 (4): 480–485.

Milman, Oliver. 2017. "A Civil Rights 'Emergency': Justice, Clean Air and Water in the Age of Trump." *The Guardian,* November 20, 2017. https://www.theguardian .com/us-news/2017/nov/20/environmental-justice-in-the-age-of-trump. Accessed March 7, 2019.

Milman, Oliver. 2018. "Environmental Racism Case: EPA Rejects Alabama Town's Claim over Toxic Landfill." *The Guardian,* March 6, 2018. https://www.theguard ian.com/us-news/2018/mar/06/environmental-racism-alabama-landfill-civil-rights. Accessed March 7, 2019.

Mintz, Joel A. 2012. *Enforcement at the EPA: High Stakes and Hard Choices.* Austin: University of Texas Press.

Mock, Brentin. 2014. "Environmental Justice Works—and These Folks Show Us How." *Grist,* September 18, 2014. https://grist.org/cities/environmental-justice-works-and-these-folks-show-us-how/. Accessed March 7, 2019.

Mock, Brentin. 2017. "At the EPA, It's the End of an Era." *CityLab,* March 10, 2017. https://www.citylab.com/equity/2017/03/at-the-epa-its-the-end-of-an-era/519246/. Accessed March 7, 2019.

Mohai, Paul, Byoung-Suk Kweon, Sangyun Lee, and Kerry Ard. 2011. "Air Pollution Around Schools Is Linked to Poorer Student Health and Academic Performance." *Health Affairs* 30 (5): 852–862.

Mohai, Paul, Paula M. Lantz, Jeffrey Morenoff, James S. House, and Richard P. Mero. 2009b. "Racial and Socioeconomic Disparities in Residential Proximity to Polluting Industrial Facilities: Evidence from the Americans' Changing Lives Study." *American Journal of Public Health* 99: 649–656.

Mohai, Paul, David Pellow, and J. Timmons Roberts. 2009a. "Environmental Justice." *Annual Review of Environment and Resources* 34: 405–430.

Mohai, Paul, and Robin Saha. 2007. "Racial Inequality in the Distribution of Hazard-ous Waste: A National-Level Reassessment." *Social Problems* 54: 343–370.

Mohai, Paul, and Robin Saha. 2015. "Which Came First, People or Pollution? A Review of Theory and Evidence from Longitudinal Environmental Justice Studies." *Environmental Research Letters* 10: 125011.

Moore, Kelly. 2008. *Disrupting Science: Social Movements, American Scientists, and the Politics of the Military, 1945–1975.* Princeton, NJ: Princeton University Press.

Moore, Wendy. 2008. *Reproducing Racism: White Space, Elite Law Schools, and Racial Inequality.* Lanham, MD: Rowman & Littlefield.

Moore, Wendy Leo, and Joyce M. Bell. 2017. "The Right to Be Racist in College: Racist Speech, White Institutional Space, and the First Amendment." *Law and Policy* 39 (2): 99–120.

Morello-Frosch, Rachel. 2002. "Discrimination and the Political Economy of Environ-mental Inequality." *Environment and Planning C: Government and Policy* 20: 477–496.

Morello-Frosch, Rachel, and Bill M. Jesdale. 2006. "Separate and Unequal: Residen-tial Segregation and Estimated Cancer Risks Associated with Ambient Air Toxics in U.S. Metropolitan Areas." *Environmental Health Perspectives* 114 (3): 386–393.

Morello-Frosch, Rachel, Manuel Pastor Jr., and James Sadd. 2002. "Integrating Envi-ronmental Justice and the Precautionary Principle in Research and Policy Making: The Case of Ambient Air Toxics Exposures and Health Risks among Schoolchildren in Los Angeles." *Annals of the American Academy of Political and Social Science* 584: 47–68.

Morello-Frosch, Rachel, Miriam Zuk, Michael Jerrett, Bhavna Shamasunder, and Amy D. Kyle. 2011. "Understanding the Cumulative Impacts of Inequalities in Envi-ronmental Health: Implications for Policy." *Health Affairs* 30 (5): 879–887.

MPCA. 2015. *Environmental Justice Framework: 2015–2018.* Minneapolis: Minnesota Pollution Control Agency.

MPCA. 2017. "Air Permit Commenting Training." Email announcement. October 13, 2017. Minneapolis: Minnesota Pollution Control Agency.

MPCA. 2018. "Air Permitting in South Minneapolis." Minnesota Pollution Control Agency. https://www.pca.state.mn.us/air/air-permitting-south-minneapolis. Accessed November 13, 2018.

Mueller, Jennifer C. 2017. "Producing Colorblindness: Everyday Mechanisms of White Ignorance." *Social Problems* 64: 219–238.

NAPA. 2001. *Environmental Justice in EPA Permitting: Reducing Pollution in High-Risk Communities Is Integral to the Agency's Mission.* December 2001. National Academy of Public Administration.

Nash, Linda. 2006. *Inescapable Ecologies: A History of Environment, Disease, and Knowledge*. Berkeley: University of California Press.

NEJAC. 1996. *Environmental Justice, Urban Revitalization, and Brownfields: The Search for Authentic Signs of Hope*. U.S. Environmental Protection Agency National Environmental Justice Advisory Council. EPA 500-R-96–002. December 1996. https://www.epa .gov/sites/production/files/2015-02/documents/public-dialogue-brownfields-1296 .pdf. Accessed March 7, 2019.

NEJAC. 2000. *Environmental Justice in the Permitting Process: A Report from the Public Meeting on Environmental Permitting Convened by the National Environmental Justice Advisory Council, Arlington, Virginia*. EPA/300-R-00–004. July 20, 2000. U.S. Environmental Protection Agency National Environmental Justice Advisory Council.

NEJAC. 2004. *Ensuring Risk Reduction in Communities with Multiple Stressors: Environmental Justice and Cumulative Risks/Impacts*. December 2004. U.S. Environmental Protection Agency National Environmental Justice Advisory Council.

NEJAC. 2010. *Nationally Consistent Environmental Justice Screening Approaches*. U.S. Environmental Protection Agency National Environmental Justice Advisory Council.

NEJAC. 2011. *Enhancing Environmental Justice in EPA Permitting Programs*. April 2011. U.S. Environmental Protection Agency National Environmental Justice Advisory Council.

NEJAC. 2013a. *Recommendations Regarding EPA Activities to Promote Environmental Justice in the Permit Application Process*. U.S. Environmental Protection Agency National Environmental Justice Advisory Council.

NEJAC 2013b. *Model Guidelines for Public Participation*. U.S. Environmental Protection Agency National Environmental Justice Advisory Council.

NEJAC. 2014. *Recommendations for Integrating Environmental Justice into the EPA's Research Enterprise*. June 30, 2014. U.S. Environmental Protection Agency National Environmental Justice Advisory Council.

NIEHS. 2017. "Research to Action." National Institute for Environmental Health Sciences. https://www.niehs.nih.gov/research/supported/translational/peph/prog/rta /index.cfm. Accessed June 21, 2017.

NJDEP EJAC. 2009. *Strategies for Addressing Cumulative Impacts in Environmental Justice Communities*. New Jersey Department of Environmental Protection Environmental Justice Advisory Committee.

Noonan, Douglas S. 2015. "Assessing the EPA's Experience with Equity in Standard Setting." In *Failed Promises: Evaluating the Federal Government's Response to Environmental Justice*, ed. David M. Konisky, 85–116. Cambridge, MA: MIT Press.

NRC. 2009. *Science and Decisions: Advancing Risk Assessment*. Washington, DC: National Academies Press.

Nweke, Onyemaechi C. 2011. "A Framework for Integrating Environmental Justice in Regulatory Analysis." *International Journal of Environmental Research and Public Health* 8: 2366–2385.

Nweke, Onyemaechi C., Devon Payne-Sturges, Lisa Garcia, Charles Lee, Hal Zenick, Peter Grevatt, William H. Sanders III, Heather Case, and Irene Dankwa-Mullan. 2011. "Symposium on Integrating the Science of Environmental Justice into Decision-Making at the Environmental Protection Agency: An Overview." *American Journal of Public Health* 101 (S1): S19–S26.

NYCREDC. 2011. *Strategic Plan*. November 14, 2011. New York City Regional Economic Development Council.

NYSDEC. 2003. "Environmental Justice and Permitting." Commissioner Policy CP-29. New York State Department of Environmental Conservation.

NYSDEC. 2011. *Application and Instructions: Environmental Justice Community Impact Grant Program for Communities Exposed to Multiple Environmental Harms and Risks in New York State*. Albany, NY: New York State Department of Environmental Conservation.

NYSDEC. 2015. "Environmental Justice Grant Application Information." New York State Department of Environmental Conservation. http://www.dec.ny.gov/public /41460.html. Accessed January 8, 2015.

NYSDEC. 2016. *New York State Environmental Justice Community Impact Grant Program 2016 Request for Application*. New York State Department of Environmental Conservation.

O'Brien, Mary. 2000. *Making Better Environmental Decisions: An Alternative to Risk Assessment*. Cambridge, MA: MIT Press.

O'Connor, James. 1998. *Natural Causes: Essays in Ecological Marxism*. New York: Guilford.

ODEQ. 1997. *Environmental Justice: Principles and Implementation*. Oregon Department of Environmental Quality. https://www.oregon.gov/deq/FilterDocs/DEQeJpolicy.pdf. Accessed March 3, 2019.

Omi, Michael, and Howard Winant. 2015. *Racial Formation in the United States*. 3rd ed. New York: Routledge.

O'Neill, Catherine A. 2000. "Variable Justice: Environmental Standards, Contaminated Fish, and 'Acceptable' Risk to Native Peoples." *Stanford Environmental Law Journal* 19 (1): 3–118.

OPM. 2017. "Profile of Federal Civilian Non-Postal Employees." U.S. Office of Personnel Management. https://www.opm.gov/policy-data-oversight/data-analysis-documenta

tion/federal-employment-reports/reports-publications/profile-of-federal-civilian-non
-postal-employees/. Accessed June 5, 2018.

OPM. 2018. Federal Employee Viewpoint Survey. U.S. Office of Personnel Management. https://www.opm.gov/fevs/. Accessed April 24, 2018.

Ottinger, Gwen. 2013. *Refining Expertise: How Responsible Engineers Subvert Environmental Justice Campaigns*. New York: NYU Press.

Ottinger, Gwen, and Benjamin R. Cohen. 2011. *Technoscience and Environmental Justice: Expert Cultures in a Grassroots Movement*. Cambridge, MA: MIT Press.

Ozymy, Joshua, and Melissa Jarrell. 2017. "Administrative Persistence in the Face of a Hostile Regime: How the Environmental Protection Agency Can Survive the Trump Administration." *Environmental Justice* 10 (6): 201–208.

Pache, Anne-Claire, and Felipe Santos. 2010. "When Worlds Collide: The Internal Dynamics of Organizational Responses to Conflicting Institutional Demands." *Academy of Management Review* 35 (3): 455–476.

Pache, Anne-Claire, and Felipe Santos. 2013. "Inside Hybrid Organization: Selective Coupling as a Response to Competing Institutional Logics." *Academy of Management Journal* 56 (4): 972–1001.

Paris, Britt, Lindsey Dillon, Jennifer Pierre, Irene V. Pasquetto, Emily Marquez, Sara Wylie, Michelle Murphy, Phil Brown, Rebecca Lave, Chris Sellers, Becky Mansfield, Leif Fredrickson, and Nicholas Shapiro. 2017. *Pursuing a Toxic Agenda: Environmental Injustice in the Early Trump Administration*. Environmental Data & Governance Initiative. September 19, 2017. https://envirodatagov.org/publication/pursuing-toxic-agenda/. Accessed March 7, 2019.

Park, Lisa Sun-Hee, and David N. Pellow. 2004. "Racial Formation, Environmental Racism, and the Emergence of Silicon Valley." *Ethnicities* 4 (3): 403–424.

Park, Lisa Sun-Hee, and David Naguib Pellow. 2011. *The Slums of Aspen: Immigrants vs. the Environment in America's Eden*. New York: NYU Press.

Pastor, Manuel, Robert D. Bullard, James K. Boyce, Alice Fothergill, Rachel Morello-Frosch, and Beverly Wright. 2006. *In the Wake of the Storm: Environment, Disaster and Race after Katrina*. New York: Russell Sage Foundation.

Pastor, Manuel, Rachel Morello-Frosch, James Sadd, and Justin Scoggins. 2013. "Risky Business: Cap-and-Trade, Public Health, and Environmental Justice." In *Urbanization and Sustainability*, ed. Christopher G. Boone and Michail Fragkias, 75–94. Dordrecht: Springer.

Pastor, Manuel, Jim Sadd, and John Hipp. 2001. "Which Came First? Toxic Facilities, Minority Move-In, and Environmental Justice." *Journal of Urban Affairs* 23 (1): 1–21.

Pautz, Michelle C., and Sara R. Rinfret. 2011. "Making Sense of the Front Lines: Environmental Regulators in Ohio and Wisconsin." *Journal of Environmental Studies and Sciences* 1: 277–288.

Pautz, Michelle, and Sara Rinfret. 2014. "State Environmental Regulators: Perspectives about Trust with Their Regulatory Counterparts." *Journal of Public Affairs* 16 (1): 28–38.

Payne-Sturges, Devon, Amalia Turner, Jessica Wignall, Arlene Rosenbaum, Elizabeth Dederick, and Heather Dantzker. 2012. "A Review of State-Level Analytical Approaches for Evaluating Disproportionate Environmental Health Impacts." *Environmental Justice* 5 (4): 173–187.

Peck, Jamie, and Adam Tickell. 2002. "Neoliberalizing Space." *Antipode* 34 (3): 380–404.

PEER. 2017. "EPA Criminal Pollution Enforcement Withering Away." Public Employees for Environmental Responsibility. August 24, 2017. https://www.peer .org/news/press-releases/epa-criminal-pollution-enforcement-withering-away.html. Accessed March 7, 2019.

Pellow, David N. 2000. "Environmental Inequality Formation: Toward a Theory of Environmental Injustice." *American Behavioral Scientist* 43 (4): 581–601.

Pellow, David Naguib. 2004. *Garbage Wars: The Struggle for Environmental Justice in Chicago*. Cambridge, MA: MIT Press.

Pellow, David Naguib. 2007. *Resisting Global Toxics: Transnational Movements for Environmental Justice*. Cambridge, MA: MIT Press.

Pellow, David Naguib. 2014. *Total Liberation: The Power and Promise of Animal Rights and the Radical Earth Movement*. Minneapolis: University of Minnesota Press.

Pellow, David Naguib. 2018. *What Is Critical Environmental Justice?* Medford, MA: Polity Press.

Pellow, David Naguib, and Robert J. Brulle. 2005. *Power, Justice, and the Environment: A Critical Appraisal of the Environmental Justice Movement*. Cambridge, MA: MIT Press.

Perkins, Tracy. 2015. "From Protest to Policy: The Political Evolution of California Environmental Justice Activism, 1980s–2010s." PhD diss., University of California, Santa Cruz.

Petrella, Christopher F., and Ameer Loggins. 2016. "Standing Rock, Flint, and the Color of Water." *Black Perspectives*, November 2, 2016. http://www.aaihs.org/standing -rock-flint-and-the-color-of-water/?utm_content=bufferf074f. Accessed March 7, 2019.

Pezzullo, Phaedra C., and Ronald Sandler. 2007a. "Introduction: Revisiting the Environmental Justice Challenge to Environmentalism." In *Environmental Justice and Environmentalism: The Social Justice Challenge to the Environmental Movement*, ed. Phaedra C. Pezzullo and Ronald Sandler, 1–24. Cambridge, MA: MIT Press.

Pezzullo, Phaedra C., and Ronald Sandler, eds. 2007b. *Environmental Justice and Environmentalism: The Social Justice Challenge to the Environmental Movement.* Cambridge, MA: MIT Press.

Phillips, Nelson, and Cynthia Hardy. 2002. *Discourse Analysis: Investigating Processes of Social Construction.* Thousand Oaks: SAGE Publications.

Popovich, Nadja, Livia Albeck-Ripka, and Kendra Pierre-Louis. 2018. "78 Environmental Rules on the Way Out under Trump." *New York Times*, January 31, 2018. Updated December 28, 2018. https://www.nytimes.com/interactive/2017/10/05/climate/trump-environment-rules-reversed.html. Accessed March 7, 2019.

Pratt, Michael G., Majken Schultz, Blake E. Ashforth, and Davide Ravasi. 2016. "Introduction: Organizational Identity: Where We Have Been, Where We Are, and Where We Might Go." In *The Oxford Handbook of Organizational Identity,* ed. Michael G. Pratt, Majken Schultz, Blake E. Ashforth, and Davide Ravasi, 1–18. Oxford: Oxford University Press.

Principles. 1991. "Principles of Environmental Justice." First National People of Color Environmental Leadership Summit. http://www.ejnet.org/ej/principles.html. Accessed December 3, 2017.

Pruitt, Scott. 2017. "Oklahoma Office of the Attorney General E. Scott Pruitt: About the Attorney General." http://web.archive.org/web/20170108114336/https://www.ok.gov/oag/Media/About_the_AG/. Accessed August 25, 2017.

Pulido, Laura. 1996. "A Critical Review of the Methodology of Environmental Racism Research." *Antipode* 28 (2): 142–159.

Pulido, Laura. 2000. "Rethinking Environmental Racism: White Privilege and Urban Development in Southern California." *Annals of the Association of American Geographers* 90 (1): 12–40.

Pulido, Laura. 2015. "Geographies of Race and Ethnicity I: White Supremacy vs White Privilege in Environmental Racism Research." *Progress in Human Geography* 39 (6): 809–817.

Pulido, Laura, Ellen Kohl, and Nicole-Marie Cotton. 2016. "State Regulation and Environmental Justice: The Need for Strategy Reassessment." *Capitalism Nature Socialism* 27 (2): 12–31.

Raffensperger, Carolyn, and Joel Tickner, eds. 1999. *Protecting Public Health and the Environment: Implementing the Precautionary Principle.* Washington, DC: Island Press.

Rea, Chris. 2018. Panelist comments in "Panel on Critically Interrogating the Environmental Regulatory States: Methodological and Ethical Challenges." Association of American Geographers Annual Meeting. April 2018. New Orleans, LA.

Rechtschaffen, Clifford, Eileen Gauna, and Catherine A. O'Neill. 2009. *Environmental Justice: Law, Policy and Regulation*. 2nd ed. Durham, NC: Carolina University Press.

Rhodes, Edwardo Lao. 2003. *Environmental Justice in America: A New Paradigm*. Bloomington: Indiana University Press.

Richter, Lauren. 2018. "Constructing Insignificance: Critical Race Perspectives on Institutional Failure in Environmental Justice Communities." *Environmental Sociology* 4 (1): 107–121.

Rinfret, Sara R., and Michelle C. Pautz. 2013. "Attitudes and Perspectives of Front-Line Workers in Environmental Policy: A Case Study of Ohio's Environmental Protection Agency and Wisconsin's Department of Natural Resources." *Journal of Public Affairs* 13 (1): 111–122.

Ringquist, Evan J. and David H. Clark. 1999. "Local Risks, States' Rights, and Federal Mandates: Remedying Environmental Inequities in the U.S. Federal System." *Publius* 29 (2): 73–93.

Robertson, Morgan. 2010. "Performing Environmental Governance." *Geoforum* 41: 7–10.

Rogers-Dillon, Robin H., and John David Skrentny. 1999. "Administering Success: The Legitimacy Imperative and the Implementation of Welfare Reform." *Social Problems* 46 (1): 13–29.

Rose, Nikolas. 1999. *Powers of Freedom: Reframing Political Thought*. Cambridge: Cambridge University Press.

Sandweiss, Stephen. 1998. "The Social Construction of Environmental Justice." In *Environmental Injustices, Political Struggles: Race, Class, and the Environment*, ed. David E. Camacho, 31–57. Durham, NC: Duke University Press.

San Francisco. 2010. *Grant Program 2010–12 Grant Solicitation*. San Francisco, CA: City and County of San Francisco Department of the Environment.

Santoro, Wayne A., and Gail M. McGuire. 1997. "Social Movement Insiders: The Impact of Institutional Activists on Affirmative Action and Comparable Worth Policies." *Social Problems* 44 (4): 503–519.

Save EPA. 2017. *Save EPA*. http://saveepaalums.info/. Accessed March 1, 2019.

Sbicca, Joshua. 2018. *Food Justice Now!: Deepening the Roots of Social Struggle*. Minneapolis: University of Minnesota Press.

Scammell, Madeleine Kangsen, Peter Montague, and Carolyn Raffensperger. 2014. "Tools for Addressing Cumulative Impacts on Human Health and the Environment." *Environmental Justice* 7 (4): 102–109.

Scandrett, Eurig. 2007. "Environmental Justice in Scotland: Policy, Pedagogy and Praxis." *Environmental Research Letters* 2: 045002.

Scarce, Rik. 2000. *Fishy Business: Salmon, Biology, and the Social Construction of Nature.* Philadelphia: Temple University Press.

Schlosberg, David. 2007. *Defining Environmental Justice: Theories, Movements, and Nature.* Oxford: Oxford University Press.

Schmelzkopf, Karen. 2002. "Incommensurability, Land Use, and the Right to Space: Community Gardens in New York City." *Urban Geography* 23 (4): 323–343.

Schnaiberg, Allan, and Kenneth Alan Gould. 1994. *Environment and Society: The Enduring Conflict.* New York: St. Martin's.

Schwalbe, Michael, Sandra Godwin, Daphne Holden, Douglas Schrock, Shealy Thompson, and Michele Wolkomir. 2000. "Generic Processes in the Reproduction of Inequality: An Interactionist Analysis." *Social Forces* 79 (2): 419–452.

Scott, W. Richard. 2014. *Institutions and Organizations: Ideas, Interests, and Identities.* Los Angeles: SAGE Publications.

Sellers, Christopher, Lindsey Dillon, Jennifer Liss Ohayon, Nick Shapiro, Marianne Sullivan, Chris Amoss, Stephen Bocking, Phil Brown, Vanessa De la Rosa, Jill Harrison, Sara Johns, Katherine Kulik, Rebecca Lave, Michelle Murphy, Liza Piper, Lauren Richter, and Sara Wylie. 2017. *The EPA Under Siege: Trump's Assault in History and Testimony.* Environmental Data and Governance Initiative. June 2017. https://envirodatagov.org/publication/the-epa-under-siege/. Accessed March 1, 2019.

Selznick, Phillip. 1966. *TVA and the Grass Roots: A Study of the Sociology of Formal Organization.* New York: Harper and Row.

Senier, Laura, Phil Brown, Sara Shostak, and Bridget Hanna. 2017. "The Socio-Exposome: Advancing Exposure Science and Environmental Justice in a Postgenomic Era." *Environmental Sociology* 3 (2): 107–121.

Sexton, Ken, and Stephen H. Linder. 2011. "Cumulative Risk Assessment for Combined Health Effects from Chemical and Nonchemical Stressors." *American Journal of Public Health* 101 (S1): S81–S88.

Sexton, Ken, and Stephen H. Linder. 2018. "Cumulative Risk Assessment: An Analytic Tool to Inform Policy Choices about Environmental Justice." In *The Routledge Handbook of Environmental Justice*, ed. Ryan Holifield, Jayajit Chakraborty, and Gordon Walker, 264–282. London: Routledge.

Shadbegian, Ronald J., and Ann Wolverton. 2015. "Evaluating Environmental Justice: Analytic Lessons from the Academic Literature and in Practice." In *Failed Promises: Evaluating the Federal Government's Response to Environmental Justice*, ed. David M. Konisky, 117–142. Cambridge, MA: MIT Press.

Shear, Michael D. 2017. "Trump Discards Obama Legacy, One Rule at a Time." *New York Times*, May 1, 2017.

Shilling, Fraser M., Jonathan K. London, and Raoul S. Liévanos. 2009. "Marginalization by Collaboration: Environmental Justice as a Third Party in and beyond CALFED." *Environmental Science and Policy* 12 (6): 694–709.

Shrader-Frechette, Kristin. 2002. *Environmental Justice: Creating Equality, Reclaiming Democracy*. Oxford: Oxford University Press.

Skocpol, Theda. 1985. "Bringing the State Back In: Strategies of Analysis in Current Research." In *Bringing the State Back In*, ed. Peter B. Evans, Dietrich Rueschemeyer, and Theda Skocpol, 3–43. New York: Cambridge University Press.

Skrentny, John David. 1998. "State Capacity, Policy Feedbacks and Affirmative Action for Blacks, Women, and Latinos." *Research in Political Sociology* 8: 279–310.

Slesinger, Scott. 2014. "EPA Spending in the President's Budget: Where Does the .22 percent of Federal Spending Go?" *Expert Blog*, NRDC. March 21, 2014. www.nrdc.org /experts/scott-slesinger/epa-spending-presidents-budget-where-does-022-federal-spend ing-go. Accessed March 7, 2019.

Smith, Christopher M., and Hilda E. Kurtz. 2003. "Community Gardens and the Politics of Scale in New York City." *Geographical Review* 93 (2): 193–212.

Solomon, Gina M., Rachel Morello-Frosch, Lauren Zeise, and John B. Faust. 2016. "Cumulative Environmental Impacts: Science and Policy to Protect Communities." *Annual Review of Public Health* 37: 83–96.

Soule, Sarah A. 2012. "Social Movements and Markets, Industries, and Firms." *Organization Studies* 33 (12): 1715–1733.

SSB. 2015. Sustainable South Bronx. https://www.ssbx.org/. Accessed March 7, 2019.

Szasz, Andrew. 2007. *Shopping Our Way to Safety: How We Changed from Protecting the Environment to Protecting Ourselves*. Minneapolis: University of Minnesota Press.

Sze, Julie. 2006. "Toxic Soup Redux: Why Environmental Racism and Environmental Justice Matter after Katrina." Social Science Research Council. June 11, 2006. http:// understandingkatrina.ssrc.org/Sze/. Accessed March 7, 2019.

Sze, Julie, and Jonathan London. 2008. "Environmental Justice at the Crossroads." *Sociology Compass* 2 (4): 1331–1354.

Targ, Nicholas. 2005. "The States' Comprehensive Approach to Environmental Justice." In *Power, Justice, and the Environment: A Critical Appraisal of the Environmental Justice Movement*, ed. David Naguib Pellow and Robert J. Brulle, 171–184. Cambridge, MA: MIT Press.

Taylor, Dorceta E. 2000. "The Rise of the Environmental Justice Paradigm: Injustice Framing and the Social Construction of Environmental Discourses." *American Behavioral Scientist* 43 (4): 508–580.

Taylor, Dorceta, 2014a. *Toxic Communities: Environmental Racism, Industrial Pollution and Residential Mobility.* New York: NYU Press.

Taylor, Dorceta. 2014b. *The State of Diversity in Environmental Organizations.* Ann Arbor: University of Michigan. July 2014. http://vaipl.org/wp-content/uploads/2014/10/ExecutiveSummary-Diverse-Green.pdf. Accessed March 3, 2019.

Taylor, Serge. 1984. *Making Bureaucracies Think: The Environmental Impact Statement Strategy of Administrative Reform.* Stanford, CA: Stanford University Press.

TEDxMidwest. 2010. "Majora Carter: 3 Stories of Local Eco-Entrepreneurship." *TEDxMidwest.* September 2010. https://www.ted.com/talks/majora_carter_3_stories_of_local_ecoactivism. Accessed March 3, 2019.

Teeger, Chana. 2015. "'Both Sides of the Story': History Education in Post-Apartheid South Africa." *American Sociological Review* 80 (6): 1175–1200.

Tennessee, Denise. 2016. "EPA Celebrates Inaugural Environmental Justice Academy Graduation." *The EPA Blog.* U.S. Environmental Protection Agency. June 1, 2016. https://blog.epa.gov/blog/2016/06/ej-eja_graduation/. Accessed March 7, 2019.

Tesh, Sylvia Noble. 2001. *Uncertain Hazards: Environmental Activists and Scientific Proof.* Ithaca, NY: Cornell University Press.

Thornton, Joe. 2000. *Pandora's Poison: Chlorine, Health, and a New Environmental Strategy.* Cambridge, MA: MIT Press.

Tickner, Joel A. 2003. *Precaution, Environmental Science, and Preventive Public Policy.* Washington, DC: Island Press.

Tierney, Kathleen, Christine Bevc, and Erica Kuligowski. 2006. "Metaphors Matter: Disaster Myths, Media Frames, and Their Consequences in Hurricane Katrina." *Annals of the American Academy of Political and Social Science* 604: 57–81.

Tilly, Charles. 1978. *From Mobilization to Revolution.* London: Longman Higher Education.

Tolbert, Pamela S. 1988. "Institutional Sources of Organizational Culture in Major Law Firms." In *Institutional Patterns and Organizations: Culture and Environment,* ed. Lynne G. Zucker, 101–113. Cambridge, MA: Ballinger.

Tolich, Martin. 2004. "Internal Confidentiality: When Confidentiality Assurances Fail Relational Informants." *Qualitative Sociology* 27 (1): 101–106.

Turkewitz, Julie. 2017. "Trump Slashes Size of Bears Ears and Grand Staircase Monuments." *New York Times,* December 4, 2017. https://mobile.nytimes.com/2017/12/04/us/trump-bears-ears.html?referer=. Accessed March 7, 2019.

UCC. 1987. *Toxic Wastes and Race in the United States.* New York: United Church of Christ Commission for Racial Justice.

UCS. 2008. *Voices of Scientists at the EPA*. Union of Concerned Scientists. https://www.ucsusa.org/sites/default/files/legacy/assets/documents/scientific_integrity/epa-survey-brochure.pdf. Accessed March 3, 2019.

UCS. 2018. *Science under President Trump: Voices of Scientists across 16 Federal Agencies.* Center for Science and Democracy. Union of Concerned Scientists. August 2018. https://www.ucsusa.org/sites/default/files/attach/2018/08/science-under-trump-report.pdf. Accessed March 4, 2019.

UCS. 2019. *The State of Science in the Trump Era: Damage Done, Lessons Learned, and a Path to Progress.* Center for Science and Democracy. Union of Concerned Scientists. January 2019. https://www.ucsusa.org/sites/default/files/attach/2019/01/ucs-trump-2yrs-report.pdf. Accessed March 4, 2019.

U.S. CCR. 2016. *Environmental Justice: Examining the Environmental Protection Agency's Compliance and Enforcement of Title VI and Executive Order 12,898.* Washington, DC: U.S. Commission on Civil Rights.

USDA. 2015. *Environmental Justice Annual Implementation Report.* Washington, DC: U.S. Department of Agriculture.

Vajjhala, Shalini P. 2010. "Building Community Capacity? Mapping the Scope and Impacts of EPA's Environmental Justice Small Grants Program." In *Environment and Social Justice: An International Perspective*, ed. Dorceta E. Taylor, 353–381. Bingley, UK: Emerald Group.

Vajjhala, Shalini P., Amanda Van Epps, and Sarah Szambelan. 2008. *Integrating EJ into Federal Policies and Programs: Examining the Role of Regulatory Impact Analyses and Environmental Impact Statements.* Resources for the Future Discussion Paper 08–45. Washington, DC: Resources for the Future.

Vogel, Sarah. 2012. *Is It Safe?: BPA and the Struggle to Define the Safety of Chemicals.* Berkeley: University of California Press.

Wacquant, Loïc. 2009. *Punishing the Poor: The Neoliberal Government of Social Insecurity.* Durham, NC: Duke University Press.

Walker, Gordon. 2012. *Environmental Justice: Concepts, Evidence, and Politics.* London: Routledge.

Ward, Roger K., and Janice F. Dickerson. 1995. *Environmental Justice in Louisiana: An Overview of the Louisiana Department of Environmental Quality's Environmental Justice Program.* April 1995. Louisiana Department of Environmental Quality.

Washington, Sylvia Hood. 2008. "Mrs. Block Beautiful: African American Women and the Birth of the Urban Conservation Movement, Chicago, Illinois, 1917–1954." *Environmental Justice* 1 (1): 13–23.

White, Monica M. 2011. "Sisters of the Soil: Urban Gardening as Resistance in Detroit." *Race/Ethnicity: Multidisciplinary Global Contexts* 5 (1): 13–28.

Whiteside, Kerry H. 2006. *Precautionary Politics: Principle and Practice in Confronting Environmental Risk*. Cambridge, MA: MIT Press.

WHO (World Health Organization). 2016a. "WHO Releases Country Estimates on Air Pollution Exposure and Health Impact." September 27, 2016. http://www.who .int/news-room/detail/27-09-2016-who-releases-country-estimates-on-air-pollution -exposure-and-health-impact. Accessed March 3, 2019.

WHO (World Health Organization). 2016b. *The Public Health Impact of Chemicals: Knowns and Unknowns*. International Programme on Chemical Safety, World Health Organization, Geneva, Switzerland. http://www.who.int/ipcs/publications/chemi cals-public-health-impact/en/. Accessed March 3, 2019.

Wilson, Sacoby, Frank Howell, Steve Wing, and Mark Sobsey. 2002. "Environmental Injustice and the Mississippi Hog Industry." *Environmental Health Perspectives* 110 (S2): 195–201.

Wing, Steve, and Susanne Wolf. 2000. "Intensive Livestock Operations, Health, and Quality of Life among Eastern North Carolina Residents." *Environmental Health Perspectives* 108 (3): 233–238.

Winne, Mark. 2008. *Closing the Food Gap: Resetting the Table in the Land of Plenty*. Boston: Beacon.

Wynne, Brian. 1992. "Misunderstood Misunderstanding: Social Identities and Public Uptake of Science." *Public Understanding of Science* 1 (3): 281–304.

Yang, Tseming. 2002. "Melding Civil Rights and Environmentalism: Finding Environmental Justice's Place in Environmental Regulation." *Harvard Environmental Law Review* 26: 1–32.

Zald, Mayer N., Calvin Morrill, and Hayagreeva Rao. 2005. "The Impact of Social Movements on Organizations: Environment and Responses." In *Social Movements and Organization Theory*, ed. Gerald F. Davis, Doug McAdam, W. Richard Scott, and Mayer N. Zald, 253–279. New York: Cambridge University Press.

Index

Urban and Industrial Environments

Series editor: Robert Gottlieb, Henry R. Luce Professor of Urban and Environmental Policy, Occidental College

Stephanie Foote and Elizabeth Mazzolini, eds., *Histories of the Dustheap: Waste, Material Cultures, Social Justice*

David J. Hess, *Good Green Jobs in a Global Economy: Making and Keeping New Industries in the United States*

Joseph F. C. DiMento and Clifford Ellis, *Changing Lanes: Visions and Histories of Urban Freeways*

Joanna Robinson, *Contested Water: The Struggle Against Water Privatization in the United States and Canada*

William B. Meyer, *The Environmental Advantages of Cities: Countering Commonsense Antiurbanism*

Rebecca L. Henn and Andrew J. Hoffman, eds., *Constructing Green: The Social Structures of Sustainability*

Peggy F. Barlett and Geoffrey W. Chase, eds., *Sustainability in Higher Education: Stories and Strategies for Transformation*

Isabelle Anguelovski, *Neighborhood as Refuge: Community Reconstruction, Place Remaking, and Environmental Justice in the City*

Kelly Sims Gallagher, *The Globalization of Clean Energy Technology: Lessons from China*

Vinit Mukhija and Anastasia Loukaitou-Sideris, eds., *The Informal American City: Beyond Taco Trucks and Day Labor*

Roxanne Warren, *Rail and the City: Shrinking Our Carbon Footprint While Reimagining Urban Space*

Marianne E. Krasny and Keith G. Tidball, *Civic Ecology: Adaptation and Transformation from the Ground Up*

Erik Swyngedouw, *Liquid Power: Contested Hydro-Modernities in Twentieth-Century Spain*

Ken Geiser, *Chemicals without Harm: Policies for a Sustainable World*

Duncan McLaren and Julian Agyeman, *Sharing Cities: A Case for Truly Smart and Sustainable Cities*

Jessica Smartt Gullion, *Fracking the Neighborhood: Reluctant Activists and Natural Gas Drilling*

Nicholas A. Phelps, *Sequel to Suburbia: Glimpses of America's Post-Suburban Future*

Shannon Elizabeth Bell, *Fighting King Coal: The Challenges to Micromobilization in Central Appalachia*

Theresa Enright, *The Making of Grand Paris: Metropolitan Urbanism in the Twenty-first Century*

Robert Gottlieb and Simon Ng, *Global Cities: Urban Environments in Los Angeles, Hong Kong, and China*

Anna Lora-Wainwright, *Resigned Activism: Living with Pollution in Rural China*

Scott L. Cummings, *Blue and Green: The Drive for Justice at America's Port*

David Bissell, *Transit Life: Cities, Commuting, and the Politics of Everyday Mobilities*

Javiera Barandiarán, *From Empire to Umpire: Science and Environmental Conflict in Neoliberal Chile*

Benjamin Pauli, *Flint Fights Back: Environmental Justice and Democracy in the Flint Water Crisis*